CLASS PRIVILEGE

"With this extremely timely and immensely readable book, Harry Glasbeek does for the lay reader what he has done for generations of his law students. Deploying loads of fascinating cases from Canada and around the world with great felicity, profound insight, and charming wit, he lifts the veil of legal jargon to explain in the clearest terms how corporations and states intertwine through laws and regulations, courts and tribunals, to allow corporate executives and directors, shareholders and investors, to systematically screw workers, consumers, and citizens, and to accumulate wealth and power at the public's expense."

— **Leo Panitch**, senior scholar and emeritus distinguished research professor, York University

"Through his consistently forensic use of legal methodology, real conceptual sophistication, and via a wealth of data, Glasbeek comprehensively—with fury, irony, disgust, and humour—reveals how corporate capitalism is no more and no less than a system that privileges the shareholding class. Challenging the bases of toxic class privilege—the edifice that is the corporation, and the subservient complex of bourgeois law—this majestic text reinvigorates the belief that a better world remains within our grasp."

— **Steve Tombs**, professor of criminology, The Open University, UK

"With deep insight and biting humour, Glasbeek exposes the ideological myths of corporate law, which allow flesh and blood capitalists to voraciously pursue profits without responsibility for the inevitable harms their activities impose on the rest of us. This book is essential reading for anyone who wants to understand how law belies its promise of equal justice for all and instead protects the interests of the few."

— **Eric Tucker**, professor, Osgoode Hall Law School, York University

"*Class Privilege* provides a stunning critique of corporate capitalism and the controlling shareholders hiding behind the bourgeois legal categories of corporate personhood and limited liability to reap massive financial rewards whilst routinely evading responsibility for the many and devastating harms generated by *their* corporation. Glasbeek's work is a much-needed corrective to the "thinking capitalists" and their state enablers who desperately plead their case for saving corporate capitalism and to the corporation's many academic cheerleaders who naively cling to the belief that we can somehow rid the corporation of its predatory instincts so that it might finally realize its social and economic benefits. *Class Privilege* is a must-read for those who find themselves questioning the legitimacy of the modern corporation and for those currently struggling against the capitalist status quo in the hopes of realizing a better, more just alternative."

— **Steven Bittle**, associate professor, Department of Criminology, University of Ottawa

"Harry Glasbeek has written an accessible guide to how the law creates and sustains class privilege through corporate capitalism. Shining a light on controlling shareholders, this book exposes how, through law, the real human beings behind the corporate veil are shielded from accountability for social and economic harms. In demystifying this technical knowledge, Glasbeek identifies practical points of leverage and legal principle that can be harnessed for real change."

— **Fay Faraday**, social justice lawyer , visiting professor, Osgoode Hall Law School, and Packer Visiting Chair in Social Justice, York University

"Harry Glasbeek's meticulously argued and supremely convincing book exposes one of the great political and economic deceptions of our time: that the corporation is somehow autonomous from the people who own and profit from it. *Class Privilege* literally tears away the corporate veil with finely crafted analytical precision that allows us to see exactly how shareholders hide behind a machinery of economic growth and human waste that is quickly pushing us to extinction. In demystifying this dehumanizing machine that we call the corporation, Glasbeek shows us how we can be truly human again: by taking back control of our lives and livelihoods from the wealthy minority who hide behind the corporation. This book does not trivialize or oversimplify the enormity of the task that confronts us in beginning to dismantle corporate power; by not shirking from a full exposition of what needs to be done, Glasbeek gifts us with a clear set of instructions that tell us where to start."

— **David Whyte**, professor of socio-legal studies, University of Liverpool, UK and co-author of *Corporate Human Rights Violations: Global Prospects for Legal Action*

"This book is a contemporary *Mirror for Magistrates* for all professionals and regulators who could expose the falsehoods, fictions, and fallacies of corporate law and regulation but choose not to. It is the current honest politicians' and ethical citizens' guide to corporate capitalism and the reform of its unethical and unsustainable values. It highlights the legal incentives for controlling shareholders to be careless with others' lives and well-being. It illustrates how limited liability and separate legal personality confer immunity for their dishonest conduct. It illuminates how they lead to unfair inequalities in wealth. It sets out in plain and urgent language the necessary reforms to make controlling shareholders, like other citizens, responsible and accountable for their actions refuting the arguments that this is too hard."

— **Neil Andrews**, professor of law, Victoria University, Australia and past editor of the *Australian Journal of Corporate Law*

CLASS PRIVILEGE

HOW LAW SHELTERS SHAREHOLDERS AND CODDLES CAPITALISM

HARRY GLASBEEK

BETWEEN THE LINES
Toronto

Class Privilege: How Law Shelters Shareholders and Coddles Capitalism

First published in 2017 by
Between the Lines
401 Richmond Street West
Studio 277
Toronto, Ontario M5V 3A8
Canada
1-800-718-7201
www.btlbooks.com

LIBRARY AND ARCHIVES CANADA CATALOGUING IN PUBLICATION

Glasbeek, H. J., author
    Class privilege : how law shelters shareholders and coddles capitalism / Harry Glasbeek.

Includes bibliographical references and index.
Issued in print and electronic formats.
ISBN 978-1-77113-307-4 (softcover).—ISBN 978-1-77113-308-1
(EPUB).—ISBN 978-1-77113-309-8 (PDF)

    1. Corporations—Corrupt practices. 2. Corporate power. 3. Social responsibility of business. 4. Capitalism. I. Title.

HV6768.G54 2017   364.16'8   C2016-907422-6
                                           C2016-907423-4

Text and cover design by David Vereschagin, Quadrat Communications
Printed in Canada

We acknowledge for their financial support of our publishing activities the Government of Canada through the Canada Book Fund, the Canada Council for the Arts, which last year invested $153 million to bring the arts to Canadians throughout the country, and the Government of Ontario through the Ontario Arts Council, the Ontario Book Publishers Tax Credit program, and the Ontario Media Development Corporation.

To my parents,
who taught me an unshakeable optimism,
and to *la famille* Souquet,
who showed me the decency and compassion
of which people are capable.

Contents

Introduction

CONFRONTING FLESH-AND-BLOOD TARGETS

ANTI-CAPITALIST ACTIVISTS ARE PREOCCUPIED WITH THE FOR-PROFIT corporation. Their language makes this plain: the corporate agenda, corporate culture, corporate rule. In many progressive circles, it is a put-down to describe a way of doing things as "corporatized." And the modern corporation is all around us. Its presence and potency influence everything we do. It is in our minds when we think about social, political, and economic activities. It crops up in any conversation about economic growth, technological innovation, employment, or taxation. It factors in sport sponsorship, government regulation, social programs, philanthropy, and funding of political causes, parties, or candidates. The corporation is accepted as a vitally important institution. We have been taught to think of the modern corporation as a normal, natural, and pivotal component of our society. And to a goodly extent, we have internalized this message.

It is understandable, then, that anti-capitalist activists demonize the corporation. An identifiable enemy is needed to coalesce resisters, and the vehicle through which perceived wrongs are wrought appears to be a good target. But this tendency to focus on the corporation as the enemy is, conceptually, a misreading of the situation. The corporation is only an instrument for the system; it is not itself the system. It is capitalism's tool, and it has identifiable beneficiaries. The corporation is the tool through which individual capitalists maintain and perpetuate their dominance, the instrument which they use to enrich themselves obscenely and to impoverish almost everyone else.

Capitalism's agenda, the endless pursuit of private accumulation of socially produced wealth, is felt by many to be unjust. But in daily life, capitalism appears as a concept, not as a target with a defined shape or body. Capitalism—as a system, as an "ism"—is indifferent as to how wealth is created and accumulated. We are to compete with each other to get more; we are to exploit our physical and cultural environments to get more. This competition is not waged on an even terrain. Riches and talents were unevenly distributed from the start, leading to increasing imbalance over time. While oft-noted, the validity of those unequal starting points has not come under serious challenge. Thus it has come to pass that today, a very few people, those we call capitalists, control vast amounts of wealth. The system, capitalism, imbues them with a spirit of indifference to others and to their cultural and physical environments.

Greed is the pivot of the system that maintains and drives capitalists. It is a carcinogenic starting point. In 1921, British historian R.H. Tawney observed that it made for sick social relations:

> By fixing men's minds ... upon the exercise of the right to pursue their own self-interest, it offers unlimited scope for the acquisition of riches, and therefore gives free play to one of the most powerful of human instincts.... It assures men that there are no ends other than their ends, no law other than their desires, no limit other than that which they think advisable.... Under the impulse of such ideas men do not become religious or wise or artistic; for religion and wisdom and art imply the acceptance of limitations. But they become powerful and rich. They inherit the earth and change the face of nature.[1]

The few, the capitalists who own the bulk of the means of production, rule the roost. They dictate how we live, materially and spiritually. They idolize money and the power it gives them. They prosper in a system of naked self-interest and impose its logic on all of us. This is wrong. It is a system that abjures ideals such as sharing, mutuality, respect, and compassion. It denies our potential for nobility. As French Resistance fighters Stéphane Hessel and Edgar Morin have lamented, "humanity is unable to attain humanity."[2]

But knowing that something is wrong is not enough. We need to know how to change it. It is hard to fight the system as a system. We are not only subjected to it, we are part of it. We are both coerced and co-opted into compliance and acceptance. This makes it difficult to see capitalism as a tangible enemy. What we see is its tool, the corporation for profit.

Capitalists have made their dominance appear natural and unchangeable, in large part, by hiding themselves from legal view. They have succeeded in making the invisible, ethereal corporation into a shield behind which, if seen at all, they are seen as passive beneficiaries of corporate activities. But if capitalism is so great and capitalists are so good for us, why such a great need for conjuring tricks? Why the need to hide? The corporation serves the capitalists' purposes much as the ink-like fluid emitted by an octopus serves it to fool its enemies. Capitalists are like the Romulans of television fame who are equipped with a cloak that renders them invisible to their favourite prey, the Starship *Enterprise*. For a capitalist, the corporation is what the ink is to the octopus; it is what the cloaking device is to the Romulans. It is meant to hide, to distract so that they can do what they like. If we want truth and justice, the shield of the for-profit corporation needs to be removed. This book argues not only why this should be done but also how it might be done.

The book's focus is, as it should be, modest. I am a lawyer who studied labour and corporate law. I want to assist, first, those who want to defend us against the immediate impacts of corporate capitalism, and second, those who want to change it forever. The work utilizes such expertise as I have to highlight how, whatever goals they have set themselves, whatever tactics and strategies anti-capitalists choose, their cause might be advanced by changing the ideological context of their resistance.

While the corporation serves market economic functions that supposedly yield material benefits for all of us, the brute fact is that the corporation ensures that the owners of wealth will get the lion's share of that material welfare. Moreover, because of its centrality to the political economy, the corporation also has political and cultural impacts. Through it, dominant capitalists hold sway over elected politicians and moulders of public opinion. We are conditioned to live within a corporate political culture, largely reduced to fighting its excesses from within its self-perpetuating logic. This deepens the power of the corporations' hidden masters. Political theorist Hannah Arendt observed that corporate culture is "the rule of nobody and for this reason perhaps the least human and most cruel form of rulership."

Capitalists, as we will see, benefit enormously from the transliteration of capitalism into corporate capitalism. The corporation is portrayed as a mechanical device created by the state to serve its functions and, therefore, as one expected to behave in accordance with that state's goals and aspirations. This suggests that capitalists employing the corporation share the values and norms of the state's citizens. When the workings of the corporation are examined, though, they reveal that they necessarily involve a betrayal of the very values and norms that, for their legitimacy's sake, capitalists purport to share.

One of capitalism's potential weak spots, then, is the perverting economic, political, and ethical role played by the prime instrument of private wealth accumulation, the legal corporation. Once the corporate mask is ripped off, those who hide behind it become visible. Stripped of their protective garb, capitalists—the few who own the means of production—will be as naked as the rest of us are when we face their corporations. The enemies may become more real, less distant, and weaker.

This book sets out to humanize capitalism. Not to make it more acceptable, not to make it gentler and kinder, not to help it to perpetuate itself. The aim is the very opposite: to help people rid themselves of the system which, because all of us are enveloped within its embrace, does not present us with easily hittable targets. I set out to help activists identify some of their powerful antagonists, the few who truly profit from capitalism's reign, namely those who control corporations. Corporate capitalism is not an ungoverned, naturally existing system, but one that is run by and for the benefit of a very few human beings.

We should go after controlling shareholders. This goal should have visceral appeal, and it may help militants confront capitalist relations of production more effectively. The task is difficult because law, an institution of unparalleled prestige, allows capitalists wrapped in corporate clothing to convey the impression that they are just as helplessly bound by the iron laws of capitalism and its corporations as its more obvious victims and opponents are. Law suggests that flesh-and-blood capitalists should rarely be blamed for the many hurts inflicted by corporate capitalism.

The argument is not that the law instrumentally sets out to favour capitalists and their corporations over everyone else. Law could not fulfill its primary functions if it was so blatant. It is more subtle. In Anglo-American jurisdictions—Canada, New Zealand, Australia, the United States, the United Kingdom, as well as other jurisdictions that share a common legal historical and cultural background[3]—law portrays itself as the institution that protects and maintains liberal values, values that posit the equal sovereignty of all individuals and eschew coercion of any kind. This is most obviously reflected in the adherence to what is called the rule of law.

Law is wedded to fair processes and neutral applications of the law by neutral adjudicators who treat all individuals as equals before, according to, and under the law. As law is both created by the state and provides the mode of exercising state power, it plays a role in ensuring that that state's inherent coercive power does not undermine the goals of law and its liberal project. That coercive state power is kept in check by judges and constitutional bills of rights. More directly relevant here, as the state is the only legitimate repository of coercive powers in a liberal polity, the state's use of those powers to punish errant citizens, to treat them as criminals, is sought to be contained by law and its attendant processes.

It is an attractive, seductive message. Law—and thereby, the institutions it spawns and the activities it controls—is given a difficult-to-challenge authority. Law's edicts have sway with the public. Adherence to the ideal of liberalism permits law to legitimate actors and activities that it promotes and regulates. Law holds out the promise that capitalists and their corporations are subject to its principles and authority.

Law goes out of its way to fortify the view that its creation and oversight of the capitalism-promoting vehicle, the corporation, are mere exercises in legal technology by means of which lawful and useful ends may be pursued by virtuous actors, namely, capitalists. If any corporation or capitalist offends the law, they will be held to legal account, as would any other actor. Capitalists and their corporations are under control. Law's prestige, derived from being seen as a class-transcending institution, as being above politics, renders this starting point seemingly unassailable. In this way, as social historian Doug Hay observes, law is the rhetorical and instrumental mode by which the powerful both justify and enact their predations.[4]

The point of departure of this work is that this position is false. To maintain the legitimating notion that capitalists and their corporations are bound to follow the same agreed-upon rules we all do requires accepting a host of ill-based assumptions and pretenses. Once they are stripped away, corporations will no longer hide their masters from our gaze.

To this end, part I of the book gives an account of the chief characteristics of the creature law has created to make the world safe for capitalists, the for-profit corporation. Corporate law masks those capitalists in a legal guise, one that showers special legal advantages on them. They are transformed into shareholders. This enables capitalists to satisfy their insatiable greed while minimizing their risk of material or reputational losses. The legal sleight of hand that turns capitalists into shareholders of a machine called the corporation furnishes capitalists not merely with the capacity to inflict harms but also, shockingly, with incentives to do so.

Part II will show that, acting on these incentives, capitalists do inflict harms in spades and that law has to be contorted grossly to allow them to do so with impunity. When exposed, these contortions need to be defended by adherents of the status quo.

Part III tackles their justifications. It shows what arguments are proffered by corporate capitalism's cheerleaders to justify the flagrant betrayals of legal principles, the persistent denial of our supposed economic preferences, and the negation of society's more deeply held values. Such arguments whitewash the ever more visible fact that corporate actors deny us our sovereignty and dignity. I evaluate these justifications. The evidence shows that they are profoundly flawed, both in conceptual and empirical terms. The latter matters greatly; corporate capitalists' predations and their distortions of legal and economic principles are justified because they are said to yield more positive welfare than they do harm. No other system of wealth production could yield as many benefits.

There is no alternative (TINA) is the empirical claim. If this empirical claim is false—as the evidence marshalled in this book will show it is—the uglinesses wrought by corporate capitalism can be condemned and dealt with as if they were homicides, thefts, and coercions perpetrated by mere human beings. The octopus's ink will be washed away, the Romulans' cloaking device destroyed. We will be in a position to blame and stigmatize the legally privileged class, the shareholders who control corporations. We will be in a position to confront those controlling shareholders who get corporations to slash and burn everything around us to allow them to satisfy their vulgar lust for money and power.

PART I

THE CORPORATION: LAW'S GIFT TO CAPITALISTS

In which the way that the law creates an extraordinary tool to further the private accumulation of socially produced wealth is sketched out. That tool, the corporation, is given attributes that enable its beneficiaries to impose costs and risks on non-capitalists with little fear of personal consequences for abuses of shared political and economic norms and values.

A Corporation Is Born

THERE MAY BE AS MANY AS TWO MILLION INCORPORATED FIRMS IN Canada. Though these corporations vary widely in business and size, they share some essential legal features. One of the most important is that they are characterized as self-standing creatures, distinct from the promoters who create them, from the functionaries who operate them, and from the intended beneficiaries of their operations.

CONDITIONS FOR CREATING A CORPORATION

Section 5 of the *Canada Business Corporations Act* provides that any eighteen-year-old who is not bankrupt at the time and has not been adjudged insane by a court is entitled to form a corporation. (In Canada, correspond-ing provincial statutes each have a similar provision—and these require-ments are typical of Anglo-American jurisdictions in general.) All applicants need to do is to fill out a form and, accompanied by a small fee, file it with a government official, called a registrar (or sometimes a director). That official must then issue a certificate of incorporation. The details the government requires are minimal.

Applicants have to suggest a name for the firm. The name must not already be in use by anyone or anything else, or likely to be confused with another one already in use. Applicants must pay for a search of databanks listing names in use. If they cannot think of an original name, they may simply use a unique number. This is not very catchy, to be sure, but the low visibility a numbered company provides may be useful to miscreants. Thus, 630903 Ontario Inc. was a wage-stealing corporation whose human owners were held unaccountable for receipt of benefits produced by unpaid labour; and 550551 Ontario Limited ran the Westray mine, the mass killer of coal miners in the 1992 Nova Scotia disaster, whose functionaries and beneficiaries were left untroubled by the law.[1]

In addition, applicants must furnish the registrar with a postal address for the corporation-to-be and the names of one or more directors. The application must also indicate how the promoters intend to share the proceeds of any corporate activity.

It is much easier to incorporate a firm than it is to become a citizen or to obtain resident or refugee status; it is much easier to incorporate than it is to become a member of a trade or profession or to establish a trade union. A union seeking to be certified must prove that its objectives include the pursuit of harmonious relations between employers and employees, that its prime objective is to improve conditions of work for employees who could not be more easily organized by another union, and that it will remain at arm's length from the employer. These kinds of requirements matter in all other requests to a government for a special status. It matters who is asking for special privileges from the state, what kind of people they are, and how they propose to use the privileges they seek. The identity, character, track record, and intentions of the applicants matter, and the oversight body is given discretion to accept or reject the application.

The promoters of a corporation, by contrast, only need to prove that they are over eighteen, sane, and not bankrupt. The objectives of the corporation-to-be are irrelevant unless they are overtly illegal. Once these very low hurdles are cleared, the registrar has no choice but to grant a certificate incorporating the firm.

A magic trick is performed. A "person" is created. Out of thin air.

THE CORPORATION AS PERSON

The governing *Business Corporations Act* says that, once the certificate is granted, the newly established corporation has the capacity, powers, and privileges of a natural person. In a liberal capitalist legal system, persons (that is, real human beings) are entitled to own private property and to deploy it as they decide is best for them. They are expected to pursue their own interests. When the law says, therefore, that a corporation has the capacities, powers, and privileges of a natural person, it is bestowing attributes on an incorporated firm that enable it to act as a full-blooded capitalist in its own right.

It becomes part of classical liberal economics' constellation of unwitting do-gooders. "It is not from the benevolence of the butcher, the brewer, or the baker that we expect our dinner," Adam Smith wrote in *The Wealth of Nations*, "but from their regard to their own interest." The corporation, then, is created as a virtuous person, as a legitimate market participant. And acting in its own interests, indifferent to ours, it is expected to contribute to our welfare.

Even though the law says it has the capacities of a natural person, the corporation has no physical presence; it has no brain or muscles. It is like ectoplasm, the substance a medium's body is said to emit during a trance. It is a blob—like the alien mass of jelly in the 1958 horror movie that landed on earth, intent on consuming everything in its path.

To act as a sovereign capitalist, the new corporation needs someone to think and act for it. This is why the promoters of a corporation need to name directors. They are to form a board that directs, that is, a group that thinks and causes its thoughts to be implemented on behalf of the corporation. The law imposes duties and obligations on these directors. They are to act in the best interests of the corporation they run, and they are to use reasonable skill and diligence. The content and meaning of these duties and obligations are contestable, and indeed, they are frequently contested. Much of corporate law litigation has to do with their interpretation and enforcement. What is more pertinent here is that it is the board of directors that is in charge of the deployment of the corporate person's assets.

But first, it must get assets. After all, if the corporation is to act like a natural person does when engaged as a capitalist, the corporation needs capital.

SOURCES OF CAPITAL

There are two main sources of capital for a corporation. First, the corporation could decide, via its directors, to borrow money to start off its profit-seeking ventures. It enters into a loan contract with one or more lenders. The borrowing corporation issues an IOU, often called a debenture or bond. The borrower undertakes to repay the money borrowed, plus interest, within a given time, sometimes by arranging for periodic repayments.

As is the case with other loans, the lender has nothing like a legal owner's interest in the borrower's business. Thus, when a consumer gets a loan from a bank to purchase, say, a car, the bank has no interest in how the car is used or in what else the borrower owns or does with their life. It is interested only in the borrower's ability to repay the loan on time and, to safeguard itself, it may take a lien over the car or some other property of the borrower. In case of default, the bank can then try to recoup its loss by enforcing its contractual right to get part of the value of the property over which the lien was taken.

Similarly, a lender to a corporation may secure its loan by taking a legal interest in an asset of the borrowing corporation. But this limited contractual right is its only legal entitlement to the corporation's assets or over its daily doings. It is an outsider to the corporation's property and operations. This is a very different relationship to that created between the corporation and the second main source of capital.

The other principal source of contributions comes from people who have no contractual expectation of repayment. To the contrary: they are willing to risk the property that they invest in the corporation. They are gamblers. The gamblers bet that the corporation will succeed and make a profit. What they want is a share of that profit, referred to as dividends. Their share of any distributed profit is measured by the proportion their bet bears to the total amount of bets made. They are given a certificate by the corporation that indicates the proportion of the profits to which any one contributor is entitled. It is evidence of the investor's promised share. The gambler is that certificate's holder and is, therefore, dubbed a shareholder.

THE ROLE OF THE SHAREHOLDER

Shareholders' dependence on profit-making means that they have good reason to be concerned about the way in which, and the efficacy with which, "their" corporations chase profits. This is why they get the following rights:

- To vote on the appointment and dismissal of the corporation's directors.
- To vote on plans to make profound changes to the corporation. For example, if it is suggested that the corporation sell a substantial portion of its assets, or agree to a takeover by another entrepreneur or a merger with another corporation, these issues are likely to affect the value of shareholders' certificates.
- To call meetings and make proposals (non-binding recommendations) to guide the board of directors.
- To share in any assets left after a corporation has met all of its obligations and has ceased operations.

A number of vital features of the legally created entity have now emerged. First, the corporation is treated as a sovereign individual and the funds contributed to it become its property to do with it as it wishes. It is, via its directors, an operating capitalist. As such, it is self-standing and self-serving. Those who lend it money, its creditors, are outsiders. Unlike them, gamblers who bet on the corporation are treated as insiders. These shareholders have a serious interest in, and considerable legal control over, corporate operations and decision-making.

Other consequences follow from the legal incorporation processes, all of them somewhat miraculous.

THE CORPORATION AS IMMORTAL ADULT

The law says that, once incorporated, a firm has the attributes of a natural person. But in fact, it features many characteristics that we, mere human beings, do not possess. As soon as a registrar grants a certificate, the corporation is born, and it is, instantaneously, fully adult. It is ready to participate in market capitalism. There is no pesky growing-up period, no demand that it wait at least eighteen years before engaging in adult or market activities. Nor does it have to worry about aging. It is created to be potentially immortal. Corporations die only if they decide to cease operations (commit suicide) or if they are eaten by another corporation or assassinated by its creditors.

And, because they are adults when they are born, they can instantly reproduce. There is no puberty period to endure, none of the awkwardness of finding a mate, none of the nausea and discomforts that accompany a period of gestation. Conception and birth-giving are virtually simultaneous. As soon as a certificate of incorporation is granted, a corporation can apply to the appropriate registrar to form another corporation. The directors must follow the easy-to-satisfy rules of incorporation set out above. Upon acceptance of the application, a "child" will be born.

This child (born, too, as a potentially immortal adult) can, of course, give instant birth as well, while its parent can continue to spawn siblings for the first-born. Extended families of corporations with all the capacities, powers, and privileges of a natural person can be produced at will. Being bloodless blobs, their ties are legal and functional, not strained by human emotions such as likes, dislikes, jealousies, and other human foibles. Their relations are more stable than those of flesh-and-blood families. They have a greater congruence of purpose, unaffected by personal goals and ambitions.

Thus, unencumbered by frailty, operators of an integrated group of legal persons can plan to maximize the corporate family's opportunities for profit-making. They are in a position to compartmentalize, to departmentalize, to distribute the group's operational functions and assets and obligations as they see fit. It is a recipe book fit for fancy cooking. And the corporation's cooks are ready to go to work.

Cooking the Books

IN 2013, THE MEDIA WERE BUZZING WITH NEWS OF THE U.S. Government Accountability Office revelation that a small edifice in the Cayman Islands called Ugland House had, in 2008, had 18,857 residents. One might have thought that these living conditions would be unacceptable. They were not. The residents were all corporations.[1] Not one of them needed its own bed, a separate kitchen, a bathroom, or a quiet spot to read, listen to music, or watch television, to chat with a friend or relative.

This makes plain what should never be forgotten. Much as the law says that a registered for-profit corporation has all the legal capacities (and more) of a human being, it is not a sentient person. It is not a flesh-and-blood creature that lives, eats, washes, thinks, hopes, hates, and loves as we do. It is a device, one established by law. When the tenants are corporations, a small, very densely occupied building does not turn into a slum dwelling.

THE LETTER OF THE LAW

Occasionally, liberal law does acknowledge this self-evident proposition. The law drops its pretenses when the use of its creature, the corporation, is useless from a market capitalist perspective. Thus, when in 2013, the Californian anti-corporate activist Jonathan Frieman, while driving by himself, drove in the car pool lane, he was fined for this offence. He defended himself by asserting that it only looked as if he was alone. In fact, he had an invisible passenger, and this entitled him to use the lane. Next to him, on the passenger seat, were the articles of incorporation of his business firm. That is, a person was sitting there.

His argument was rejected.[2] Presumably, his technically persuasive argument offended the spirit of the law. Apparent compliance with the letter of the law could not be allowed to negate its purpose. If only this common sense principle were applied consistently to, say, the tenants of Ugland House!

We know why all these legal persons congregate in one little building on the Cayman Islands. It is not the climate, the view, or the good rental conditions that attract them. They are there to take advantage of the letter of the law, regardless of its purpose. They are there to reduce their tax bills.

Corporations that engage in productive activities that generate profits should pay taxes to the government of the locale of production. This helps the government to fund its programs and corporations to repay their hosts for the use of their resources and trained workforces. Ugland House is built to undermine this reasonable expectation.

A FAMILY AFFAIR

As we have already seen, corporations have been enabled to create corporate families. They can persuade their near relatives to live elsewhere. By pressing a button on a computer, they can install one of them on, say, the Cayman Islands. Once their relative is there, it can be credited with the wealth generated by the parents' productive activities in the parents' home country. That wealth can now be used to generate more wealth while using this friendlier environment as a base.

The Cayman Islands exacts a corporate tax of zero per cent. So, no tax has been paid where the wealth was gathered, and no tax is to be paid by the relatives lounging about in Ugland House, collecting returns on the money if it is deployed. Of course, should any of this money be claimed by those persons or corporations who reside where it was initially earned, taxes will have to be paid. But the volume of money returned and the timing of the return depend on the family's decision-making.

Until any of it is credited back to the parents and its human controllers, the tax is deferred. And, when the money is finally brought back and accounted for, the rate at which it is taxed is at the mercy of the tax-paying corporation. More often than not, the corporation can arrange for minimal taxes to be paid in foreign jurisdictions which will greatly minimize the tax rates when the profits are repatriated. For example, in 2013, *Business Day* reported that Google paid the U.K. government only 2.4 million pounds on its 2.5 billion pounds of income.[3] In response to criticism, Google's executive chairman noted that the corporation had not acted illegally.

There are variants on this model, all established to achieve the same ends. For instance, a multinational corporation doing business in one jurisdiction might contract out part of its income-earning operations to a corporation that it forms and registers in a low-tax jurisdiction, say, Ireland. That corporation then moves the proceeds to another low-tax jurisdiction, say, the Netherlands, where it is taxed, making the impost of tax when the remaining money is returned to headquarters risibly low. The scheme's name describes its shifty nature: "Double Dutch Irish Sandwich."

These are clever schemes. President Obama was less polite when he called Ugland House the "largest tax scam in the world." It, and schemes like it, are very popular. Journalist Carl Gibson reports that, as of 2013, The Bank of America had over 300 foreign subsidiaries, 115 of them in tax havens like the Cayman Islands and Bermuda.[4] And it is not just Ugland House that offers these fine incentives to move income around. There are many other tax havens (more than sixty by some counts) to which large corporations can shift their assets to avert the incidence of taxation in their home country.

Money seeks out the most money-preserving layabout spots. This is why Microsoft's foreign holdings were boosted by $16 billion in 2012, its total foreign holdings rising to a staggering $60.8 billion by June 30, 2012. Oracle used low-tax-jurisdiction Ireland to avoid U.S. taxes to the tune of $272 million. Abbott Laboratories moved $8.1 billion of its U.S.-generated profits to foreign tax havens, enough to allow it to make a pre-tax loss on its American income. It proudly noted that it had saved itself $1.6 billion in U.S. taxes. Johnson & Johnson managed to move almost all its cash out of its home jurisdiction, the

United States: it had $14.8 billion out of its total cash holdings of $14.9 billion in foreign locales with more generous tax regimes. Investigative reporter Robert Scheer noted that General Electric had $108 billion of its massive assets enjoying spa-like conditions in less threatening tax jurisdictions, helping it to avoid paying any tax at all in the United States in the years 2010 to 2012.[5]

And the trend shows no signs of abating. The *International Business Times* reported in August 2014 that Microsoft, in its report to the Securities and Exchange Commission, admitted to having increased its offshore assets to $92 billion, an amount that would have been taxed at the rate of 31.9 per cent in the United States rather than the 3.1 per cent it was paying, costing the American taxpayer $29 billion.[6]

TAX TOURISM

There are a surprising number of locales where bankers and authorities do not ask for the names of depositors willing to come to their jurisdiction, enabling them to avoid the incidence of taxation. Many of them are neither exotic islands nor economically insignificant. Hong Kong and Switzerland top this rather unadmirable list, followed by the United States—many of the states, scrambling for revenue, offer easy incorporation and maximum secrecy to those who use their services. Journalist Jana Kasperkevic avers that U.S. states such as Delaware, Wyoming, and Nevada make it easier to incorporate a shell corporation—a legal entity devised to pursue business goals, with no productive purposes of its own—than to get a library card. The states require less information, showing themselves willing to render applicants virtually invisible to taxing authorities.[7]

The potential for nations, or states within nations, to make a buck out of helping corporations not pay taxes elsewhere has spawned an industry of incorporation. For instance, one report of the International Consortium of Investigative Journalists (ICIJ) found that the British Virgin Islands, a British-controlled micro-state in the Caribbean, has incorporated more than one million offshore entities (that is, offshore vis-à-vis the United Kingdom). The fierce competition for fee-paying and wealth-yielding registrants appears to push nation states to disregard all prudence.

The amount of taxes that might be collected should these pyrotechnics be unavailable to the corporate sectors would make a sizeable difference to national budgets and, therefore, to national decision-making. Diana Gibson, president of the not-for-profit organization Canadians for Tax Fairness, estimates that Canadians have parked $175 billion in tax havens. If that sort of money were taxed at the rates set by democratically elected Canadian governments for Canadians enjoying the business opportunities afforded them by this country, massive amounts of revenue would be available for improvements to welfare, public education, and health. The paper-pushing schemes have budget-affecting impacts. These clever exercises are not harmless peccadilloes.

Recently, the law- and policy-makers who sat by while all these tax avoidance schemes evolved have been newly embarrassed by the revelations known to the media as the Panama Papers. A whistleblower associated with a now famous Panama law firm, Mossack Fonseca, leaked millions of documents to the ICIJ, which shared them with the *Süddeutsche Zeitung* in 2016 and thence with mainstream media all over the world. The sheer number—and in some cases the fame—of corporations and people who used Mossack Fonseca's services to safeguard their money from their home jurisdictions' tax and criminal laws was staggering. Unsurprisingly, as more and more investigators like the Tax Justice Network and the ICIJ report their findings, there are pushes to find ways and means to put a stop to these kinds of manipulations.

In September 2013, the leaders of the G20 met to discuss, not for the first time, developing tools to help authorities combat international tax evaders. The Panama Papers have given these efforts more impetus. Pivotal to the strategies urged by reformers is to entice or force financial institutions to surrender information on customer assets to tax authorities so that they can follow the money and then, perhaps, bring it back to where it belongs. To demand that this happen does not ensure that it will. But let me focus here on why such a plan is needed at all.

THE PROBLEM: PERSONHOOD

It is the apparent unchallengeability of the notion that each corporation is a sovereign person, distinct from its relatives and promoters, that causes the headache. Each corporate person may, as any human might, do as it likes with its property. This, we firmly believe, will ensure its optimal use of resources. It is recognized, of course, that such freedom might lead to abuses and, in some narrowly defined circumstances, the law will prohibit the transfer of assets to foreign jurisdictions. In legalese, a distinction is drawn between the evasion of taxes, which is not allowed, and the avoidance of taxes, which is. Both, of course, lead to the minimization of tax burdens. From the public's perspective, they are hard to keep apart. Indeed, lawyers and courts do not find it easy to do so. But it is widely accepted that there may have to be some constraints on the use of the corporation; the line in the sand is drawn between evasion and avoidance.

Here is an example used by author Gabriel Zucman.[8] He observes that evasion is an attempt by owners of wealth to hide its very existence and, thereby, the owners' interest in it. To do this, they might set up a shell corporation in the Cayman Islands and equip it with a bank account in Switzerland. The creators of the scheme might then get the shell corporation to bill them in respect of an alleged transaction, with the invoice to be paid by depositing the money "owed" into the corporation's bank account in Switzerland. The creators' money will, for all practical purposes, have disappeared from view, snatched away from the clutches of any authority. Criminals such as drug sellers, thieves, and politicians who steal from the national treasury can hide their ill-gotten gains in this way.

This evasion is characterized as an abuse of the grant of legal personhood: the corporate form is not meant to be used for overt criminal purposes. Prosecutors and tax departments can have such schemes set aside if they ever find out about them. But this kind of abuse is not the core problem. It is when corporate decision-makers, for ostensible operational reasons, move their openly acknowledged and properly acquired assets around to other jurisdictions that it becomes difficult to hold any accompanying tax minimization to be wrongful.

Such schemes are legal. Corporations are staying within the letter of tax laws and relying on the formal rules of corporate law. Their astute use of law allows corporations to lower their tax bills, almost to the vanishing point. Governments could change these kinds of laws any time they chose. But they come under fierce pressure from those very corporations that benefit from the current state of play, the same pressure that will make it very hard for strategies such as those the G20 has promised to develop to succeed. Large corporate manipulators contend that inhibiting their tax scheming would put them at a competitive disadvantage and that this would be bad for the government and the people it serves. And of course, the same corporations had lobbied law-makers to allow them to lower their tax obligations by taking advantage of tax havens in the first place.

Corporate logic mandates that these kinds of pressure tactics will be employed to reduce the costs of government interference with the unfettered market. There is a continuous push to reduce government-imposed costs that are intended to avert harms to, or to bestow benefits on, the overall welfare of the citizenry. This goes on in all spheres of regulation, whether it be tax laws or consumer, environment, or workplace protections. In the last thirty years or so, these attacks have become so common and so effective that, in public discourse, they are referred to by one (misleading) word, deregulation.[9] Deregulation is praised as reform by capitalists and bemoaned as regressive by advocates for non-wealth owners. And the latter have been fighting losing battles as the law has handed capitalists weapons of mass destruction.

INVISIBLE INFLUENCE

The corporation, created as the equivalent of a natural person, may hold property and, as a sovereign individual, do with it as it wills. This has led to a widespread internalization of the belief that, just as human beings in a liberal market democracy are entitled to do, corporations are entitled not to invest their property. These blobs, especially the very large ones, are able to exercise extraordinary influence over policy-making, effectively pushing governments in directions that force them to change their priorities. The larger the corporation, the greater the fear it induces in politicians.

It is rarely necessary for corporations (via their human mouthpieces) to threaten a government directly. It is seldom essential for a corporation to explicitly declare that, unless it gets its way, it will withhold its capital. An occasional closure of a plant, a speech by one or more noted capitalists that they, or the blob with which they are associated, have lost confidence in the government's policies, or the publication of a learned paper to this effect by some think tank, all supplemented by slick blandishments by wallet-carrying lobbyists, will do the trick.

Large for-profit corporations routinely use their dominant economic position to bias the political and legal system in their favour. These kinds of corporations are fairly characterized as political actors, not just economic ones. They do not respect the supposed separation of the economic from the political sphere. This should be a source of anxiety for intellectual defenders of liberal market capitalism, who hold fast to the pretense that politics and economics are separate spheres.

The mantra is that the economy is at its most efficient the less political intervention there is with market operations. Not only should private profit-seekers not be asked to act on behalf of others, but governments should also be loath to do so. The political economy as a whole works best when the economic and political spheres are kept distinct.

This perspective is heavily propagandized by the corporations' cheer-leaders. So when large corporate blobs set out to destroy the basis on which these views are said to be founded, its political legitimacy comes into question. The tax haven phenomenon is one such cause for angst. Concern about the relationship between the political and the economic also comes up when a government opposes foreign state-owned investment funds. That kind of investor, it is feared, might be prone to direct a corporation to serve a foreign state's political purposes rather than the mere maximization of corporate profits. This potential use of economic power for political purposes is portrayed as anathema, not just because it advances a foreign nation's goals but also because it muddies the pure waters of the market.

The separation of acceptable economic actions by corporations from their exercise of political power is important to our system of liberal law.

The system pretends that the political sphere of decision-making is subject to the rule of law and democratic practices. Private economic actors can be left to chase their dreams, as they will never be allowed to take over the political authority of law and the state. But the brief sketch above makes it all too plain that the largest corporations do seek to get politicians to act on their behalf and do so effectively by using their economic clout. It is particularly obvious in the United States—where the watchdog Sunlight Foundation reports that from 2007 to 2012, the two hundred largest politically active corporations spent six billion dollars on lobbying and were rewarded with four trillion dollars in government contracts and other assistance, a return of $760 for every dollar spent—but it is true everywhere.

The viability of our electoral democracy—in which numbers supposedly matter more than dollars, in which human electors should matter rather than legal artificial beings—comes under scrutiny. In daily political discourse, there are ceaseless debates about the dysfunctional use of lobbyists, the distortions spawned by campaign and political party financing, and the venality and corrupting influence of the revolving door between large corporate influence-seekers and the political and senior bureaucratic classes. It is conventional wisdom that these shenanigans undermine, and have the potential to destroy, our democratic values and legal institutions. It has become trite to say that we know that large corporations will try to act politically, and that this is wrong because our one-person, one-vote electoral system is put at risk by their disproportional political clout.

The responses we make, however, are less than radical. We try to limit corporations' ability to act politically by attacking the instruments they use. We concentrate on limitations on the use of lobbyists, on financial contributions to politicians and their parties and causes. These attempts are meritorious, but they do not challenge the source of the corporations' political power. Their control over the means of production gives them inherent political and economic clout. The right of those owners of wealth who seek to have this clout used to their advantage is not put in issue. Our reforms are aimed narrowly; they focus on the regulation of the ways corporations exercise their powers to dominate us while the disproportionate influence wielded by the capitalists who control the corporate world is not confronted directly.

This explains stories like Ugland House and the Panama Papers. They are examples of how large for-profit corporations possess an eagerness, indeed, a zealous desire, to avoid the legal responsibilities governments seek to impose on them by the expressed will of society. This, in turn, attests to their willingness to reject any notion of a duty of reciprocity or mutuality, the kind of virtue that human members of any would-be cohesive society embrace. As Nobel Prize–winning economist Joseph Stiglitz put it, "Multinational corporations … call on the federal government to negotiate favorable trade treaties that allow them easy entry into foreign markets and to defend their commercial interests around the world, but then use these foreign bases to avoid paying taxes."[10] These corporations have no sense of national pride and, more importantly, they reject any idea that they might owe legal or moral obligations to their government and the citizenry it serves.

PROFESSIONALS FOR SALE

Corporations' behaviour reveals a kind of anomie. Large for-profit corporations act as if compliance with existing laws is all that should be expected of them and, in addition, put their considerable resources to work to ensure that the laws that they will obey crimp their profitability as little as possible. The best we can hope for is that they will abide by the strictest, narrowest meaning of the law, even as that behaviour defeats the law's purpose and spirit. Moreover, they display little concern for the adverse impact that their drive to minimize their obligations has on anyone else or on the political system. It is fanciful for reformers to expect these kinds of corporations to care about anyone but themselves, a point to which we shall return again and again.

This strongly suggests that the tremendous efforts exerted by well-intentioned reformers into developing socially responsible corporations that have regard for non-corporate stakeholders are not having—and will not have—much impact. If these tax- and regulation-averse corporations were asked to justify their self-regarding behaviour, they would contend that, if left as untaxed as possible, as unregulated as possible, not just they but everyone would benefit. Unblushingly, they call themselves job creators. Whatever the merit of this theoretical argument (based, as it is, on a pristine laissez-faire doctrine), it is the opposite of the positive altruistic action called for by the social responsibility/corporate stakeholder movements. This points to another feature of the blob's many machinations and obligation-avoiding stratagems.

Large corporate capitalists, precisely because they are soul-less, bodyless entities, employ professionals to do their not-so-admirable handiwork. The Ugland House and Panama Papers stories point to an unpalatable fact. These corporate cost-reducing drives reveal the "professional-for-sale" role played by some of our elites. As corporations generally prefer to act within the law that would impose obligations on them,[11] the ensuing schemes developed by the professionals they hire are sophisticated and refined.

Corporations pay handsomely for advice that enables them to say that they are not evading the legal requirements, as a common thief does, but are merely taking the law, as written, to where lawyers and accountants say it may go. This spurs lawyers, accountants, and other financial and technical advisers to look for ways to push the legal envelopes in which elected governments have wrapped their policies. If that means subverting the integrity of those policies, the professionals excuse themselves by the mantra that it is their job to serve their clients while staying within the law. They believe, sincerely no doubt, that this can do nothing but good. To serve their clients—supposedly akin to the single-minded butchers, brewers, and bakers of the to-be-adulated Adam Smithian world—is to serve the advancement of the public good.

This justification breeds cadres of professionals determined to defeat the spirit of laws aimed at fettering the power of wealth owners, especially of large corporate blobs. They reap rich material rewards and are deemed to be very good at their job every time they think up a new scheme that dilutes the adverse impact on profits that a particular regulatory framework might have. It breeds, in other words, a powerful and often prestigious group of opinion leaders whose daily activities abjure the idea that profit-maximizers have any social responsibility other than maximizing profits. It breeds, then, a most influential layer of people whose everyday conduct, regardless of the high-blown rhetoric in which professional bodies wallow, negates the ideals and values of altruism and compassion. It is a corrosive influence.

The extent of that corrosion of our values and norms needs to be appreciated. If we want change, I will argue, a totally new approach is warranted.

Gaming the System

EFFORTS TO SHIFT COSTS BY MEANS OF THE CORPORATION IMPOSE burdens on society. They offset the economic and social benefits the corporate form is supposed to bring by its efficient chase for profits. Potentially, one could justify the incorporation of large firms as a more productive use of discrete parcels of capital contributed by different individuals that are aggregated and entrusted to a large number of functionaries and workers. But I will argue that that potential is not realized, as the minuses outweigh the pluses. And when small firms incorporate, there is no logic to any claim that incorporation improves efficiency.

SNAPSHOTS: EVERYDAY LEGAL PLOYS
Unpaid Workers: *Refac* and *Avant Lithographics*

Suppose a man runs a business supplying Ford Motor Company with parts. He loses his contract to supply Ford and, as a result, he is in the process of closing down this business, knowing that some of his employees are owed unpaid wages. This does not stop him from trying to start again: he opens a new business to win a contract to supply Ford Motor Company and, this time, other clients. Before his new business gets started, the bank from which he had borrowed to run his first business tries to recoup some of its money. It takes over the running of his first business to get whatever it can out of it before it goes under. That does not yield very much, and the bank sells the assets that first business had. Some of those assets are bought by the second business that our man is trying to get off the ground. The employees of the first business then bring actions for unpaid wages against our man and his new business.

The ordinary person in the street would find it hard to see how our man, just because he is now operating a new business, could argue that he is no longer responsible for the debts he has left behind. Those debts are owed because he has defaulted on a contract he made as an individual with his individual employees. Most of us would think that he should pay what is legally owed. Liberal philosophy and the principles of a market economy, which posit that individuals should be responsible for their conduct, would have it no other way. This is a platitude—unless a corporation is inserted into the mix. The blob makes a huge difference. Consider the legal decision in a case called *Refac Industrial Contractors Inc.*[1]

This was a case before an administrative tribunal from which the facts in the made-up case above were taken. In the made-up case, there were no corporations. In the actual case, there were. In the actual case, our man was named Keller. He ran his two businesses through incorporated firms. The first business was called Keller Ltd. When he formed the second business, he gave it the name of Refac Industrial Contractors. In law, these two blobs (Keller Ltd. and Refac) were distinct legal persons, that is, distinct from all other legal persons. Distinct, therefore, from each other and from our man Keller. Keller was the chief shareholder and manager of both corporations. In law, there was now an argument that Refac Industrial Contractors Inc. could not be held responsible for the debts left by Keller Ltd. Moreover, there was an argument that Keller himself was not responsible for the debts owed by either Keller Ltd. or Refac Industrial Contractors Inc., firms which he had incorporated and managed and in which he had bought shares in the hope of increasing their value.

Just as before, the ordinary person in the street would have little difficulty in seeing Keller as the self-seeking person who had created the debts and, therefore, should be held responsible for them. That would satisfy common sense, our sense of justice, our belief in the tenets of a liberal polity and a market economy. Only in law, only in corporate law, does the plain truth become obscured; only by law, by corporate law, are liberal and market principles endangered. The interposition of a corporation, of an inanimate entity, creates formally different relationships. This allows clever manipulators to avoid the materialized risks of their risk-creating activities.

The problem is so serious that legislatures have had to step in, again and again. The *Refac Industrial Contractors* case arose out of a 1990 adjudication under the *Employment Standards Act* in Ontario. It is one of many statutes that provide that, in certain circumstances, formally separate persons will be treated as sufficiently related to be responsible for each other's obligations. Employees' contractual or statutory rights are not to be lost because of some clever finagling of corporate law. This would give our labour laws legitimacy problems. Similar provisions exist in other areas; for instance, workers who have won bargaining rights at one place of employment might find themselves without a collective agreement or union if their corporate employer restructures the business by hiving off separate corporate entities to do some of the bargaining unit's work or by selling assets or operations to another corporate entity. The problem arises often enough for governments to have enacted related and successor employer provisions which, in certain specific cases, will safeguard existing bargaining rights.

The emphasis of the remedial legislation is that relief is to be granted in limited circumstances. Thus, in *Refac Industrial Contractors*, the corporation Refac was held responsible for Keller Ltd.'s debts because the web of businesses (which featured Keller, the man, as the spider who had spun the web) had the effect of negating the intent of the governing *Employment Standards Act*. Such a conclusion is not reached easily. Labour law students spend an inordinate amount of time studying the subtle differences which gave rise to different results in similar cases. (They thereby incidentally become acquainted with how best to manipulate the law for future clients who might benefit from avoidance practices.) The reason for the restraints imposed on remedial legislation is that, while the spirit of protecting laws—such as minimum standards and successor bargaining rights laws—is to be safeguarded from misuse of the corporate form, the corporate form itself is to be encouraged because it facilitates capitalist market actors and activities.

An example of the delicacy involved is furnished by a decision by another referee adjudicating an *Employment Standards Act* case in Ontario in 1991. In *Avant Lithographics*, employees again sought to recover unpaid termination pay. The workers argued that a newly formed corporation, doing very similar business to the original one, was sufficiently related to the original corporation to be made responsible for the debt owed to them by the original corporation. The new corporation had been launched by the principal participants in the original business. They quickly found it hard going and looked for an infusion of capital. A new major investor came along. He was the son of one of the shakers and makers of the original corporation. This helpful angel immediately appointed his father as president and a director of the new corporation which, of course, was to pay his father a salary. The dutiful son had borrowed the money for the investment from his affectionate mother. The referee determined that the second corporation, although it involved many of the same human actors who had been pivotal in the original, debt-leaving, corporation, had not relied on any capital that might have been said to come from the original business. This caused the referee to hold that the new corporate entity was not sufficiently related to the original one to be held responsible for its debts.[2] The lesson is stark.

Our legal system, designed to serve market capitalism, encourages enterprise and investment. The corporation is one of the instruments it provides to facilitate such activities. The blob's legitimacy must be maintained and its use should not be discouraged. The starting position, therefore, is that no questions are to be raised about the utility of the corporate form and there is to be no introspective inquiry as to whether its use in the particular circumstances serves any social benefit at all. Its economic and social utility is to be assumed. If clever (or, to their victims, unscrupulous) small-business entrepreneurs use the form in a way that yields shameful results, the instinct is to provide a remedy without affecting the general standing and future use of the blob.

Governments, imbued by the cult that upholds the utility of the corporate form, are very ungenerous when enacting protective legislation that may interfere with the formal logic of corporate law. Instructed in this way, judicial tribunals find it difficult to put serious restraints on the use of the corporation as a cost-shifting mechanism. And it is worth noting that, whenever it is found that the interposition of a corporation allows an actor central to risk-creation to avoid responsibility for the costs that actor imposes, those costs do not disappear. They are borne by unpaid creditors and workers and these victims' dependants, as well as by the governments that have to pick up the pieces.

Worker Safety: *Lee's Air Farming* and *Brambles*

Lee v. *Lee's Air Farming Ltd.*[3] was a case decided by the Privy Council in 1961. The Privy Council was then one of the highest courts in the Anglo–common law judicial hierarchy, and its precedents continue to be highly persuasive. Lee was a New Zealand crop duster who flew a plane to do his job. He entered into contracts with farmers who wanted their fields sprayed. For reasons unexplained in the judicial decision, Lee incorporated the business he had run as a sole entrepreneur. He became the chief director and manager of the new corporation as well as its major shareholder (his bookkeeper being given one, obviously token, share). Lee continued to fly the crop-dusting plane to fulfill contracts obtained from farmers. His plane crashed and he was killed.

The issue was whether the corporation had been his employer and liable for workers' compensation premiums and payment. To consider the corporation to be Lee's employer took a lot of imagination. It was his creature; it was created to continue his business as it had always been run by him. Lee, the man, still went out to obtain the contracts. Lee, the man, advised the corporation whether to seek a contract from a particular farmer and what to charge the farmer. Lee, the man, still flew the plane to perform the contract. To suggest that Lee was just an employee like any other, taking orders on how to carry out tasks set by his employer was, to say the least, fanciful. Yet, in a decision that still is one of the most important precedents for modern corporate law practitioners in England and its former colonies, it was held by the Privy Council that Lee's Air Farming Ltd., having been formally incorporated, was a separate person, distinct from all others in the world, including its creator and only functionary and beneficiary, Lee, the man.

The decision is so important to corporate lawyers because its logic allows them to use their imagination to alleviate many legal responsibilities their clients might otherwise bear. In the *Refac* and *Avant Lithographics* cases discussed above, the tribunals were confronted with fact situations where the supposedly distinct businesses were of the same character, served the same general market, employed similar modes of operation, and were the creatures of the same human beings. The tribunals were asked to hold that the human beings and their creatures were separate persons in law, regardless of their functional connections. The logic of, and reverence for, the holding in *Lee's Air Farming Ltd.*—and in the thousands of decisions based on it—forced the tribunals in *Refac* and *Avant Lithographics* to look for something very special to thwart the impact of the formal legal separation of such intimately related actors. This logic is even harder to overcome when there are no human and corporate overlaps, even though there is a great deal of integration between different firms and humans, between blobs and the people who create and run them, between distinct legal persons.

In one such case, a worker named Wail was an employee of a large corporation called Brambles Ltd. Brambles ran a laundering service for hospitals. It had a fleet of specially designed trucks in which trolleys could be fitted, four across. The truck was marked with the Brambles logo and was insured by Brambles. Wail's job was to use this truck to pick up and deliver laundry from and to various hospitals. After he had loaded his truck with dirty laundry, the laundry would be cleaned by Brambles and then loaded back on the same truck for return to the hospitals.

Brambles Ltd. decided to get rid of all of its truck drivers. The dismissed employees, such as Wail, were told that, if they formed a corporation, it could bid to get a contract to serve the same route that the former employee had serviced. If successful, the newly formed corporation would ask its promoter, the former Brambles employee, to use the same truck bearing the Brambles logo, fitted with its trolleys and insured by Brambles, to service the same routes, enabling the new corporation to fulfill the contractual obligations it owed to Brambles Ltd.

Wail, together with his friend Parker (who was given a token share and acted as the corporation's bookkeeper) formed a corporation they named Andar Transport Pty. Ltd. This corporation successfully bid for the contract to service the route that Brambles Ltd. had formerly allocated to Wail, its erstwhile employee.

Let us stop for a moment to stress the message being conveyed: the corporate form is being consciously used to avert existing legal responsibilities. Brambles Ltd. changed its legal relationships by getting rid of personal contractual relations with its employees. As an employer, it had borne the costs of injuries its employees suffered and caused to others when carrying out their duties; Brambles also had to make contributions on its employees' behalf to social security programs. By no longer contracting directly with the employees, it reduced its legal obligations to them and to outsiders.

To return: Wail was injured because the Brambles Ltd. truck he was driving, more specifically, the way in which the trolleys had come to be aligned, was defective. He was crushed. He sued Brambles Ltd., saying that it had breached a duty it owed him as a person who would foreseeably be affected by a malfunctioning trolley due to its failure to take appropriate care when providing the truck. After a complex legal struggle, Wail won that argument. But then Brambles Ltd., seeing all its careful scheming come to naught, sued Wail's corporation, Andar Transport Pty. Ltd., for a contribution to the damages it had to pay Wail.

Brambles's argument was that Andar Transport, like any employer, had a personal duty to take care to ensure that its workers were safe and that it had failed in this case. As in the *Lee's Air Farming* case, the contention was that the corporation, formed and controlled by Wail, was completely separate from Wail. The absurdity is gobsmacking: Andar Transport Pty. Ltd. only existed to ensure that Wail had a job, specifically, his old job. It had no other purpose.

The highest court in Australia accepted Brambles Ltd.'s argument, holding that, even though a corporation could only meet its duty to provide a safe work environment by relying on the thinking and acting of the very employee who was injured, it was stuck with a separate obligation to meet the standard of care. The employing blob created by Wail so that he could be employed was personally responsible for the failure to take care towards Wail, even though it was Wail who decided how the corporation ought to behave. As a result, Wail, having been awarded damages to be paid by Brambles Ltd., now had to direct Andar Transport Pty. Ltd., that is, his corporation, to make a contribution to Brambles. Manifestly, any loss incurred by Andar Transport was a loss incurred by Wail. Brambles's scheme, rupturing a contractual arrangement by the use of a corporate entity, had wrought a magical outcome.[4]

The profound judicial internalization of the cult of the separateness of the corporate person led, inexorably, to the acceptance of the argument that the employee Wail had directed the corporation he had created to be careless towards him. This can only be described as surreal. Unfortunately, this kind of thinking is not aberrational. Its widely accepted legitimacy has allowed anti-social manipulators to poison much of our societal relations.

Capitalist employers are always looking for means to reduce their costs and, thereby, increase their profits. Labour costs are the bugbear of all employers, and they use their economic clout to undermine workers' bargaining positions. The *Brambles* case was such an instance. For Brambles's scheme to work, it had to use its power to force its employees to set up a "separate" person through which all transactions would be conducted. In the *Refac* and *Avant Lithographics* cases, the same human actors and overlapping assets and goals tied the various businesses together, making it possible, at least, to hold them responsible for each other. In fact, Brambles was just as closely involved in the whole of the relationship as were the various actors in those cases, just as controlling as the pivotal actors in those cases—if not more, as it had forced Wail to form the separate blob—but it was harder to hold Andar Transport and Brambles to be related or associated for legal liability purposes. This exercise of control by one corporation over other discrete corporations without having to enter into a contract is a favoured piece of legal shenanigans.

Hiding behind the Supply Chain: Eliz World

Rebecca Wong had a business that made lines of clothing that were to be sold by large retailing chains. She created a corporation named Eliz World to conduct her manufacturing business. She obtained contracts to supply a line named Northern Elements. The contract to supply the line was given to her by another corporation by the name of Kenny's Sportwear. Kenny's Sportwear, in turn, obtained a contract to produce Northern Elements from another corporation called Presidio Clothing. Presidio Clothing asked Knitted Sportswear to make these garments after an order was placed for them by the incorporated retailer that would eventually sell them. The retailer was Venator.

Rebecca Wong's corporation, Eliz World, had two similar arrangements with other supply chains. At the apex of one was the retailer J.Crew. It had found one contractor to make J.Crew clothes who, in turn, found another, and so on, until eventually the task to make J.Crew garments fell to Rebecca Wong's Eliz World. Another retailer's brand of clothing, Culture Clothing, was to be delivered to the corporate retailer Modern Times. To this end, Modern Times contracted with a corporate manufacturer, Culture Clothing Inc, which contracted with another corporation to make these clothes, and so on, until the doing of the actual job got to Eliz World in Toronto.

Eliz World, being a blob, could not do the jobs. That task fell to Rebecca Wong to organize and manage. One of her choices was to hire workers who would work from home, a common practice in the garment industry. When Eliz World fell on hard times, some of those workers found they had been short-changed, another common phenomenon in this kind of set-up. There were unpaid wages; worse, the agreed rate at which wages were to be paid had been below the statutory minimum. There was also money owed for overtime and vacation that should by law have been paid.

Claims for this owed money were brought against the retailers at the top of these supply chains. The question was whether they should be held responsible as the corporate persons that had sought to benefit from the low-wage sector, indeed, from wages that were unlawfully low. In effect, the question was whether their connections with Eliz World and its employees were sufficiently strong to have them treated as related or associated employers and, thereby, legally liable to pay the workers' claims. For the ordinary citizen, brought up within a value system that holds that those who create risks and cause harm for their own benefit should be held accountable when the risks materialize, this would have been an easy question to answer. It was not for a court of law.

The court held that Venator, J.Crew, and Modern Times could not be held responsible because the workers could not establish that the retailers enjoyed common ownership of assets or shared management with the clothing manufacturers with which they contracted directly or with any other subcontracting entities down the line (with which they had no contractual relations at all). Adherence to the formality of the doctrine that each corporation is a sovereign person in its own right did not allow for a finding that, despite the close business links they had with the contractors and subcontractors, they could be considered liable for those other individuals' wrongs.

The respect paid to the sovereignty and independence of these interposed blobs is remarkable. If the contractors with the retailers had been mere human beings, each of whom, in turn, had found another human being to produce the garment, who had found another human being who, in the end, had turned to Rebecca Wong (and if her business was not incorporated), it is likely that the law would have found it much easier to categorize all those human beings along the way as the retailers' employees or agents. It would have been more obvious that all these intermediaries were part and parcel of the retailers' consciously created business organization.

What is even more bizarre is that the court understood that the set-up was deliberately designed by the retailers. It was their business plan. The court was under no illusion about the deep links and commonality of purpose of all the actors in each of the supply chains that finished with Rebecca Wong's outfit as the manufacturer. The presiding judge, Cumming, J., in the 2001 case that ensued,[5] noted that this was a common and economically efficient way to organize production, especially in the garment industry:

> The industry seeks high inventory turnover. Time is of the essence....
> Subcontractors have the ability to have jobs completed when time runs

short … [and] it is common for manufacturers to subcontract … [this] evidences an integrated industry rather than an integrated business. (para. 58).

There we have it. The economic integration of business organization in an industry is to be expected and accepted because it makes for efficiency. But in law, it is pretended that any one instance of this "natural" phenomenon will not necessarily make the corporation at the top of that particular food chain responsible for the marginalized, cheap labour resources that its minion blobs have recruited on its behalf. This legal tolerance, which seems to go out of its way to ignore the functional tightness of the links between blobs, is relied on by the Apples, Nikes, Walmarts, Gaps, H&Ms, Sears, Hudson's Bays, and so forth, as they bring us their branded goods. It allows them to satisfy our desires at prices which we can much better afford than the prices we would have to pay if the full cost of the depletion of finite resources and the harms done to workers in faraway places were paid for by them.

We will focus on this issue in more detail in chapter 7. For the moment it suffices to note that the use of the corporate form enables the costs of production to be externalized by large corporations. Others bear those costs, while the behemoths reap the lion's share of the profits.

This clever use of the blob is one to which its defenders never thought it should be put. Intellectual corporate cheerleaders are market enthusiasts, and the market is distorted by this canny and self-serving shifting of risks. They should be discomfited; they should be embarrassed by the imaginative professionals that engineer such risk-shifting schemes.

The Burden of Risk: James Hardie Group

This easy distancing between profit-chasing capitalists and the people they might harm by relying on blobs to erect barriers is even available within the framework of a corporate group with tight legal links. In a recent example, James Hardie, an Australian corporate group constituted by seventy entities—a parent and its children and grandchildren—constituted a profitable enterprise that mined and processed asbestos.[6] Out of the massive profits produced by the integrated asbestos business, it built a large and profit-able additional business that supplied building materials to the construc-tion industry. In the late 1980s, the James Hardie outfits had stopped doing any asbestos mining and processing but, by then, their balance sheets were burdened by potential liability for damages owed to many people grievously damaged by their toxic substance business. Cleverly (or unscrupulously, if you will), their lawyers and accountants restructured the corporate group.

Formally, they said that they were merely redeploying the assets and skills to be more efficient, something which capitalist law has to respect and facilitate. James Hardie moved all of its current business (mainly in building supplies) out of Australia to the Netherlands, a more favourable tax jurisdic-tion, leaving behind two corporate members of the group with no function except to hold funds to satisfy the legal obligations owed to injured, sick, and dead Australians. A trustee was to oversee the process of vetting claims and paying them. In the event, James Hardie's directors and executives tried to be too cute and left behind a risible amount of money, much too little to take care of all the potential liabilities. This led to a political uproar and gov-ernment intervention. Eventually a settlement of sorts was hammered out. There was a great deal of condemnation of the strategy employed by James Hardie to limit its liability. Yet what the James Hardie corporate group had done when it sought to restructure itself is a lawful business tool commonly deployed by corporations.

This kind of reorganization of a corporate business firm is said to be acceptable because the directors and their management team have a respon-sibility to make the best use of their assets, and their judgment is to be trusted. But if reorganization means a reallocation of assets and liabilities, this might leave some creditors with recourse to less than what had been the aggregated group's capital. Their position would be affected.

In law, a compromise has been struck between, on the one hand, giving profit-pursuing corporations freedom to manoeuvre and, on the other hand, protecting creditors of those corporations. Restructuring is to be allowed if it is the result of diligent deliberations by the corporate group's managers. Their judgment should be respected. Creditors should remain aware that changing risks are part and parcel of capital markets' efficient operations. All that creditors are entitled to expect, therefore, is that the changes wrought to the corporate group are made in good faith and after appropriate disclosure. This is what was lacking, people thought, in the James Hardie case, and that is why its restructuring did not fly. But normally, the law tolerates the reallocation of the burden of existing risks by corporate managers.

There is no equivalent doctrine in the non-corporate sphere. Individuals cannot unilaterally say to creditors that they are no longer responsible to meet the obligations their non-incorporated firm had incurred while chasing benefits. They cannot say: We have hived off some of our assets to members of our family because this makes good business sense, and it's too bad that the assets you creditors thought we had are no longer available to you.

It would be plain to one and all that to permit a human being to behave in this way would offend both liberal law and market principles. Interpose a bunch of blobs and those principles are shamelessly, effortlessly jettisoned. The law makes the easy formation of corporate families available for just such manipulations. It allows the disavowal of responsibility for harms done by profit-yielding activity by one (formally separate) member on behalf of the whole firm.

The technique is used in a dazzling array of circumstances where incorporated capitalists want to shift the risks they build into their relentless chase for profits. When an enterprise knows that its business has the potential to harm a great number of people simultaneously, it will sensibly put a ring around its assets by allocating the risk of this potential misfiring to one or more of its not-very-well-funded blobs.[7] This strategy is a favourite one.

It is all too embarrassing for sincere believers in market capitalism, and they reach out to make it all look less absurd, more in line with the general public's expectations. This, it turns out, is a tough task for believers in corporate personhood.

ATTEMPTS TO LIFT THE VEIL

Law has woven a fabric hiding from public view responsibility-shy individual actors who otherwise would be accountable in their own right. Every now and again, these shy folk might have to be held accountable; every now and again the need will be felt to peek under the blob's cloaking device. This is referred to as lifting, or piercing, the corporate veil. The impulse is resisted more often than not. The anthropomorphic approach to the corporation is so deeply embedded and the normalization of corporate capitalism so entrenched that this this lifting of the veil occurs rarely and haphazardly.

As the Supreme Court of Canada has stated, the law on piercing the veil "follows no consistent principles."[8] When it does happen, it is usually in very easy cases involving small corporations where the line between the active individuals in the enterprise and the blob is completely blurred because the active individuals do everything, get everything, finance everything. In those cases, it is easier to see the righteousness of removing the veil because its use is "too flagrantly opposed to justice," the criterion proffered by the Supreme Court of Canada, though a nebulous concept, at best. One might have thought that, whatever justice entails, it ought to have led to different results in *Lee* v. *Lee's Air Farming Ltd.* and the *Brambles* case discussed above.

Courts and tribunals find it difficult to lift the veil; they are too wedded to the cant of the sacred nature of the sovereign legal personality of corporations.[9] This is why legislatures have had to step in with remedies. Several cases that allowed tribunals to classify corporate persons as sufficiently associated to be held responsible for each other in some circumstances were discussed above. But we also saw that decision-makers, even when specifically armed with legislation, are far from gung-ho when they are asked to set aside cunningly woven veils.

Thus, the law provides some remedies against the anti-social, anti-market gyrations of corporate plotters and schemers. But the starting point of the corporate person as a sovereign one puts the harmed individuals, those onto whom the costs of corporate profit-chasing have been shifted, behind the eight ball when they seek indemnification for their losses. They must try to gather political support and, if necessary, litigate, wasting money and time, to get what is owed to them legally and morally. Few people have the resources and knowledge to pursue their claims. Given the starting position and the uncertainty about just when the law will look beyond the blob's sovereignty, there is little risk that the exploiters of corporate law will be made to account to those they hurt by their corporate manoeuvring.

In sum: corporate law, judges, and tribunals encourage the bastards. Who are they?

THE BLOB'S HUMAN MOTIVATORS

It is not surprising that an invisible, intangible creature without cognition or sensibilities will act in an anti-social manner, manifest anomie, or be heedless of the hurt it inflicts on vulnerable people. After all, a corporation is insubstantial ectoplasm. It can be moulded to take any shape, to act in any way.

But this also means that the corporation itself would have no objection if its conduct was required to be altruistic, concerned with the plight of others and their environment. While capitalism needs us to believe that it is natural for us as human beings to be self-centred and uncaring about others and their environments, and that to be greedy and aggressively competitive are worthy character traits, blobs do not feel anything. They do not have the urge to become wealthier or bigger or to change shape. There is nothing in their soul-less and bodyless existence that would make them want to compete with other soul-less, bodyless blobs. Obvious though this is, it is important to emphasize it: the corporation's motivation to conduct its business in one way or another is framed by the decisions and desires of real human beings, decisions and desires that are made and developed in a specific context.

Those who think and act on behalf of the corporation must decide how to use the corporation's capacities. They are given a legal mandate: they must pursue the best interests of the corporation. Manifestly, this directive is of little help. The corporation in its own right—as a blob, as ectoplasm—has no interests to pursue. But corporations are allowed, indeed, encouraged to be formed, because they will help capitalists to satisfy their greed which, we are told over and over, will enure to the public benefit. If corporations are to fulfill these functions, they should push to accumulate socially produced wealth for the benefit of those whose tool they are. The best interests of the corporation are served, then, if the actions taken advance the grasping tendencies of the human owners of wealth who have invested in the corporation.

During his ill-fated presidential campaign against Barack Obama, Mitt Romney, responding to a heckler in Iowa who suggested that taxes should be raised on corporations, said: "Corporations are people, my friend … of course they are. Everything corporations earn ultimately goes to the people ….human beings, my friend."

Romney, a rich and corporate-investing man, was lampooned mercilessly for equating artificial persons with flesh-and-blood human beings. The oft-repeated sound bite "corporations are people" attracted understandable derision: everyone knows that it is ridiculous to equate a real human being with a legal instrument. Of all people, politicians who offer themselves as servants of the citizenry should be aware of this. On the basis of this short and silly statement, it was right to depict Romney as being badly out of touch. But he had said something else as well, something that everyone also knows to be true: corporations do what they do to please some very special people, namely capitalists. That is, they do it for real people.

It is those special people who motivate the blobs to act as they do. It is to pursue their interests that the corporate form is used to avert responsibilities, to heap the costs and injuries of profit-maximization on others, to pervert our conventional values and norms. It is the satisfaction of these special people's goals that make corporations what they are.

In part II, I will argue that corporate law is deliberately constructed to advance the goals and objectives of a special sub-set of our community, of some identifiable human beings who could not get away with pursuing the corporations' many anti-social activities from which they benefit if they had to act without the help of the blob. So, let us talk about shareholders.

PART II

THE SHAREHOLDER:
THE PRIVILEGING
OF A CLASS

In which it is shown that shareholders in blobs want to have it all ways. When it comes to paying up for a bad bet, they want to be treated in the same way as the lazy folk who bet on horse races. They do not want to be held responsible for any wrongs committed by means of the blobs on which they bet. But the law cares about them much more than about gamblers. It treats them as if they are essential components of a productive economy. They want to be treated like human beings acting as entrepreneurs, without any of the risks of being punished as unblobbed human entrepreneurs are for wrongful behaviour. Thus shareholders become the core of a zone of irresponsibility, toxins who poison the body politic. When this becomes evident, corporate capitalism must scramble frenetically as it seeks to maintain its legitimacy.

The Shareholder
as Gambler

TO BECOME SHAREHOLDERS, INDIVIDUALS INVEST SOME OF THEIR private property in a corporation. They do this with a view to garner more property than they invested, and they expect the corporation to help. As we have seen, their invested money instantly becomes part of the corporation's capital, of its private property. The corporation—through its directors, executives, and employees—plans how best to put that capital to use so as to maximize profits which it will share with the shareholders. The blob is to be the active capitalist. What does this make the contributing shareholders?

THE PRETENSE

Shareholders could be considered real capitalists if the corporate ownership and deployment of their contributions of capital were seen as mere facilities enabling individual entrepreneurs to meld their capital with that of other like-minded folk, all of whom are better off as a result. Recall the blob's major legal attribute, separate legal personhood, and the accompanying right—bestowed on every sovereign individual—of being entitled to use its property as it sees fit. Its personhood could be read as making it merely an efficient agent for a bunch of principals, the shareholders, who had transferred their property to it. This would acknowledge the shareholders to be red-blooded capitalists.

Indeed, an influential school of intellectuals—the law and economics school—characterizes shareholders as contracting principals, as real capitalists.[1] And while I share this characterization, I do not agree with the way those scholars get to that conclusion, nor with the way in which they then put it to use. This argument will be picked up in in chapters 9 and 11. For the moment, let us simply note that many shareholders see themselves as contracting principals, as owners of the business run by means of the corporation. But this characterization of the blob as an instrument serving the shareholders/capitalists is dangerous to the corporate law project. It threatens the idea that shareholders/capitalists are eligible for the protections they crave and get. What happens next speaks to the duplicity of our legal system.

Corporate law pretends that shareholders are not what they believe themselves to be, what logic says they are, namely, principals of incorporated firms. Legal trickery is needed to ensure that shareholders are not burdened by the risks that, in all other spheres, the law demands risk-creators should bear. Whenever an agent is seen to have acted on behalf of a principal and has incurred liabilities, the principal is held responsible for those liabilities. If the corporation were an agent of the capitalists that use it, that is, the tool of shareholders, shareholders could be held responsible for corporate wrongdoing. But this would wreck everything. The attraction of a legal artifact to which entrepreneurial types hand over their hard-earned cash might be considerably lessened. Let me elaborate.

If the corporation were seen as a mere agent, its legally bestowed separate personhood could no longer hide the shareholders' role as principals. Shareholders would no longer be able to avoid or shift the burdens of doing business via the corporation. From the investors' perspective, all the fancy footwork needed to wrap a corporation inside a veil would be much less useful; it would lose considerable charm.

The rich and powerful do not want this to happen. They like the irresponsibility they enjoy as a result of the generous, and somewhat startling, legal notion that the corporate firm is a self-standing capitalist. This is why the pretense that the corporation is a sovereign, independent actor, not an agent of those who contribute capital to it, is to be kept up. Never mind common sense!

The public understands that the real entrepreneurs are flesh-and-blood human beings. But—and this is truly significant—what to the "uninformed" public is self-evidently a pretense, an obvious fantasy, is not treated by law as such. The pretense that the active entrepreneur is the blob is fiercely defended by those who command the bully pulpits that create authorized knowledge. A huge amount of effort goes into massaging the facts on the ground to ensure that the autonomy of the legally established corporation remains a sacred ideal. As a result, reality conflicts sharply with the make-believe world conventional wisdom creates. The tension of this conflict forces the dream-world creators to take positions that put shareholders in a bad light.

The mouthpieces of conventional wisdom insist that the corporation, as a sovereign person—like all sentient human beings in a liberal polity and market economy—is to be responsible for its own decisions. It decides what to do; it decides how to do it; it decides when and where to do it. In short, it formulates a profit-maximizing business plan and implements it. The corporation, therefore, must be responsible for the fallout of its actions and decisions. No one else. This is reflected in law.

DECISION-MAKERS OR LAYABOUTS?

When a corporation is created, a set of bylaws (often known as articles of association) comes with it. If the promoters decide to have a special governing and management structure, it is permissible to draft different ones. But this is rarely done. The default position, endorsed by the courts, is that shareholders, as providers of capital, are not given the legal power to participate in the daily management decisions of the corporation. In these matters, directors are to be free to override the clearly expressed wishes of a majority of shareholders.

Thus, in *Automatic Self-Cleansing Filter Syndicate Company* v. *Cunninghame*,[2] the 1906 English case that laid down this proposition, the shareholders agreed at a general meeting that they wanted to sell the property of the company in which they held their shares. They claimed that, as they had now agreed on this, this was to be taken to be "their" company's wish as well. Hence the directors had no choice but to carry it out. The court rejected this argument. Unless explicitly negated, the court held that corporate law assumes that directors are charged with the management of the company and this includes the sale of its property; therefore, they cannot be bound by the shareholders' directions. Shareholders do have some governance powers, but those powers do not include management of the company.

The welfare of shareholders, then, is to be derived from the uses made of their contributions of capital. Legally, at least, they are totally dependent on the wisdom, efforts, and luck of the corporation and its functionaries. As former owners of the amounts of capital they contributed, they are legally disempowered when it comes to the uses made of that capital. This starting position enables the law and the fantasy-world creators to hold fast to this fundamental proposition: the corporation is not a mere agent of the shareholders; therefore, shareholders are not to be held responsible for the debts and obligations the corporation incurs.

Of course, this position makes shareholders look somewhat hapless. Rather than enterprising individuals who make their own way in an idealized Adam Smithian capitalist world, law- and policy-makers portray them as innocent bystanders awaiting the outcomes of corporate decisions and conduct. They are to live in hope of receiving benefits yielded by the efforts of others. Corporate law portrays shareholders as layabouts, as not doing anything. As the well-known U.S. political scientist Michael Parenti once quipped: "Profits are what you make when not working."

Shareholders are presented as folk who have placed a bet on other people's activities. Those who defend the conventional wisdom are pushed towards this unhappy characterization by their need to pretend that the corporation is in no way the shareholders' agent. This is how it comes about that—unintentionally, certainly reluctantly—they promote the notion that shareholders closely resemble a not-so-respected segment of our population: gamblers.

Although the standard moral teachings found in biblical texts did not forbid it, for many centuries gambling was viewed as a disruptive vice, one closely associated with an unworthy search to satisfy one's greed. At various times, gambling was subjected to criminalization.[3] But as the market economy rose from the ashes of feudalism, it became acceptable to act on one's greed. Entrepreneurs pursuing their self-interest by working hard and combining their own talents and resources were admired for making a bet on the potential of their personal capacities. But the acceptability of greed was restricted—and is largely still restricted—to this narrowly bounded sphere. Greed generally remains a trait of dubious moral standing. So, therefore, does gambling.

The folk who bet on the draw of a card or a roll of the dice are trying to satisfy their greed without making an effort of any kind, with no intention of producing a good or service that others may want. Such manifestations of greed have always been regarded as ugly. People who exhibited it during the Reformation were seen as unworthy; they were the very opposite of those to be respected, who adhered to the ethic of self-reliance, hard work, and saving. Disapproval of gambling supported a good deal of repressive legislation.

But the impulse to gamble was not easily stilled. It appears to be a rather common human frailty, infecting even the respectable classes.[4] And frailties tend to be forgiven more easily when they are exhibited by the high and mighty. Despite the general denunciations of gambling, greater latitude was given to gambling by the well-to-do. Gradually, as governments realized the potential for raising considerable revenues by licensing gambling, they showed more tolerance for the gambling drive of less exalted folk. Statutory prohibition of gambling changed to regulated control of some forms of gambling. And this is where we are today.

New York University criminologist Jerome H. Skolnick suggests that gambling falls in a grey area, one in which we place vices as opposed to crimes. It resides in that murky neighbourhood that criminal lawyer Francis Allen aptly called "the borderland of criminal justice." Society regards gambling as having no moral value and little social merit. It is willing to tolerate gambling, but not to allow it to reign unfettered.

We remain dubious about the worthiness of gamblers because they seek to gratify their greed, their desire for more, by not doing anything worthwhile. The last thing on their minds is using their talents or working to get a return on their investment. They want to get lucky, that is all. They are indolent. They have no interest in developing their talents or skills, and they feel no urge to be innovative. Their focus is embarrassingly self-interested in the most glaring way. Gamblers, therefore, and unworthy of vigorous social and political protection. Mere tolerance is all that should be offered them.

USEFUL ECONOMIC ACTORS?

Those who buy and sell shares of corporations bear a striking resemblance to the socially unmeritorious gambler. This is not hyperbole. Indeed, without any apparent sense of embarrassment, the law governing shareholders describes them in those terms. In law, shareholders are defined as holders of a security. A security is a legally recognized claim on the corporation's assets and yields, a claim that can be given a monetary value and thus become marketable. The courts have held that a security is created when "a person invests his money in a common enterprise and is led to expect profits solely from the efforts of the promoter or a third party."[5]

This definition of a security is a legal acknowledgement that security holders, such as shareholders, are folk who make a bet that their investment will yield them a positive return without having to lift a finger of their own. They intend to rely on a promoter or third party, in much the same way as punters leave it to the trainer and jockey to get most out of the horse on which they have placed their bet. Why, then, do we give them respect—indeed, inordinate respect? And why do we treat them with much more tender care than we do race-goers or poker machine players? It is curious.

Our legal system sets out to advance overall welfare by providing incentives to individuals to make the most of their talents and resources. It wants them to compete with each other on as level a terrain as it is possible to create. Such a legal system should not promote effort-shy, non-competitive gamblers. Even if they are to be tolerated, they should not be encouraged. Yet this is exactly what corporate law and its accessory, securities law, set out to do. These laws are designed to invite shareholders and would-be shareholders to come forward and place their bets on what other people's efforts and talents will produce. This counterintuitive policy needs to be justified by corporate cheerleaders if they want to maintain and perpetuate their fantasy world. And it is. Vigorously.

Essentially, defenders of the status quo argue that these gamblers are crucial to the "good greed" that a market capitalist society needs to foster. Their wagers furnish real producers with the wherewithal to engage in wealth-creating activities. Obviously, this justification is based on an empirical claim. It should have no resonance, therefore, if facts on the ground do not bear out its assumptions. Does the capital raised by issuing shares make a significant contribution to wealth creation activities by means of corporations? As will be shown in chapter 12, it turns out that it does not.

Such on-the-ground facts should be devastating to those who argue that gambling shareholders play a useful part in maintaining wealth-creating activities. So the facts are largely ignored by the law and by policy-makers. They plow on, in the face of contrary evidence, as if the capital subscribed by shareholders is pivotal to a regime of welfare generation by means of incorporated firms. That is, yet another pretense is to be maintained to perpetuate the current system. That pretense justifies another astonishing benefit granted to the shareholding class.

The gatekeepers for the current system assert that, because shareholders' contributions are so pivotal to help "good greed" do its thing, potential shareholders need to be given an incentive. After all, these worthy folk have given up control over their own property to promote the welfare of all of us. Something needs to be done to convince them to continue to offset their loss of power. They deserve a deal, a good deal. And they get one.

The deal makes shareholders a truly privileged class. This is an amazing result, given the law's very low expectations of them: they are not expected to be involved in the planning, the innovating, or the doing of any work as the corporation and its other functionaries combine talents and sweat to pursue profits. These gamblers, these shareholders, really are in a class of their own.

LIMITED LIABILITY, LEGAL PERSONHOOD

To restate the ground rules: when investors contribute capital to a corporation, their contributions instantly become the property of that separate legal person, the corporation. It can now do with the capital it has so collected as it decides or, more accurately, as its board of directors decides. The corporation issues a certificate to the contributors of capital that entitles them to a share of any profits made, to vote on the appointment and dismissal of directors and on major constitutional or structural changes, to call meetings on certain issues, and to share in any assets left over when a corporation's life has come to an end and its outstanding obligations have been met. If it is a publicly traded corporation, shareholders may also sell their share certificates. Apart from the right to trade in shares, these entitlements are available to shareholders in any type of corporation, whether it be small, mid-sized, or gargantuan, no matter how diverse in nature. This should astonish us. After all, ignoring such important differences smacks of wilful ignorance.

Let us here recall the story of Lee, the major shareholder in the crop-spraying business known as Lee's Air Farming, as well as that corporation's director and only employee. The relationship between the corporation and Lee, as shareholder, director, and employee, in no way resembles the relationship of a shopping mall employee who, through her pension fund, has an interest in shares in Bell Canada, Enbridge, and Inco. Her position as an indirect shareholder is her only relationship to Bell, Enbridge, and Inco; she has no legal or other connection to the corporations' management or workforces. To insist that those very different kinds of shareholders, Mr. Lee and the shopping mall employee, holding securities in very different kinds of corporations in very different ways, should have the same fundamental rights and obligations is, at best, disingenuous.

But that is precisely the conventional starting point. The system's gate-keepers have positioned themselves to safeguard the privileges of the truly wealthy and dominant shareholders by pretending not to be doing so. They ask everyone to suspend disbelief. Let us see, then, where this twisted logic leads.

Thus far we have seen that shareholders are gamblers who have some considerable control over the outcome of their wager through their right to vote, share in profits, and share in the corporation's residual property. These indirect rights to exercise influence are allegedly needed to offset their loss of power over their contributed capital. What this means, of course, is that their bet is rendered less risky than that of a chap who bets on someone else's dog.

The shareholders' defenders often call them risk-takers, a misleading bit of advertising. They have some control over the risk. Indeed, their wager is made even less risky through one more enormous legal gift.

Gamblers can only lose the amount of money they have put down on a horse, a team, or a lottery ticket. This makes sense. After all, they are just playing their luck; they are forecasting the outcome of other people's efforts or betting on the occurrence of a particular event. They are not responsible for any of it. The horses, their owners, the jockeys, the roulette operators, and so on, all act without their input or regard for their welfare. This is why the bettors' liability is limited to the size of their bet. But why should it be so for those gamblers who have a more exalted place in our economy and legal system? Why should it be so for shareholders?

Shareholders want those who run the blob in which they have invested their capital to maximize its profits. This will improve their share of the profits distributed and add to the value the market will place on the share certificates they hold. They rely on other people to chase the profits which they intend to enjoy. So far, there is a parallel between the racehorse gambler and the shareholder. But in the corporate sector, the profit-chasing is to be undertaken for the benefit of the gamblers, the self-styled investors. This should make a difference.

The profit-seeking on behalf of the corporation and the shareholders creates risks. Corporate actions may inflict physical harms to people and the environment; those who come into contact with the corporation's conduct and goods and services may suffer monetary damages. Fiscal obligations are created as the corporation incurs debts. All these costs arise from the corporation's efforts to help shareholders win their bets. And yet, when the costs materialize, shareholders are only responsible for the amount of money they have invested. The shareholders' liability is limited to the size of their bet.

Even if the corporation's coffers are not up to pay what it owes, the shareholders' houses and yachts remain safe from claims by the blob's creditors and victims. Investors in that most capitalist of institutions, the corporation, enjoy limited fiscal risks. This is remarkable. After all, this protection is unavailable to entrepreneurs who seek profits by the use of their own talents and resources, that is, it is unavailable to unblobbed entrepreneurs. Their bets are on themselves, and they are fully responsible for them. There is no ectoplasmic blob to bear the brunt that would make them more like socially challenged gamblers than entrepreneurs.

Shareholders are a privileged lot. Their deal is sweetened even more by another feature of corporate law, one that we already have touched on. As the corporation, in legal terms, is the actor of record, as it is cast as the capitalist attempting to maximize profits, shareholders not only enjoy limited fiscal responsibility, but they also are not punishable for violations of law that the corporation may commit as it pursues profits intended to be shared with them. The shareholders are to be treated as passive beneficiaries in waiting. For those who defend this position, to describe shareholders as risk-takers is an abuse of language; to describe them as capitalists in the admirable sense is simply a distortion.

This legal state of things presents those who defend corporate capitalism—who proclaim a belief in a liberal philosophy and a market economy—with a serious headache.

A PROBLEM OF LEGITIMACY

From the beginning of the modern period, the special treatment of shareholders in a corporate setting gave rise to grave concerns. These concerns persist to this day. When it was first raised, the notion that those who contributed capital to a corporate firm could limit their liability for the debts incurred by that corporation was seen as repellent. In 1834, the *Law Times* referred to the granting of limited liability to shareholders as unprincipled. The bestowal of limited liability was nothing less than a free pass for ne'er-do-wells. The editors said that the privilege amounted to the granting of a charter to would-be deviants, a veritable Rogues Charter. At that time, many feared that the advance of market capitalism was already impairing public morality, as the search for riches was giving sinful greed too much sway.

For example, Charles Mackay, in *Extraordinary Popular Delusions and the Madness of Crowds* (1841), documented the odious enterprises to which get-rich-quick investors contributed. One company claimed it would extract silver from lead, another offered an insurance firm that would guarantee female chastity, and one asked investors to send in their money (and they did!) to fund a firm that would serve them well but in a way that could not yet be revealed.

The bestowal of limited liability, it was thought, would only aggravate this march towards irresponsibility. More, the corrosion of social responsibility would likely be accompanied by economic inefficiency, as the other main feature of the corporate form, separate legal personhood, took its toll. Adam Smith, the intellectual hero of market capitalists, had warned that directors and managers would not act as if they were real owners. He scathingly proposed that the corporate form be used only where a business required no serious effort or innovation:

> The only trades which it seems possible for a joint stock company to carry on successfully are those, of which all the operations are capable of being reduced to what is called a routine, or to such an uniformity of method as admits little or no variation ... the banking ... the trade of insurance from fire, and from sea risk and capture in time of war ... the trade of making and maintaining a navigable cut or canal ... the similar trade of bringing water for the supply of a great city.[6]

Today, this may seem no more than a quaintly amusing story about bygone times. After all, corporations are everywhere. They seem as natural as the air we breathe. Indeed, what appears unnatural is the idea that major economic activity should not be carried out by means of this sovereign person whose investors enjoy a limited liability.

Does this mean that we have abandoned the purist liberal principles that made nineteenth-century pundits think quite differently about the limited liability corporation? Today's dominant political philosophers would reject any such notion. The legitimacy of our political and economic institutions is predicated on the argument that they should uphold and enhance these liberal principles. Does it mean, then, that as capitalism entered the twentieth century, it matured and found ways to make corporate existence and operations compatible with those principles? The answer is a resounding no.

The perceived gap between legally disempowered shareholders and empowered directors and executives continues to give corporate cheerleaders heartburn. In what remains the most influential sociological research in this area, the 1932 empirical study by Adolph A. Berle and Gardiner C. Means[7] established that, in the large corporations milieu, the divorce between ownership of the property contributed by investors and their control over the incorporated firm had reached crisis proportions. A dysfunctional and inefficient system had been allowed to grow. Like Adam Smith, they feared that this likely meant that there would be less zealousness in the pursuit of profits than there should be.

But even more alarming to these researchers and their followers over the ensuing decades was that those empowered with control over other people's assets, the directors and executives, might use the capital with which they had been entrusted for their own benefit rather than for the benefit of those who had left it in their care. There was likely to be, in the characteristically colourful language of corporate law, a lot of looting and shirking by directors and executives. Today, a huge amount of effort goes into overcoming these perceived problems. Much of corporate law teaching and research is devoted to this problem and, predictably, concludes that it is not really a problem.

A voluminous literature now tells us not to be anxious about the gap between owners and controllers of corporate property: the magic of the market will save us. There will be, despite Berle and Means's fears, no gap for shirkers and looters to exploit. Directors and their executives will be forced to pursue the maximization of profits with the corporation's capital as if they were owners. If they do not, aggrieved shareholders will punish them by using their voting power to replace them.

This threat, of course, only has oomph if the belief in the efficient workings of competitive markets for goods, services, and shares is justified. If it is, directors and executives who do not work as hard as real owners would or who pay themselves noticeably more than real owners would—that is, who shirk and loot—will adversely impact the corporation's competitive position, making it less valuable to investors. It then is likely that some investors will see that, if the corporation were run by different, harder working, less self-serving people, its potential for better returns could be realized. Motivated by their own greed, these prescient investors—whether they be insiders or outsiders—may use their voting powers, given to them by their dollars already invested or yet to be invested, to gain control over the way things are done in the corporation.

Replacement of directors and executives, a takeover of the corporation, a sale of some or most of its assets, or a merger with another corporation are potential market responses. These market responses, believed to be inevitable because they are natural, should ensure that the maximization of profits for shareholders will be the principal focus of those who are appointed as directors and executives of corporations. Voila, problem solved; the gap will be eliminated by the market.

These hoped-for means to keep legally empowered non-owners in check are negative in nature; they rely on meaningful threats. They are fortified by positive means, such as making rewards for directors and their managing executives depend on the delivery of the goods for the legally disempowered shareholders. Managers are given incentives by tying their wages to increases in the value of the corporation's shares. Sophisticated remuneration formulas are devised by experts. On top of setting a basic wage, bonuses may be awarded if certain outcomes (most often increases in share value) are attained. Some of the executives' pay is to be in kind, that is, by way of being granted shares or the opportunity to buy shares at a set price, giving them a direct incentive to maximize share value. This, it is believed, will align the directors' and executives' interests with those of shareholders.

In short, elaborate justifications are necessary to aver that neither Adam Smith's nor Berle and Means's fears have merit in a well-functioning market economy. There are ways and means, we are told, to ensure that shareholders' interests will be treated as paramount, as if they had not truly lost control over the property whose potential they want to maximize. The arguments, then, made to defend the use of the corporation as a device by which practising capitalists can pursue their naked self-interest as sovereign, responsible owners of property should, for their own benefit and, thereby, to the benefit of all, are designed to tell liberal worrywarts that there is no need to worry. Despite the law's treatment of shareholders as passive former owners of property and, therefore, as deserving of special legal protections, defenders of the status quo argue that privileged shareholders still exercise ultimate control in the real world. And this implicit acknowledgement of potential shareholder control is a vital point.

The contrariness of the reasoning is plain. While the twists and turns of the arguments are much beloved by legal scholars, troubling questions remain unanswered. These questions continuously threaten the legitimacy of the corporate vehicle as a form in a liberal polity and market economy.

On the one hand:

- Corporations are treated as the legal capitalists. They are responsible for the conduct in which they engage to deploy their capital. Their legal responsibility is not limited fiscally or legally. They are fully responsible for their actions, as are any other individuals when they exercise their dominion over their property.
- Mentally and physically, corporations need to rely on individuals to deploy their capital. Directors and executives owe a duty to act in the best interests of the corporation. Their relationship to the corporation is a personal one.

On the other hand:

- In publicly traded corporations, shares are frequently sold and bought, that is, the identity of shareholders constantly changes. Corporations are not affected when shareholders exercise their exit power, that is, when they sell their interest in the corporations' existing assets and future stream of profits. The capital owned by the corporation is unaffected. It does not matter who the shareholders are. The relationship between corporations and their shareholders is, in legal terms, an impersonal one.

- Shareholders are not owners of corporate capital. They lack some of the rights that are the usual insignia of ownership of private property. They do not have the right of entry onto the corporation's property, and they cannot exclude anyone else from the use of that property or sell or lease that property. They cannot enforce debts owed by outsiders for services rendered by that property or for damage to it, nor are they employed as agents to deal with that capital. In addition to not being owners, shareholders are not managers of corporate property. As non-owners and non-managers, they bear no responsibility for the conduct of the corporation.

- Even though, legally, they are not owners of the corporation and its assets, and even though they are not allowed to act as managers, shareholders are given the right to vote. By exercising their voting rights, shareholders can change the policies and nature of the corporation. They are legally entitled to influence the way in which the corporation pursues its best interests or their own. They can use their owner-like powers to guide, push, incentivize, and sanction directors and executives into satisfying their goals. In practice, directors and executives believe that they serve the best interests of the corporation when they seek to serve the best interests of the shareholders.

- Shareholders have limited personal liability for fiscal debts left by the corporation. They are responsible only to the extent of their investment. Their relationship to the corporation is that of having an interest in the material outcomes yielded by the corporation's deployment, as a sovereign owner, of its property. They are entitled to some of its proceeds (dividends).

There is something terribly wrong with this picture.

1. Directors and executives have legal duties and responsibilities.
2. They discharge them by maximizing returns for shareholders.
3. Shareholders, as shareholders, have no duties whatsoever.
4. Shareholders are protected from the costs of the risks taken on their behalf.

Shareholders thus find themselves in an environment where self-interest and naked greed are seen as noble traits, in which getting rich without effort is considered clever and virtuous, in which they have no incentive to care how directors and executives pursue their interests. "Just show me the money" is the mantra of these gamblers. The tenderness shown to them by law leads them, at best, to have no regard to the way in which the corporation behaves and, at worst, to be callous about its fallout.

Let me offer one illustration of how disregard for others offends our supposedly shared social values.

A POISONED ENVIRONMENT

If the value of shares in a corporation eventually collapses because their value was inflated by improper machinations by the corporation and its executive team, this does not mean that all the shareholders are losers. Take the notorious bankruptcy scandals of Nortel in Canada or Enron in the United States. True, when the end came, investors still holding shares lost all of their invested money. But in between, the shares had rocketed up because of the malfeasance of the corporations and their executives. Thus, shareholders who bought when the shares were worth, say, $40 and sold them when they reached $68 made out like bandits. Those who bought at $250 and then saw the share value reduced to near zero lost big time. But no one asks all the people who made money because they profited from the lying, cheating, and manipulating on the way up to give any of their winnings back.

The logic is that, as non-owners, as non-managers, they had no responsibility to ask questions about why the corporate stock was doing so well. They were permitted, indeed, encouraged, to be indifferent to such matters, to the fact that the combination of their mollycoddled greed and heedlessness encouraged the promoters, executives, and others who lied, cheated, and manipulated. Don't ask, don't tell. To an ordinary person, uncontaminated by "corporate think," they could perhaps be regarded as the receivers of tainted or stolen goods. The law, however, treats them as fortunate gamblers.

It is a poisoned environment. Shareholders, with their capacity to pressure directors and executives to pursue their narrow goals, preferably by responsible means but by irresponsible ones if they think it necessary, provide an impetus for anti-social conduct. In a society that pays a great deal of attention to law and order, this ought to raise policy-makers' concerns. After all, they are always on the lookout for elements of society that present a clear and present danger to its values and norms.

We fight wars on drugs; we monitor, discipline, and punish refugees, religious and ethnic minorities, suspected political troublemakers, and the like. Prolific social commentator Diana Gordon identifies these groups as contemporary society's "dangerous classes."[8] This is a constant refrain in capitalist societies. Charles Loring Brace, the nineteenth-century New York social activist, listed vagabonds, waifs, predatory criminals, vagrants, and prostitutes as the members of the dangerous classes.[9] The tenor of this literature is that the poor should be considered dangerous because they provide a breeding ground for evil-doing.

In mature corporate capitalism, this should be turned on its head. It is the spoiled rotten and wealthy who constitute the most dangerous class of all. I will argue that the indolent and legally indulged gamblers/shareholders provide fertile soil for wrongdoing of all kinds. The very privileging of shareholders nurtures evil-doing.

Let us turn to the evidence.

5

The Shareholder as Toxin

DRIVEN BY THE IMPERATIVE TO ACCUMULATE PRIVATE WEALTH, capitalists invest their talents and resources. In an ideal market world, they would set out to meet spontaneously generated demands. In contemporary society, however, they play a large part in controlling the markets, in creating the demands that their talents and resources are most able to satisfy at a profit. This is what advertising—or "market education"—is all about. But, as no one directly forces consumers to demand any specific good or service, this manipulation is not perceived as a distortion that warrants correction. The scene is thus set for a continuous hunt for new investment opportunities by inventive, desire-creating wealth owners, including a ceaseless quest to get government out of providing goods and services and leave it to the for-profit sphere. There is a restless search for unoccupied markets by corporate actors who do not care very much what they have to do to satisfy their endless search for *more*.

PUSHING THE BOUNDARIES

In our daily lives, most of us draw distinctions between acceptable and offensive behaviour. But in the market, this kind of sensibility has no resonance. Anything not specifically forbidden and from which profits might be garnered is the meat and potatoes of free enterprise. To a market economy, the production of a skin lotion that people want is no less worthy than the production of a pharmaceutical drug that people need. The only issue is, is it profitable? And as long as a business gives rise to a credible hope for profits, it is sure to attract devil-may-care shareholders to gamble on a share of those profits. Shareholders wager their money on anything that might yield them more dividends or increases in the value of their purchased shares. They do not have to care about how their goal is met. And this indifference is encouraged by law.

Shareholders can say that they are mandated by law to pursue their narrow personal interests, as evidenced by their legal protections: limited fiscal liability for corporate debts and legal immunity for corporate wrongdoings. These privileges are claimed to be simultaneously efficient—as they help provide capital for capitalism—and natural—as selfishness, being close to godliness, should be furthered.

Corporate directors and executives can say that they are legally and economically bound to serve selfish shareholders and that shareholders are rightly empowered to hold their feet to the fire if they do not. This affects the setting in which those who run the corporation discharge their responsibilities. Rather eagerly, because often they are substantial shareholders of the corporation they run or of other similar corporations, directors and executives have internalized the idea that the norms and morals of their context are defined by the shareholders' legitimated culture of indifference to social welfare.

A symbiotic, perniciously anti-social, arrangement emerges. The corporation becomes a vehicle in which the major actors—directors, executives, and shareholders—encourage each other to focus as little as possible on the impacts the pursuit of their mutual goal is likely to have on outsiders. The corporation is a mechanism through which the directors, executives, and shareholders pressure each other to be single-minded profit-maximizers, first and last.

The resulting disregard for the outside world is vocally defended by the dominant elites of the corporate world. Their cant is that the plight of others is the concern of the public/political sphere. The actors and institutions in the private/economic sphere are not equipped to deal with them. They are to do the only thing for which they are fit and for which they have come together, namely, to maximize profits by deploying their talents and resources in any area that is not forbidden to them. Let law-makers determine what should and should not be allowed, their gurus say. Anything else would be inefficient and undemocratic.[1]

Much too conveniently, the fact that corporations do participate in the political processes that determine whether private operators are permitted to engage in a business is ignored. And their clever argument that they bear no responsibility for what is allowed is largely accepted by our governments and policy-makers. Corporate capitalists are free to roam the world seeking profit-making opportunities. The formalized encouragement of greed and the protections bestowed on shareholders whose interests are to be given primary attention leaves corporate actors in total darkness. And, as Victor Hugo would have it, "if the soul is left in darkness, sins will be committed. The guilty one is not he who commits the sin but he who causes the darkness."

SNAPSHOTS: ENCOURAGED INDIFFERENCE
Licensed to Kill: The Presumption of Innocence

Lee Drutman and Charlie Cray, political scientists associated with the Center for Corporate Policy in Washington, tell a story about anti-tobacco lobbyists who in 2004 asked the corporate registrar of the State of Virginia to accept their application to incorporate a business.[2] Its name was to be Licensed to Kill; its articles of incorporation stated its purpose as the "manufacture and marketing of tobacco products in a way that each year kills 40,000 Americans and 4.5 million other persons worldwide." Virginia registered the applicants' firm as a corporation fit to conduct the proposed business. The anti-tobacco incorporators then asked what would have happened if, as human beings, they had requested state authorization to go on a killing spree. They might have been sent to a psychiatric institution or worse, they speculated.

Lesson: The presumption of innocence is given amazing scope. A brilliantly flashing green light is shown to wealth owners, even if the outcomes of their corporate business are likely to be harmful. Corporate capitalism is not required, or expected, to be feely-feely. Directors and executives and the shareholders they serve are not required, or expected, to be socially conscious. Their job is to maximize profits by hook or by crook. This is what drives businesses like tobacco.

In this atmosphere, it is unsurprising that corporate apologists stand ready to make eye-popping arguments. The *Wall Street Journal* reported in 2001 that a tobacco company lobbyist had asked the Czech Republic not to force Philip Morris to disclose the adverse effects of smoking more graphically than it was already required to do because, as elderly people used the health and welfare system more than other groups, allowing them to die earlier than they would if they did not smoke would be cost-efficient for the government. Whatever decent character traits corporate leaders display in their familial and social lives when acting outside the blob are easily jettisoned when they act as corporate functionaries.

The Perilous Game: Amoral or Worse

Henry Blodget was a financial adviser who became notorious in the early 2000s for having brazenly misled prospective investors who had put their trust in him. He was fined and banned from participating in the securities industry. Having accepted the stigma and punishment that came his way, he has become a widely published and broadcast financial commentator. Blodget pontificates from the vantage point of one who knows how perilous the investment game really is. In that guise, addressing green ethical investors, he wrote:

> If you could go back ... 50 years and retroactively add one stock in
> the Standard & Poor's to your retirement portfolio, which would it be?
> IBM? DuPont? Philip Morris? If your goal is to generate the highest
> possible investment return, the choice would be easy: tobacco giant
> Philip Morris—the single best-performing stock in S&P index for the 46
> years through 2003.[3]

Lesson: As a class, shareholders are at best amoral, perhaps worse. They are more than happy to profit as tobacco corporations peddle a harmful drug. After all, it is a good business: the drug is addictive and this makes for strong market performance. The corporate architecture is designed so that shareholders need have no qualms about their choices, as they will not be held to account for them. It is clear that legally supported irresponsibility and the incentive of easy profits constitute a recipe for cooking up moral-lite businesses.

Viatical Insurance: Anything Goes

Michael Sandel, the Harvard political philosopher, reports on a roaring trade in what are called viaticals in the United States.[4] This is the name given to a species of transactions based on existing life insurance policies. It begins when someone who has purchased a life insurance policy has a need for the money that their family would receive upon their death. They can sell the policy to a third party who will collect whatever the insurance policy will pay out when they die. The original purchaser of the policy will be paid less than the policy would have yielded, but this sacrifice enables them to get cash immediately.

Of course, the purchaser of such a policy must pay the premiums to keep the policy viable until it is terminated by the original policyholder's death. As the buyer is to make a profit on the difference between the price paid and the full benefit when the originally insured person dies, less any premiums paid until then, the buyer has a macabre interest in the early death of the seller. To many people, perhaps to most, this might appear unseemly. Not to profit-seekers.

Sandel—who tells this story to illustrate how an economic system that treasures monetary gains will convert anything and everything into a commodity—reports how purchasers of discounted policies were truly miffed when policyholders who were known to suffer from AIDS began to live longer because medical treatments had improved. Premiums had to be paid for longer periods. Now it was harder to convince the share market players that there was much future in continuing to invest in corporate brokers of viaticals. One such firm saw its share price plunge from $14.50 to $1.38 before going out of business.

The share-buying community, therefore, had to be reassured about these kinds of undertakings. The executive director of the Viatical Association of America proclaimed that the death futures business was still a good one: "Compared to the number of people with AIDS, the number of people with cancer, severe cardiovascular diseases, and other terminal illnesses is huge."[5]

Lesson: Corporate capitalists look high and low for opportunities to make profits. As the famed English economist E.J. Mishan put it, "A society in which 'anything goes' is ipso facto a society in which anything sells."[6] Capitalists do not care whether a particular opportunity is disgusting or even immoral, as long as it may yield profits. Worse, shareholders indicate their disapproval of directors and executives if a repugnant business fails to deliver the goods. They will stiffen the directors' and executives' spines by disciplining and sanctioning them and, in the process, push them to be as indifferent to the social good as shareholders evidently are. This is why even corporate functionaries think that shareholders' sense of corporate responsibility is poorly developed and why they think it appropriate to appeal to their venal instincts, as they did in the case of viatical insurance.

Private Prisons: The Construction of Markets

When governments deliver services, they generally do so without a thought to monetary profit. The services are perceived to be needed and, therefore, are made available to the extent that the government is willing to allocate funds to them. Often, this becomes burdensome. For example, the intensification of law-and-order programs has led to bulging prisons, and costs have become a problem. Governments have sought relief by turning to the private sector. This has happened in all Anglo-American jurisdictions, but it is most pronounced in the United States, where both the push for law and order and the devotion to the private sector are the most developed.

Giant corporations have emerged to take advantage of these for-profit opportunities. In the United States, in 2010, the two largest prison corporations received nearly three billion dollars in revenues for services rendered, and their top executives earned circa three million dollars each. Their shareholders were kept happy.[7] In 2000, Corrections Corporation of America's shares were valued at one dollar each. Then the federal government began putting immigrant detainees into private prisons. By 2013, the shares were valued at $34.34. In its annual report, filed with the Securities and Exchange Commission, Corrections Corporation of America disclosed to the share and bond markets, as it was required to do, what risks its business might have to deal with in the immediate future:

> The demand for our facilities and services could be adversely affected by the relaxation of enforcement efforts, leniency in conviction or parole standards and sentencing practices or through decriminalization of certain activities that are currently proscribed by our criminal laws. For instance, any changes with respect to drugs and controlled substances or illegal immigration could affect the number of persons arrested, convicted, and sentenced thereby potentially reducing the demand for correctional facilities to house them.

In 2012, the American Civil Liberties Union (ACLU) reported that the three largest private U.S. prison companies had spent $45 million lobbying state and federal governments to maintain the law-and-order policies that enrich them. And private prison corporations contributed to the campaigns of thirty of the thirty-six legislators who supported Arizona's notorious "show your papers" law that targeted so-called undocumented aliens.[8]

Lobbying is not the only private prison industry initiative. The advocacy group In the Public Interest reports that, when they enter into a contract to run prisons, these profit-hungry corporations are paid per inmate.[9] They are always anxious lest, because of some government "relaxation" or "leniency," they will be left with empty cells. As even heavily lobbied governments are unpredictable, the prison corporations, when negotiating with governments, ask that they guarantee a certain occupancy rate, regardless of the vagaries of law-and-order policies. Sixty-five per cent of contracts examined by In the Public Interest have clauses that specify that the government guarantees between 80 and 100 per cent occupancy rates. Unless governments deliver enough prisoners for enough time, they must pay the private prison firms for keeping empty cells available. Given that governments are accountable to their taxpayers, they are thus under pressure to maintain tough law-and-order programs.

Unsurprisingly, pressure to deliver profit-yielding poor and desperate people to private prisons has some strange fallouts. The ACLU's 2011 *Banking on Bondage* report[10] refers to one case where a jury found a judge guilty of all sorts of crimes, including conspiring with private prison corporations to ensure that they would get more inmates for longer periods. Perhaps this sad episode should be seen as an extreme, unlikely to be repeated outcome of the commodification of tasks that should rightfully be left to the public sector.

Lesson: Owners of wealth are driven to find investment opportunities. Frequently, they get such opportunities when services delivered by the public sector are turned over to the private sector. The specific example of private prisons provides evidence for a more universal truth: there is no such thing as a natural market. All markets—like that for private prison operations—are constructed. Governments have political constraints when setting up programs but, unlike legally created blobs, they are not bound to serve a privileged class of investors that has a singular focus on getting more bang for the buck. And while corporations must chase profits, they have no political constraints. They are not, after all, part of public decision-making, not part of the formal political institutions of our liberal democracy. But this claim is a transparently self-serving one: corporations have it both ways.

While not politically accountable, private corporations play an active role in creating markets, for example, by pushing for the privatization of prisons. And when a market has been created, they push and shove to change policy goals that an elected government might have wished to pursue when it provided the service in the first place.

Corporations engage, then, in politics to get and improve private profit opportunities. They are de facto active political players, not just economic vehicles that have little to do with the setting of social and legal norms. Their shareholders benefit from these machinations, while purporting to be uninvolved in them. They are more than content to have the corporate functionaries be commercially and politically zealous on their behalf, even as this has serious impacts on public policies and values.

Corporate-Owned Life Insurance: No Shame

To buy insurance protection against damage or injury to a thing or person, the law requires that buyers of such insurance have a pecuniary interest in the continued safety of the thing or person. They must be able to show that they would suffer financial loss should damage or injury materialize. It should follow that it should be impossible to insure the life of another person. Over time, however, large corporations became entitled to insure the personal safety of their senior employees. The notion behind this concession was that these folk have special skill sets, specific to the corporate enterprise and, therefore, like other valuable property, would be very costly to replace. Once they were given that inch, corporate capitalists have pushed to go a mile, in fact, many miles.

A series of exposés[11] tells the story of how, in the United States, this insurance coverage of corporate executives has blossomed into something tellingly known as "janitors' insurance" or "dead peasants' insurance." Corporations now insure the lives of their lowly employees. They had to lobby legislatures to allow them to do so, as the law's original requirement for a purchaser of insurance to have an insurable interest in the thing to be insured appeared to stand in their way. But they succeeded and were able to construct a new market.

Sandel[12] records that, by the 1990s, the taking out of insurance policies worth hundreds of thousands of dollars over paid workers' lives had become a common practice among major, respected corporations such as AT&T, Dow Chemical, Nestlé USA, Pitney Bowes, Procter & Gamble, Walmart, Walt Disney, Winn-Dixie, Bank of America, and JPMorgan Chase. The formal name for these kinds of repellent insurance policies—which give employers an interest in the early demise of their employees—is corporate-owned life insurance (COLI). When their employees die, employers collect. After 9/11, some of the life insurance payments taken out on victims' lives went to their employers, leaving the dependants empty-handed.

Lesson: Corporate directors, executives, and shareholders know no shame. If there is a buck to be made and the law does not forbid it, they will chase it. If the law does prohibit it, they will try to change the law. Neither the integrity of a law designed to protect the public good nor the majority sensibility of the surrounding community distracts them from their capitalist obsession: to get more, no matter what it costs anyone else.

The corporate vehicle makes this dismal mindset seem normal. This makes it easier for shareholders to feel that theirs is not to question why or how profits are generated, they are merely to sit and collect. It is a sad and corrosive situation. The COLI saga has a horrible spectre hanging over it, one that is a natural corollary to the systemically designed quest to get *more.* The scheme puts corporate employers in a position where it is in their notional interest not to protect workers from harm. This does not mean that they will deliberately harm them. But to foster potential nonchalance about people's lives runs counter to public policy and offends widespread notions of common decency.

THE DEGRADATION OF SOCIAL STANDARDS

For capitalism to triumph, society's deep, longstanding antipathy to avarice had to be overcome. This had an impact on human behaviour and on social relations. By means of the corporation, the push to satisfy greed now defies all remnants of restraint. Once inside a blob, directors, executives, and shareholders are encouraged to behave in ways that defy the civilizing bonds and values society developed over the centuries. And those on whose behalf this push is taking place bear an uncomfortably close resemblance to gamblers, whose vice is still considered somewhat sinful when it isn't wearing a corporate cloak.

The people who inhabit the corporation claim that they are merely doing what they ought to do in a market economy. They say they are to advance their own interests, acting like Adam Smith's butcher, brewer, and baker. This necessarily enures to the benefit of all. What is ignored is that, from inside the blobs, they work to change the laws that reflect and protect important values and interests. They ignore that, unlike the butcher, brewer, and baker, who act alone and competitively, they act collectively and often in a competition-challenged environment. They ignore the fact that, unlike the butcher, brewer, and baker, they are rarely personally responsible for their actions. This is especially true of the intended beneficiaries of corporate enterprises: shareholders.

Yet despite its contestability, the assertion that, although they use a corporate form to do their thing, corporate actors are just Adam Smithian marketeers is rarely challenged by the mouthpieces of conventional wisdom. As a political economy, we tolerate, often promote, reprehensible outcomes of aggressive, greedy behaviour, provided it is legal. As the political journalist Michael Kinsley told CNN's *Crossfire*, "The scandal isn't what is illegal—the scandal is what is legal." This situation gives profit-maximizers way too much leeway. All of the examples recounted above were stories about legal, if ugly, activities. It has become the norm not to question what is right and wrong.

The University of California's G. Geis, in his own work[13] and in his research with sociologist R.F. Meier,[14] tells the story of a notorious corporate crime, the heavy electrical equipment conspiracy. Major firms, led by General Electric, engaged in a gigantic price-fixing scheme. The judge who in 1961 sentenced the guilty-pleading offenders felt he had to be tough because they had brought the American economic system into disrepute at a time when the United States and the USSR were fighting for the world's hearts and minds. The admitted facts were embarrassing. Executives of the offending corporations were childish and shameless as they tried to hide their wrongdoing. They communicated with each other by sending messages about what prices to set as if they were members of a Christmas carolling group. These subterfuges were used because they were aware that they were violating laws. Their corporate consciences, however, were not troubled. When asked why he had participated in this conspiracy, one executive responded that, while he knew it was against the law, it was not such a horrible thing to do: "Illegal? Yes, but not criminal."

The conspiring corporations were fined and some executives got minor jail sentences. But no shareholders, many of whom undoubtedly benefited from the profits swollen by the illegal behaviour, were held to account in any way.

Corporate functionaries and shareholders—continuously told that their drive for *more* is a public good and that they are unlikely to be personally responsible—come to live in a moral fog. They seem to worry only about whether their conduct is legal and, when it comes down to it, have a low regard for law. In the ethically muddled world of directors, executives, and shareholders, the violation of law is not necessarily a serious wrong. To wealthy corporate actors, many laws are believed to be unnecessary fetters on their innovation, on their efforts to advance the wealth creation the economy needs. This belief is bolstered by the fact that it is shared and promoted by many of those responsible for law-making.

Many in government and a majority of policy-makers pay increasing homage to the natural superiority and efficiency of the for-profit sectors. Their starting point is that the laws governing profit-chasing activities are to be classed as regulatory laws, rather than as criminal laws. Regulatory laws look like criminal laws because they set standards which, if violated, attract penalties, but these regulatory laws are seen and treated very differently from criminal laws. Regulatory laws are characterized as rules facilitating and moderating business. They are designed to help wealth creators do their thing, while ensuring a modicum of restraint to protect the public from unfortunate outcomes. These laws are the result of compromises made after capitalists and governments, preoccupied with making capitalism work, have negotiated what is best for capitalism in the circumstances. Accordingly, the standards they set are not seen as reflecting a consensus about the sacredness of some specific shared values.

By contrast, true criminal law standards purport to embed and reinforce our shared morality, and offences against those standards are treated as grave wrongs. Violations of regulatory laws are seen as technical failures to abide by useful rules, not as attacks on fundamental social principles. Unlike true criminal acts, breaches of regulatory laws, therefore, do not attract opprobrium. They do not alarm governments and, as a corollary, governments rarely insist that these regulatory laws be policed or enforced strictly. This is a hallmark of Anglo-American corporate law regulation.

In 2007, English criminologists Steve Tombs and David Whyte[15] reported that the fine for killing a worker in the United Kingdom fluctuated between 20,000 and 45,000 pounds; the largest fine, imposed in respect of the killing a family of four in Scotland, amounted to less than 2 per cent of the firm's after-tax profits and 0.16 per cent of its annual revenues. If the corporation had been a mere human being, earning 25,000 pounds, the equivalent fine would have been 36 pounds. Directors (as the English name members of the board of directors and executives) were the target of only 3 per cent of all prosecutions. This feeble record of prosecutions of corporations and major decision-makers is in line with the U.S. record as reflected in the heavy electrical equipment conspiracy, where General Electric, its counterparts and executives were treated with kid gloves. Current data show that that pattern has remained the same, because the thinking has remained the same in Anglo-American jurisdictions: sanctions are rarely imposed and, when they are, they are usually risible.

Our system, then, provides incentives and facilities for the pursuit of profits and, to these ends, has created an elaborate corporate law apparatus. The devotion to for-profit initiatives is so profound that we permit and encourage the search for profits even if it involves anti-social behaviour, provided it is done within the strict letter of the law. In the corporate sector, actors are legally permitted to be amoral and encouraged to be cavalier about the significance of obeying the law. They live in murky world, one in which there is little incentive to ask whether behaviour is right or wrong, moral or immoral, legal or illegal. Even though corporate actors are from time to time sanctioned for crossing the regulatory line, such prosecutions are relatively rare and the punishments doled out are, for the most part, derisory.

This is how it comes about that wrongdoing by corporations is rife, indeed, epidemic. It is not aberrational. It is misleading, when wrongdoing occurs, to label it deviance.

CORPORATE DEVIANCE AS CORPORATE NORM

A voluminous literature describes the extent to which truly ugly, unethical, and sometimes illegal corporate activities occur. The largest study to date on breaches of laws to which penal sanctions are attached found that 40 per cent of the five hundred largest corporations in the United States, as ranked by *Fortune*, did not violate any such laws; 60 per cent did. Many were repeat offenders.[16] Later and earlier studies in a variety of Anglo-American situations all paint the same picture.[17] Why, then, do we not treat corporate directors, executives, and shareholders as we do members of a dangerous criminal class requiring serious monitoring and restraint?

One reason many violations do not incite anger is that they may be technical, administrative lapses—even if harmful. We are asked not be too vexed. Such "minor" illegal conduct can be safely left to the regulatory framework that promotes profit-seeking initiatives, while reining in some of their more dangerous aspects. For the most part, when violations of such rules occur and cause some damages, they are treated, as Brandeis, J., famously wrote, as "the inescapable price of civilized life and, hence, to be borne with resignation."[18]

But many of these benignly viewed corporate activities take an enormous toll on the well-being of people and their physical environments. In those cases, the argument that they were undertaken as part of to-be-welcomed wealth-creating initiatives does not serve its customary cleansing function. Mere compensation of victims and their families may not do the trick either.

There are a lot of these situations.[19] A very short list of well-known malfeasances includes the following:

- the selling of thalidomide to pregnant women when its horrendous side-effects should have been know, leading to thousands of infant abnormalities
- the use of highly explosive isocyanates in a manner not used by the same corporation in the United States, causing a massive explosion in the impoverished Indian town of Bhopal with, again, thousands of victims

- the peddling of the birth control device Dalkon Shield after it was known to lead to miscarriages and deaths, leaving hundreds of injured people
- the keeping of the known-to-explode-on-touch Ford Pinto on the road, having calculated that it was cheaper to pay off victims than to fix the car's known defect, immolating dozens of car owners and passengers
- the peddling of powdered milk by Nestlé to people in poor countries who, Nestlé knew, would have to mix the product with impure water, harming an unknown number of babies who would have been healthier if they had had breast milk
- the pesticide manufacturers whose products kill traditional agriculture and destroy ways of life across vast swaths of the globe
- the heedless asbestos miners and processors, and their millions of victims

Corporate malfunctioning also inflicts serious environmental and accompanying physical damage and harm—the *Exxon Valdez* in Alaska, Esso Petroleum in Bass Strait, BP in the Gulf of Mexico, Shell in Nigeria, Unocal in Burma, BHP at Ok Tedi, Hooker Chemical Company at Love Canal... Then there are the many cases in which multinationals rely on foreign governments to allow them to wreck environments and abuse local populations and workers as they extract resources. Often security or police forces supplied by compliant governments are enlisted to move or repress people who get in the way of profit-maximization. People are dispossessed and sometimes killed.

Ian T. Shearn, a journalist who specializes in corporate accountability, reports that ExxonMobil, through a subsidiary that, in turn, employed other contractors, had been mining limestone for use in the construction of a pipeline for a nineteen-billion-dollar liquefied natural gas project undertaken for the Papua New Guinea government. Shearn records[20] that the excavators were warned about the grave danger their method of digging was creating. The warnings were ignored, and Tumbi Mountain came tumbling down. The landslide buried a village. Twenty-seven people are known to have been killed; more may be buried under the rubble. ExxonMobil needed the road, now blocked by the landslide's debris, to be cleared in order to get on with its project. When as-yet-uncompensated and angry landowners refused to give access to the road, the government called on its ruthless mobile police squads to help ExxonMobil get the "consents" it needed.

Law being what it is, it is not clear whether these interrelated events amounted to prosecutable crimes committed by ExxonMobil or its functionaries. But a great tragedy, still unfolding, was caused by the obsession of a group of corporations and their human operators with profit-maximization for the shareholders at whatever cost to others. Shearn's thoroughly researched story in the *Nation* reveals a degree of recklessness that speaks to a systemic indifference to human beings' welfare and to that of their natural environment.

Such stories of people being dispossessed and, sometimes, killed are all too common. Organizations such as MiningWatch Canada and the Canadian Centre for International Justice keep a close eye on Canadian multinationals that set out to extract resources in nations where governments are not too worried about the human or natural costs this might entail. Often, these resource extractors know they would not be given the same latitude by the jurisdictions they come from.

To illustrate: a petition on MiningWatch Canada's website urged the attorney general of Guatemala to refer a matter to a human rights tribunal.[21] The concern was the use of force by the Guatemalan police to evict protestors who had set up a camp some six kilometres from a mine to whose operations they objected. The mine was Tahoe Resources' Escobal mine. Tahoe Resources is a Canadian corporation, 40 per cent of whose shares are owned by Goldcorp corporation, a large Canadian resources firm. The Guatemalan objectors had assembled because of their concern about the impact of the mine on their environment, on their traditional way of life, and on their health. They wanted to be fully informed and consulted before they would give approval to mining taking place in their long-lived-in lands. Tahoe Resources cried out for help from the Guatemalan authorities. The use of force by the police followed a declaration by the government that the encampment constituted a state of siege. As the police drove the objectors away, a young girl was fatally shot and other people were injured. The former head of security at Tahoe is facing charges for having shot at protestors.

The point here is not that it is clear that Tahoe Resources and the controlling Goldcorp corporation behaved illegally. Much more evidence is needed for a lawyer to make such an assertion, although one might think that it all smells bad enough to warrant stigmatization or some sanctions. A civil class action alleging deviant behaviour has been launched. Whatever the outcome of these legal processes, the story, as told by MiningWatch Canada and the Canadian Centre for International Justice, does allow some pertinent observations to be made.

First, it is an example of a recurring problem. Often, poverty-stricken governments—some of which can be easily bribed—will aid corporations headquartered in the more mature capitalist nations to make profits in ways that are, to say the least, ethically controversial. Second, this is rarely, if ever, a concern for the shareholders of the parent corporation.

In this case, activists tried to bring the Guatemala events to the attention of Goldcorp's directors, executives, and shareholders by holding a memorial for the killed girl outside Goldcorp's head office in Toronto at the same time as a memorial service was being held at Tahoe Resources' locale in Guatemala. In Guatemala the activists were trying to persuade the Guatemalan government to act against the perpetrators. In Toronto, Canadian activists were pleading with shareholders to have their directors do something remedial. At this time, it is unknown whether this pressure will have the desired impact on shareholders of Goldcorp. What is clear is that resort is being made to indirect action because no one seems to believe that we can hold shareholders to account directly or that we can make them disgorge any profits made by Goldcorp through the activities of Tahoe Resources in Guatemala.

There it is again. Shareholders are understood to be immune from the fallout of corporate wrongdoing, while possessing the potential to wield influence over such conduct, which, it is equally understood, is intended to benefit them. This should be seen as truly embarrassing. Our self-proclaimed liberal society holds that risk-creators are to take responsibility for those risks that materialize. Yet, well understood though the gap between the ideal and reality is, corporate law is designed to maintain it.

Inevitably, corporate law's fiat to create zones of irresponsibility is exploited by directors, executives, and shareholders. They have potential control but choose to pretend they do not. This is all made obvious when shareholders do not gain from this kind of exploiting behaviour in foreign lands but, instead, stand to lose because of it. Then they remind everyone that they have entrusted their money to the corporations in which they have invested on the basis that they will be efficient in exploiting the poor of the world.

In April 2014, MiningWatch Canada reported that some shareholders might express anger at Barrick corporation's annual general meeting to be held in Vancouver that May. Shareholders were upset because the head office's corporate directors and executives had allowed those in charge of an operation in far-off Chile to be heedless towards local concerns when they should not have been. The operations in Chile had threatened the environment and the local population, leading to vociferous objections. The damn-the-torpedoes approach of Barrick's Chilean subsidiary had forced the Chilean government and the Chilean judiciary to intervene. This led to costly overruns and, back in Canada, to a loss of money for Barrick shareholders.

At the time of writing, there is talk of a billion-dollar class action being brought by these miffed shareholders. That is, when shareholders lose money directly because of excesses and abuses, they are then prepared to flex their muscle. MiningWatch Canada points out that these disappointed Barrick shareholders could have prevented their losses if they had used their influence earlier. After all, some of the affected Chilean people had come to an earlier AGM in Canada to voice their concerns to the very same shareholders. But, as is nearly always the case when these kinds of complainants come calling, they had been treated as irritating malcontents who were interfering with the serious business of money-making.

MiningWatch also relates that Barrick is involved in a controversy eerily similar to that which engulfs ExxonMobil in Papua New Guinea. In the last week of April 2014, a Barrick subsidiary was dealing with violent protests at a mining site in Papua New Guinea. It had called on the government to deploy a hundred special police and army personnel to ward off incursions by poor people trying to get some gold from Barrick's field of operations. This should not have surprised Barrick shareholders. In 2009, protests against Barrick's operations in Papua New Guinea had caused it to rely on government repression; three hundred houses of Indigenous people were burned down in the ensuing fracas.

Again, it is impossible to make a bald statement that Barrick or any of its human agents have engaged in criminal activities in these cases. But it is crystal clear that they have been involved in questionable behaviours, perhaps highly unethical ones, that have inflicted and continue to inflict a great deal of harm. And that their silent beneficiaries, their shareholders, have exhibited a remarkable indifference to this suffering. The shareholders are content to be hands-off, mindless, money-making bystanders. If they were asked, they likely would plead ignorance or helplessness—unless and until they lose money. Then they sit up and become knowledgeable; then they assert themselves.

Can shareholders make a difference? With apologies to Barack Obama, Yes, they can!

6

The Shareholder as Victim

THE SHAREHOLDERS' SENSE OF ENTITLEMENT COMES TO THE FORE most explicitly when corporations or their directors and executives act in ways that rip off the financial investors. Then their cries for help are heard with sympathy by the powers that be, which go out of their way to ensure that shareholders will not be victimized. Owners of wealth are to be protected. Let us revisit the James Hardie affair, referred to in chapter 3.

THE NEED FOR GREED

The James Hardie Group had mined and processed asbestos in Australia for over fifty years before it became obvious that this kind of poisonous enterprise had reached its nadir.[1] Anticipating claims by both identified and as-yet-unknown victims, James Hardie's planners changed the nature of the business, left a fund in a set of legally self-standing corporations in Australia, and moved the rest of their vast assets to the Netherlands. There they would be able to seek profits in a building materials undertaking while assuring investors that this relocated business was unburdened by demands for asbestos compensation. In corporate language, they fortified the capital markets' confidence in their undertaking. The intention was to make it easier for James Hardie to attract investors and lenders to contribute funds to the relocated, and now debt-liberated, business. But things went awry.

Too little money was left behind in Australia to deal with the compensation bills. It came to be popularly believed that the underfunding had been if not intentional then, at best, due to rank incompetence at calculating the number of deserving victims. A political furor led to a commission of inquiry. Its findings were scathing about the indifference, incompetence, and callousness of the directors of this major public corporation when it came to injured and killed workers. The directors' nonchalance contrasted sharply with the zealousness on display when the same directors were boosting the corporation's reputation in financial houses and share markets. The directors and the corporation were portrayed as eager to comfort a lot of rich, unpoisoned people. The distaste was palpable. Some horse dealing ensued and James Hardie agreed to make some more money available for future payments to its Australian victims. That part of the James Hardie problem, the compensation scandal, was now considered to have been resolved.

Corporate and security law regulators, however, were not satisfied. After all, it was on their watch that directors and executives of a significant public corporation had behaved so badly that they had been chastised by a public body for not complying with the basic requirements that those regulators supposedly patrolled. Implicitly, this damned the regulators. Their legitimacy stems from ensuring that the requirements for directors and executives to exercise reasonable judgment and provide accurate information to investors are met. This is what capitalists need to believe. To show they cared about investors, about capitalists, the regulators brought actions against James Hardie's directors for flagrant abuses and violations of these rules.

After years of litigation, the regulators succeeded, and financial pundits appeared satisfied that the regulatory system had worked and respect for it was restored. Directors and executives had been told that they must not depart from the golden rule: to exercise due diligence and good faith to serve the interests of investors. The punishments imposed on the disciplined directors and officers, though, were paltry. They were asked to pay some risible fines (some covered by corporate insurance) and disbarred from serving as directors on corporate boards. Other than that, their lives, unlike those of the asbestos victims, were undisturbed. So not only is it harder to hold capitalists and their functionaries to account, they also get special treatment when, finally labelled wrongdoers, it comes to punishment.

To many people, these political machinations and protracted legal processes were less than satisfying. Not one director, executive, or shareholder was brought to justice for knowingly exposing workers to appalling physical risks during over half a century of profit-making. This is particularly galling as some of the major shareholders during James Hardie's long life had acted as both directors and executives. They were not sanctioned in any way. It is only when shareholders might be adversely affected—in this case, there was no evidence that investors had lost money because of the failures of the prosecuted directors—that the might of the law steps in to teach corporations and their chief actors a lesson.

To recapitulate: the law does not directly say that the satisfaction of shareholders' interests and, more generally, of the stock markets in which they play are to be the principal goals of those who manage a corporation. But it is nonetheless clear that this is perceived to be the rightful focus of directors and executives. Certainly, it is clear that shareholders act as if they are entitled to this kind of attention, and the law ensures their welfare. But shareholders are never truly safe from the dangers that inhere in a system that elevates the satisfaction of greed to a virtue.

There is a symbiotic relationship between, on the one hand, directors and executives and, on the other, shareholders. But there is also the possibility of conflict between them. Shareholders can profit in two ways. First, by choosing a corporation that is likely to prosper over the long term and thereby return good dividend payments and improved share value. Second, by pushing directors and executives to improve share values in the short term, allowing investors to sell their shares at a profit and use the realized capital to start over again in some other venture that will be also pushed to improve share values instantly.

For either path to riches, shareholders have to rely on directors and executives. Shareholders must entrust decision-making powers over the deployment of corporate assets and policies to directors and executives. Their actions might harm shareholders.

When discussing the Berle and Means study, we noted that the danger presented by directors and executives loafing on the job or enriching themselves at the expense of the corporation and its shareholders has always been a source of concern. Shirking and looting is not only possible but is also to be expected, because those who climb the corporate ladders and become major directors and executives are likely to have internalized the idea that selfish behaviour is normal, indeed, laudable. It would be surprising if a goodly number of them were not tempted to use their decision-making powers to suit themselves as much as possible.

This has forced regulators to jump in. The task of drafting appropriate rules is a delicate one. First, it is necessary to acknowledge that some of the most powerful and to-be-respected people in our society are not quite trusted by equally to-be-respected people. Second, there is a need to say that their decision-making is to be curtailed to some extent. The question is, to what extent?

Our adoration for private profit-seeking requires that we honour the decisions made by individuals looking after themselves. We are to respect their judgments and exercises of discretion. This means that directors and executives, acting on behalf of a corporation, are to be given room to make business judgments as they see fit. If they stand to profit from decisions made on behalf of the blob, this does not automatically mean that their decisions should be second-guessed. It is very difficult to show that their decisions were solely or primarily for their own benefit, rather than for the benefit of the corporation or of its shareholders. The balancing required to deal with these tensions leads regulators to draft corporate governance rules that are rather vague in nature.

Directors, executives, and specified officers of corporations are to use due diligence and make reasonable decisions as they worry about how to advance the best interests of the corporation. They are urged not to think about their own interests and to avoid conflicts between their personal interests and those of the corporation they are paid to serve. These hopeful prescriptions allow directors and executives a good deal of room to make choices. The to-be-averted dangers of self-dealing and indolence have not been met head-on.

An added complication is that, because directors and executives are considered to be important people, people with heft who are worthy of respect, it is hard for anyone, including regulators and judges, to think of them as we think of ordinary workers. Yet the duties of care, skill, good faith, fidelity, and the need to do one's best for the corporation, not for oneself, are identical to the duties imposed on any employee in any low-level position. When it comes to non-managerial staff, employers, aided by law, enforce these duties ruthlessly. Any vagueness as to how they should be applied tends to be read in favour of the employer.

This tells us two things. First, to the blob and to shareholders, it is important to remind directors and executives that, despite their highly regarded and highly paid positions, they are to do the utmost with their talents to serve their masters; they are to curb their desire, natural as it is, to benefit themselves. They are to play second fiddle to shareholders. Second, these special rules had to be put into words because directors and executives are not seen simply as employed workers. In part, this is because, unlike in most employment situations, no one tells them how to do their job. Their job description is necessarily unspecific, except that they are to maximize profits. Also, they are not seen as employees because it is more accurate to see them as belonging to a hybrid category. They serve the capitalists—the corporation, and through it, the shareholders—but simultaneously belong to the capitalist class, as they are often shareholders in the very corporations they run on behalf of shareholders.

In recent times, it is the shareholders themselves who have insisted that directors and executives be paid in shares, thereby aligning their personal interests with those of the capitalist shareholders. This dual character of directors and executives—as capitalists/employers when deploying the workers, a task which is part of their duty as servants of the corporation and its shareholders, and as shareholders/capitalists in their own right—goes a long way towards explaining the fusses around executive remuneration.

If it is seen as excessive wages that have been paid to executives who are only glorified employees, it becomes tempting to compare executive remuneration to that of the lesser employees in the same corporation. The executive pay, then, is easily characterized as overpayment, or as proof of shirking and looting. This breeds envy among the corporation's waged workers and a sense of anger among shareholders whose share values and dividends are disappointing at the same time that their supposed servants do pretty well. Employees are not meant to do well when their employer does not.

But as we have seen, "employee" is a disputable characterization of executives; this makes so-called excessive remuneration an intractable problem. After all, there is no such thing as excessive profits for a shareholder. And all too often, executives are significant shareholders who see themselves, and are seen by shareholders, as fellow travellers. Then, even obscene remuneration is hard to attack.

Tensions between directors/executives and the shareholders they are meant to serve are built into the architecture of the for-profit corporation. The law goes to a considerable extent to create corporate governance rules that protect shareholders who are forced to rely on powerful directors and executives. These functionaries are to be discouraged from favouring themselves. At the same time, they are to be encouraged to be aggressive in their search for profits. Shareholders encourage the same directors and executives to be ruthless towards others and heedless of the environment, often by promising them a cut should their harm-causing risk-taking lead to more profits for shareholders.

That is, shareholders want directors and executives to be loyal to them but not to interests or values that protect outsiders. The rules governing directors and executives reflect these rather tension-filled, sometimes clashing, objectives: restraining the animal spirit prized by those who choose them and want their own animal spirit satisfied. Drawing this line requires delicately drafted rules that ensure that shareholders are not unduly disadvantaged.

For those shareholders who make money by the purchase and sale of equities rather than by hanging onto shares in any one corporation, there is a need to be given access to all the relevant information at the same time as everyone else is and to have the same opportunity as anyone else to sell and buy. To these ends, elaborate rules force directors to set up reporting and auditing regimes. An imposing set of agencies has been spawned to oversee the complex structures. This is what the rules of stock exchanges such as the Toronto Stock Exchange, the Securities Commission of Ontario, the Investment Dealers' Association, and the like set out to do.

Directors and executives must pay attention to these agencies' protocols and rules. It is the failure to honour them sufficiently that was called into play in the James Hardie case. Here, then, there is some clarity. The scheme is focused on heightening the directors' and executives' awareness that their primary responsibility is towards shareholders. From society's point of view, the downside is that this leads them to be solicitous of shareholders' goals even if the means used to meet this objective lead to anti-social results. For example, Colin Mayer, a professor at Oxford's Said Business School, records that a "survey of thirty-four directors of US Fortune 200 companies reported that thirty-one of them would cut down a mature forest or release a dangerous unregulated toxin into the environment to increase corporate earnings."[2]

Of course, while they are largely indifferent about the outcomes for outsiders, the directors' and executives' zeal on behalf of shareholders may be blunted somewhat if they see an opportunity to use their decision-making powers to advance their personal cause. They might be tempted to shirk and loot if this can be masked in some clever way. This threat is made more of a danger than it might otherwise be because a large number of influential people have an interest in moulding the director/executive restraining rules to their advantage, inducing directors and executives of corporations to leave the straight and narrow of the path set out for them. This lessens the efficacy of the myriad rules designed to make corporate governance honest, fair, and transparent. On occasion, indeed, many occasions, these moulding exercises reduce the investors' faith in the markets for capital, defeating the very purpose of the rules.

ENTER THE INTERMEDIARIES

To bring sellers and buyers together, brokers of all kinds are paid commissions. They sell corporate equities and bonds, and other rent-yielding instruments based on them. They have a stake in having many purchasable instruments available to many willing purchasers of these instruments. They have an interest in the markets being seen as both safe and as returning high yields. They want corporations to go to the investing public more often; they want that public to feel that this is a meritorious way to generate wealth for all, as well as for each investor. As they push these adventurous undertakings, they need to be trusted.

We've already mentioned the regulatory and monitoring institutions, both internal and external, that are developed to make potential participants feel sanguine about the capital markets. In addition, intermediaries who facilitate the sale and purchase of financial instruments have set up their own associations that claim to discipline their members and, thereby, to protect investors. These associations deploy a dazzling number of professionals and advisers meant to reassure investors:

- analysts who give assurances about the quality of the products designed by corporations and their professional helpers for sale by the commission agents
- clever mathematical whizzes who develop such products for the capital markets, finding new and more ways to invest in future income streams from corporations
- lawyers and accountants who draft instruments that accord with the letter of the law while exploiting the ingenuity of the mathematical whizzes

And without belabouring the point, note that the word "product" is used for arcane instruments that, in some way, constitute a claim on future corporate income. The instrument being sold and bought is only tangentially related to the production of actual goods or services by a corporation.

There are, then, a lot of sophisticated folk whose economic well-being stems from the movement in financial instruments based, in some unspecified way, on the corporation's business. In promoting transactions that will earn fees, the system creates what Nancy B. Kurland, of the Franklin & Marshall school of organizational studies in Pennsylvania, has termed "blatant conflicts of interest," as brokers and commission agents encourage trades without much regard for their clients' or society's interests.[3] The emphasis is on transactions, on puffery and on the massaging of information, on exaggerating the soundness of an investment. It is on proffering (or pretending to proffer) early information to some clients, on seeking advance information from directors and executives and rewarding them with a better opportunity to sell or buy than others might have. All of this becomes part and parcel of the daily game, a game that gives a lot of people incentives to distort, to lie, and to cheat.[4]

Naturally, they prefer hyperbole and distortion to outright cheating. The latter is not only illegal, but it is also offensive to their professional codes. A bit of exaggeration, of cleverness within the rules, however, is commendable. It is portrayed as merely pushing legal boundaries to their logical conclusion to attain the best results for their clients and themselves, both laudable goals in a for-profit economy. A veritable phalanx of financial professionals and underwriting finance houses profit—in terms of reputation and hard cash—from pushing the envelope.

They manipulate regulatory restrictions. They find ways to bestow advantages that abide by the letter of the law while clearly bending its spirit—such as tax havens and the creation of group organizations to minimize taxes or avoid liabilities. They devise new products for shareholders whose highly speculative nature is likely to escape close scrutiny by regulators—subprime mortgages being a great illustration—or that shift responsibility for imposts or contractual obligations—here, the integrated garment retail/production industry is a poster child.

Parasitic professionals justify their well-paid machinations by holding out that they are merely zealously serving their clients' rightful chase for profits. Their only duty is to use their skills within the letter of the law. *The Smartest Guys in the Room*, a book about the Enron scandal, illustrates the dynamic this way:

> Say you have a dog, but you need to create a duck on the financial statements. Fortunately, there are specific accounting rules for what constitutes a duck: yellow feet, white covering, orange beak. So you take the dog and paint its feet yellow and its fur white and you paste an orange plastic beak on its nose, and you say to your accountants, "This

is a duck! Don't you agree that it's a duck?" And the accountants say,
"Yes, according to the rules, this is a duck." Everybody knows that it's a
dog, not a duck, but that doesn't matter because you've met the rules
for calling it a duck.[5]

These ethically troubling and well-paid machinations lead to soul searching from time to time. But they persist as parasitic professionals justify the
use of their peculiar skills by maintaining that, as long as they stay within the
bounds and metes of professional protocols and the letter of the law, they are
zealously furthering their clients' rightful desire to maximize profits.

INCENTIVES FOR CARELESSNESS

The ordinariness and acceptability of this approach constrains the efficacy
of the rules and the agencies that enforce them. The always frail fabric of the
financial markets is stretched and stretched, inevitably leading to its occasional tearing. One of the destructive forces is the symbiotic relationship
between the equity market operators and financial institutions, on the one
hand, and the corporate directors and managers, on the other.

Corporate directors and executives rely on the financial service render-
ers to promote and sell their equities; they depend on them for valuations
and, thereby, credit ratings and the like. Financial services depend on managers to get the business of offering shares to the public, to be involved in
any acquisition, takeover, or merger plans, and so on. This interdepend-
ence is not, in itself, a dangerous circumstance. Indeed, it may be an efficient one if the corporate managers remain loyal to the corporation and
its needs, and if their loyalty is supported by the financial service industry's professionalism.

But just as those who make a living from promoting the stock markets
have incentives to be careless about the products they offer the investing
public, so do executives and directors of corporations. First, the intensify-
ing pressure of shareholders to maximize value without much regard for
the productive activities of the corporation may, in a very general sense,
cause the pressured managers to lose sight of the long-term viability of the

enterprise and of the social impact of its operations. It is conventional wisdom that Anglo-American business has a short-term horizon, that it has too much regard for share value maximization and not enough for long-term prosperity. Inasmuch as this is true, it may, in part, be the consequence of judging management by its ability to yield satisfactory share valuations, quarter by quarter.

Second, if the ability to maximize share values is the measure of worth of directors and executives, they are under pressure to present the state of the corporation in an appropriately favourable light. Here the symbiotic relationship with financial institutions and professionals who have a similar agenda may become problematic. There will be premiums for those who can push the envelope of legal and ethical presentation to its limits. The line between acceptable and unacceptable accounting is likely to be blurry and, therefore, crossed, often unintentionally, sometimes wilfully. This amoral-to-immoral spectrum of behaviour is all the more likely to manifest itself if directors and executives, like their external advisers and partners, have much to gain personally from innovations and imaginative portrayals. Sometimes the results are arrestingly gross. The *Wall Street Journal* reported in 2011, for example, that Shaw Engineering entered into a contract to pay its chief executive officer seventeen million dollars for not competing with the corporation after he died.

These excesses outrage policy-makers. The paradox is evident: the drive to maximize shareholders' interests puts weapons into the hands of folk who may use them against those very shareholders, even as the law and lore of the land seek to promote and protect their interests. The alarm is raised: investors of wealth, shareholders, are being injured. Not workers, not consumers, not the environment—but shareholders. This should not happen.

Yet none of this should surprise. All the undesirable features associated with the generation of markets to raise capital by and for corporations were visible from the beginning. In 1696 the English Board of Trade declared that, while useful, the novel entrepreneurial vehicle, the company form, invited shysters to the party. The invention was being abused by the sale of stock "to ignorant men, drawn in by the reputation, falsely raised and artfully spread, concerning the thriving of stock."[6] The lesson was plain then and should be plain now: deviance by corporate actors' abuse of the corporate form is not aberrational.

There is no shortage of examples of such built-in, sleazy, society-imperilling behaviour today. Despite the sophistication of the rules and the countless overseeing agencies, both governmental and voluntary, the amount of shamming and scamming has never abated. In at least one respect, it is worse: more of our economy is tied to the functioning of financial markets. The huge amounts invested in them and the interrelatedness of so many major corporate and financial houses threatens not only the well-being of shareholders, but also that of our economies.

OUTBREAKS OF ROGUERY

Sometimes, because of our desire to let the market set conditions, certain corporations are put in a position to rig the market in their favour. When their functionaries exploit such opportunities, it may seriously impact a huge number of investors who operate under the market conditions created by a few actors for their own benefit. It will be hard to identify them, but countless victims will arise out of this abuse of market power. Consider LIBOR.

Just after the world-shaking subprime mortgage scandal led to the 2008 financial crisis, it was revealed that some of the same major banks involved in the subprime mortgage scams had been manipulating something called the London Interbank Offered Rate (LIBOR). This caused losses of billions of dollars. LIBOR is a postbox where, every day, major banks report the interest they expect to be charged for loans from other banks. In effect, they are making a statement about their financial health, and LIBOR administrators are able to promulgate an average of the prevailing interest rates. LIBOR is an announcement to the capital markets about the financial health of major banks; at the same time, the average set affects countless transactions worldwide.

If a particular bank says it expects to be paying a lower rate than it actually is, and this is accepted by the LIBOR people, that bank's balance sheet will look a lot better than it otherwise would. This facilitates lending and borrowing on terms more advantageous than should prevail to the bank and worse for borrowers and lenders. As it also affects the average rate of interest communicated to the capital markets, the distorting impact eddies outward.

LIBOR is a mechanism that is easily gamed. All that's required is for someone at a bank to convince someone at the LIBOR offices to make a deal. When that happens, it is clearly a betrayal of the investors' trust. But the engineers of falsehoods revel in their exploits, much like teenagers who think they have fooled their substitute teacher in letting them go home early. Matt Taibbi's *Divide* reports the following exchange between a LIBOR agent and a Barclays Bank "fixer": "For you ... anything.... Always happy to help, leave it to me." A little later: "Done ... for you big boy." To which the contented Barclays Bank officer replied: "Dude. I owe you big time! Come over one day after work and I'm opening a bottle of Bollinger."[7] And when some of the big banks finally admitted that they had been guilty of rigging the LIBOR rates, Jenny Anderson of the *New York Times* reported that one trader at Barclays Bank had written in an online chatroom, "If you ain't cheating, you ain't trying."[8]

Shortly after the LIBOR revelations, reports of a similar scam hit the business pages. This time it concerned a scheme to fix the benchmarking of currency rates on which the lucrative market for buying and selling currencies on the international markets is based. Referred to in the media as the WM/Reuters currency rates scandal, it too involved a falsification of rates that everyone is asked to trust. Reliance on the accuracy of the currency rates set by the benchmarking system is pivotal to the huge market in currency trading. If some people can push the rate up or down by a fraction and know about that before anyone else, gobs of money are to be made by selling or buying currency. Testosterone-imbued bravado accompanies this scam as well. *Business Day* noted in January 2014 that the alleged manipulators had answering machines that responded with identifying names such as The Cartel; The Bandits Club; One Team, One Dream; and The Mafia. The traders gave themselves names like the Three Musketeers, and the A Team. A crude kind of locker-room culture drives the makers and shakers activating financial capital's entrails. Their crudeness does not make them any less dangerous. And the outcry that follows each set of revelations does not do anything to prevent the next episode of skullduggery.

The deceit, the bombast, the lying, and the cheating are endemic. When there is an outbreak of roguery, there is a tendency to present it as if something has gone wrong with an otherwise trustworthy system. Nothing could be further from the truth. Deceit and cheating are par for the course. As Bernie Sanders told Hillary Clinton in a CBS Democratic Primary debate on November 13, 2015: "The business model of Wall Street is fraud, that's what it is." The system is structured so that it is easy to make the trusting and ignorant, namely the vast majority of us, suckers.

In the last two decades or so we have seen the debacles involving BCCI, Barings Bank, Long-Term Capital Management, Enron, Adelphia and World-Com, Northern Rock, Bear Stearns, Lehman Brothers, Parmalat, RBS, AIG, the subprime mortgage and savings and loans scams. In Canada, the names of Bre-X, Nortel, and Hollinger are associated with odious behaviour. Before that, T. Hadden, reporting on the United Kingdom in the 1980s, wrote:

> Recent reports ... have highlighted a number of abuses: ...the making of improper payments and perks to directors and their associates, the window-dressing of company accounts by intra-group dealings and questionable revaluations of company assets, and the more general tendency of those in control of companies to treat their assets as if they were own personal property. There also has been a continuing series of frauds and improprieties on the securities market, from cases of insider trading, both by those in control of established companies and their associates, to the rigging of markets in association with apparently fictitious take-over bids by collusive bidding.[9]

There were similar scandals in the United States at that time, the essence of which is captured in headlines collected by two American economists, W. Adams and J.W. Brock: "Boesky Goes to Jail," "Levine Cooperates with Investigators," "US Indicts Singer's Bilzerian in Raids on 3 Firms," "Superstar Lawyer Sentenced for Insider Trading," "Drexel Burnham Lambert

Pleads Guilty; Agrees to Pay Out a Record $650 Million."[10] The 1980s, like the 1990s, the 2000s, and 2006–2009 were seen as a period of out-of-control greed. So, of course, was the decade preceding the Great Depression and the depression of the 1880s/1890s, the 1840s and its shocking railway scandals, as was the period of the South Sea Bubble and that of the Tulip Bulb mania. There has been no shortage of scandalizing avarice run amok during corporate capitalism's reign. And after each episode, legislators have run to fortify the barricades, to set up new and higher hurdles to ensure that such ugliness would never occur again. Not too successfully, it appears.

Charles H. Ferguson—the maker of the popular film *Inside Job,* which chronicled the lying, cheating, and arrogance of the banks, the directors, executives, brokers, analysts, and academic pundits who brought us the subprime mortgage scandals that crippled the world's economies—undoubtedly hoped that his vivid exposé would lead to some effective reforms and better behaviour. He has been disappointed. His new lament, *Predator Nation: Corporate Criminals, Political Corruption and the Hijacking of America*, documents how, again and again, the same wrongdoers who brought us the excesses described in his film are lying, cheating, and arrogantly ripping off society and flouting its laws all over again.[11]

Ferguson calls for more jailing of chief executives who are able to use the legal corporate shields which protect them and major shareholders against personal responsibility and allow them to wield the political influence of their corporations' economic assets. This leads, he says, to the enrichment of the few at the expense of the many, often by unethical or illegal behaviour.

Similarly, Matt Taibbi's recent investigation concluded that, on any single day, Wall Street is awash in embezzlement and fraud.[12] This is not new. John Kenneth Galbraith, writing about the 1929 crash, noted that, at any one time, there was a hidden treasure trove of undetected embezzlement in American corporations. With his usual flair, Galbraith suggested we honour it by giving it a name, a "bezzle," something that expanded when times were good and shrank when times were tough.[13] This is the reality: the numerous frauds and lesser deceits and ethical lapses are not abnormal occurrences.

To illustrate, one day in the *New York Times*, June 7–8, 2014, yielded the following:

- "Love of Risk Leads Many over the Line," a sympathetic article by James B. Stewart, explains that the numerous excesses and egregious gambles taken with other people's money, as well as their own, is attributable to an inherent desire to wager, rather than naked greed. Many examples of outrageous conduct are offered and characterized rather gently by the reporter, much as one might describe gamblers as people who cannot help themselves.

- "BNP Paribas Executive May Leave" reports that a chief executive may leave and the corporation pay six billion dollars to "settle" a case being brought against it for laundering money for foreigners on the U.S. terrorist list, folk from Sudan, Iran, and the like. The story reports a similar case and settlement involving Credit Suisse. The story might have referred, but did not, to a similar and even larger settlement with HSBC for allegedly laundering money on behalf of known drug dealers, criminals, and people on terrorist lists.

- "More Risks for Deutsche Bank's Profits" describes the bank's alleged involvement in a five-trillion-dollar currency rate scam and global benchmark manipulation.

That is just one day, a day that also saw the *Times* report "GM's Response to a Fatal Defect Was to Shrug," a story about a shoddy product knowingly put on the market and reportedly involved in numerous deaths. This is a non-financial bit of deviance, but it, too, speaks to the repeated wrongdoing done by our captains of industry and finance hiding under the umbrella of corporations and undertaken for the benefit of shareholders who are also hiding behind those corporations.

ASKING NICELY

There are efforts to remedy the many widely acknowledged downsides of relying on the for-profit corporation as a principal generator of welfare. After every new set of scandals—and its associated damage to society and the economy—comes to light, the jurisdictions and powers of various agencies and monitoring bodies are revised. In addition, there are many earnest efforts to persuade corporations to be, well, nicer. The corporate social responsibility and stakeholder movements are pleas to the corporations to abandon their singular focus on the welfare of selfish and uncaring shareholders. But so deeply ingrained is the understanding that the need to chase profits must remain a primary goal that these movements seek to reassure policy-makers and corporate actors that, while asking them to be nicer, they do not, in any way, intend to delegitimize the profit-chasing paradigm. To the contrary: corporate social responsibility advocates claim that to consider interests other than those of shareholders while chasing profits is not only a decent thing to do, but it will also add to the profits available.

Unsurprisingly, the movements have had little traction. It is difficult for any one corporation to see how it should make choices that will ensure it meets both profit-maximization and undefined social goals. The aspirational nature and vagueness of corporate social responsibility contrast sharply with the guidance given by prevailing practices, vested interests, and the law that governs corporate behaviour. The central actors in the blob-o-sphere are issued firm and precise instructions: they are to pursue a narrow maximization-of-profit agenda, rather than costly, blurry goals that just might serve the outside world. The British American Tobacco Australia website, for example, advances this rather tortuous argument: "If a business is manufacturing products that pose real risks of serious disease we believe that it is all the more important that it does so responsibly."[14]

"Shareholder Democracy in Canada," a 2010 National Bureau of Economic Research working paper offers this analysis:

> Of course, corporations should be run ethically, but what does this mean? The most outspoken advocates of ethical behaviour in any country are often its most religious citizens, but no one would seriously advocate turning Canada's great corporations over to priests or ministers, let alone evangelists. An ethical metre-stick of corporate performance needs to be both easily readable and marked in in a way

acceptable to the majority of citizens in a democracy. At present, we are only in the earliest stages of building a better metre-stick.

And, as Eduardo Porter pithily noted in the *New York Times*, there are more precise metrics around: "Corporate executives are paid to maximize profits, not to behave ethically."[15] Even John Maynard Keynes had to admit that, in business, "foul is useful and fair is not. Avarice and usury must be our gods for a little longer still."[16]

This goes a long way towards explaining why corporate governance— the protection of investing capitalists from unfair market conditions and from the opportunistic management of corporations—rather than corporate social responsibility has won the hearts and minds of corporate cheer-leaders and legislators. This is why all these agencies require directors and executives to abide by specific duties that should benefit the best interests of the corporation, equated with the maximization of profits and shareholders' welfare, and why so many institutions and organs set enforceable rules that govern the raising of capital.

There are, of course, also rules that impose duties on directors and executives to ensure that their corporations comply with regulations concerning worker health and safety, consumer and environmental protection, and so on.[17] The corporation must obey the laws of the land. In earlier work, I have detailed how poorly enforced these rules are, but, even if they were more successfully enforced, this would not mean that corporations would be socially responsible. Think of corporations' lawful engagement in industries such as tobacco, asbestos, and private prisons, where they cause great harm to the physical integrity and welfare of people and their environments. Lawful behaviour, as we will examine in more detail, is not necessarily ethically or socially acceptable.

To return: the laws by which corporate actors must abide are regulatory, poorly enforced, and often co-written by corporations.[18] That is, these demands on directors and executives, even if they are made to stick, fall well short of satisfying those who would like corporations to be more socially responsible, let alone altruistic. This has been documented by David Vogel, the well-known political science and business ethics researcher from Berke-ley.[19] He noted that, in 2005, a Google search yielded more than thirty thou-sand sites on corporate social responsibility, there were more than fifteen million pages on the Internet addressing aspects of the topic, and Amazon listed more than six hundred books on the subject. He studied all the studies and found that the movement had failed to make a positive impact and that, if the goal was to improve the assumption of social responsibility by corpora-tions, government intervention was indicated. The blob was unlikely to do this voluntarily, the evidence showed.

Much ink has been spilled to push the corporate social responsibility/stakeholder agenda. But it is fair to say that current corporate practices, policy emphases, and legislative efforts furnish persuasive testimony that, more than ever, the primacy of shareholder interests governs our corporate thinking and doing. Though not without causing thinking members of the elite some embarrassment. Some of them push to put a gentler and kinder face on corporate capitalism, without wishing to abandon it.

There is a movement in the United States to push for legislation at the state level that allows corporations to register themselves as having goals other than shareholder satisfaction.[20] They may name other goals in their bylaws; their directors are then to take these additional goals into account when exercising their discretionary powers. Failure to do so will allow the corporation to bring an action against its directors for having breached their duties towards the so-called benefit corporation, or B-corporation. Such corporations are monitored by an outfit named B-Lab. It reports that twenty-seven U.S. states have enacted enabling legislation and that many corporations have enrolled themselves as B-corporations.

It is a modest movement. If, say, one of the defined benefits is to take the physical environment into account, a failure by directors to do so does not give anyone in the damaged environment an action against the deficient dir-ectors. The wrong is done to the corporation, and it may or may not punish one of its directors. Ingenious and encouraging though this movement is, it appears that the default position remains that profit-maximization is cru-cial and that shareholders' irresponsible search for profits is still at the core of corporate capitalism. But it is a positive step that, as corporate excesses become ever more visible, implicitly acknowledges the need for reform.

THE INTRACTABLE CONTRADICTION

We have seen that, when it is shareholders and the capital markets in which they play that are likely to be injured by opportunistic corporate directors and executives, a large variety of rules are imposed, monitored, and enforced by government regulators and a host of professional institutions. Transparent and accountable corporate governance is widely seen as an important policy issue. The concern is that investors might lose confidence in the game they are asked to play. Shareholders might be in a position to make directors and executives behave better towards them. But we continue to pretend that they have no powers and should be given considerable public assistance to reward them for their sacrifice and to stop them from being victimized by the people they have put in charge of what was once their property.

It is very different when market manipulations affect those who are not members of the corporations, outsiders like workers, consumers, and other such stakeholders. Not only are the regulatory protections that do exist relatively feeble and poorly enforced, but more pertinent to the point being made here, they are not to be used against shareholders. Shareholders are not to be seen as motivators of harm-causing conduct to outsiders. They are not to be the target of actions aimed at redressing harms inflicted by the corporations that sought to shower benefits on them as shareholders.

All this serves to make avaricious directors and executives look like the bad guys in the story. That claim has great resonance with elites because it is often supported by the plaintive claims of victimized shareholders. On those occasions reformers note that a reason for roguish behaviour by directors and executives is that the many rules and regulations they have to deal with are not enforced as rigorously as they should be. A new leaf is to be turned over. As day follows night, more precise regulations, more promises of tougher enforcement follow each scandal. To little effect. The corporate leaders play a role in drafting the new rules; they have symbiotic relations with the regulators who have been taught to treat them as honest and important people because they are wealth creators and because the discretion left with these functionaries is perceived as necessary for true entrepreneurialism. The never-ending rounds of reforms founder on the internalized belief that too strict a system of oversight might kill the geese that lay so many golden eggs for the shareholding class.

The mechanisms we have are not working. We have horrible outcomes, economic losses, physical injuries, deaths, environmental carnage, the rending of our supposedly shared values, and financial scandal after financial scandal. But we keep putting band-aids on the problems. We do not try to find the reason for the abuses and wrongs done by means of the blob.

Here, then, is the situation: shareholders are to be benefited and protected, even if this defeats social expectations. All of the law's instruments and implementing institutions are based on the premise that we owe shareholders a debt of gratitude. They willingly contribute capital to another "person" who, through directors and executives, will deploy the combined capital in a more efficient manner than would otherwise have been possible. Not only do shareholders no longer own their property, but they have given power over it to others. This generosity must be appreciated. It contributes to social welfare, by increasing everyone's wealth. It justifies a reward or, as it turns out, many rewards. Most pertinently, limited fiscal liability and legal immunity.

These benefits are bestowed even if the need to satisfy the shareholders' desire to get the most bang for their buck militates towards ensuring that the corporate professional classes will likely engage in ethically challenged, often illegal, behaviours. These regrettable outcomes are treated as unavoidable aspects of a virtuous activity, namely, the contribution of capital to a marvellously efficient institution, the blob.

At the same time, we need to protect these bounty-providing shareholders from those very people selected for their aggression when pursuing profits. They are chosen for their focused rapaciousness, and it should not be surprising that they might seek to profit themselves. If this also benefits the shareholders, it may not matter. But if it does not—watch out! Moral, contractual, and legal fetters are put in place so that directors and executives know how they are to use their powers. This strengthens the belief of directors and their managers that anything goes if they please shareholders. Restraints, whether morally or legally imposed, are only to be treated as serious ones if violations displease shareholders. As a result, shareholders are truly a privileged class.

Why it is that, if we sincerely desire corporations to behave better, we do not try to change the shareholders' understanding of what are and are not appropriate interests to pursue? This might be done by making them more responsible for the actions of the corporations in which they invest. Or at least, we could try to hold to account, criminally or civilly, those shareholders that we believe are able to change the behaviour of a corporation by exercising their influence and power over directors and executives.

The legal conventional wisdom does not countenance this possibility because of the way in which it conceptualizes the corporation. But really, this wisdom is intended to preserve the privileges of capitalists, of shareholders. It is an argument of political convenience that must be rejected if real political change is to be put on the agenda.

And because the argument to be confronted is cloaked in legal garb, it is that legal garb that must be ripped off. The next part of this book is an effort to do just that.

PART III

THE CORPORATE ACTOR: PIERCING THE VEIL

In which it shown that liberal law staunchly defends the value of individual responsibility until it gets to the blob-o-sphere. Then law pretends that application of this fundamental value is worth ditching because it would do more harm than good to be rigid about the principle of individual responsibility in the corporate sphere, because accountable individuals are too hard to find, and because the corporation makes a necessary contribution to the public welfare. All three propositions, it is shown, are empirically very threadbare.

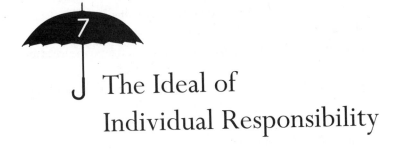

The Ideal of
Individual Responsibility

WITH THIS CHAPTER, I BEGIN A QUINTESSENTIALLY LEGAL ARGUMENT to identify the flesh-and-blood actors who hide behind the corporate veil and give them their due. A deviation from standard legal interpretations is proposed. It is important to understand that this deviation is not only politically and morally meritorious, but it is also defensible in terms of traditional legal methodology.

THE APPLICATION OF PRECEDENT

Much of common law's legitimacy depends on even-handed processes and the conceit that judges merely apply principles of existing law. Judges find those principles by looking to decided cases in the same area as the dispute before them. Theirs is presented as an apolitical, technical task. But of course, finding and interpreting so-called precedents demands the exercise of discretion.

In the corporate law sphere, the judiciary has adopted one of the two major methods of exercising discretion and interpretation. It is a formalistic one that reads precedents as written, as if they were texts of a religion that must be read as they have always been read. The alternative method would be one that judges often use in other areas of law. It allows them to group together a host of differing precedents, analyzing them and concluding that, although as single instances they were treated by judges as belonging to different categories, with the benefit of time and under the pressure of new social conditions, the old decisions reveal an underlying principle that unites them all. This new principle, unarticulated until now, can form the basis for new decision-making.

This approach is neatly expressed in an article by legal academic Joachim Dietrich:

> It is not uncommon for different areas of law to deal with essentially similar problems in different ways. Indeed, in an era of increasing legal specialization, it is easy to remain oblivious to developments and approaches in other areas of law.... By surveying the different approaches the law has taken to essentially similar questions, it may be possible to identify some common problems and, perhaps, possible solutions to such problems.... The fact that accessorial liability in different contexts are not identical in all details does not mean that they are not different species of the same genus, and able to be subjected to *similar* analysis.[1]

THE BUCK STOPS HERE

"Top Brands Shut Bangladesh Factories" was the headline in the *Toronto Star*.[2] The story chronicled the actions taken by the Alliance for Bangladesh Worker Safety. This alliance had been formed by major North American retailers after the dreadful Rana Plaza factory collapse that took 1,129 lives in April 2013. The purpose was to save the retailers' newly imperilled reputations. They use suppliers from Bangladesh and other low-cost labour jurisdictions to make huge profits, as western customers take advantage of cheap goods. After Rana Plaza (and quite a few other similar events), there was a widely shared perspective that these major retailers should insist on better conditions for their suppliers' workers. The retailers agreed to set up monitoring systems and, should their suppliers fall short of some requirements, to stop ordering goods from them. The *Star* recorded some suspended orders after the alliance had received unsatisfactory reports on conditions at some suppliers' workplaces.

The story is retold here to illustrate what we all know. As individuals, we are expected to take responsibility for our actions. This is why huge corporate retailers felt themselves pushed to form a disciplining association. As part I made clear, they could mount a plausible legal argument that they had no legal duty to oversee the behaviour of the supposedly sovereign entities with which they had contracted for supplies. And they had relied on this line of reasoning for years. But now, too many highly publicized dramas had occurred.

After Rana Plaza, they had to show their customer base that they knew they were socially bound to exercise such influence as they could. They needed to ensure that production, undertaken to fulfill their orders, met the standards that responsible corporate citizens would be expected to meet if they undertook the production themselves. The prevention of harms at the supplying sources, or at least, a demonstration that they had told their suppliers that they cared about preventing such harms, had become crucial. A deeply embedded social value had forced these corporations to set up a monitoring and disciplinary system.

That social value is so well known and well accepted that it is reflected in law. As a general rule, the law encourages all individuals—provided they stay within whatever boundaries of behaviour have been drawn over time—to think and act as they please to satisfy their needs and desires. The law holds individuals accountable if their conduct violates existing standards and rules and leads to harm.

Because of the complexity of our interactions, it is not always clear whether a person who is not directly involved in a plan or act that causes harm should be held accountable for the violation. Could or should that person have exercised influence or control over the direct actor or actors? Manifestly, the principle of accountability might be undermined if powerful people are able to exploit this uncertainty. This gives the courts and lawmakers headaches from time to time. But the ingrained principle is that those who do something or have influence over another, and who hope to benefit from the ensuing conduct, are responsible for its safe implementation. The law will go to great lengths to give this principle life.

Take the English case of the Borstal Boys. In the 1960s, the Borstal system kept juvenile offenders in low-security detention and set out to rehabilitate them by education and recreation. One group of Borstal Boys escaped from their rather lax guardians and, on their "night out," vandalized a yacht. The yacht's owner wanted to be compensated. Clearly the thrill-seeking delinquents were responsible for the damage they had caused. But they were not worth suing. So the yacht owner brought an action against the Home Office, the governmental institution that oversaw the Borstal Boys. He succeeded, even though the Home Office argued—rightly and understandably—that the boys were agents in their own right, that the Home Office had not intended that they should act as they did, and that the system which provided for low security was democratically chosen and reflected a sound policy.

In the end, the House of Lords found in favour of the yacht owner.[3] That decision reflected the felt need for the law to hold accountable those who could exercise control over other people's conduct and could reasonably be expected to do so. This was the case even though the other actors had behaved contrary to the known wishes of the person now held responsible. A similar decision was reached in another case in which the Home Office was held responsible for conduct by police officers that amounted to misfeasance in public office.[4] These decisions echo the public's widely held belief that we all should take responsibility for our own actions and for actions we influence others to take.

This belief is reflected in such popular sayings as "The buck stops here" and "Whoever pays the piper calls the tune." In the parliamentary system, ministers of the Crown are expected to take responsibility for the behaviour of the bureaucrats who implement the ministers' policies. When Maxima, a truly iconic supermarket in Riga, Latvia, collapsed in 2013, killing fifty-four and injuring many more, the Latvian prime minister felt he had to resign, as this disaster had happened on his watch.[5]

The media express outrage when some horrific, violent act is perpetrated by militants who seek to attain a political goal by blowing themselves up and others with them. The media report on, or demand, an acknowledgement of responsibility by those who instigated or controlled the actual wrongdoers. Even people considered to be beyond the pale are expected to take responsibility for their actions: we expect people to stand behind their conduct. Both lore and law treat this principle as a cherished one. When an employee's carelessness, while working for an employer, causes harm to other people or their property—say, by driving a truck into someone's front room—not only will the employee be responsible for the wrong, but the employer will also be held responsible. Lawyers call this vicarious liability. It has a special name because, on the face of it, it is an exception to the rule that, in an individualistic society, each of us should be responsible only for our own conduct.

It is tempting to attribute the judiciary's development of the vicarious liability doctrine to its well-honed sense of pragmatism. Most employees, much like the Borstal Boys, are not in a position to satisfy substantial claims for compensation. This deep-pocket justification for imposing liability for the costs of compensation on "innocent" employers, however, would be an unprincipled one. Indeed, the chief justice of the Supreme Court of Canada, in a case called *Bazley* v. *Curry*,[6] decided in 1999, stated that mere expedience should not be allowed to diminish the importance of that most fundamental of liberal legal principles, namely, individual responsibility for individual fault. She was adamant that employers (and similarly placed principals) should only be responsible for the conduct of others when another equally important principle of law justified such a finding. Then, unsurprisingly, she and her fellow judges identified an overarching principle that explained vicarious liability, or legal responsibility for acts committed by others.

As found in leading law books and approved of by justices of the Supreme Court of Canada, the argument is as follows. The employer has established a risk-laden enterprise and should bear the losses when the risks materialize, not only because this is fair but also because the employer is—as a creator and calculator of risks—in the best position to prevent them. It is the employer who determines what level of skills employees ought to have, what technologies are used, how the work is organized, and so forth. The imposition of liability on employers, then, is not one that expediently allocates responsibility to a person without fault. It anchors responsibility in the extent of control a person has over events.

This is not only a principled approach, but it also makes good legal policy sense: it supports society's interest in deterring the creation of unwarranted risks. Thus, in the employment case, the employer is—because of its knowledge and funding of the enterprise—the best insurer against the risks built into the undertaking. When risks do materialize, this makes for more efficient cost allocations. Thus, while employment relations have been thought to give rise to a special category of liability, this turns out to be far too categorical a view.

The above reasoning suggests that the liability rests with the real controller over an undertaking and with that controller's failure to exercise sufficient care in making its undertaking as reasonably safe as practical. This is what makes it responsible for the acts of sovereign "others," be they employees or other individuals acting within the framework of the undertaking.

This doctrine's principle is thought important enough to be applied even if the conduct of the employee amounts to an intentional wrong, one not meant to benefit the employer. Thus, when an English law firm's employee unlawfully appropriated clients' money, the employing law firm was held accountable to the clients.[7] It had not authorized its employee's conduct; indeed, it was horrified by it and saw it as a gross violation of the employee's contractual obligations. But it was held accountable, nonetheless. This mirrors the approach taken in the Borstal Boys example.

Such responsibility for the intentional wrong of another resembles the identification doctrine commonly used to attribute criminal responsibility to corporations. A corporation may be held criminally responsible if its directing minds and wills acted with the appropriate intention when breaching a standard of criminal law. The law likes to pretend that those guiding minds and wills are not persons in their own right, that they are "really" the corporation. But this only makes sense to those who fervently believe in the pretenses that surround corporate legal personhood. To them, corporate criminal liability is imposed on the corporation because *it* did the wrongful act. This awkward make-believe is unnecessary if we accept the general principle that any undertaking, whether run by an individual or any other not-for-profit organization, may be responsible for its failure to adequately prevent other actors from inflicting harms arising out of its operations.

Indeed, this line of thinking is reflected in the latest amendments to Canada's *Criminal Code* that came into effect in 2003 as a remedy for the shortfalls revealed by the Westray disaster (a tragedy that will be discussed in more detail in the next chapter). Those amendments provide that organizations (including corporations) will be criminally responsible as before, that is, when guiding minds and wills, now called senior officers,[8] did a wrongful act with the appropriate criminal intent. In addition, organizations will also be criminally responsible if senior officers failed to take reasonable steps to prevent representatives (that is, other employees) from breaching a duty of care they have to people they supervise or to others likely to be affected by the operations.

The message is clear. An organization is to be held responsible because those responsible for its system of operations, knowing of the risks created on behalf of the organization, did not, on its behalf, take appropriate care to eliminate them. The organization is to be criminally responsible because it creates the risks, and it can and should reduce them. Once again, the law is saying that an overarching principle of liberal law is to be applied. Those who create risks and are in a position of control have a duty to avert the materialization of those risks; it is right and proper to hold them responsible if they fail to meet the standard of this duty. They need not do anything positive to invite the wrath of law. An omission to ensure that appropriate care is taken may be enough to attribute criminal responsibility.

Of course, an organization will not be responsible for its senior officers' wrongdoings or omissions if they are aimed at harming the organization. Analogously, an employer or principal should not be held civilly responsible for the acts of others if those others were not acting within the umbrella of the employer or principal's activities. This is liberal law 101. This is why, when it comes to a demand that an employer be held liable for an employee's wrong, the employer may claim that the employee was not acting within the course of their duties or had been engaged in a frolic of their own.

The potential to engage in this kind of fine line-drawing is welcomed by lawyers, and it leads to some fiercely contested litigation, giving impetus to the misleading idea that vicarious liability is some special branch of law. But while this kind of finding-angels-on-the-head-of-a-pin exercise makes for interesting and remunerative legal disputations, it does not negate the basic principle that liability could be imposed on a risk-creator when another acts within that risk's ambit and inflicts injury. This holds true even if the harm-doing actor was self-interestedly abusing an opportunity furnished by the organization to which they belonged. The need to find a justification, a special reason, to exempt an employer from such liability only serves to endorse the basic principle. And precisely because it is a basic principle, the risk-creator's responsibility is the basis for liability in a whole series of different circumstances.

SNAPSHOTS: CONTROL AND LIABILITY

Bazley v. *Curry*: The Opportunity to Control the Risk

The general principle has been applied in a number of recent cases in which organizations have been entrusted with the welfare of vulnerable persons, such as children left in their care. That was the context of the *Bazley* v. *Curry* decision cited above. There the issue was whether the provincially funded, not-for-profit Children's Foundation should be held liable for the acts of Curry, a long-term employee who turned out to be a pedophile and who was convicted for the abuse of children in the foundation's care. Bazley was one of Curry's victims. Curry was viewed as a person of authority by the children, who were left alone with him for long periods; some of the children were bathed by him.

The Supreme Court of Canada found the Children's Foundation responsible, not simply because the wrong took place on the foundation's property or because there was bound to be some incidental connection between its employees and the children. More was needed. That more was that a risk had been created by setting up the operation, and that there was an opportunity to control that risk through the way in which the Children's Foundation organized its operations. By not exercising its control over the built-in risks—or, to use the language of the court, those risks tangibly connected to the organized undertaking—the organizing Children's Foundation had laid itself open to successful legal action by Curry's victims.

The lay reader will be struck by the rather vague nature of this formulation. What is meant by a significant connection between the creation or enhancement of a risk that then materializes and causes injury is not defined with any precision. Only when an employer is sought to be held vicariously responsible for the conduct of an employee acting within their scope of employment is this not true. There strict liability as connectedness is assumed because the law implicitly acknowledges that employees are much like inorganic equipment for which the employer is responsible. Other than that, there is little clarity about what will be held to be sufficient connectedness to establish liability.

Shamefully, this lack of precision is a staple of law. Lawyers like to give themselves room for manoeuvre. They talk about the need for flexibility that can be used to adapt the law as needed to analogous circumstances. This leads to some uncertainty about how existing law will be applied in any one case. But rarely does this deliberately built-in elasticity question rights and duties that underpin the basic principles of liberal law.

Kofi Patrong: Sufficient Connection

The nature of the debate this flexibility spawns is illustrated by litigation launched in 2016 by Kofi Patrong, a young man who was wounded by a shooter who mistook him for a member of a rival gang. Patrong contends that the Toronto police were aware of the gang war and that the shooter was a major threat to public safety. They suspected him of a previous shooting, wire-tapped his communications, and trailed him as he went about his life. Patrong argued that the police had had ample grounds on which to arrest the shooter, and that their failure to do so led to Patrong's being shot. Patrong argued that the Police Services Board, the chief of police, and the two detectives tasked with dealing with the feuding gangs should compensate him for his injuries.

The defendants successfully argued at trial that there was no evidence that made Patrong a likely victim entitled to expect care from them. Patrong issued another claim specifying how the gangs' public-endangering activities took place in the locale in which he lived. This time, a trial judge and a reviewing court found sufficient connection between those with potential control over the acts of others (even if they were free, wrongdoing agents) and the victim to base a legal claim for liability.[9]

What is not vague, then, is the acknowledgement by the judiciary that those who originate risky situations to satisfy their own goals should be held to account for regrettable outcomes if they do not exercise their knowledge of, and power over, the organization in a reasonable manner. It is not sufficient for them to say that they plainly did not desire such outcomes. In *Bazley*, for instance, it is obvious that the Children's Foundation did not desire or expect its employees to be abusive. If it had been necessary to make its expectations explicit, it is obvious that it would have forbidden any of its employees from acting as the pedophile Curry did. But its perfectly reasonable assumption that there was no need to spell this out in the employment contract could not get it off the hook.

In the judges' opinion, the foundation did not do enough to minimize the risk that was built into the undertaking. It is the omission to try to minimize the risk that makes outfits like the Children's Foundation and the Toronto police potentially liable. The pressure to hold them responsible reflects a widely shared and deeply embedded social value, the same value that impelled the garment retailers to set up systems to control the risks that they took by hiring cheap contractors in impoverished countries. The same approach is detectable in a wide variety of circumstances.

A Night on the Town: All Reasonable Precautions

The courts have repeatedly found that the owners of bars and commercial hosting businesses have a duty to prevent patrons from drinking too much lest as a result of their inebriation they harm someone. The Supreme Court of Canada has declared that operators of these businesses have a duty to take affirmative action to prevent reasonably foreseeable risk to third parties.[10] They have to establish means to diminish or eliminate the risks built into their enterprises or face the consequences of their omissions.

Thus, in an Ontario case in 2001, an underage young man was observed to slur his speech, spill drinks, and grope another patron after he entered a tavern. Yet he was served several drinks. When he drove home, he struck a pedestrian. The driver was required to compensate the injured person. But the tavern operator was held to be partially responsible as well, because it was established that the tavern's organizational practices made it hard for it to identify underage patrons, and that, while a bouncer had thrown out the drunken young man for violating the dress code and for being drunk and angry, nothing had been done to prevent this reckless young man from driving his car.[11]

As usual, there are many cases in which the rule is difficult to apply. There must be a failure of the commercial host to set up an appropriate set of protocols that led to the injuries suffered by a third person. After all, the direct cause of the hurt is the conduct of a reckless, negligent other person. Liberal law clearly expects that other person, as a sovereign actor, to be held accountable. But the commercial host setting up an undertaking that may give an opportunity for the infliction of harm by another leads to the imposition of a legal duty to take appropriate care.

This legal reasoning is derived from the widely shared social value of holding accountable those who organize their affairs for self-serving purposes and create risks for others. This is why a person holding a dinner party where liquor will be consumed will not normally be held liable if one of the guests imbibes too much and causes harm to another. Such a host has not created an organization where risks are built in to attain some purposes of their own. In most of these situations, the blame will be borne by the wayward guest.

Society's values and expectations, so clearly reflected in these judicial rulings, have been internalized by legislatures. Operators of alcohol-serving businesses need to be licensed. The statutory criteria to gain and maintain such a licence include provisions that no licensee shall serve liquor to any person who appears to be intoxicated. The licensee will be civilly liable should a patron commit suicide or meet death by accident if there were signs that the patron was likely to lose control over their behaviour. In addition, licensees will be held civilly accountable if injury is incurred by another as a result of such intoxication having been permitted to occur.

Lawyers fiercely debate whether the common law and legislative tests are slightly different in adjudicating whether a licensee is to pay compensation to a third person. But there is no doubt whatsoever that both the common law rules and the statutory rules are based on the same principle: entrepreneurs organizing undertakings for their personal benefit must use their knowledge and control over the risks they inevitably create to prevent harm. They are to take all reasonable precautions, including overseeing the wilful conduct of other actors, if they wish to be legally immunized from the fallout of the conduct of those others.

Further Applications: Safety and Clean-up

This is the approach taken in much of our regulatory laws. Statutes require entrepreneurs and their executives to adhere to standards for consumer services, health and safety at work, or maintenance of a clean environment. They typically also impose responsibility for controlling the acts of others, in a manner analogous to the duties of tavern keepers, institutional guardians of the vulnerable, and the like. One difference is that, in the statutory situations, the burden of showing that due diligence was exercised frequently falls on the enterprise and its managers. This can be an onerous burden.

When, in March 2013, a fence around a construction site fell on three passersby and killed them in Melbourne, Australia, the outfit that ran the construction site had hired another firm to erect the safety fence that separated the sidewalk from the site. It was not allowed to say that, by relying on a reputable contractor, it had done everything it could to abide by the prevailing safety standards. Its legal obligation was its own, and it could not avoid liability by merely delegating a task to others. While another tribunal might have come to a different conclusion on somewhat similar facts, the principle that the creation of risks for others carries responsibility towards those others was once again unquestioned.

The ethos reflected in these legal developments is to be found in every nook and cranny of law. In the United States, for instance, a large number of environmental statutes impose responsibility for clean-ups on those people who might have the power to influence the polluters. The most prominent of these statutes is the *Comprehensive Environmental Response, Compensation, and Liability Act* (CERCLA).[12] It imposes liability on those who own and operate a waste-producing facility, including in the definition of such a facility a parent corporation whose subsidiary carries on such a business. In one case, the court determined that a secured creditor of a polluting corporation was liable for the costs associated with a spill, because it had the potential to affect the waste-producing facility's operations.[13] Again, involvement in the creation and control of a risk-laden organization is fingered as a sufficient link between the injured world and the harming business. The pattern is clear: it does not matter whether the ultimate defendant was a direct actor when the harm was inflicted.

RESPONSIBILITY FOR OVERSEAS WRONGDOING

Thus it is that, in recent times, an eighteenth-century U.S. statute has been used to give more life to the general principle that those who create and organize risk-taking activities should be held accountable when others have been given the opportunity (and/or the incentive) by them to inflict injuries and harms. The *Alien Tort Claims Act*[14] allows aliens to bring actions in U.S. courts against controlling persons or corporations in respect of conduct by persons and corporations that inflicted harm in foreign locales and that violated the accepted law of nations (that is, the basic principles of law that all modern states acknowledge to be inviolable). This has amazing potential to curb major wrongdoing by U.S.-based multinationals operating in foreign lands.

Unocal was sued by Burmese people and their allies in 2002 because its subsidiary in Burma allegedly had been implicated when the Burmese government and army used forced labour, displaced people, and engaged in murder and rape. These horrendous acts, it was alleged, helped the Unocal subsidiary build and secure a pipeline. The litigation wound its way through a number of U.S. courts as Unocal's clever lawyers used various procedural, jurisdictional, and substantive points to derail the complainants' case.[15]

While no final decision was rendered, most of the judges made it clear that it was legally plausible to hold the U.S. parent responsible for the wrongdoings in faraway Burma. The bases on which the different judges thought such liability should be founded, however, varied a good deal.

Some judges contended that it had to be shown that the corporation had directly engaged in wrongful conduct by, say, giving practical assistance to the Burmese government and army. Others insisted personal involvement be proved by establishing that the corporation both knew that violations of the law of nations were occurring and had purposely assisted the violators. There were also opinions indicating that much less would suffice. For instance, that it would be enough if it was shown that the corporation had been involved in something of a joint venture with the Burmese authorities or had used the Burmese authorities as agents to attain its purposes. Or simply, that it had acted with reckless disregard as to whether its project might lead to human rights violations.

Legally, then, the many judgments delivered in the *Unocal* litigation that was eventually settled left it unclear whether a U.S. corporation would be held responsible only if it came to be viewed as a direct actor in foreign wrongdoing or whether a less direct role would suffice. But the potential to hold a U.S. corporation responsible for acts elsewhere, committed by legally distinct persons, was undoubted. Indeed, this view was supported by the U.S. Supreme Court in a 2004 case called *Sosa* v. *Alvarez-Machain*.[16] This enunciation of principle came down while the *Unocal* case was still winding its way through the labyrinth of lower courts. It caused Unocal to settle the case. The company was fearful of losing, and its allies were concerned that an adverse judicial pronouncement in the *Unocal* case might make them all more vulnerable. Alarm bells had been set ringing in major corporate circles. With good reason.

Notre Dame presidential fellow Doug Cassel reports that, since the mid-1990s, about 150 lawsuits have been launched under the *Alien Tort Claims Act*, involving corporations having connections to conduct engaged in by other legally separate but closely related actors in sixty countries.[17] There was an action against Caterpillar for selling bulldozers to Israel, allegedly used in violation of the established law of nations by Israelis against Palestinians. A suit was brought against Chiquita for paying paramilitary forces, allegedly to safeguard its banana plantations in Colombia from legitimate labour unrest.[18] Banque Nationale Paris Paribas was alleged to have provided funds to Saddam Hussein in breach of the United Nations' "oil for food" humanitarian program. Many corporations were sued for doing business with the anti-humanitarian apartheid regime in South Africa.

It is a long list and, while successes have been rare, there has been a growing tendency in U.S. courts to entertain such actions. This trend heightened the public perception that, all too often, the corporate sectors have behaved unethically and should be held accountable. It is becoming costly and embarrassing. Unsurprisingly, corporations and their representatives have set out to reverse this dangerous legal trend.

In 2013, in *Kiobel*,[19] a decision of the currently pro-corporate U.S. Supreme Court, it was decided that the *Alien Tort Claims Act* should not automatically be given extra-territorial effect. To come to the view that, in the future, the legislation was to be applied more sparingly, the court read the wording of the statute as narrowly as possible, ignoring the many judicial pronouncements that had read the same language more broadly. This holding could well slow the flow of cases brought under the statute.[20]

But for the purposes of the argument being made here, it is important to note that, corporate-friendly though the U.S. Supreme Court showed itself to be, it relied on jurisdictional arguments, arguing that the U.S. courts were not a proper place to fight these cases. It took refuge in procedural rather than substantive reasoning. It did not assert that the theory that parent corporations could be made liable for the conduct of formally separate actors had made the *Alien Tort Claims Act* inoperative in the case before it. As it turns out, that theory has allowed similar actions to go forward, despite the *Kiobel* holding. What seems to spur the judiciary on is the sheer ugliness of the corporate actors in these later cases.

In 2007, Chiquita had settled a criminal complaint against it by the U.S. government. It admitted that it had made payments to a paramilitary organization in Colombia, where Chiquita conducted its business. The paramilitary outfit, known as AUC, had been classified as a terrorist group by the United States. Chiquita agreed to pay a $25-million fine. Subsequently, it was also revealed that Chiquita had also made payments to FARC, a militant resistance force in Colombia. Some four thousand Colombians have since initiated an array of actions under the *Alien Tort Claims Act* in U.S. courts. Eventually they were consolidated into one action. These complainants variously allege that they or their dead loved ones were targeted by the AUC and FARC, and had been victims of extra-judicial killings, torture, forced disappearances, crimes against humanity, and war crimes. The allegations go on to say that Chiquita had made payments to these groups to help it pursue profits, and that Chiquita and/or its executives should be held responsible in U.S. courts.

The litigation that began after Chiquita publicly admitted payments in 2007 is still unresolved. The corporation has used a host of defences. Chiquita has denied knowledge of the wrongdoings. It has claimed that its payments to these groups were extorted from it—that is, it did not pay the groups to have them do favours for Chiquita, but rather paid protection money to allow Chiquita to escape harm. And of course, it relied heavily on *Kiobel* to contend that the U.S. courts were not the appropriate forums in which to bring actions.

This led to many cases in many courts. But in June 2016, a U.S. judge allowed the complainants to bring some of their actions in U.S. courts. While this decision does not signify that they will win, it does show that, when push comes to shove, it is extremely difficult to deny the strength of the proposition that undertakings that create risks for their own benefit must face the music for harms that arise out of this risk-creation, even if the immediate inflictors of the harms, like the AUC and FARC, are not in any formal way a legal part of the undertaking.

A similar struggle arising out of the U.S. *Alien Tort Claims Act* is being fought in Canadian courts. It is a claim by some Ecuadorians against Chevron.[21] In brief: Texaco, with the help of a friendly Ecuadoran government, embarked on oil exploration. It left behind 916 unlined open toxic pits. The locals, thirty thousand of them, brought actions against Texaco under the *Alien Tort Claims Act* in New York. Texaco successfully argued that this was not an appropriate forum. So, back to Ecuador, where Texaco hoped a corporate-friendly government and judiciary would favour it. But after long delays, the plaintiffs won an award of nearly nineteen billion dollars.

Chevron, having taken over Texaco, had no assets in Ecuador, and now argued in a New York court that the Ecuadoran decision be set aside. Among the reasons Chevron offered was that the Ecuadoran court had allegedly been corrupted by the claimants' lawyer. Kaplan, J., the presiding judge in New York, found this to be a credible argument and set aside the complaint. The judge also held that no action could be brought against Chevron to enforce the Ecuadoran judgment anywhere in the world.

A U.S. Court of Appeal said Kaplan had gone too far. This spurred the claimants to bring actions in Argentina and Canada, where there are Chevron subsidiaries with plenty of assets. Chevron's counter-claim is that its seventy-three revenue-producing subsidiaries throughout the world cannot be sued to get at its coffers, just because it was those subsidiaries' parent. It argues that there is no legal basis for a Canadian court to take jurisdiction over the dispute.

After an Ontario Court of Appeal declared that the Ecuadoran villagers were entitled to seek enforcement in Canada of the judgment they had obtained in Ecuador, Chevron asked the Supreme Court of Canada to review the matter. Intriguingly, the Canadian Bar Association determined that it would support Chevron's jurisdictional argument, but angry members of the bar forestalled this unusual intervention.[22] In the event, on September 4, 2015, some twenty years on, the Supreme Court of Canada determined that a Canadian court could take jurisdiction over the dispute, and the matter is now to go to trial.

Of course, any outcome is likely to be appealed. Chevron had sworn to fight the original judgment in Ecuador against it "until Hell freezes over, and then we'll fight it out on the ice." Even more troubling, the Supreme Court acknowledged that, should the plaintiffs win, it would not automatically follow that Chevron's Canadian shares or assets would be available to satisfy the debt owed by the parent company to the Ecuadorian victims. That prickly issue might have to be decided in court later. But these manoeuvres nonetheless show that the basic principle argued for in this chapter is not to be seriously challenged. The holding by the Supreme Court, with all its practical drawbacks, endorses the widely accepted notion that it makes good social and legal sense for a creator and controller of risk to be held responsible if those risks cause injury as a result of a related violation of a law subscribed to by the nations of the world, even if that violation was the direct result of legally independent actors.

CRIMINAL APPLICATIONS

The cases under the *Alien Tort Claims Act* seek a civil remedy for damages. Of course, a victory also serves to label the defendant as a wrongdoer, the outcome sought by a criminal prosecution. This conceptual congruence makes it unsurprising that adherence to the principle is to be found in analogous criminal settings. It might be expected that in a criminal law setting, the imposition of liability for the acts of sovereign others would be approached with more caution. The use of the principle here might lead to lasting stigma and serious punishment. Nonetheless, the principle is so basic that it has criminal applications.

In the Zyklon B case fought through the Nuremberg trials in 1946, two men were prosecuted for being accessories to Second World War crimes.[23] The accused had been leading members of a firm that had sold poisonous gas to the SS. The gas was used to exterminate people. The prosecutors did not try to prove that the accused acted with the intention of assisting the SS in its horrible project. Rather, they argued that the accused sold the gas to make a profit and, as they knew what use it was likely to be put to, the elements of the crime had been proved. The accused were convicted. They had knowingly enabled conduct that violated shared social norms.

In an even more explicit application of the principle, Lothar Fendler, the second-highest-ranking officer in a Nazi organization, was proved to have admitted that he knew that people were found guilty of various offences as a result of processes he knew to be "summary," that is, that he knew to be contrary to existing laws.[24] There were serious consequences: people found to be guilty by this flawed process were executed. Fendler was convicted of participating in war crimes. He had been in a position to act, and his omission to do so, given his knowledge, made him criminally culpable.

This decision is important to the argument that controlling shareholders should be held responsible for not taking action to prevent abuses by the corporation in which they hold shares. While it is proper to acknowledge that the Fendler decision is rather unusual, and possibly handed down because of the sheer horror the Nazi outrages had generated, it does dovetail with a larger principle. Not taking appropriate care for others when it is within one's power to do so is a moral and legal justification for the imposition of liability.

A vivid illustration is furnished by the recent acquittal of an Ontario prisoner charged with four counts of assault with a shank, as a result of a fight with rival gang assailants. The judge found that, if anyone should be held responsible, it should be the institution that ran the maximum security facility that allowed the people it controlled to have weapons and to behave violently towards each other. "The system put him [the accused defendant] in this situation, and the system cannot blame him for resorting to his own means of defence," wrote Morgan, J., of the Ontario Superior Court. Potential control over others may lead to the imposition of a legal duty to exercise actual control.[25]

In a similar way, the U.S. Supreme Court has observed that wilful blindness should lead to culpability if defendants had deliberately shielded themselves from taking note of facts that a reasonable person would have ferreted out. Shielding oneself behind a corporate veil might well, in the right circumstances, amount to this kind of wilfulness. Again, it will depend on the way in which we look at facts—but the principle itself is unquestioned.

There is, of course, much room to differ on whether the right level of connection or wilful blindness exists in any one case. The two international criminal law decisions discussed—Zyklon B and Lothar Fendler—do not appear to require more than knowledge of a potential violation. Others, however, require practical assistance, encouragement, or moral support by the person accused of aiding and abetting. Some other adjudicators have looked for evidence that the person so accused had the same purpose as the actor who committed the crime. This requirement is sometimes diluted: the main purpose of the person accused of aiding and abetting the act need not necessarily be to further the criminality.

As is to be expected, then, there are attempts to fetter the open-ended application of the general principle. The constraints imposed depend on the world view of the decision-makers. That is, they depend on policy, on politics, not on rules of law. And the decision-makers do not question the essential elements of the general principle. They do not reject the notion that persons who organize themselves in a way that allows the costs of harms spawned by such organized undertakings to be imposed on third parties may be held accountable to those third parties and society at large. What they differ on is how substantial the connection between the organization and the harm needs to be. In the end, this question is determined on a political basis or, when it is done by a court, by preferring one policy over others. The principle is to be given life unless there are good reasons why it should not be. This was acknowledged in an Ontario court's decision.[26]

Hudbay Minerals Inc. is a large Canadian mining company. Through wholly owned and controlled subsidiaries in Guatemala, it ran a mining operation, called Fenix, in that country. To operate the mine, it had been necessary to get the co-operation of the government to relocate Mayan residents who had lived in this area for centuries. There had been evictions, not-so-peaceable ones. The Mayans had returned, arguing that their legal rights had been wrongfully taken away. This disrupted the mining project, and several incidents allegedly occurred. They led to legal actions currently being fought against Hudbay Minerals and its subsidiaries in Ontario.

The complaints include allegations of a gang rape of eleven women by mining company security personnel and military, the beating and killing by Fenix's chief of security of an Indigenous leader who opposed the project, and the shooting and subsequent paralyzing of another man by the mining operations' security people. Hudbay took the position that there could be no legal case to answer. To hold it responsible for the conduct of its subsidiaries and their employees would require a court to pierce the sacred veil of the subsidiaries. After all, those blobs in Guatemala were sovereign, independent legal persons. In short, Hudbay reasoned that, once a corporation is inserted, the normal rules that make employers liable for the behaviour of their employees should not apply. They relied on the formalism and rigidity of corporate law.

The Ontario court agreed that, as a rule, the special rules devised for the blob-o-sphere should remain intact. Lifting the veil was to be reserved for very special circumstances. It should only be done where a controlling corporation completely dominates a subsidiary to the extent that it has no independent life, or where the subsidiary is used by its parent to commit a fraud that unjustly deprives claimants of their rights. Here there was neither evidence that the subsidiaries were totally dominated, nor that they were being used as a shield for improper conduct. It is worth noting how much more stringent these tests for corporate liability are than those applied in the non-corporate cases and circumstances discussed earlier. The ordinary rules, once again, are recast when we enter the blob-o-sphere. But, let us leave that and return to the decision in Hudbay.

The court went on to observe that, while it would be wrong to make Hudbay responsible by piercing the veils wrapped around its subsidiaries, it could be made legally responsible for its own wrongs. As we have seen, corporations, their directors, their executives, and/or their employees often are held to account as legal persons in their own right. The only issue is whether they have violated the appropriate standards of law. In the kind of complaints brought against Hudbay, the pertinent legal questions were whether the injuries had been reasonably foreseeable and, if so, whether they were proximate enough to the conduct of the defendant (Hudbay Minerals) to hold it responsible.

The court found that, at this preliminary stage of the proceedings, Hudbay, as shown by its own documentation and actions, had been sufficiently aware of the dangers, pitfalls, and disputes at the Fenix project that the harms might have been both foreseeable and proximate. This forced a new tack onto Hudbay's defence team.

It argued, correctly, that it was not sufficient to say that the harm might have been foreseeable and was not too remote. More was needed to hold that a defendant was in breach of a legal duty of care in circumstances where no such duty had previously been imposed in decisions involving comparable actors. In the absence of such a precedent, a court would have to find that there was now a good policy reason to impose a duty of care where none had existed hitherto. To show that there were no such good new policy reasons, Hudbay told the court that various attempts had been made to introduce statutory laws to require Canadian extraction corporations to abide by international norms and human rights standards, as well as efforts to pass legislation that would make Canadian corporations liable to be sued in Canada by foreign plaintiffs. The failure to pass this kind of legislation, said Hudbay, showed that Canadian policy-makers wanted to protect Canadian extracting corporations and to preserve their competitive positions. This was a good policy reason to refuse the establishment of a novel duty of care; the trial judge should, therefore, not let the case proceed to trial.

The plaintiffs, aided by Amnesty International, argued the opposite point of view. A court might well hold that it should support governments in enacting rules of the kind thus far rejected. In fact, it was, in part, the role of tort law (the civil branch of law involved here) to advance public policies of this kind, and the role of judges to develop the law in line with changing circumstances.

In the upshot, the presiding judge said that, while she could not tell which of the two competing versions of policy the court charged with making a decision in the final litigation would choose, it might decide that there was no good policy basis to reject the finding of a duty of care. That question should be tested in court. The defendant's claim that the matter should not proceed was, therefore, rejected. The plaintiffs could proceed to trial.

Once again, in liberal law, only the nature of the necessary connection between the creator of a risk and the materialization of the risk is in play. The notion of a prima facie responsibility for the creation of risk is not. No matter how the issue is finally resolved in Hudbay, one thing is crystal clear. The controversy was not about whether the principle that a person who seeks benefits and who controls the pursuit of such benefits could be held responsible even if it did not directly inflict the harm. The starting point, as it has been in all of the legal situations considered in this chapter, was that the controller should be held accountable unless there is another reason, a policy or political reason, why it should not be.

THE "IMPERMEABLE" SHIELD

The principle of accountability is crucial to the legitimacy of both a liberal polity and a market economy. It is, therefore, vital to the legitimacy of a corporate capitalism that sells itself as acceptable because it lives within the confines of liberal and market precepts. Corporate law's vigorous attempt to undermine the principle by granting immunity to all shareholders—just because some do not play any part in, or influence, operational decisions—flies in the face of corporate capitalism's own claims. The tensions created are clear.

We have seen that law will hold controllers, including controlling shareholders, responsible for corporate acts, although it does not expressly acknowledge that it does this. In the Borstal Boys, the pedophile at the Children's Foundation, and the tavern keepers decisions, this principle was used to hold controlling individuals or institutions responsible. In the *Alien Tort Claims Act* cases or in the Hudbay one, the controlling person held to account was a corporation. These blobs are held responsible because their shareholding gives them control over the acts of other corporations and their functionaries. It is their capacity to exercise influence over these others that makes them appropriate targets for the application of the general fundamental principle of accountability. The interposition of separate other persons, other corporations, is not seen as a basis to prevent holding a shareholder (that is also a corporation) legally responsible.

There is, then, a legally permissible route to get past the supposedly impermeable shield of legal immunity. The normal assumption is that the interposition of a corporation gives even obvious risk-creating and risk-controlling shareholders a free pass. We have just seen that this need not be so. And more importantly, the law does not insist that it always be so. There are many circumstances where it is offensive for the law to permit a free pass.

The next chapters set out to provide the evidence and to buttress the argument that controlling shareholders should be held responsible for anti-social behaviour engaged in by corporations on their behalf. That is, a moral and factual basis is laid to make the argument that there are good policy reasons why the law should allow one of its basic principles—taking responsibility for one's undertakings—to govern the corporate world that benefits from a formalistic shielding of its movers and shakers.

Let us remove that veil!

The Ideal
Abandoned

ALTHOUGH SOCIETY GREATLY VALUES THE IDEAL OF HOLDING INDI-
viduals to account for the results of their actions, in the case of corporate
shareholders, this ideal suddenly dissolves. When it comes to holding anyone responsible for corporate activities that harm workers, consumers, the
environment, or any other non-corporate interests, shareholders disappear
from legal sight.

SNAPSHOTS: EVADING BLAME
Westray: The Standard Does Not Apply

The Westray mine explosion in Nova Scotia in 1992 caused the death of
twenty-six miners. The tragedy led to a public outcry and, eventually, to
amendments to the *Criminal Code of Canada*. Amendments were necessary
because the failure to hold anyone to account for the killings was attributed
to the impoverished state of the law, rather than to the law's unwillingness
to hold corporate actors accountable. The need for changes arose because,
in the Westray case, there had been no successful legal actions—yet there
were plenty of blameworthy people around. Supervisors at the mine ignored
workers' frequent complaints about health and safety. Government inspect-
ors failed to follow through on any of the fifty-two health and safety violations

they recorded prior to the explosion. There was the seemingly heedless corporation itself—and then there was C.H. Frame.

Frame had been a partner in a firm that was sold to a corporation whose only name was a number. In due course, it became a publicly traded corporation with the name of Curragh Resources. Curragh came to own 90 per cent of the shares of another numbered corporation, 630903 Ontario Inc. This camouflaged corporation became the licensee of the mine operation popularly known as the Westray Coal Mine Project. Prior to the sale of its shares to Curragh, 100 per cent of the shares in the licensee had been owned by a corporation named Frame Mining Company. In turn, 74 per cent of the shares in Frame Mining had been owned by a corporation called Westray Mining Corporation, and 70 per cent of the shares of Westray had been owned—surprise!—by C.H. Frame. Westray Mining Corporation owned 519,737 multiple voting shares in Curragh; Frame Mining held 678, 887 multiple voting shares in Curragh; and the licensee corporation, the rather ghostly 630903 Ontario Inc., owned 14,523,113 multiple voting shares in Curragh. That is, C.H. Frame had a huge amount of voting power in the affairs of all of these companies, including Curragh Resources. Curragh, unsurprisingly, had seen fit to name C.H. Frame as its chief executive officer. Intriguingly, the management of Curragh had given a separate corporation a richly remunerated consulting contract to advise its CEO, C.H. Frame, on the development of the Westray Coal Mine Project. That consulting firm's name was C.H. Frame Consulting Services.

Before the licence to mine was granted by the government, C.H. Frame hobnobbed with major politicians in the Nova Scotia and federal governments, persuading them to subsidize his mining project with taxpayers' money. As a result of these wheelings and dealings, Frame became a bit of a business media darling. He was profiled in photo-heavy articles describing him as something of a pioneer. He was a prominent, celebrated man. Until the killings.

The commission of inquiry that was set up to uncover what had happened found the obvious: the corporation and its management team, in pursuit of profits, had been reckless of human life. The government, in its desire to facilitate and promote private accumulation, had been lax in its enforcement of the law. The commission recommended that, in the future, criminal prosecutions should be laid in these kinds of cases and that, to this end, novel legal tools would have to be devised. The existing ones were not effective. In the Westray case, charges under the mine safety legislation were brought against the corporation, some government staff were let go, and criminal charges of manslaughter were brought against hands-on managers. But the corporation declared bankruptcy, the mine safety charges disappeared, and the criminal charges against the mine's managers were dropped because of procedural mistakes by the prosecution.

Lesson: It was acknowledged that the corporation, as a legal person, and its directors, executives, managers, and employees, as natural persons, could be held accountable for the materialization of the risks they had built into the project and had personally controlled and operationalized. As we have seen, this is liberal law 101. But the saga also shows, somewhat startlingly, that the standard of liberal law was thought not to apply to C.H. Frame, the major shareholder, functional owner, and master of the corporation and its managers' fate.

Imagine what the result might have been if Mr. Frame had not had a whole bunch of corporations hiding him. Would anyone have thought that the law should not attribute responsibility to him, that he should not be subjected to sanctions for running a business in a manner scathingly decried as heedless, as wilfully reckless of the danger to human lives? Would he have been able to mount any argument that, as a functional controller of an enterprise, he should not be held legally responsible because he had left some of the operations to others?

As far as can be told, the authorities did not feel that the controlling shareholder, C.H. Frame, should be in the legal frame. Yet it is manifest that, before the killings at the Westray mine, it had never occurred to anyone, least of all to the same authorities, that anything happened there without his say-so. The disjuncture is jarring. A major shareholder, deeply implicated in reckless corporate conduct that had inflicted horrendous and highly foreseeable harms, was not considered a target for legal retribution.

In his *History of the World, Part I*, Mel Brooks plays a self-indulgent French king who knows that his unforgivable behaviour will not be punished, crowing "It is good to be king." In the blob-o-sphere, it is good to be a controlling shareholder.

Bre-X: Not All Victims Are Equal

A British company owned a piece of land with mining potential in Busang, Indonesia. It asked John Felderhof, a geologist, to help it sell this property. At that time, several established mining companies had explored the area and had not found it worth exploiting. Felderhof provided David Walsh, a promoter of mining ventures in Canada, with a report from a geologist called Michael de Guzman. That report, contrary to earlier reports by mining firms, said that the site contained a minimum of a million ounces of gold. Walsh set up a corporation, Bre-X, which bought the property. Exploratory drilling began and the findings were very promising, largely because—as the world was to find out—the area had been salted with gold dust.

This happened again and again, the deposit being reported as containing 30 million ounces of gold in 1995, 60 million in 1996, and 70 million by 1997. Analysts and the media jumped aboard the golden galleon called Bre-X amid these reports of richer and richer findings. There was a frenzied buying of the corporation's shares. This occurred during a boom time for shares in nickel, copper, and cobalt ventures in Labrador, adding to the excitement. Bre-X shares jumped from being worth pennies (the corporation had begun life as a speculative venture, literally as a penny stock), to having a market value of $280 each. This meant that the corporation was assigned a capital value of $4.4 billion by the all-knowing market. In fact, it was worth next to nothing. It announced its bankruptcy in 2002, some five years after the scam came to light.

The geologist de Guzman was said to have fallen out of a helicopter when all this was about to be exposed. Walsh and his family had moved to the Bahamas by 1998; he died that same year. Felderhof was living in the Cayman Islands where, like Walsh, he persistently claimed that he had not been a party to the salting or the false reports put out by the corporation.

Lesson: There are a large number of willing, non-productive gamblers out there, eager to place bets on the hoped-for success of the work done by others. Their greed and indolence means that they are easily misled, despite legislators' efforts to provide them with adequate and timely information. This built-in flaw becomes a major problem for corporate capitalism when some promoters are not just overly optimistic or incompetent, but deliberately mislead the investing public. This legitimacy problem is exacerbated because frequently—as in this case—some of the misled investors are not unlovable, indolent gamblers. In the Bre-X fiasco, some of the biggest losers were people who got involved in the gamble without knowing that they would be taking this kind of risk.

Many investors in the share markets are there because they need a way to provide for themselves when they can no longer work for wages. They entrust some of their savings to supposedly savvy investment fund managers who study the markets and have access to the highly technical information that is publicly provided. Armed in these ways, they are to invest these savings prudently. But the managers of those funds (unlike the depositors) belong to the class of investors and traders who run the corporations in which they are to invest, a class to which profit-seeking by taking risks with other people's money is second nature. They have an incentive to seek rich returns on their depositors' investments. It is likely to bring them more business. Despite their brief to be prudent, they tend to follow market trends because they share the zeal for profits that imbues the actions of self-standing gamblers. Moreover, they always worry that, should they not take notionally imprudent action, their less cautious competitors will win a greater share of the institutional investment markets. In the end, these savvy investment house managers are likely to be just as easily gulled and bedazzled as out-and-out self-standing gamblers are.

Thus it came about that public sector funds lost a great deal of vulnerable savers' money by jumping on the bandwagon of the financial markets' enthusiasm for Bre-X's prospects. The Ontario Municipal Employees Retirement Board claimed to have lost $45 million, the Quebec Public Sector Pension fund $70 million, and the Ontario Teachers' Pension Plan $100 million.

These losses of money invested with them by non-gamblers, by information-starved and trusting workers, added to the fury engendered by the Bre-X fiasco.

Many others also saw their money disappear. Some estimate that investors left with the Bre-X stock after its collapse may have lost as much as six billion dollars. Many class action suits were launched to try and recoup some of the losses. Little has been achieved thus far. The corporation had no valuable assets out of which to meet the many claims made. Of course, some shareholders made money out of this finagling, as they sold their shares at a premium to buyers feverishly clamouring for this glamour stock.

It might be pushing it too far to argue that those who sold Bre-X shares at a profit should be asked to disgorge their profits to some of the less fortunate punters. After all, it is likely that these sellers into a good market did not know that their shares had become so desirable because of the scams perpetrated by Bre-X. There was no evidence that they were or could have been possessed of knowledge through being in control of the enterprise and the risks it had created. But that was not true of all the shareholders.

David Walsh, as CEO, and John Felderhof, in charge of the Indonesian operations, had been at the helm of Bre-X from its inception. They did much to boost its reputation as a new El Dorado. While Bre-X was riding high, so were they. Our capitalist society celebrates those who rise from rags to riches, showering them with accolades and respect. Walsh and Felderhof were given Man of the Year awards by the mining industry, and Felderhof got the prestigious Prospector of the Year award in 1997. They were widely and rightly seen as the driving forces behind Bre-X. The understanding that they were major operators and controllers of the corporation was fortified by the knowledge that they also were major shareholders.

The year before their public recognition, both Felderhof and Walsh (and his spouse) had sold a lot of their Bre-X shares, netting an estimated thirty million dollars each. Why should they not have been asked to make good some of the losses others suffered? Even though they now argued that they were ignorant of the flagrant fraud, of the actual operations of Bre-X, they did not claim such ignorance when fame and fortune was showered on them, and when they bought Bre-X shares cheaply and sold them for a profit. Like C.H. Frame, the ownership of shares was not seen as the basis for the attribution of responsibility, neither to compensate those hurt, nor to be punished as major players in a fraud. As we asked in the Westray case, if Walsh and Felderhof had behaved exactly as they did without the help of a corporation, would they not have been legitimate targets for the law as owners and controllers of the business?

It must be noted that, though some of the Bre-X events—in particular, the salting and the heedless exaggeration of the amount of gold found—have been described here and in the popular media as a fraud, no criminal charges were laid against anyone. Indeed, the RCMP announced in 1999 that it was ending its criminal investigation. But some charges were brought.

The Ontario Securities Commission charged Felderhof with insider trading. That is, it alleged that Felderhof, as a major actor inside Bre-X, had used his position to advance his own benefit by cashing in his shares while not sharing information as to why he might have thought it timely to do so with other shareholders and potential investors. In short, the charge was not for the exaggeration about deposits and the falsified reports that ensued. Rather it was the possibility that a man at the core of operations had been unsporting towards other capitalists, towards other shareholders and prospective shareholders, that attracted law-makers' ire.

The anti-social, truly offensive aspects of wrongs done by and within Bre-X were not to be stigmatized by law. Harm to the capital markets was seen to be the sin which demanded the harshest of legal denunciations. We saw a similar approach in the James Hardie Australian asbestos case, where the directors were punished for misleading members of their own class, the capital market participants, but the role of the shareholding family that controlled the corporation that killed countless numbers of people while they were in control of it was ignored. We care about shareholders; we will even protect them from other shareholders. We will rarely protect anyone else from them.

In the event, after one of the longest trials in history, one at which the defendant Felderhof did not give evidence, Felderhof was acquitted. Whatever the reason for this result, it is part of a long tradition: insider trading,

Felderhof's supposed sin, is rarely punished in Canada. The scholar Arturo Bris reports that Canada is the least draconian of all jurisdictions seeking to inhibit insider trading.[1] A possible explanation is proffered in the next chapter.

Class action suits launched by people who had lost money by betting on Bre-X have also failed to provide joy to anyone. On April 23, 2014, seventeen years after the legal actions were lodged, the Ontario Superior Court discontinued them. It accepted evidence that any money that had been resting in the Cayman Islands had been spent by the Walshes (who had declared bankruptcy) and Felderhof on living expenses and massive legal fees. Felderhof is living in the Philippines and is said to have a mere $250,000 in the bank. The lawyers had collected $850,000 in fees, a pittance given that the presiding judge said that normally the work done would have yielded them $2.6 million.[2]

As an educative force, as a deterrent tool, as an instrument affirming shared social values, law performs poorly in the blob-o-sphere.

WHO IS HELD TO ACCOUNT

It is not true to say, as the illustrations above demonstrate, that law does not work at all. Corporations, their directors, their executives, and/or their employees are held to account as legal persons in their own right. But note that shareholders are not. The insertion of a legal corporate "person" between shareholders and the actual operational organization and its functionaries appears to inhibit the application of conventional legal principles. This is one impact of treating the corporation as the equivalent of a natural person. It has reverberations for the legitimacy of law, as the real beneficiaries and stimulators of wrongful conduct appear to be protected from fiscal liability for the costs, and in addition, are rendered immune from punishment for the wrongdoing.

Because it is understood by defenders of the status quo that this is not very satisfactory to the public, they mount a defence. In essence it is that corporations and directors and executives are more appropriate targets than shareholders. This is a problematic response.

When blobs are held responsible (as any legal person running an undertaking might be), their ethereal nature, their capacity to pass the costs on, their potential to restructure, that is, to disappear and reappear in a new corporate vestment, all mean that the public may still be left with the feeling that justice has not been done. This disappointment stems from the obvious lack of even-handedness and from the failure to satisfy the desire for vengeance that outrageous deceptions and frauds inspire. Punishing a disembodied being just does not do the trick. And it turns out that the alternative, making directors and executives responsible, occurs more often as an exception than a rule.[3]

In recent times there have been many screaming headlines in the United States and the United Kingdom about the huge fines and settlement payments imposed on miscreants during the notorious subprime mortgage scandals. Taku Dzimwasha reports that twenty global banks have paid $235 billion in fines since the 2008 financial crisis.[4] In absolute terms, the amounts are huge. They include $141 billion in fines for the mis-selling of U.S.-originated mortgages to U.K. customers, as well as $44 billion by way of compensation to those English purchasers. Ravender Sembhy has reported that, after guilty pleas in 2015 in respect of the foreign exchange manipulations, banks—including Barclays, the Royal Bank of Scotland, Citigroup, and JPMorgan—were hit with $5.7 billion worth of fines, following an earlier set of payouts amounting to $4.4 billion in November 2014.[5]

Staggering though these sums are, the following must be noted:

- The fines are dwarfed by the amounts lost as a result of the corporate shenanigans.
- The government had bailed out these same corporations when their earlier predations and subsequent inability to meet their obligations threatened the financial well-being of the globe.
- Some components of some of these payouts may be tax deductible as, in the United States, when settlements are reached with wrongdoers, some of the remedial payments are permitted to be treated for tax purposes as an expense of doing business. Matt Taibbi reports that Chase Manhattan was allowed to claim $7 billion of the money it had to pay as remedial payments,

reducing its tax by some $2.7 billion.[6] This kind of "adjustment" often leads to a rise in the price of shares of the penalized banks, as the cost of their wrongdoings turns out to be less than antici- pated. (And note, again, that the shareholding class continues to invest, obviously not upset by the ugliness of the corporations in which they buy shares.)

- It has not stopped some of these punished corporations from awarding their senior executives handsome bonuses.
- The corporations do not have to admit their culpability when entering these kinds of settlements and, even if they do, they are rarely banned from doing business as usual.
- Major directors and executives have not been charged with any wrongdoing.

The last point in that sorry list needs a rider. This work argues that it is controlling shareholders that should be held responsible for not using their influence over the corporation and its executives to avert harmful con- duct. This notion is implicitly shared by the wider public, even though it is unpunished executives that attract its immediate attention. The distinction between executives and major shareholders is not always that sharp in fact, and certainly not in the public mind. Often, the anger about unpunished executives is because these major executives *are* significant shareholders as well as hands-on employees. They are seen to be using their control, or more accurately, as not exercising their control, to ensure that all is done as it should be done. The executives' indifference to how profits are to be made is motivated in part by their status as significant shareholders and in part by the view of the world they share with controlling non-operative sharehold- ers. That is, the publicly made argument to hold senior executives respon- sible rests on the same ground as the claim made here that we should hold controlling, but non-operative, shareholders responsible.

In the end, the failure to go after actual human beings who are more obviously responsible for the scandalous conduct, or after any of those whose large shareholdings put them in a position of influence to ensure the common good, amount to a signal to those who operate and control the ectoplasmic blobs. They have been told that they are free to resume their virulent behaviours. The shareholders, who were not even thought of as targets of legal redress after the recent financial rip-offs, have been told that it remains safe to sit by, like so many Pontius Pilates, wash their hands, and profit from the zealously aggressive and, if need be, anti-social management of corporate businesses. The results are inevitable: the same kind of wrongdoing will recur again and again.

The *New York Times* recorded that, between 1996 and 2011, fifty-one major banks had entered into settlements that allowed them to pay some money and to avoid legal punishment on the promise not to misbehave again.[7] These same banks, the *Times* found, had had to enter into new similar settlements because they had violated the same laws that had led to the earlier settlements with their promises of "never again."

On another front, Kara Stein, a member of the U.S. Securities and Exchange Commission, heard a request by misbehaving banks that, despite their previous wrongdoing, they should continue to enjoy the privileges of their standing as Well-Known Seasoned Issuers. This privileged status is granted to promote efficiencies. It gives large companies advantages over smaller ones in the capital markets. Such privileged firms are supposed to lose this status automatically when they have breached basic rules, although the regulator is given discretion to give wrongdoers a waiver, allowing them to retain their status. Stein observed that five wrongdoing banks making an application to her to retain their Well-Known Seasoned Issuer status had had the benefit of waivers by the commission twenty-three times in nine years. She was outraged.[8]

The stories add to the evidence that the basic principle of deterrence is largely ignored when we enter the sphere of very large corporations' wrongdoing. This tolerance for corporations and their personnel and beneficiaries is so widespread, and this soft-hearted approach clashes so violently with the law-and-order agendas of so many of our governments, that one critic, Ezra Wasserman Mitchell, of the Shanghai University of Finance and Economics, sees them as evidence of institutional corruption.[9]

The reluctance to prosecute vigorously may be due, in part, to the fact that it is not always easy to prove that reckless or negligent acts were criminal in nature. Though regulators may believe this, there is some reason to be sceptical. Many of the settlements entered into after the recent financial scandals revealed that toxic loans whose risks were knowingly misrepresented were sold to ignorant investors. That sounds awfully like fraud or deliberate deception. Yet the tendency remains strong not to act against active individuals, not to see them as criminals. Increasingly, the preferred route is to look to the corporations (rather than major executives, let alone major shareholders qua shareholders) for redress and retribution.

In previous periods, say during the savings and loans and Enron days, some major directors and senior functionaries had been stigmatized and sanctioned. Charles Keating, Jeff Skilling, Kenneth Lay, Bernard Ebbers, Michael J. Rigas, L. Dennis Kozlowski, and other luminaries were made to take the "perp" walk in front of rolling television cameras before they were tried and jailed. The public was assured that the government and the law, like the average citizen, agreed that these deviants deserved to be punished as much as burglars are. Of course, the public was baying for their blood because they were not only hands-on executives, but also shareholders who benefited directly from their corporations' egregious behaviours.

One of the striking aspects of the aftermath of the 2008 financial shenanigans has been that easily identifiable and much-celebrated CEOs and their acolytes have been left untouched as their corporations were first protected by bail-outs and then entered into deals to pay fines and compensation. In the book that serves as a sequel to his famous documentary *Inside Job*, Charles H. Ferguson wrote: "Three years after a horrific financial crisis caused by massive fraud not a single financial executive has gone to jail. And that's wrong ... the bad guys got away."[10]

"Too big to fail, too big to jail" is not a legal principle. Indeed, it is an anti-legal principle and does not apply across the board. It is not true that major executives are never prosecuted, as the Felderhof case illustrates. But what is true is that if it is done, it is mostly done in smaller corporations where directorship and ownership are often more closely and obviously intertwined. And even then, it is the role played by a person as a director rather than their role as an owner that is the target of the law. The law goes to great lengths to keep up the myth that shareholders are not, and should not be, accountable actors.

SNAPSHOTS: THE LIMITS OF BLAME
Metron Construction: Reduced Responsibility

In the notorious Metron Construction tragedy in Toronto, a swing stage, a sort of suspended platform, crashed. At the time there were six people on it, and they fell fourteen floors. It was designed to carry only two. It was equipped with two life lines, but only one of the workers had the required life line attached to his body. Four of the workers died; one was seriously injured. The public might have expected some kind of homicide charges to follow.

Metron Construction Corporation, the blob—a legal person to be sure, but one that could not be jailed—pled guilty to a charge of criminal negligence causing death, a charge brought under the amendments to the *Criminal Code* enacted to respond to the Westray legal fiasco. In accepting a guilty plea, it was agreed that the site supervisor directing the swing stage operation was a senior officer within the definition of the *Criminal Code*. Under that amended law, the acts and intentions of such a senior officer could make a corporation criminally responsible if there had been a breach of a duty of care by the officer or representatives the officer knew or should have known were violating that duty of care. Here that duty had been violated in many ways. The evidence showed that three of the four deceased workers and the site supervisor had used marijuana, the number of workers on the swing stage was too great, the weight was excessive, there were not enough life lines, and the equipment was faulty.

Vadim Kazenelson, a senior officer of Metron Construction, employed as the building project's manager, also was charged with having committed crimes leading to deaths.[11] This led to a separate criminal trial.

Lesson: As the facts emerged, the authorities understood that they had to do something to show that they cared about workers' lives, that they were serious about the protective laws they had enacted. After all, the breaches of those laws were gross and four people were dead. Obviously, the corporation and its managers had fallen well short of the required precautions. The corporation was the immediate and main target of the prosecutors. Initially, the corporation was fined $200,000. The trial judge took into account the assets and prospects of the corporation, noting that the fine imposed was three times the income earned by the corporation in the previous year. The Crown was disappointed. It had made much of the seriousness of the case and had asked for a fine of $1 million. It appealed the trial judge's award and had a considerable victory.

The Court of Appeal increased the fine to $750,000, a sum that was beyond this guilty-pleading blob's capacity to pay. The Court of Appeal said it did not care if this fine might bankrupt the company. The judges noted that the corporation was no longer paying any employees and thus it was not obvious that deserving and vulnerable people would be adversely affected by the size of the fine. In effect, the goals of denunciation and deterrence were front and centre in the Court of Appeal's decision. Yet it should be noted that, despite the Court of Appeal's strong language, Metron Construction, even though it had killed four people, had been allowed to plead to one charge of criminal negligence causing death. The vigour of the message sent might be diminished further by the likelihood that the eye-popping fine might never be paid by the excoriated wrongdoer or by anyone on its behalf.

More importantly, the demonstration effect of the Court of Appeal's decision on the blob-o-sphere is reduced greatly because it is well known that there is little chance that many corporations will be charged as Metron Construction was. The first ten years of operation of the amended *Criminal Code* provisions indicate that, despite the number of fatalities in workplaces remaining constant, there has only been one prosecution per year. In statistical terms, each year there is a mere 0.1 per cent chance that a prosecution will be initiated after a workplace death has occurred.[12] And even then, a prosecution is more likely to be launched against a senior officer than a corporation. So, while the Court of Appeal gave voice to its outrage in Metron Construction, its decision may not have all that much impact.

Nonetheless, it is plain that the Court of Appeal was sincere in its intent to send corporations the strongest of messages. It stated that the trial judge's penalty of $200,000 was "manifestly unfit," given the "high degree of blameworthiness and gravity" of the "extreme" negligence of the swing stage's direct supervisor, negligence that could be attributed to the corporation. Such behaviour was deserving of serious punishment. Could that message have been strengthened?

This brings us to Joel Swartz. The press frequently referred to him as Metron's owner. He was the sole director of the corporation and its controlling shareholder. This very corporation had pled guilty because of its managers' delinquencies. Their recklessness had so deeply offended our shared values that the most senior of them, Kazenelson, has been charged with homicide offences. For its part, the corporation when pleading guilty acknowledged that it had no choice: it could and should be held criminally responsible for the conduct of its managers. It was charged and convicted. But not Swartz, that same corporation's guiding mind and will.

Swartz had established the organization, set up its workings, built in its risks, and had ultimate control over how the organization worked and how its risks were managed. As everyone else was being charged with homicide, the public might have expected some kind of homicide charges to be launched against Swartz. There were none. Now, Swartz did not escape altogether. His centrality had to be acknowledged by the legal authorities; his intimate connection to the horrific happenings could not be ignored.

Swartz was held responsible, not as a major shareholder, but as a director, that is, as manager and employee. (Sort of as his own employee, as in the Lee's Air Farming case discussed in chapter 3.) He pled guilty to violations of the duties that the occupational health and safety regulatory laws imposed on him as a director. A heavy fine was agreed to between the government and Swartz. To be penalized for a breach of a regulatory standard is, of course, a punishment. But it does not have the connotation attached to a true criminal conviction.

In form, regulatory laws resemble criminal ones. But while the central goals of criminal law—deterrence, retribution, and denunciation—are also goals of any regulatory regime, regulatory law remains distinct from criminal law proper. Laws against theft, assault, sexual assault, and murder are aimed at preventing conduct; by contrast, regulatory laws set out to facilitate competitive conduct that may cause harms. They are concerned with the promotion of what is prima facie desirable conduct, rather than with the inhibition of what is viscerally deemed to be bad conduct. The regulated standards set for behaviour are outcomes of a political process which is preoccupied with cost-benefit analyses and is influenced by political clout. Unlike criminal law prescriptions, the standards are not enacted to protect our most important shared values and social mores.

Thus, to take an everyday example, a man who gets into his car after drinking to excess and who kills a person whom he does not know and towards whom he bears no animosity may be charged under the regulatory offences that constitute the rules of the road. But he also will be charged with a crime, such as reckless and dangerous driving, manslaughter, or criminal negligence. He will be charged criminally, not because he intended to kill, but because his conduct was heinous, revolting to us; it indicated that he was indifferent as to whether he might hurt someone.

Let us here imagine what the result might have been if Metron Construction had not been an incorporated firm. Is it not likely that the prosecution would have looked to make Swartz—as the guiding mind, will, and very heart and soul of this unincorporated firm—responsible both under the regulatory law covering workplace safety and the criminal law safeguarding all of us from reckless disregard for our physical well-being? Once a corporation was inserted between Swartz and what functionally remained his firm, this was not on the agenda. For responsibility, for punishment purposes, he disappeared, at least as a controlling shareholder. He was now only visible as a director. In that guise, he was allowed to plead to the less stigmatizing, much less seriously punished, violations of the *Occupational Health and Safety Act*.

It is possible that this indulgence made it easier for the prosecution to get the blob, Metron Construction, to plead guilty to the severe criminal offence that the authorities wanted to impose on someone or something. After all, who but the controlling shareholder and only director was in a position to agree to such a deal? The deal served the purposes both of the prosecution and of Swartz. The Crown wanted to show that it had set out to get a serious penalty imposed. This explains why it appealed the disappointing fine stipulated by the trial judge. From Swartz's point of view, while he was to bear some responsibility as a major actor in the corporation, it was less than that of other managers. Kazenelson, as senior officer in charge of the overall project, has now been convicted on four counts of criminal negligence causing death and one count of criminal negligence causing bodily harm. He is facing serious jail time as well as stigmatization. Note that Swartz was in a position to discipline Kazenelson, but was much less severely punished, less publicly held to blame than either his inferior or the bloodless corporation.

Once the blob-o-sphere is entered, basic legal principles and normal reasoning are suspended. The conventional mindset leads to a pretense that controlling shareholders, the quasi-owners of the blob, do not exist or are impotent. They are not effective actors. To save face, we might have to hold them responsible as directors/executives; but then it is likely that, precisely because they are shareholders, we will treat them kindly. All of these manoeuvres lead to twisted thinking and practices. This is exemplified again by the way in which the legal events around the Lac-Mégantic case are developing.

Lac-Mégantic: Systemic Failure

The Transport Safety Board of Canada released the first authoritative overview of what happened when a runaway train, loaded with volatile crude oil, exploded in Lac-Mégantic, Quebec, in 2013. The train blew up the centre of a small town and killed forty-seven people. Transport Canada found that there had been a systemic failure; all concerned shared the blame. The government's oversight had been non-existent, and it had failed to audit the railway operator to ensure that it was managing the inherent risks of the enterprise. The railway operator, Montreal, Maine & Atlantic railway (MMA), was run like a shoestring operation. It exhibited a weak safety culture as it failed to manage the risks of transporting volatile crude oil. In particular, its training of employees was shoddy, as were its monitoring and maintenance practices. Corner-cutting was the order of the day, and a much-too-cozy relationship between government as regulator and the railway corporation as regulatee was allowed to prevail.[13] In this context, the culminating incident was a disaster waiting to happen.

The engineer, the sole operator of the train, had left the train unattended, with its brakes on, while he went to a nearby hotel to sleep. The locomotive was kept running to secure the brakes. This was the usual practice. Unfortunately, the brakes stopped functioning. Several possibilities could explain the malfunctioning. One is that the train should have two people to operate it to ensure that all safety precautions are taken. It had become the practice to do away with two-person crews some time ago. A second is that there had been a fire on the train while the engineer was sleeping, which had required the attention of some firefighters. Their rescue work may have affected the situation; so also might the way in which the engineer had put the brakes on, or the condition of the brakes.

The government, the corporation, its senior executives, the hands-on operators, possibly others; all were players in this drama. There was plenty of blame to go around. Who, thus far, has been singled out?

The Government of Canada has said that, primarily, we should look to the corporation and its operators. The government, it has argued, did everything by the book as it was written at the time. Undoubtedly, the book might have to be rewritten, and the government assures the public that it is vigorously doing so. Tougher standards and better enforcement will ensue. No heads have rolled. True, governments are paying a price as the federal and Quebec governments pour aid money into Lac-Mégantic to help the town and the victims get back to some normality. Taxpayers, rather than government actors, are on the hook.

MMA became bankrupt. Two years after the events, the *National Post* reported a bankruptcy settlement reached in the United States.[14] The settlement is the result of negotiations by claimants (governments and victims) with more than twenty companies. This speaks again to the way in which integrated webs are established that make it difficult to ascribe blameworthiness or to attribute accountability to any one actor. At this stage, it has not yet been determined how much each Lac-Mégantic claimant will receive, but there already have been murmurs about how great the costs of the negotiations have been and how much lawyers are going to make. As is so often the case, this kind of deal may do little to assuage the angered victims of corporate misbehaviour, especially as the major corporation involved is now out of danger.

This case should have been a good candidate for charges to be laid under the post-Westray *Criminal Code* provisions. The acts of representatives were, to the actual or reasonably attributable knowledge of the senior officials of the corporation, likely to lead to violations of the existing duty of care. Indeed, the police investigated to this end, but no criminal prosecutions against the corporation were initiated. The Crown prosecutors publicly announced that they have chosen to prosecute other folk.[15] What criminal prosecutions did they lay? Who are the persons being blamed by the law and its officials?

Workers, of course. Charges of criminal negligence causing deaths have been brought against the train engineer, Thomas Harding, MMA's railway traffic controller, Richard Labrie, and its train manager, Jean Demaître. Each is charged with forty-seven deaths, not just the one out of four to which Metron Construction was allowed to plead in the swing stage case. It is, to say the least, passing strange that workers are to wear the serious and stigmatizing criminal responsibility for terrible outcomes widely attributed to the systemic facilitation and promotion of for-profit activities by persons who were in command of these workers. It should outrage us, especially the people of Lac-Mégantic. The media reported that some would have liked to see more significant actors brought to justice. They may have been thinking of Ed Burkhardt.

Burkhardt was the president of a U.S. corporation called Rail World, the parent and controller of MMA. Thus, Burkhardt exercised major influence over MMA. Burkhardt became the poster child for everything that went wrong in the aftermath of the dreadful explosion. It took him four days to get to Lac-Mégantic. He expressed his condolences and regrets and noted that he, too, was a victim as the value of his shares had diminished. He blamed the train engineer. The announcement that neither he, nor Rail World, nor MMA were to be criminally charged is remarkable. Once again, controllers who, for their private gain, systematically established a risk-rich organization are not to be held accountable in the same way as a mere mortal unenveloped in corporate garb would have been.

As if to underline the point being made, it was announced on June 25, 2015, that further charges would be brought against MMA and six of its senior executives. But these charges are not for causing deaths and injuries by criminal negligence, charges laid against the workers which leave them facing the possibility of imprisonment for life. Not at all. These executives and the defunct MMA are being charged with two violations of the *Rail Safety Act*, namely a failure to set the necessary number of handbrakes and then to perform a test to ensure that the train was unable to move.[16] Obviously, if convicted, the stigma will not be the same as that associated with conviction for a crime designed to punish wrongful killing. The maximum penalty available reflects this: these individuals are facing the imposition of a maximum of six months in jail and/or a penalty of fifty thousand dollars. As well, they will face charges laid by Environment Canada under the *Fisheries Act* for causing oil and other dirty substances to leak into a nearby lake.

These charges are something, but not much. They are very different from the ones workers are facing, and they are not at all proportionate to the horrible harms inflicted by this corporation and its senior executives as they sought—with considerable help from a non-watchful government—to maximize profits at any cost.

WHO'S IN CONTROL

These cases suffice to illustrate what we do not do. When it comes to shareholders, we do not apply the usual rules of law. The rules reflect our socially shared desire to hold accountable those who have a direct connection to materialized risks that they are in a position to control. But they are not to be applied. Even when the circumstances cry out for such accountability, the law- and policy-makers go to great lengths to avoid it. We will hold other corporate actors, the corporations and their functionaries, responsible for their personal actions, but not those who impel them to behave as they do. Those wilfully ignorant motivators are made to disappear from the normal sphere of allocation of blame. It is an extraordinary privileging of one class of people.

The extent of this privilege is revealed when it is shareholders who are likely to be hurt by controlling shareholders. In that case, as if by magic, controlling shareholders make an appearance as legitimate targets. The law sets out to redress wrongs, to exact retribution from wrongdoers. All of a sudden some shareholders are appropriate targets for blame-laying precisely because they are more powerful than other people just like them: other shareholders. Their deployment of influence and power over the corporation is no longer a permitted use, but may be viewed as an abuse because it is exercised not at the expense of consumers, workers, or the environment, but to the disadvantage of other deserving capitalists.

Directors, in charge of policy-making and the daily operations of a corporation, may well take a tack that some members of the corporation see as harmful to them. But as the directors are given very wide discretion to take action on behalf of the corporation, they are only vulnerable to restraint if the corporation can show that their choices and actions are not in the corporation's best interests. Here the gyrations imposed by corporate law come out of the closet. How does a corporation determine that the directors' policies and actions are hurting it? Through its guiding minds and wills, that is how. And who can bring the actions on behalf of the corporation that has been advised that it is being harmed? Why, the very same guiding minds and wills. As they are the ones whose exercise of discretion and judgment are said to be harmful to the corporation, they will not be eager to help the corporation bring an action against themselves.

In earlier times it was, therefore, almost impossible for anyone to have a corporation bring an action to protect itself from its wayward guiding minds and wills. Today, legislation has come to the rescue. It allows shareholders to bring an action on behalf of the corporation, without having to get the help of the guiding minds and wills to make the corporation initiate such an action. They do, however, have to satisfy a court that they should be entitled to do so, leaving the remedy somewhat enfeebled. The availability of the remedy underscores the point: it acknowledges that the interests of the corporation and its shareholders are not only deeply intertwined, but that the corporation is seen as an instrument created to pursue the shareholders' objectives.

The reforming legislation was necessary because, in its absence, it was plain that corporate law was out of whack with other areas of law. Directors are in control of a person, the corporation, and can cause it to act to their benefit and to the disadvantage of others whom the law wants to protect. We have seen that the law acknowledges the need to protect victims of licensed alcohol vendors who, in a self-serving way, serve customers all too well to the detriment of others. The integrity of the fundamental legal principles that ground this kind of attribution of responsibility had to be honoured in the blob-o-sphere, and the new rules go some way towards this goal. But the derivative action, as the remedy is called, still does not provide a very effective remedy, especially not for minor shareholders, as courts are rather persuaded by the need to give the guiding minds and wills latitude as they exercise their discretion. This has led to the development of another remedy to counter wilful actions by major shareholders and senior executives who use the corporation as their plaything. It is called the oppression remedy.

The oppression remedy gives a complainant a right to go to a court to undo harms done by directors or other functional controllers of the corporation. They need no one's permission, and they need not prove that it is the corporation that is being harmed; they are entitled to enforce their claims directly. They can call a spade a spade. They have to show that, as a result of corporate decision-making and activity, they have been "unfairly prejudiced" or that their interests have been "unfairly disregarded."

As usual, these weasel words are a delightful source of revenue for lawyers and a prestige-enhancing field of research for academics. But even if the remedy's ambit is controversial, its purpose is plain enough. It is intended to give a remedy to all those who have a claim on the corporation, balancing that kind of claim against the need to leave managers with sufficient room to run the corporation "efficiently." This remedy is to be available against those who would injure third parties by the use of their disproportionate influence in the corporation. The typical oppression case is fought by minority shareholders against majority shareholders who try to have their desires satisfied by directors and senior managers at the expense of others. The remedy is also available to other stakeholders. This is the fig leaf behind which legislators hide their principal aim—protecting shareholders as a special class. Stakeholder actions are comparatively rare.

Similarly, when a takeover is in the works, the notion that other shareholders might be legitimate targets for the attribution of responsibility is front and centre. Special rules kick in when an investor comes forward and looks as if it is going to buy a substantial number of shares in a publicly traded corporation and actually obtains 10 or 20 per cent of its share capital. The threshold varies from jurisdiction to jurisdiction—but note how relatively small a proportion of the voting shares is seen to be significant when it comes to control of a corporation. In this case, the investor is required to make a bid for other shareholders' holdings. All shareholders are to be given an equal opportunity to take advantage of a takeover bid.

To ensure that shareholders have sufficient information to make a decision as to whether to sell their shares or to resist the takeover bid, a refined set of rules has been developed. This indicates that it is presumed that it matters who owns the shares. A new shareholder with voting clout might use its power to change the direction of the corporation, it might push for new directors and obliging executives, it might demand that the corporation get rid of some assets or do business with different people. In brief, it is openly acknowledged that some shareholders exercise functional control and that, when a new set of controlling shareholders comes along that, in legal terms, have no rights or duties to run the operational aspects of the corporation, they may change the nature of the business and affect the interests of other shareholders. For these purposes, it is understood that shareholders are far from hapless bystanders who have no capacity to control the way in which a corporation is run.

Often, governments are candid about this. Prone to boast that they are open to business, governments will not allow certain foreign corporations to take ownership of shares of a corporation within their jurisdictions, even though the shareholders of such a private domestic corporation may be eager to sell their interests to the foreign buyer. Governments feel they must deny some foreigners the opportunity to control certain industries. They will spring into action when they think that a foreign investor is a state-owned enterprise, one whose main shareholders may use the control over the assets they are buying to advance the interests of the state the corporation calls home. It is understood and feared that shareholders with a controlling interest (here, foreign states) may guide the corporation as they wish. Share ownership gives power to the owners if they have enough shares.

Shareholders disappear from legal sight when it comes to holding anyone responsible for corporate harm, unless that harm is to other shareholders. Can the law believe that there are not some situations in which they are not as effectively in control as, say, employers are of their employees or churches or schools are of those functionaries charged with meeting the organization's goals? As we have seen, when the victims are themselves members of the shareholding class, the power of those same shareholders is legally acknowledged. The only reasons that could justify this differential treatment would have to be based on empirical claims. Indeed, empirical claims tinge much of the justification proffered to treat shareholders as innocent bystanders when corporations maim, kill, despoil nature, or deceive investment markets.

One such claim is that there are very few cases in which shareholders have enough power to guide, influence, or control corporations or their directors and management teams. So it is not worthwhile to turn the law upside down. Implicit in this argument is that that existing corporate law is beneficial and ought only to be overturned if absolutely necessary. A second, closely related claim is that, even if enough such situations existed, holding shareholders responsible (as if they were just ordinary folk!) would do untold harm to our economic well-being. On the whole, the laissez-faire approach to shareholders is a small price to pay for the awesome contribution they make to our economies. The benefits vastly outweigh the cost of applying basic legal principles to their activities.

If factual, these arguments would explain and, in pragmatic terms, justify the special legal treatment given to shareholders as a class. But both are untrue. The next chapters set out to demonstrate that the number of corporations controlled by a handful of shareholders is vast, and that suggesting that shareholders as a class make a serious contribution to general welfare is mere puffery.

9

Too Hard to Find?
The Anecdotal Riposte

IN LEGAL AND OFFICIAL CIRCLES, IT IS CONSIDERED TO BE UNCHAL-lengeable that shareholders have given up their birthright as investing capitalists to manage their own property and, therefore, are no longer responsible for its uses and abuses. That's corporate law 101. Yet to people on Main Street, the idea appears weird. It is not the way they have been taught to think. Even on Bay Street or Wall Street, the corporate-serving folk and their business media do not think or talk that way. The legal and official version is at odds with public perception. And the public is right: the notion that it is too hard to identify controlling shareholders and give them their due is simply untrue.

TREES BUT NO FOREST

When businessman Paul Desmarais died in 2013, Canadian media were awash with accounts of his achievements. Everyone who was anyone attended the funeral. Four Canadian prime ministers, a former French president, and five Quebec premiers were there; also in attendance were the former Bloc Québécois leader, a former and current Liberal party leader, as well as the *crème de la crème* of large business interests. When it came to the affection and respect shown M. Desmarais, party allegiances and business rivalries did not matter.

Now, it is true that he was a man of many achievements. Desmarais had been active in setting up foreign trade deals, promoting federalism, and supporting cultural endeavours. He was, everyone agreed, an admirable person. He was also, of course, a man who had become exceedingly wealthy by his success in business. He had pursued his self-advancement by making excellent use of the corporate form. The *Globe and Mail* summarized his business career as follows (emphases mine):

> Desmarais' path to power began in Sudbury, where he was born in 1927. He left law school to take over the family's ailing bus company in 1951. A series of smart moves resulted in the creation of a holding company that in 1968 made a shareholder exchange with Power Corp. With the company's diversified holdings in insurance, transportation, paper, media, and financial services, *Desmarais was one of the most notable members of his province's business elite, often referred to as Quebec Inc. His empire* included Great West Life, London Life and Canada Life in the insurance industry; the Investors' Group and Putnam Investments; the Gesca newspaper chain, with its flagship, Montreal's La Presse, and stakes in the oil company Total S.A. and the Pernod Ricard liquor company.[1]

Many people participate in the promotion of good causes, in pursuing cultural and political ideals. Likely some of them, perhaps many of them, are as well intended, as intellectually gifted, and as energetic as Desmarais was. Yet Desmarais had been much more influential than most: it is manifest why. Desmarais had economic power. That personal economic power derived from his control and influence over his many business corporations. In turn, those corporations were significant actors in various important economic sectors. Their demands and voice mattered and, therefore, Desmarais's demands and voice mattered.

A similar story could be told about the Thomsons, the Murdochs, the Westons, the Bronfmans, the Irvings, Jim Pattison, about the people and families that both Main Street and Bay Street recognize as being in control of major corporations and, therefore, of swaths of the economy. And then there are the books, dozens of them.[2] They teach us how Canadian capitalism developed, how an entrepreneurial elite took risks, engaged in profit-seeking ventures, and massaged and manipulated its political environments. And how all of this was done by the promotion of and control over corporations. The stories are fascinating: they tell of derring-do, of alliances between captains of industry and their corporations, of intricate networks, of corruption, of the deep integration of government and business. Different though they are in detail, all speak to the influence and power wielded from within the confines of corporations.

Some of the books are scholarly, some snarky or fawning, some hagiographies. But none leave any doubt that, at least in Canada, we have individuals and families who, through corporate networks, exercise enormous influence over our economic, political, and social worlds. Some of the titles are revealing. Diane Francis's *Who Owns Canada?* and *Who Owns Canada Now?* Peter C. Newman's *The Canadian Establishment, volume I: The Inheritors, volume II: The Acquisitors*, and *volume III: Titans*, and his trilogy on the Hudson's Bay Company that concludes with *Merchant Princes*. Wallace Clement's *The Canadian Corporate Elite*. It is plain that these politically very different authors believe that there is a class, the corporate class, that dominates Canada's political economy.

The Canadian people in general have internalized this understanding of their society. And the Desmarais funeral hoopla told them that nothing has changed or is likely to change any time soon.

SNAPSHOTS: THE NATURE OF CONTROL
Tim Hortons: The Good Boss?

If anything qualifies as an iconic Canadian establishment in recent years, it has been the Tim Hortons chain of coffee shops. So it was understandable that, when it was announced that Burger King, an American outfit, was about to buy Tim Hortons, there was much public handwringing. Not only were Burger King's stated motives crass—they were said to be doing this to take advantage of Canada's lower tax rates, as if we were a tiny island serving as a tax haven— but the takeover would also be bad news for Canadian workers. The new owners were unlikely to be as kind as the old ones.

The bid on behalf of Burger King was engineered by its main shareholder, a corporation called 3G Capital. Mainstream Canadian media were quick to denounce its standard mode of operations. Its business plan is to acquire successful companies and then squeeze extra profits out of them. It does this by cutting employees and fancy offices, putting limits on office supply spending, on printing, on the use of electricity (all of which it did when it came to control Heinz). It does away with expensive furniture and accoutrements and entitlements such as private studies, end-of-year luxury parties, and fancy executive desks. It asks employees to use Skype instead of cell phones and reduce their use of expensive courier services (as it has done at Burger King). This business plan was contrasted with that of Tim Hortons, which was said to concentrate on constant reinvestment to build a business firm intended to last a long time.[3]

Lesson: Note the frank acknowledgement that it makes a difference who the controlling shareholders of a corporation are. In this case, our beloved Tim Hortons is to be controlled by another corporation. It is that corporation's character that draws commentators' ire. It is the attributes that make up the nature of the soul of a blob—known to the world as 3G Capital—that worry our nationalistic media.

3G Capital is a private equity company that was founded by three Brazilians. They were identified in the press as Jorge Paulo Lemann, Carlos Alberto Sicupira, and Marcel Herrmann Telles. Their combined wealth is estimated by the *Bloomberg* Billionaires Index at $45 billion, Lemann alone being worth $24.1 billion. Their way of doing business had made them rich, and it has given 3G Capital its character. This notionally soulless blob could, and should, be expected to act as its hard-driving Brazilian founders would if they were in business by themselves. This, our pundits whined, would change the essential character of another notionally soulless blob, Tim Hortons.

As an aside, it is passing strange for market capitalist cheerleaders to scorn 3G Capital's approach. After all, saving on costs to earn more on each dollar invested is the lifeblood of capitalism. In any one case, such penny-pinching may not work, but that should be left to the entrepreneurs. If they get it wrong, the market is bound to punish them and all will be put right in due course. The caterwauling about 3G Capital's mean-spiritedness, then, indicates that not very deep down, those who argue that the market should be left to its own devices do not really believe that this form of regulation always works very well.

On January 26, 2015, CBC News reported that the Cassandras may have been right. There has indeed been a change of culture and character. Tim Hortons, having promised the government that there would be no loss of front-line staff after the takeover, announced that it would lay off a large number of headquarter staff to satisfy what the CBC reported to be the new owners' desire to run a tight and mean ship.

The signal is clear: when capitalists see their preferred way of practising capitalism as likely to be affected by a corporation's behaviour, they want to know who controls that corporation. They want to know who, in the end, is responsible for its decisions; they want to know who gives this blob its character. They, the real capitalists, are not fooled by any legal cant that shareholders cannot be influential. They believe that it is worth the pain to look for who the controlling shareholders are so that they can assess a corporation's attributes and determine who will be responsible for how its chosen management, and therefore, the corporation, will behave.

Postmedia Network: Media Diversity

A similar signal was given when, once again, patriotic fervour was shown over the 2014 proposed Postmedia Network takeover of Sun Media newspapers and websites. Here the argument was that, should the bid succeed, there would be markedly less competition among news outlets. Note how well understood it is that ownership of media businesses matters. The owners—that is, the major shareholders—will colour the presentation of information and opinion and, in a pluralistic society, this can only be offset by having a large number of owners imparting their diverse views via their media outlets. In this case, the anxiety was not only about lack of competition, but also that something as important to Canadian democracy as control over media might be lodged in the keep of foreigners. This was so even though Postmedia Network is a well-established Canadian corporation.

Postmedia Network arose from the ashes of the bankrupt Canwest Global Communications. To resurrect what remained of its assets and to begin publishing again, investors, led by the enterprising Paul Godfrey, needed finance. They turned to Golden Tree Asset Management, a blob from New York, and to Silver Point Capital, a blob that hailed from Connecticut. These two hedge funds supplied the finance. In return, the two corporations took ownership of 92 per cent of the assets of Postmedia Network, and they also were issued non-voting shares. The voting shares in Postmedia Network were issued to Canadian citizens; Canadian citizens also occupied the seats on Postmedia Network's board of directors. The funding deal was structured in this way because Canada has special rules about media ownership that seek to limit foreign ownership. In legal terms, it was a Canadian corporation, albeit largely indebted to foreigners.

The business media's concern was that, regardless of the legal power of Canadian shareholders to run the corporation through their appointed Canadian directors, Postmedia Network was factually subject to the wishes of foreigners. Although the guiding mind of Postmedia Network, Paul Godfrey, had said that the U.S. hedge fund investors were "hands-off investors," this was countered by unnamed sources who claimed that Godfrey would not make any major moves without checking with the hedge fund managers first.

Lesson: Once again, brute reality tore up the fabric of legal make-believe. The business media so often defends the corporate shield on behalf of influential controllers. But they made it clear that they knew that, in many cases, such control and influence could be exercised by people who are legally considered bystanders when it comes to corporate decision-making. Here it should be emphasized that the persons feared, the U.S. human beings behind the hedge funds, did not have any voting rights to help them influence the senior managers of the blob they were seen as controlling. But they could influence those who held voting rights. What was important was not their technical legal status but their functional ability to make the blob do what they wanted it to do. Control is what counts. As President Nixon is reputed to have said: "If you have them by their testicles, their hearts and minds will follow."

The Stronach Trust: Democracy Undermined

Frank Stronach's career is one of those success stories that make capitalism attractive to many people. Over some thirty years, he built the largest automobile spare parts manufacturing firm in Canada. Magna International is a major multinational in this sphere. As it grew, it employed thousands of people, used large managerial staffs, and attracted many investors. Those investors contributed capital to the corporation in order to earn positive returns. Despite—or better, because of—Magna's success, they began to feel that the shares traded at lower prices than they should.

One contributing factor was the way in which the corporation's shareholding register had come to be structured. The corporation issued two classes of shares to investors. Owners of Class A shares were allotted one vote for each share they held. This is common when a corporation issues shares to attract capital. The corporation had also issued Class B shares. The holders of those shares were allotted three hundred votes per share. This meant that three hundred Class A shares were needed to match the voting power of a Class B shareholder with one share.

Class A shares of the type issued in the Magna case are commonly known as subordinate shares, Class B shares as superior ones. As an aside, this dual share structure is a distortion of the already distorted notions of democracy that characterize the corporate world. Even when all shares carry the same voting power, when it comes to corporate voting, it is not a tally of the number of people who vote in favour of a proposition that matters. It is the number of shares cast in favour of that proposition that counts. As a small number of people may have most of the shares, a minority of human beings and legal persons may control the majority of votes. Inside corporations, democracy is of the one-dollar, one-vote variety, not one-person, one-vote. The use of a dual share structure, as employed in the Magna case, further exacerbates this deeply undemocratic culture.

In its wisdom, the directors and management team of Magna had seen fit to issue the superior Class B shares to an entity called Stronach Trust. It was controlled by its chairman, Frank Stronach, and other members of the Stronach family. That meant that the Stronach Trust needed to contribute a risible 0.6 per cent of the equity funding of the corporation to control 66 per cent of its votes. A large number of hefty capital contributors had much less sway than Stronach Trust—and Frank Stronach—did. Many of them saw this corporate structure as undesirable.

It depressed the value of Class A shares, as their holders had less influence over the board of directors—and therefore, over management—than their contributions should warrant. The shares were, in part, valued less than they would be if corporate governance had been more efficient and allowed for more transparency and accountability. In addition, shares had less value than they otherwise would have because the share structure impeded the possibility of a takeover by a bidder, that is, it diminished the possibility of getting a premium for the shares that the bidder would have to buy. As well, inasmuch as all this made the purchase of shares less attractive than they would otherwise be, the corporation's access to capital funds was constrained.

Note that these objections to the peculiar corporate structure at Magna did not revolve around Magna's failure as a manufacturing enterprise. They centred on the fetters Magna imposed on financiers to whom the successful corporation that Frank Stronach built was the substratum for money-making endeavours. This is a significant issue to keep in mind as we investigate claims about the desirability of the corporate form.

To return: these allegedly undesirable features of Magna's share structure led Magna's management team to approach Frank Stronach to suggest changes. Only one meeting was convened and, after some internal work by a committee of the board of directors, a plan of arrangement (that by law required court approval) was put to the shareholders. Under the plan, Frank Stronach would give up his voting control by allowing Magna to buy, and then abolish, his Class B shares. A value, therefore, had to be put on the Class B shares. They were determined to be 1,800 per cent more valuable than Class A shares.

In the upshot, Frank Stronach was to be paid $863 million. That sum was to be a combination of nine million ordinary shares (of the one-share, one-vote variety, now to be the only kind of shares) plus $300 million in cash. In addition, Frank Stronach was given a five-year contract to act as a consultant to Magna, and an equity position in a partnership between Magna and Stronach Trust to operate an electric car manufacturing business. A number of large institutional investors in Magna, including the Canada Pension Plan Investment Board, the provincial asset managers of Alberta and British Columbia, and the Ontario Teachers' Pension Plan, objected vigorously. Among other things, they thought that the increase in the number of ordinary shares would, over time, dilute the value of all of the shares. This estimate was based on the history of what happens when large-scale dilution takes place, not on any evidence of a decrease of share value in the immediate aftermath of the deal. The objectors felt that Stronach had used his controlling position unfairly. But a majority of votes cast by shareholders approved these arrangements and, on that basis, they were given court approval.

Lesson: In one sense, even as the demand for an 1,800 per cent premium attracted much attention and some opprobrium, it does not seem unreasonable that the founder and energetic force behind Magna's success should profit from his efforts. That, after all, is what motivates capitalists. It is the way in which Stronach reaped his reward that attracted attention here. He used his influence inside the corporation—that supposedly separate and sovereign person—to give himself special deals, even if they came at the expense of others who had entitlements under that corporate envelope.

The first deal was engineered when he got those superior shares that gave him a lot of power without having to tie up much of his personal wealth. This happened in 1978. Such a deal had to be approved by the corporation's board of directors. It is hard to document, but easy to guess, that the directors were likely very sensitive to Frank Stronach's wants and needs. The second deal was initiated by a management team when Belinda Stronach, the well-known businesswoman, political figure, and philanthropist—and Frank Stronach's daughter—was executive vice-chair of Magna.

There is no indication of her using improper influence. Indeed, it is only fair to note that Belinda Stronach was not around when the Class B share structure was established. But it is not a huge leap to think that the directors and managers of Magna were conscious of Frank Stronach's interests, even as they did their best to serve the overall interests of the corporation, and even as they made a recommendation ostensibly designed to improve the governance of the corporation and its attractiveness to investors. Frank Stronach's strong bargaining position as a controlling shareholder, seen as not easily challengeable because of the invisible and historic links between him and the directors and managers, led to a proposal that some felt allowed him to hold more vulnerable shareholders to ransom.

In functional terms, Frank Stronach had control and he used it. There would have been no issue if the firm had not been incorporated. It would have been his firm, his property, to do with as he wished. But legal corporate rules hold that those private property principles should not be applied when investors cease to be legal owners of the invested capital. Stronach should not have been able to advance his own interests as if he were the owner of the firm. Yet something very much like that did happen because, despite the law's best efforts, it is quite possible for one or more persons to influence corporations into acting as if they were not self-standing, self-interested persons. One of the lessons of the Magna tale is that this retention of control can be achieved by structuring the corporation one way rather than another.

Corporate law creates opportunities for some investors to use the risk-shifting corporate form while not giving up any of their power over their risk-creating property. This is why corporate law has had to furnish more general remedies. In the United States, courts have imposed a fiduciary-type duty on majority shareholders like Stronach to ensure that they do not use their voting power to the disadvantage of minority shareholders. In Canada, we have developed an elaborate oppression remedy to attain those needs. This is not a book about the workings of law, and it is not to the point to examine how effective these rules are (although I will assert that there is much more litigation and scholarly writing about the oppression remedy than tangible, positive results). What is to be noted is that, even within the framework of corporate law, it is understood that some corporate actors remain well placed to exercise influence and control over the activities of a corporation even though, legally and technically, they are deemed not to have such powers.

In sum, it is commonly and sensibly believed that there are people out there who are able to use the corporation for their own ends—and that they do so. Indeed, everything in our experience tells us that there are a great number of such folk. This widely held perception, however, does not have much purchase when it is contended that shareholders might be held accountable for corporate practices. The basic principles underlying both our liberal legal culture and our market economy's logic scream out that the citizenry have a right to demand that something be done when they learn of corporate deviance. They feel, often strongly, that controlling persons should be held responsible for the harmful outcomes of their corporations' conduct. Yet, law and the dominant class's intellectual gatekeepers continue to argue that, should these controllers be mere shareholders, as opposed to hands-on directors or executives, they should be left alone. This requires a lot of justification. It comes in sophisticated forms, but the arguments are ultimately less than persuasive.

THE BLOB AGAINST THE MARKET

An incorporated firm is a vehicle in which a group of people combine their assets and talents in order to pursue the goal of making a profit. It is the "legal entity" feature that differentiates it from a partnership. As the U.S. Supreme Court has said, "A corporation is, after all, only an association of individuals under an assumed name and with a distinct legal entity."[4]

The statute books define a partnership as a relationship between persons carrying on a business in common with a view of profit, a definition that, on its face, describes an incorporated firm. But the partnership statutes go on to state explicitly that, where persons are carrying on a business in common with a view to profit and have registered their firm with an incorporating registrar, they will not be covered by partnership law. This is significant.

If they were partners, the members of the firm would be responsible, as individuals, to make good on any of the obligations incurred by the firm as a result of their own acts or those of the other partners. In this kind of firm the character, reputation, and reliability of the persons with whom one associates matter. Partners owe each other fiduciary duties precisely because they can make each other responsible. They undertake the business as individuals who are to accept full responsibility for things done for the partnership, so their individual wealth can be called on by anyone pursuing losses inflicted by the partnership. Partners do not have limited liability. Simply put, they are sovereign individuals who, by participating in competitive market activities as they pursue their self-interest, are expected to take personal responsibility for any breach of accepted standards, even though, for efficiency's sake, they act in concert with others.

If the partnership does not pursue profits by exploiting the efforts of others, the partners are classic examples of Adam Smith's welfare creators, the self-standing and self-interested butcher, brewer, and baker. They are prototypical market actors. And should the partnership pursue profits by exploiting the work and resources of others, the partners would be classic capitalists who, in the idealized market world, also must be treated as sovereign individuals whose control over an enterprise makes them responsible for outcomes arising out of violations of acceptable legal norms. Chapter 7 was replete with the ways in which the law affirms this proposition.

But the moment we put a corporate envelope around the same association of people, all of this personal responsibility disappears. Everything remains the same: the association of investors, their efforts, their exploitation of others (if any); everything is the same except the responsibility they owe for the obligations of the firm or its functionaries or those of fellow investors. In a corporation, they do not have to care about who those other investors are or about their character, reputation, or reliability.

Turning a firm into a legal corporation, into an ectoplasmic blob, gets flesh-and-blood capitalists off the market's personal responsibility hook. The corporate envelope gets rid of most of the risk arising out of their greed-driven activities. Unsurprisingly, many people who, for public policy reasons, are not allowed to use corporations because they are expected to be responsible to the larger public for their private acts would like similar protections. In recent years, self-regulating professional law and accountancy firms have turned themselves into variants of corporations. Law and accountancy firms' names are frequently followed by the acronym LLP. Standing for limited liability partnership, it signifies that members of the legal or accounting firm's partnership will not be responsible for the conduct of other partners unless they played a part in, or in some way controlled, those other partners' conduct. But note that they are to remain responsible *if* they exercised or could have exercised control. This dovetails with the basic premise of liberal law. It is not something entrepreneurs embrace willingly. They prefer to limit their liability—and this is what they love about the blob.

The drive to satisfy this desire explains why partnership statutes must state that an incorporated association of persons carrying on a business with a view to profit is not a partnership. Corporate law, as opposed to partnership law, insists that none of the fundamental rules of partnership—specifically, the rules about personal responsibility—are to apply to corporations. This is a frank acknowledgement that one major purpose of corporate law is to create a safe haven for some actors. Investors, that is, owners of capital, are not to be subjected to the ordinary laws of the market.

This is a good juncture at which to remind ourselves that the market's tenets of personal responsibility for one's choices, as idealized by Adam Smith, provide a major justification for an economic scheme of private ordering and wealth creation. The fundamental premise is that, as long as the market's basic principles reign, we can expect responsible and efficient behaviours. This bestows legitimacy on the search for private profits. It would evaporate if no persuasive reason could be offered as to why practising capitalists, simply by adopting a corporate guise, should not be subjected to the normal rules of the idealized market. A series of justifying reasons have had to be crafted.

The first response is that, as a matter of law, the corporation is an individual, like a natural person. It is a legitimate participant in the market, just as human beings are. It follows that, if the corporation and its agents are held responsible for violations of market standards, the market's principles are being honoured. But this is a bootstrap argument. The reason any justification is required in the first place is that the corporation is understood to be an association. It is a collection of actual persons who should, if the market rules, be responsible for their choices as individuals.

A second response, similar but more nuanced, has been proffered by libertarian economic scholars and policy-makers. The argument is that the personhood of the corporation doesn't matter after all. No matter what the law says, these scholars and policy-making elites contend, the corporation is just a convenience used by entrepreneurs associating with others like them to do their personal thing. The corporation is really a network of individuals who are associating with each other by contracting how they should combine their talents and resources, how to deploy them, and how they are to share out the profits, if any. That is, the corporation is not the market actor; rather, the individual contracting human beings are the real market participants.

This approach brings a plus for the defenders of the status quo. By barging their way past the corporate form, the promoters of the firm (technically incorporated, to be sure) come back to life. It can now be claimed that it is appropriate to treat shareholders as owners who have given up some of the managerial rights to their agents. Thus, it is perfectly appropriate for law to bestow property-ownership-like entitlements (share in profits, voting rights regarding directors and significant changes in the nature of the firm) on non-managerial shareholders. It allows investing shareholders to be treated as the real owners of the business, even as the law says that they are not the owners of the corporation's capital. And it allows the law and economics school adherents to bemoan the fact that, over time, these individual owners, as shareholders, have lost control.

For them, of course, the problem is that non-owners may exercise too much control, something that may turn the supposedly convenient corporate form—much as Adam Smith had feared it might—into an inefficient vehicle. As well, this otherwise useful giving up of control by the real owners to directors and their management teams might permit these directors and their managers to shirk and loot. The law and economics devotees who normally rebel against governmental regulation of markets are pushed to favour legal interventions to inhibit unacceptable gouging by non-owning directors, executives, senior officers, and lowly workers. They conclude that the corporate device can serve capitalists well, as long as its potential failures are kept under control.

But treating the corporation as a mere form, as a useful but conceptually insignificant device, also brings a minus for those same scholars and policy-makers. If the shareholders are really contracting owners and risk-takers, and the incorporated firm is merely a facilitating tool, then why should these contracting owners not be held responsible when the conduct of the firm violates market or social standards? Those scholars and policy-makers answer that this approach makes sense in principle, but that it would be inefficient. Their argument is that making shareholders responsible—even though they are the individuals who constitute the incorporated firm—is fraught with practical problems. It is too difficult to make individuals responsible. There are so many of them and the individuals holding shares often change; they are hard to find; and it is quite likely that some should be held more responsible than others, and it is difficult to identify the right ones. For these reasons, the corporation, rather than the shareholders, should be held responsible for violations of accepted standards while chasing profits.

That it would be more efficient to have a corporation to sue rather than the associating individuals whose activities had injured others was argued by those who, in the nineteenth century, tried to persuade legislators to allow firms to register as non-partnerships, as corporations. The contention was that incorporation of what were in effect partnerships—then known as unincorporated joint stock companies—would provide a tangible, identifiable "person" to target legally. It would make it easier to provide remedies when they were needed. This argument, based on legal pragmatism rather than conceptual purity, was central to the enactment of modern corporate law.

The law and economics school's adherents use the same argument in an elaborated manner. They assert that nothing will be lost in principle if corporations, rather than their real owning or contracting individuals, are held responsible. The law's and the market's goals of keeping the individual as the linchpin of a social and economic system of personal responsibility will be honoured. Given a well-working market, attributing responsibility to the corporation will provide redress for those injured and serve both to educate that corporation and corporations in general. The market will punish those corporations that have to pay compensation, that lose licences, or that are convicted of regulatory or criminal offences. It will be more difficult for them to get credit and to attract new investors. The value of their shares may fall, thereby punishing shareholders who may include directors, executives, and other managers. It may become harder to inveigle talented people to join the firm... All the actual individual actors will be taught lessons.

These are two clever lines of reasoning. The corporation is first characterized as a mere convenience, a facilitating tool, one that does not negate the fact that the market is still peopled, as it should be, by rugged entrepreneurs. The essence of this argument is that reality is not changed by the use of a legal cypher. But then that cypher is revived to say that one of its many conveniences is that, as a holder of the capital funds of the contracting association of individuals, it can act as an effective proxy for the attribution of individual responsibility. Clever though it is, this reasoning does not satisfy.

Targeting the corporation as a proxy, even if the market is functioning perfectly, will touch individual shareholders only indirectly and their non-invested assets not at all. More importantly, the laws dealing with breaches of contract—aimed at compensation for injured third parties, those regulating productive and commercial activities, and those designed to prevent and punish criminal behaviour—all imagine that wrongs are committed by individuals who are capable of forming an intent, acting upon it, and feeling remorse and pain. Corporations do not fit the bill. They think and act through others, feel nothing when funds are lost, experience no shame or pain when punished. And when asked to pay up, corporations are often able to pass on the cost or, if unable meet their obligations, simply fail to do so.

For the corporation, as such, there is no serious downside. After all, it is a blob. It feels nothing, even if it is killed. Indeed, it may be deregistered and its promoters may have it recreated in slightly different garb, a process that may not persuade the public that justice has been done. All this means that the fundamental objectives of law's oversight roles—namely, compensation, specific and general deterrence, rehabilitation, and revenge—will rarely be met when corporations become the proxy for those who controlled and sought to benefit from the blob's activities.

The argument that the market will take care of everything that needs to be taken care of by holding the corporation—that mere tool—responsible, rather than its functional owners, pretends that the markets work perfectly, or at least well, and that individuals will feel the corporation's pain and react appropriately. This is at best a romantic view of the markets; at worst, an uninformed one. The inevitable inability of the markets to do their thing leaves most of us dissatisfied. It ignores the way we think and live. It ignores the need to satisfy our sense of justice.

There is a visceral desire, one promoted by law's claim of neutrality and even-handedness, to attribute meaningful responsibility to those human beings who did us harm. It is this sensibility that fuels the anger and generates pressures on law reformers and politicians when folk like C.H Frame, David Walsh, John Felderhof, Ed Burkhardt, the Reid family (initial owners and operators of the James Hardie corporations), the retailers astride a bunch of subcontractors who exploit vulnerable garment workers, the Brambles who force employees to form their own companies to shift liability on to them, and so on, are allowed to hide behind the blobs they control. Those who intended to benefit from the manipulations and who could have prevented their use are left off the hook. It is this sense of unfairness, of injustice, that has led so many commentators, like Charles H. Ferguson and Matt Taibbi, to bemoan the acceptance of financial compromises with deviant corporations that allowed them to put their financial wrongdoings behind them and their controllers (senior managers and considerable shareholders) to continue to live the good life. As a *Moyers and Company* program said when talking about the resignation of U.S. Attorney General Eric Holder:

> He will leave behind a mixed scorecard: A for civil rights, C for civil liberties and F for failing to prosecute the banking executives who brought

about the financial calamity of 2008. Holder let the bankers off the hook individually.... The billions of dollars in penalties the banks are paying will largely be borne by shareholders and by taxpayers as the banks write off the fines as the cost of doing business. The executives get off scot free.[5]

Thus, while the clever, nuanced conceptual arguments of law and economics scholars and like-minded policy-makers are bound to be popular with the wealthy, dominant class, they do not fare so well in other circles. This forces the status quo's intellectual gatekeepers to strengthen their case by making empirical claims. They contend that, despite the anecdotal evidence in this chapter that points to some easily identifiable controlling shareholders, it is simply unworkable to hold individuals who associate by means of a corporation personally responsible for the firm's and its functionaries' wrongs. They claim that, even if it might make sense to hold the real owners responsible, this would never work. There are too many owners, they say, they are all different in kind and influence, and those few that could fairly be lumbered with responsibility for the blobs' conduct will be too hard to find. Thus, attempts to do so would needlessly discourage this most efficient way of doing business.

This set of claims is based on a grossly mistaken understanding of the world of corporations in most of the jurisdictions in which they flourish. The next chapters are devoted to establishing this point: there are controlling shareholders inside corporations who can and should be held responsible for the blobs' excesses and abuses.

Too Hard to Find?
The Empirical Riposte

THOSE WHO ADVOCATE LESS REGULATION BY GOVERNMENT SING A repetitive refrain: regulation is bound to be inefficient. Private actors, chasing profits, know better how to discern what goods and services are in demand and how many of them should be produced at what cost. Each, as an individual, with special talents and resources, is better placed than a government to make those kinds of decisions. Some will make mistakes and fail, others will succeed. Overall, they say, as every actor, under competitive pressure, reacts to spontaneously generated demands, the optimal use of our aggregated talents and resources should result.

ONE SIZE FITS ALL?

The best thing for government to do, in this way of thinking, is to stay out of the way, once it has created conditions that give everyone an equal opportunity to participate in competitive markets. As a corollary, it is also wrong for government to hand out welfare to those who do not participate well, or at all, in the marketplace. Such subsidies reduce incentives to contribute to the general welfare; they induce laziness and undermine self-reliance. And they deplete the resources of those who are willing and eager to generate wealth by their own efforts. In short, anti-regulation activists proudly trumpet their individuality, their willingness to take risks and to compete with other rugged individuals. It is a mark of being worthy; it gives them the right to be contemptuous of those who supinely rely on the paternalism of a nanny state.

All this bravado is ditched when we enter the blob-o-sphere. Those who contribute capital to, in return for shares in, a supposedly distinct market actor, the corporation, are intent on becoming, legally speaking, market bystanders. They position themselves to become legally passive persons who seek to profit incidentally from the productive, profit-chasing pursuits by the corporation and its controlling management. They willingly jettison their claim to respectability arising from their exercise of control over their talents and resources and their readiness to stand behind its impacts. If anyone is to be responsible for the use of their contributed capital, it is the corporation. The corporation is the market actor; *it* is the entrepreneur.

Formerly proud, risk-taking investors have transliterated themselves: they are no longer principals in charge of their own destiny but hopeful, somewhat vulnerable, passive bystanders. But because they are still contributing something, some capital, they want to be treated well, especially as they are facing new dangers. In fact, they demand extraordinary privileges, and they get them. Government intervention, on a grand scale, privileges them.

As we have noted, corporate law allows shareholders to vote on major issues, to share in the profits, to sell the shares unless they have agreed not to do so, to enjoy limited fiscal responsibility and legal immunity from actions arising out of the corporation's conduct. This is the kind of government regulation these capitalists like. They see it as deserved; after all, they support corporations by giving them resources to play with, and they give up their right to control the way in which their contributed capital is used.

This argument is seen as so obviously right that this regulatory set of privileges is made available to any member of any corporation, no matter its type or size. All shareholders in all kinds of corporations are deemed to be worthy of limited liability and legal immunity because, technically speaking, they are not in control of the corporation's conduct. "One size fits all" is acceptable when it suits capitalists. Liberal economists and lawyers sing from a songbook that they normally relegate to the bin labelled "bad ideas."

This privileging of the shareholder makes no sense. It ought to be absurd on its face to make the entitlements available regardless of whether

- the corporation is tiny, medium-sized, or huge
- it raises capital by asking the general public for contributions and allows its shares to be publicly traded, or prefers to restrict its contributors to specific individuals, allowing sales and purchases of shares only as agreed to by the members of the firm

According to the rationale, shareholders' relationship to a corporation is always of the same kind, no matter its type or size. They are, therefore, deserving of similar legal treatment. To put it mildly, the credibility of this rationale is hollow. It is a thoroughly counterintuitive starting point.

SMALL CORPORATIONS: MOST OFTEN CONTROLLED BY IDENTIFIABLE SHAREHOLDERS

As should be expected in a market capitalist society, there are so many would-be entrepreneurs in Canada that it is hard to get a fix on the exact number of individuals who set out to use their resources and talents to supply what they deem to be unmet demands. Many incorporate the firm through which they conduct their business. This does not mean that they give up control of the firm, that they are people who should not be held responsible—if liberalism and liberal law are to mean anything—for the obligations their firm incurs or the wrongs it does. Industry Canada, a statistical department of the federal government, notes that the size of a business can be measured in several ways: by the value of its annual sales, by its gross or net revenue, by the value of its assets, or by the number of people it employs. Since we are most interested in whether some investors in a firm may be deemed to have potential or actual control over it, the number of employees is the most germane of these measures. The more people who act on behalf of the firm, the more who may have discretionary powers, the less easy it will be to attribute control to one or more persons.

The data are clear: there are relatively few Canadian firms where so many people are involved in the firms' activities and decision-making that potential and actual controllers cannot be identified. Industry Canada states that, as of December 2012, there were 1,107,540 businesses in Canada that it described as "employer businesses," that is, businesses with a number of employees. They ranged from what Industry Canada calls small to medium to large businesses. Small businesses are those that employ 1 to 99 employees, medium ones boast 100 to 499 employees, and large ones 500 or more. Of the 1,107,540 employer businesses, 1,087,803 were small. A staggering 98.22 per cent of employer businesses employ fewer than 99 people! Medium-sized businesses make up 1.64 per cent of employer businesses, and large businesses a paltry 0.14 per cent.

Obviously, the range of small employer businesses, 1 to 99 employees, does allow for an argument that some small businesses may engage enough folk to make easy identification of controlling persons somewhat tricky. But not so. It turns out that most of the small businesses lag at the bottom of the range. Of the 1,107,540 employer businesses, 55.1 per cent have only 1 to 4 employees. And the range of 1 to 19 employees accounts for 87.4 per cent of all employer businesses for which Industry Canada provided data. Even more arresting is another set of data provided by Industry Canada: a great number of establishments do not employ anyone at all. These are in effect owner-operated businesses that, often, are incorporated. The owners, who may do most of the needed work, do not pay themselves wages as if they were employees of the company. They may have workforces that consist of non-traditional workers, such as occasional contract workers or family members.

There are, then, a huge number of incorporated firms for which it is dead easy to find a controlling person, one who in all likelihood may act as a major shareholder, director, manager, and employee. We have encountered such situations: for example, the crop-spraying pilot in the *Lee's Air Farming* case or Wail, the laundry service driver who was forced to form his own company to keep his job in the *Brambles* case, and many other situations discussed in part I. The conclusion is plain. In a huge number of incorporated firms, it is almost impossible not to be able to identify the major shareholder or shareholders who act as the real controller or controllers of the firm. Often, they are made up of a handful of related people, family members, or friends. They are in a position to direct—or be—the directors.

Factually, they are not constrained by the limits on their legal power to set policy or run operations. They may indeed behave without regard for the norms of corporate law that require that only directors, as directors and/or executives, may make policy and operational decisions on behalf of the corporation. When they do so, they are using their structural power in a legally unauthorized manner. They have crossed a technical line and courts—with their rigid adherence to the sanctity of the separate legal personality of corporations—may feel that they must make them honour that line. A judge may, then, remove the protection the corporate umbrella gives to human beings trying to hide behind it.

The bulk of the judiciary's rare corporate veil piercing decisions occur in the small, close corporate setting. It is usually so obvious in those cases that controlling individuals run the corporation as they see fit that one acute observer has suggested that the corporation is more like an employee of the controlling shareholders than it is anything else.[1] In those cases even the ultimate defenders of corporate law's pretenses, the courts, cannot deny that some people are in complete control over that supposedly sovereign legal person, the blob. In sum, the Industry Canada data indicate that most small incorporated employer businesses will be the compliant creatures of major shareholders who personally are directors and executives, or have their closest relations and friends as directors. In liberal law, the obvious makers and shakers should not be immunized from liability for the harms inflicted by the corporation they control. Nor should they be from a market economic perspective.

The huge number of truly small firms is frequently celebrated by defenders of the status quo. Knowing that capitalism is best legitimated if it can be equated with the idealized Adam Smithian market regime, the proliferation of small firms helps keep up the pretense that we have a true market economy. Mainstream politicians regularly pronounce that small business is the backbone of the economy. But this claim rests on the assumption that these businesses are really run by individuals, competing fiercely with each other. Its proponents should not also be allowed to argue that small-business operators are not to be held responsible for the way in which the activities of their blobs are conducted. The small-is-beautiful assertion rests on the fact that there are real persons, real individual competitors out there.

Factually, then, in the small corporate setting—that is, in the majority of cases in which businesses are incorporated—the situation is not different, and should not be treated differently, from the non-corporate spheres in which the doctrine of responsibility for the exercise or potential exercise over the conduct of others is accepted as the legal norm. Yet this differential treatment persists. Contrary to all evidence, much of corporate law scholarship and policy-making is based on the notion that the picture of the disenfranchised shareholder and widely dispersed shareholding is *the* accurate representation of the corporate world.

Perhaps an excuse is the belief that the most important corporations are constituted by hapless shareholders and that it is impossible to find their controlling investors. And that this is what should guide our policy-making in respect of all corporate firms. Let us turn to the first part of that proposition.

LARGE CORPORATIONS: OFTEN HAVE EASILY IDENTIFIABLE CONTROLLING SHAREHOLDERS

Bookmakers of all sorts offer odds on how a race will go, who will win a tournament or championship, who might win the next election. But nothing gets as much publicity as the odds-makers on the stock exchanges. "Frenzy in stock market.... The stock exchange was gripped by euphoria," reports the *Hindu*. "Stocks Swoon in Frenzied Trading ... investors scrambling to buy set-term bonds," gasps the *Wall Street Journal*.[2]

Up! Down! Sideways! Radio, newspaper, and television outlets and countless specialized newsletters tirelessly give running accounts of the value gambling investors put on the shares issued by large publicly traded corporations. There is a sense that, somehow, these valuations are connected to the state of the economy. This belief, in turn, is fed by the fact that these corporations are behemoths. They own and control large parcels of assets and issue millions of shares to thousands of people as part of their efforts to raise capital and employ a huge workforce.

Jordan Brennan, a researcher for the Canadian Centre for Policy Alternatives, has reported on their centrality.[3] He found that the top sixty Canadian-based firms accounted for 67 per cent of equity capital on the markets and produced 60 per cent of all corporate profits. Indeed, their profits were twenty-three times as large as the profits of the average firm trading on the Toronto Stock Exchange. It is understandable why some folk contend that it is impossible to look for controlling shareholders in these vast organizations. They claim that, whatever the situation might be in small incorporated firms—whose position in the economy is neatly described by American political philosopher Robert Paul Wolff as "a domain [that] flourishes ... like the flora that live under the soaring canopy in an Amazon rain forest"[4]—it should not be seen as applicable to the world of giant corporations. Is this claim that no one investor or small group of investors could ever control these corporations warranted?

In Canada, as in most countries, it is not. Indeed, the data make it staggeringly untrue. For this discussion of the data, I've made some conservative assumptions about what constitutes concentrated ownership of corporations:

- Corporations in which no single shareholder or group of shareholders owns, directly or indirectly, more than 20 per cent of the voting shares are defined as *widely held corporations*. These are the corporations in which the conventional wisdom that no shareholder is capable of controlling the acts of the corporation or its functionaries holds true.
- Corporations in which a single shareholder or group of shareholders, directly or indirectly, owns up to 49.9 per cent of the voting shares are described as corporations in which one shareholder or group of shareholders has *effective control*.
- Corporations in which a single shareholder or group of shareholders, directly or indirectly, owns more than 50 per cent of the voting shares are described as corporations in which one shareholder or group of shareholders has *legal control*.

In the last two situations, effective or legal control, there are easily identifiable shareholders who can exercise control over corporate behaviour. Are these situations rare? Not in Canada![5]

Randall K. Morck, David A. Strangeland, and Bernard Yeung, using data gleaned from the *Financial Post* surveys of 1988, show that of the 246 publicly traded corporations in the list of the top 500 firms measured by sales, only 67 (which included traded subsidiaries of widely held firms) were publicly traded. A mere 67 out of 246 fit the preferred portrayal of huge corporations in which shareholders are hapless bystanders with little influence and much to fear from the corporation's machinations. This fact is a central feature of Canada's business topography. In 1996, P.S. Rao and Lee Sing reported that 75 per cent of large publicly traded corporations were effectively or legally controlled by a single shareholder or a group of connected shareholders. The 2014 *Financial Post Magazine*'s ranking of Canada's largest and most profitable corporations showed that this pattern of concentrated ownership persists (although the methodology used in that survey may not have been the same as in the older academic studies).

All of this should be unsurprising. Beginning with the conscious intertwining of government and business, commencing with *l'ancien régime* and then the Family Compact period, Canada's economy has always been characterized by a few dominant corporations controlled by a few major players who often were related by family ties. For instance, in their study "The Rise and Fall of the Widely Held Firm," Randall Morck and his co-authors found that in Canada, by 1910, "the greatest part of the corporate sector, forty percent by assets and forty-five percent of firms, belonged to pyramids controlled by wealthy individuals or families. A substantial number of smaller firms are independent corporations controlled by a family or an individual." They also found an apparent lessening of concentration somewhere near the middle of the twentieth century, but that this turned out to be a blip. John Porter's study of fifty-five major corporations, published in 1956, found that only four were widely held. Tom Hadden, Robert Forbes, and Ralph Simmonds record that, in 1982, of the fifty largest corporations in terms of sales revenue, only nine were widely held. The historical consistency of the picture is clear.

It is difficult to see how anyone can maintain that Canada's blob-o-sphere is constituted by a majority of corporations with widely dispersed shareholding. The accompanying assertion that it is not worthwhile to try to attribute responsibility for the outcomes of the corporation's doings to leading shareholders is, therefore, far from convincing. Indeed, when you remember that the documentation recited above understates the degree of control exercised by a few investors inside corporations, the evidence for such an absolution of shareholders reaches the vanishing point.

Thus, the first survey mentioned, that presented by Morck, Strangeland, and Yeung, was based on a study of 246 publicly traded corporations on a list of the 500 largest Canadian corporations. Another 254 corporations of considerable size were government-controlled or private corporations, that is, corporations that limited the number of people who could hold shares. Private corporations resemble partnerships more than they do a firm that is a separate entity, a different person to its functionaries and contributors of capital. They are, par excellence, corporations in which one shareholder or group of shareholders has control over corporate conduct. Moreover, privately run corporations may well be used to lord it over widely held ones, rendering the apparently dispersed shareholding in some of them less meaningful in terms of control than it would seem to be.

Consider this situation. The business pages of the *Toronto Star*[6] reported in 2014 that the U.S.-based Sears Holdings Corporation had announced a sale of shares it held. Among its assets, this major U.S. corporation owns the Sears and Kmart retail chains in the United States. Its board of directors, seeking a needed an infusion of cash, had agreed to sell some of the shares it held in Sears Canada. It held 51 per cent of that Canadian corporation's shares. When the U.S. corporation made its announcement, a man called Eddie Lampert said that, as a current shareholder in Sears Canada, he would exercise an option he had to subscribe to any sale of its shares. And he told the market that his private firm, the Florida-based fund manager ESL, would exercise its options to buy some of the shares to be sold. That privately owned company, ESL, was already Sears Canada's second-largest shareholder, second only to the American Sears Holdings Corporation which was now selling some of its shares. The *Star* pointed out that "ESL ... controlled by Lampert is also the largest shareholder of Sears Holdings with 24.8 per cent while Lampert directly owns 23.7 per cent of Sears Holdings." Thus, even though Sears Canada's shares are publicly traded, is it difficult to imagine that Lampert and his ESL do not play a major part in decisions made by Sears Holdings Corporation and by Sears Canada, decisions such as, say, determining that the former should sell its shares in the latter to the public, including to Lampert and his ESL?

And to probe a little more closely, let us use a hypothetical. Sears is a retailer. Let us imagine that some of its foreign suppliers are found to have breached internationally acknowledged norms. Would it be difficult to find persons of influence and control in the Sears organization? Note that a year earlier, *Fortune* had reported that the surprise departure of the CEO of Sears Canada may well have been due to the differences he may have had with Lampert.[7]

On-the-ground facts, established again and again, make it clear that the claim that shareholders in large corporations have given up the inherent right of owners, namely to control the uses made of their property, is nonsense on stilts. It is not germane here to examine why, politically, socially, and culturally, the concentration of ownership has been part of the historic fabric of Canadian corporations. It is, however, noteworthy that this level of concentrated ownership makes Canada ordinary, not exceptional. Canada's corporate world looks much like that found in Australia, Hong Kong, India, Indonesia, Israel, Japan, Korea, Malaysia, the Philippines, Singapore, Taiwan, Thailand, and Turkey, in Argentina, Brazil, Chile, Colombia, Ecuador, Mexico, Peru, or in most European countries, such as Austria, Belgium, Denmark, Finland, France, Germany, Greece, Iceland, Italy, the Netherlands, Norway, Portugal, Spain, Sweden, and Switzerland. While the legal relationships between controllers and the corporations differ in these jurisdictions, the eventual outcome—concentrated power exercised by a small number of actors—is similar.

In their study "Corporate Ownership around the World," Rafael La Porta, Florencio Lopez-de-Silanes, and Andrei Shleifer found that it is only in the United States and the United Kingdom that shareholding is so dispersed that it is hard to identify controlling shareholders. This suggests that when it comes to the question of shareholder accountability, the heavily peddled but profoundly anti-empirical conventional wisdom—stemming from the naturally influential powers in the Anglo-American legal sphere—that there are few if any controlling shareholders to be found in Canada and many other jurisdictions is to be resisted. Even in the United States, where the claim of dispersed ownership seems most justified, studies show that most U.S. corporations have a small number of substantial shareholders, which might in turn be corporations themselves.[8] The U.S. and U.K. circumstances ought not to control our mindset or imagination when it comes to the question of the practicality of identifying potentially responsible shareholders, even as other, more credible empirical and conceptual commonalities with U.S. and U.K. corporate practices and laws merit our respect as we address other governance issues in our jurisdictions.

THE PROMOTION OF CONCENTRATION

A certain legal misperception moulds the mindset of Canadian defenders of the status quo and inhibits Canadian activists from trying to hold identifiable controlling shareholders responsible for corporate conduct. Those who benefit from that status quo are happy to encourage the misperception, even as they support instruments that enable the few to attain the heights of command in large corporations. They are engineers of a system of control they want the world to believe does not exist. They live happily with a series of laws and policies that promote concentrated ownership of major corporations.

One such set of instruments is the availability of different voting rights for different classes of investors. Canadian corporate law allows the establishment of restricted voting rights. This makes it possible for shareholders whose shares carry more votes per share than those of other shareholders to have an amount of control that is disproportionate to their contribution of capital. Ownership without control acquires a new and different meaning: when it comes to control and influence, some owners are less important than other owners. The Stronach Trust affair examined in chapter 9 provides a good, if extreme, example. This mechanism allows some investors to safeguard their control over a corporation while taking less risk. It is a principal tool deployed by individuals and families to perpetuate their hold on a corporate enterprise, even as it grows. And shamelessly, it has the blessing of the same law-makers who want us to see shareholders as people without power and as legally unaccountable for corporate activities.

Similarly, our laws and practices promote the use of pyramids. Here two things have to be remembered. First, corporations can toss off newborns with no effort whatsoever. Second, while initially it was not considered appropriate for a corporation to hold shares in another corporation, those days are long gone. These starting points make it possible for pyramids to be constructed.

Typically, a holding corporation formed by an individual or family—frequently a non-traded one, such as Lampert's fund manager in the Sears example above—will own enough shares in a second tier of firms to control them. Then, those second-tier firms may hold controlling blocks of shares in another level of firms, and so on and so on. This enables the initiating individual or family to have control over a large number of corporations and their assets without having to invest huge amounts of money to get such control. Morck, Strangeland, and Yeung cite a calculation that shows that a "control pyramid ten layers high, with 51 percent ownership at each level, magnifies a billion dollars of wealth into control over $840 billion."

Enormous economic and political power flows through such structures to a few individuals or families. And to add insult to injury, they will remain legally hidden or, better put, protected from legal responsibilities. This power arises from the ways in which the dispersed assets are deployed. La Porta, Lopez-de-Silanes, and Shleifer, in their study of worldwide practices, found this pattern replicated pretty well everywhere, except in the United States and the United Kingdom, where the capacity to use pyramids has been stultified. This is one reason why the power to influence the use of corporate power in Canada resembles that in Asia, Latin America, Australasia, or Europe far more than it does that of the two countries to whom it looks for economic and legal leadership, the United States and the United Kingdom.

In fact, even defenders of the status quo know that arguments based on the powerlessness of shareholders as a class are misplaced. This shows up in two ways. First, because the imbalance between controlling shareholders and others is such a frequent occurrence, they have had to devise a set of remedies to protect shareholders from bigger shareholders. Second, in their own critiques of corporate structures, they betray anxiety over the undue control of a handful of people in so many dominant corporations.

As we've noted, the oppression remedy (albeit mostly used in the small corporate setting and available also to stakeholders other than shareholders) is there to help out the less-powerful shareholders. Notionally, this remedy is available both in tightly controlled corporations and in those with widely dispersed shareholding. But it is most effectively used in the former. The less-powerful shareholders are also helped out by "dissent and appraisal" remedies. When a majority of shareholders approve of a major change to a corporation—such as an alteration or restriction on the firm's business, an alteration or restriction on the issue of shares of a particular class, an amalgamation with another corporation, the relocation of the business to another jurisdiction, or the sale of a substantial amount of the corporation's assets—the minority will be given the right to lodge a notice of dissent. If this dissent is ignored by the majority, the majority may be forced to buy out the shares of the dissenting shareholders at an appraised value.

The notion is clear: some "owners" may have their desires blocked by others and are to be given relief. It sounds democratic until you remember that the majority is usually constituted by a small number of shareholders. The availability of the dissent and appraisal remedy suggests that policymakers are well aware that controlling shareholders may rob other shareholding capitalists of their entitlements. The same observation may be made about the takeover rules that have been devised to ensure that insiders or major shareholders cannot deny minority shareholders their opportunity to get a premium for their holdings.

One reason for the reluctance to admit that so many economy-dominating publicly traded corporations are controlled by a handful of shareholders is that, for those who believe in market capitalism, this is anathema. It suggests that the market is not working as it should be. An example is provided by the work done by B.E. Eckbo in the 1980s[9] which found that, in the United States, when a takeover bid is announced, the price of the shares of the target corporation goes up sharply as the newly informed stock market reacts swiftly to the possibility of an until-then-unanticipated premium for shareholders' holdings. In Canada, there typically was no sudden spike but rather a steady, little-noticed upward movement over time. Eckbo's findings suggested that in Canada a number of insiders were in control of takeover negotiations and could use their insider position quietly and effectively.

This dovetails with the findings of scholar Arturo Bris (see chapter 8), who argued that Canada was a safe harbour for insider trading. While it has led to little action by policy-makers, the apparent capacity by the few to exercise undue influence inside corporations is a grave problem for those who portray the corporation as an uncontrolled site. On other fronts, Morck, Strangeland, and Yeung, after examining a plethora of studies, concluded that entrenched, tightly knit owners were poor managers, favouring self-serving, but not welfare-serving, transfers of assets and wealth from firm to firm under their control. Overall they performed less well than did widely held corporate businesses, spent less on innovation, used their economic powers to block new market entrants by lobbying for entry barriers, and so forth.

The point here is not that tightly controlled corporations undermine the operation of the efficient markets. Rather, the emphasis is that the many studies done and the debates they generate indicate that it is well understood that concentrated ownership is common and that, to the proponents of the market, it is deeply problematic. Indeed, it is somewhat embarrassing at times.

One of the weaknesses of concentrated control is that it is difficult for non-controlling investors to dislodge executives and hands-on decision-makers whom they feel to be poor managers. The controllers may like them because they themselves are hands-on directors or executives or because they are their friends or family members who have been appointed to plum jobs. The tendency to appoint one's own to one's economic power base speaks to loyalty, but not to merit as measured by market criteria. Coziness may well lead to inefficiencies or, just as important, to the appearance of inefficiency and mollycoddling.

In one famous public squabble, the McCain brothers, the controllers of a mighty Canadian corporate organization, feuded over which of their children should get which part of the corporate pyramid to run. Were they the only potential managers available, or was this just a case of a corporation being treated as the private plaything of major shareholders? It may well be the case that Belinda Stronach deserved to be a captain of industry, or that the children of Paul Desmarais, the Bata family's members, or the winners of an internal competition between the Bronfman offspring were the best people for the jobs they were awarded in some major corporations. But one should not jump to conclusions.

During the much-hyped 2014 mayoral election in Toronto, feminists argued that the eventual winning candidate, John Tory, was not much of a feminist. They observed that he had been a CEO of Rogers Communications and was currently a member of its board of directors and that, although there were four women on that board, three of them were Rogers family members.[10]

The United Food and Commercial Workers Union took out a full-page ad in the newspapers on September 26, 2014. It addressed Galen Weston Jr. directly, imploring him, as the man who runs the Loblaw grocery group, to be fairer to Loblaw workers. The union was in no doubt that he was in control, not just because he was the senior hands-on manager, but because he and the members of his family are the controlling shareholders. This family ownership is part of the reason that Galen Weston Sr. is the second-wealthiest man in Canada. By all accounts, his son is an accomplished businessperson, so this may be one case (perhaps one of the few) where connections and ability coincide.

David Macdonald, writing for the Canadian Centre on Policy Alternatives in 2014,[11] reported that 86 Canadians, a mere 0.0002 per cent of the population, owned as much wealth as the poorest 11.4 million Canadians. Of Canada's top-paid CEOs, only 10 made it into the top 86 owners of wealth, and all were related to the founder of the company that generated that wealth.

Such facts make it very difficult to maintain the pretense that there are few identifiable major shareholders controlling some very important corporations. This is why Diane Francis's 2008 work on the subject, *Who Owns Canada Now*, reads like one huge sigh of relief. She finds that, since she wrote back in 1986 about the thirty-two families that owned Canada, there has been a sea change. There are new kids on the block, new enterprisers who run major corporations in Canada. They did not inherit their control; they earned it by hard work, prescience, innovation, and the like. But it remains the case—as Francis shows—that identifiable controllers of corporations dominate the scene, persons who could be saddled with liability for corporate outcomes if there were a political will for it. This will is what is lacking.

THE "OTHER" SHAREHOLDERS

In addition to controlling shareholders, major corporations do have a great number of other investors, some of whom hold shares directly, others through intermediaries. The Canadian Securities Administrators' *2012 CSA Investor Index* reports that only 55 per cent of Canadians have savings outside a company-managed pension plan, RRSP, or RRIF. The three most commonly held investment products by these savers are mutual funds (owned by 62 per cent), term deposits or GICs (45 per cent), and individually held shares (33 per cent). The first two categories will include some indirectly owned shares. But the large number of non-controlling shareholders, as individuals, purchase relatively small numbers of shares in any one corporation.

Many of us invest in share markets because we need to save. Many, perhaps most, of us are not investing as risk-taking capitalists; many, perhaps most, of us are not in the share market because we want to participate in the affairs of the corporations. We are, for the most part, individuals who need to provide for our welfare when we stop working or have to deal with ill health and the like. If we act as individuals, the amounts invested, spread across a variety of corporations, will give us very little voting clout in any one corporation. Small investors might have more influence if an institutional investor combines their holdings in a corporation with those of other similar small investors. This happens because many small investors turn to intermediaries, financial institutions that claim expertise and that, by gathering various pools of money, will be able to get better returns for them.

The institutional investor who has the legal voting power attached to those pooled shares might have an effective voice in corporate affairs. But it is doubtful whether this potential will often result in the loss of influence by controlling shareholders. Inasmuch as the institutions that gather our premiums and invest them on our behalf do exercise a voice, their interests in no way coincide with our own. They want as many fee-paying clients as possible. They want to show good, immediate returns on their investments, to keep their clients and to gather more. As Adam Harmes writes in *Unseen Power*, a 2001 book about the mutual fund industry:

> [Money managers] are paid and evaluated on their ability to retain old clients and attract new ones ... they must produce strong performance numbers on a ... quarterly basis. So while the retirement savings that make up mutual funds and pension funds may have long-term horizons, the men and women who manage these funds do not.[12]

They favour directors and executives who push for improved share values or good dividends, whether or not this encourages cost-cutting by excising labour or by avoiding investment in expensive technologies that would yield returns in the long term. For many institutional investors, the greater a corporation's emphasis on short-term positive returns, the better it is for them. They are unlikely to push for more costly social responsibility. Their desire to interfere is most likely to be aroused when executive remuneration is high at a time when shares lose value or dividends dry up. Their motives, more often than not, coincide with those of the controlling shareholders who push for the maximization of profits at other people's expense. The title of Jennifer Taub's evaluation of a host of studies, "Able but Not Willing,"[13] captured her conclusion that intermediary funds rarely used their voting clout to direct managers.

By design, institutional investors are discouraged from using the many shareholder votes they control to bring about more desirable corporate behaviours. As a complementary dynamic, institutional investment houses are themselves corporations with directors and executives who have a need to be on-side with the corporations in which they invest as they scramble for advantage. They have more in common with them than with their many anonymous, uninformed, and largely passive customers.

The Canada Pension Plan Investment Board, for example, a Crown corporation that invests our Canada Pension Plan assets in the markets, sided with the Mining Association of Canada, the Canadian Chamber of Commerce, private mining corporate spokespersons, and various Conservative party members when they opposed the introduction of a legislative proposal requiring Canadian miners to respect international human rights and to subject themselves to a regime of corporate social responsibility. The guardians of our pensions wanted the corporations in which they invested to be competitively placed when pursuing profits, even if most of us might balk at making money out of the dispossession of vulnerable people elsewhere. The logic of the market aligns institutional investors with all other greedy shareholders and reckless corporate functionaries.

Sometimes institutional investors manage some aspects of the business of the corporations in which they are invested, and they profit handsomely from managing such things as corporate pension plans and various insurance coverages. This adds to the reasons for not upsetting the managements of the corporations in which they invest.[14] Sydney Law School's Jennifer Hill has concluded that, when they do not like a particular set of decisions or the state of a corporation, institutional investors tend to choose what she calls "the Wall Street walk," that is, they sell their holdings and place their investments elsewhere.[15]

The fact that institutional investors are more likely to bolster the controllers' powers than they are to attack them should put a damper on those who see institutional investors as a means to make corporate decision-makers more sensitive to diverse stakeholders or less short-term oriented. Indeed, some have come to the view that it is shareholders, including institutional ones, who push the economically inefficient short-term agendas. These observers call for a lessening of shareholder democracy, a lessening of shareholder power.[16] However justified such an approach might be, it is yet another acknowledgement that shareholders are the real motivators impelling corporate actions. It thereby provides more fodder for the argument that controlling shareholders should be held accountable for corporate behaviour.

OWNERSHIP AND CONTROL

Let us review the legal status of the shareholder.

- It is *legally accurate* to say that, once investors become shareholders by contributing capital to a corporation, the capital becomes the property of the corporation and the shareholders become former owners, that is, not owners at all. It is legally accurate to say that all they own is a call on future profits. This is evidenced by a share certificate which, if the corporation is a publicly traded one, they may sell.
- It is *legally plausible* to argue that, because they are asked to give up those rights of ownership, they need incentives. Offering them limited fiscal liability of their contribution may thus be defensible. Once they have that, it is less persuasive, though still plausible, to argue that they deserve some further reward. The right to a share of the profits made with their former property makes sense as an implied term of the giveaway. The right to vote on the appointment of directors who manage the property they used to own also makes some sense. The right to register dissent with major changes in the corporation engineered by the directors also makes some sense, as it reflects the notion that they did not expect such a change when they gave away their property.
- It is *not legally plausible* to argue that it is necessary for directors charged with serving the best interests of the corporation

to maximize profits to satisfy shareholders. This is why the law does not explicitly impose that duty on directors. When directors nonetheless equate the best interests of the corporation with the best interests of the shareholders, it suggests that, legal plausibility aside, the working corporate world sees shareholders as real owners.

- It *would be legally plausible* to argue that, because they have no formal right to direct or manage the corporation in their guise as shareholders, shareholders should not be held responsible as owners and controllers of their own property would be. But that conflicts with the real-world view of the corporate world of shareholders as the real owners.

- It is *factually inaccurate* to maintain that all shareholders have become former owners without control. Most small corporations (that is, the bulk of all existing corporations), most private corporations (some of which are among the largest enterprises in the land), and a huge majority of large publicly traded corporations are controlled by one shareholder or a small group of shareholders. In these cases, the most significant feature of ownership has not been given away to supposedly autonomous directors and their executives who manage the corporation for its own sake and who may have a distinct agenda from that of major shareholders.

In sum, then, Canadian corporations legally seem to fit the model of ownership without control. But functionally, Canadian corporations exhibit the retention of control by non-legal owners. This is why it makes sense to directors and executives to maximize shareholders' interests, rather than those of another supposedly distinct entity, the corporation, that may clash with those of shareholders. The bases for special privileges, and most importantly for legal immunity for corporate conduct, disappear when the real facts of corporate life in Canada are acknowledged. And as we have seen, the same is true in a huge number of other jurisdictions, whether they draw on the common law or some other legal approach.

It turns out that the supposedly ignorant public, the media, and popular books get it right: there are identifiable people who run corporations as if they are the real owners, with all the decision-making power that we associate with property ownership. Legal scholars and corporate cheerleaders are out of step with both Main Street and Bay Street. For example, when it was anticipated that Pierre Karl Peladeau might make a bid for the leadership of the Parti Québécois, the Quebec Federation of Labour intimated it would oppose his aspirations because Quebecor Inc. had engaged in fourteen lock-outs when fighting its workers. The Quebec Federation of Labour saw Peladeau as responsible for this conglomerate's anti-labour activities, as he was its controlling shareholder.[17]

These identifiable controllers are the very opposite of impotent bystanders. Why does the law not treat these identifiable corporate controllers as it does owners of licensed premises, charitable organizations, churches, schools, and the like, who know that their operations may affect vulnerable people, or as it does knowing, reckless, or indifferent creators of circumstances that lead to violations of accepted international norms? The reasons examined thus far are unsatisfactory.

We have yet to confront another defence of this unholy position. It is that, should we make controlling shareholders of corporations legally responsible for the outcomes of corporate conduct, more harm will be done than good. We are told that the quest for even-handed application of fundamental principles of law to the blob-o-sphere might satisfy our desire for logic and for revenge, but that it would undermine the material bounty we enjoy because of the wealth-generating capacities of the corporate firm. This empirical claim, too, does not stand up to the light of day.

The Role of
Limited Liability

IT HAS BEEN ARGUED THAT, IN ORDER TO HOLD THE RIGHT PEOPLE accountable, the corporate veil must be stripped away. That would reveal those who give the corporation its character and who are in a position to determine how the corporation attains its—and their—goals. It would take away their legal immunity for conduct they inspired, controlled, or could have controlled. Inasmuch as legal attempts to do this succeed, it is more likely to be when civil, rather than criminal, liability is sought. If shareholders become personally responsible civilly, they will have lost their limited fiscal liability privilege. Unsurprisingly, this would be anathema to those who want to maintain the status quo.

SUPPOSED BENEFITS OF LIMITED LIABILITY

To proponents of the corporate and legal status quo, stripping away the corporate veil is a dangerously harmful notion. Limited liability, in this view, is a public good that must be preserved. In fact, in 1926 the *Economist* predicted that "the economic historian of the future may assign to the nameless inventor of the principle of limited liability … a place of honour with [James] Watt and [George] Stephenson, and other pioneers of the Industrial Revolution."[1]

This line of reasoning needs to be confronted. It has three limbs.

1. Limited liability is a boon to the economy because it promotes investment in productive activities and spurs innovation.

2. To remove its protection from some shareholders, depending on their degree of control over corporate decision-making and choices, will lead to uncertainty as to who might be able to continue to claim to be protected by limited liability. Therefore, it would be detrimental to the goals of promoting productive enterprises and innovation.

3. Without the protection of limited liability, corporations would come to be seen as less useful and be used less. This would have an adverse impact on the overall welfare of our economy.

These claims turn out to be overblown, to say the least. Limited liability did not come without a fight, but today it is well established. The proponents of this boon for shareholders point to its many advantages. It inveigles owners of wealth to invest more of that wealth in other people's ventures than they otherwise might. The combined capital of many players who view an undertaking by a corporation as worthwhile creates a greater potential for efficient, profit-making investment than the investment of many separate fragments of capital in discrete businesses. And, as any residual amount of wealth investors have has not been put at risk, they are free to contribute some of this residue to other profit-chasing firms. Perhaps to many. Not only, then, does the benefit of limited liability make more capital available to any one firm, but it also promotes a diversity of productive activity.

Also, from an investor's point of view, limited liability frees investing shareholders from the burden of involving themselves in the daily operations of the corporation. The contributed capital is transferred to the corporation, where a board of directors and executives are to take charge of it. The corporation is duty-bound to chase profits, that is, the very efforts the investors would have made on their own account will still be made. But the contributors of capital do not have to expend any effort of their own. In other words, limited liability is good because shareholders do not have to do anything.

Two further arguments are made in favour of limited liability. The first arises directly from the fact we are supposed to like the idea of a thriving market in which shares can be sold and bought. Limited liability helps that cause by eliminating some of the volatility that might otherwise prevail. In the absence of limited liability, less-well-off investors might invest in higher-risk investments than would wealthier ones, because they have less non-invested assets to lose. Wealthier investors would then have a different appraisal of what makes a share's price affordable than their less wealthy comrades would. This could lead to unpredictability in the valuation of shares and, therefore, to less attractive stock markets.[2] Here the assumption is that robust stock markets are a plus for the economy—a highly contestable assumption.

The second remaining argument is that, because a corporation is an aggregate of many people's wealth and talents, it is a more orchestrated and larger unit than would otherwise be formed by investors acting on their own. This allows for more of the repeatedly necessary functions to be done in-house, that is, there will be less need to contract with outsiders for needs such as transport, advertising, trade supplies, expertise, and so forth. There should be considerable savings in transaction costs, making the corporation more efficient than a business based on a single investor's capital input could hope to be. Again, although the argument deserves to be acknowledged, it is not on its face overly persuasive. Increasingly, as the massive outsourcing of production to poorer countries demonstrates, increased transaction costs are vastly outweighed by the savings to be made from getting access to unprotected and cheap foreign labour or from the acquisition of coercively low-priced foreign resources.

All in all, there are a number of plausible arguments that support a proposition that the piercing of the veil accompanied by the elimination of the protection of limited liability for the revealed controllers of a corporation would be a regressive step. Let us confront these arguments by looking at on-the-ground facts.

LIABILITY IN SMALL CORPORATIONS

From the outset, sceptical voices have been raised on the principle of limited corporate liability. Edward Cox wrote, in 1856, in *The Law and Practices of Joint Stock Companies*:

[In partnership law] there is a moral obligation, which it is the duty of the laws in a civilized nation to enforce, to pay debts, to perform contracts, and make reparation for wrongs done. [Limited liability] is founded on the opposite principle ... permitting man to avail himself of his agent's acts if advantageous to him, and not be responsible if they should be disadvantageous; to speculate for profits without being liable for losses; to make contracts, incur debts, and commit wrongs, the law depriving the creditor, the contractor, and the injured remedy against the property or person of the wrongdoer, beyond the limit, however small at which it may please him to determine his own liability.

John McCollish, in 1859, added: "Were Parliament to set about devising means for the encouragement of speculation, over-trading and swindling, what better could it do?" And Ambrose Bierce's 1911 *Devil's Dictionary* proclaims, "A corporation is an ingenious device for obtaining individual profit without individual responsibility."

As we have seen, the bulk of firms registered as corporations are tiny businesses. Registering this genre of firms as corporations attains none of the lauded aims of incorporation. In many cases, there is no combination of many small pools of capital to create a large, more productive fund; in most of these cases there are very few, if any, transaction cost reductions. And their shares are rarely traded publicly, making it irrelevant whether limited liability is a stabilizing force in share markets. In all those cases—and let it be stressed that they represent the majority of incorporated businesses—none of the major purposes of the bestowal of limited liability are served. Limited liability plays no beneficial role. It plays a pernicious one. The effect of combining the privilege of limited liability with the grant of separate legal personhood promotes a lot of unproductive and harmful behaviours by incorporated small firms.

Using the blob and its limited liability allows for the splitting of incomes and denial of revenues to the government, and permits loading the costs of doing business onto third parties. Those risks of responsibility-shedding are so well known that those who can avoid them will. Large lenders, typically banks or powerful suppliers, will demand personal guarantees from those who run small incorporated firms. They then will not have to care when such a corporation is unable to pay its debts; they can go directly to the controlling shareholder for satisfaction. They know that there are such people, and they will not allow a mere blob to obscure this fact. They have the power to avert the risks incorporation poses to outsiders. Small traders, creditors, and wage earners, however, are not in a position to enter into contracts that will protect them from the risks of dealing with a limited liability firm.

This is characteristic of a capitalist system: self-reliance only works for the rich. The less-well-off are, all too often, coerced into accepting the risks posed by dealing with small incorporated businesses. This obvious lack of equality in results is a cause for anxiety among corporate capitalism's intellectual gatekeepers. The efficiency of the markets and the fairness and evenhandedness that elites pretend to desire are seriously undermined by the limited liability doctrine's potential to illegitimately externalize costs in the small-business sectors. Moreover, that doctrine offers no compensating benefits, either economically or socially, in those sectors. The more reflective defenders of limited liability can see that removing limited liability from some of the prime actors in these kinds of incorporated businesses would be unlikely to have an adverse impact on our economy. Indeed, they understand that it is more likely to improve business culture, as self-styled entrepreneurs will have to act as both risk-creators and risk-bearing individuals.

It is well known that clever manipulation of the blob to shift the risk from risk-creator to outsiders is the norm, not the exception. One of the United States' leading corporate scholars, Mark J. Roe, observes that it is logical for corporate groups engaged in highly risky activities to organize themselves so that all the liabilities for the risks would burden one of the group's members, one whose financial reserves can be kept discrete and minimal.[3] Similarly, in their study of small and medium-sized corporations, A. Ringleb and S. Wiggins found the use of the corporate form to shift responsibility to relatively judgment-proof vehicles to be a frequent driver of incorporation.[4] That is, a major impulse for incorporation is obtaining limited liability, but not for any of the justifying reasons offered by its advocates. It is all too embarrassing—enough to cause some corporate cheerleaders heart-burn. Typically, they worry most when the small corporation's victims are third parties who never had an opportunity to do a self-protecting deal with the corporation.

One suggestion has been that corporations set a mandatory fund aside to meet liabilities to vulnerable non-contracting victims. With some embarrassment, serious corporate scholars and policy-makers argue that, for some purposes, the corporation should act not only as a risk-creator but also as a guarantor of risk materialization. Others argue that, in some situations, limited liability should not be available to the persons behind the corporation.[5] But as these suggestions are made within a framework that retains the legal corporation as the primary wealth-generating institution, the scope of offered reforms is narrow. Mostly it is tailored to aid non-contractual victims. Many potential victims of risk-shifting by corporations are in similar circumstances, even though, in formal terms, they may have contracts with the corporation. This is likely to be true for some suppliers, some independent contractors, some customers, and all workers.

Indeed, while employees are frequently taken to have voluntarily agreed to the terms of employment contracts, this is a misrepresentation of what actually occurs. Workers, by definition, must offer their labour to someone in order to live. If they are fortunate, they may have a choice of to whom they can sell their labour. It is a stretch to call the ensuing contracts of labour voluntary. But if the removal of limited liability were made available to workers because they are to be characterized as involuntary risk-takers, as people who have not freely chosen to work for another, it would open up a debate about the nature of the work-for-wages contract, a debate that no defender of the status quo wants to put on the agenda. Hence, the reforms are restricted to formal non-contractual situations, to circumstances where the harm sought to be brought home to the corporate actors is inflicted on parties who have no formal legal connections to the corporations. The remedies on offer are usually not available to contractual relations that functionally bear identical risks.

Still, this modest set of proposals amounts to an admission. Limited liability may not be all it is cracked up to be; it may have horrible impacts.

Indeed, the cautious proposals acknowledge what is blindingly obvious to the lay person not weighed down by a pro-corporate mindset. To ordinary people, educated as they are to be responsible for their own conduct, it seems clear that those who cannot protect themselves against corporate wrongdoers by contracting with them should nonetheless be able to hold to account those actors with deeper pockets who had control over the corporate activities. To the unpolluted mind, this seems a logical application of an established legal principle.

In sum, despite extravagant claims in support of limited liability, it is clear that, at least in the small incorporated firm setting, the promised benefits of granting this extraordinary legal privilege are not delivered. Indeed, this has been acknowledged by many prestigious spokespeople for the conventional wisdom, including some more thoughtful judges. As Rogers, J., for example, wrote:

> Does limited liability serve a socially and economically useful purpose for ninety percent of incorporated companies? Should it not be restricted to public companies and such others as may be able to convince the regulatory authorities they require that privilege for the purposes [of] their trades?[6]

Let us now face that question.

LIABILITY IN PUBLICLY TRADED CORPORATIONS

A pivotal argument of limited liability advocates is that it provides a marvellous incentive for many shareholders to make contributions to create a more diverse universe of efficient corporations. It is these contributions that allow the flourishing of large publicly traded corporations. This turns out to be yet another claim that runs contrary to the on-the-ground facts. Limited liability does little for capital-raising.

In a much-noted article entitled "What Good Are Shareholders?," Justin Fox and Jay W. Lorsch startlingly answered their own question: "Little to none." They explained their negativity:

The most straightforward job of the shareholder is to provide funds.
In practice ... corporations do need capital ... but they don't get it in
aggregate from shareholders. Net issuance of corporate equity in the
U.S. over the past decade has been negative $287 billion.... Factor in
dividend payments, and we find a multi-trillion dollar transfer of cash
from U.S. corporations *to* their shareholders over the past 10 years.
Established corporations tend to finance investments out of retained
earnings or borrowed money. They don't need shareholders' cash.[7]

There were two reasons this article attracted so much attention. First,
it brought back a question that had forced itself on the agenda when it
was thought that management teams, not shareholders, were in control
of corporations, suggesting that shareholders were irrelevant to corporate
welfare. Back in 1963, Adolf A. Berle castigated shareholders as indolent
welfare recipients:

Why have stockholders? What contribution do they make, entitling
them to heirship of half the profits of the industrial system? Shareholders toil not, neither do they spin, to earn that reward. They are beneficiaries by position only.[8]

But this early interrogation of the utility of shareholders had died down,
and conventional wisdom had returned share ownership to a pedestal. It was
thought to make a significant contribution and, therefore, to deserve both
privileges and protections. This confidence was eroded by a series of market
manipulations and fiascos, culminating with Enronitis—the scandals that
swirled around Enron and the ensuing angst in elite circles. This led to new
regulations and solemn pronouncements that the capital and stock markets,
being so essential to corporate well-being, would now work better. But, clearly,
Fox and Lorsch were raising renewed doubts about the efficacy of the reforms.
This brings us to the second reason for the attention gathered by their article.

The writers were mainstream and highly respected ones; the article
was published in that most established of journals, the *Harvard Business*

Review. It was written in the aftermath of the financial crisis that became clearly visible in 2008. Regulators, pundits, and politicians were bemoaning the gyrations and manipulations of the stock and financial markets, even more than they had during the days of Enronitis and its ensuing reforms. Having talked themselves into believing that the days of uncertainty and skullduggery had been left behind, their invigorated reappearance was a source of concern. How could the markets for corporate securities be saved?

While Berle had asked whether shareholders made any contribution at all, Fox and Lorsch asked whether the positive answer that since then had ruled the roost was still correct. Or more sharply, if the answer was no rather than yes and whether, therefore, stock and financial markets deserved to be saved, to be so well respected and so well promoted? They thought not. Coming from them, this was news. But it was not new news.

Well before Fox and Lorsch burst onto the scene, leftist critics of the stock and financial markets had made similar findings. They had been largely ignored by the elites, as this cadre of naysayers usually are until it is too late. Looking at data from the 1980s, Doug Henwood had concluded that the then contemporary stock markets counted for "little or nothing as a source of finance" for corporate purposes.[9] Marjorie Kelly and William Greider had come to the same conclusion.[10] They found that, of all the dollars traded on the U.S. stock exchanges, less than 1 per cent ever reached the corporations to fund growth or operations.

Part of the story they tell is that corporations are active traders in shares. They buy back their own shares, "cleaning up" their balance sheets and increasing the value of outstanding shares. When a corporation buys back its shares, they are cancelled, reducing the total number of issued shares. This favours those who retain their shares, many of which may be owned by corporate insiders who made the decision to have the corporation buy back its shares. Kelly and Greider noted that the U.S. Federal Reserve calculated that, if the money spent by corporations on buy-backs were deducted from the value of new shares issued by them to raise new productive capital, the net amount of capital raised by publicly traded corporations was negative. This, of course, is what worried Fox and Lorsch. It was hard to see how the issuance of shares by corporations does much for the raising of capital.

While corporations need start-up capital, the empirical evidence makes it clear that investors who purchase the issued shares do not contribute anywhere near as much as corporate cheerleaders would have us believe. The buying and selling of shares after a corporation has got going is about making money by trading among bettors on the direction of the shares' future values. To them the corporation becomes a substratum for money-making. The bestowal of limited liability on would-be contributors of capital appears to have lost its raison d'être. It has little to do with its supposed purpose, namely encouraging investors to fund productive ventures. This does not mean that issuing shares serves no useful productive function, as the otherwise critical, but rigorous Fox and Lorsch acknowledge:

> Without shareholders who are willing to take risks that a bank or bondholder would not, [small, young, growing] corporations might remain stuck in low gear.... The investors who provide [them with] cash are usually granted clout.... Venture capitalists and angel funds get board seats and sometimes veto power over management.... and [are] given a say in strategic decisions.... But ... most corporations don't fit these descriptions.

In short, facilitating the raising of capital by giving limited liability to all and any contributors of capital to all and any corporations serves its stated goals only in a narrowly circumscribed set of circumstances.

The Marxist political economists Leo Panitch and Sam Gindin make a case for the utility of raising finance,[11] but it is not based on the idea that limited liability for shareholders' investment in specific corporations is a *sine qua non* to achieve this aim. Rather, they see equity investors as part of an overall scheme of financial wheeling and dealing that aims to create large pools of finance for the sake of capitalism as a whole, rather than for the well-being of individual corporations. They argue that financial capital (whatever its source) bears a symbiotic relation to productive capital, that is, capital that contributes directly to the generation of wealth by the production of goods and services. While at this time, potentially productive corporations are flush with money and do not need financial capital for production, the boom in financial speculation means that corporations find it easy to obtain credit for mergers and takeovers. This is important for the necessary restructuring of markets, and it also furnishes access to finance for venture capitalists and new firms. The abundance of financial capital also makes that capital available as a hedge against currency fluctuations and other shocks.

This analysis sees limited liability as a minor cog that accidentally helps a much larger engine do its thing. But the utility of limited liability to the functioning of corporate capitalism is extremely limited. It does not support an argument that shareholders, alone among our risk-creating individuals, should be granted a special privilege.

AN INDEFENSIBLE PRINCIPLE

Capitalism's project is the private accumulation of wealth which is socially produced. It is greatly advanced by the creation of the corporation for profit. The collectivization of assets and people within one umbrella makes it a useful tool to this end. Law enhances this usefulness in the following ways:

- It treats the corporation as if it were a single person, despite the undeniable fact that it is, and acts as, a collective. This legal sleight of hand allows the corporation to be deemed to be a natural and legitimate player in a market system peopled by actual individuals. This bestows a huge bargaining advantage on those who own and operate corporations.
- To ensure this unfair advantage can be enjoyed by wealth owners, law promotes the formation of corporations by providing enormous incentives to investing capital contributors, allowing them to profit while taking no legal responsibility and limiting their fiscal risk. These legal privileges are defended on the basis that they will lead to more investment in corporations and to a proliferation of more kinds of incorporated businesses.

What is now clear is that this scheme is based on fantasy and falsehoods. A corporate person is not the equivalent of a sentient human being. Claims that the privilege of limited liability contributes in any significant way to the economic efficiency of corporations are not based on facts. Not only does the grant of limited liability not serve the market capitalist purposes for which it is supposedly designed, but it also has a profoundly negative impact, both in market and socio-political terms.

In chasing profits for the privileged investors—whose contributions are so marginal from an efficiency perspective—corporations abuse the spirit of government policies and shift risks to people who have little to no redress. This is why legislators have to step in to give workers, who would otherwise be unsecured creditors, protection. They would not need this protection if the shareholders hiding behind the corporate veil were not safeguarded. That is, the bad publicity for legal immunity and limited liability arising out of the callous treatment of workers has made necessary a search for remedies that will dissipate anger.

A similar thrust is revealed by those who argue that, in some circumstances, third parties who have no opportunity to protect themselves from the harms inflicted by corporations—typically victims of mass torts—should be covered by a contingency fund set aside for those purposes. Interestingly, in a few jurisdictions, this kind of fund is also the protection provided for workers in the case of a corporation's insolvency, acknowledging the great similarity between many voluntary and involuntary creditors. Other commentators have suggested that it might be appropriate to remove the privilege of limited liability for shareholders in these kinds of cases. But whatever solution is proposed, its purpose is to leave the principle of limited liability intact, while warding off the oft-justified dismay and anger caused by its more obvious abuses and nasty impacts.

In short, there is plenty of evidence, especially in the small-business sectors, that many people know that the privilege being defended is indefensible both in principle and in fact. In this sphere, there is no net benefit and there is much unredressed harm. But the intellectual gatekeepers for the limited liability corporation keep on truckin', despite their misgivings. One fear is that if limited liability were abolished in the small-firm setting, that would give rise to similar empirically based challenges in the large, publicly traded blob-o-sphere. And in the large publicly traded sectors, we have seen that the role of limited liability hardly ever serves the major purpose its adherents claim, namely the raising of needed capital. That is, the issue of the inutility of limited liability in so many circumstances would push itself to the front and centre of the political debate.

This is not to be countenanced. The unacknowledged purpose of the whole corporate capitalism exercise is to serve the owners of most of the wealth, the dominant class. Mere economic efficiency for the general good is a fig leaf. Under it, the owners of wealth are trying to accumulate as much as possible for their private coffers, efficiency and general welfare be damned.

Once the question about the utility of limited liability does arise, however, it bites. The fig leaf is not very well fastened. We know that little of the capital provided by shareholders contributes to the actual production of goods and services. And historically, the granting of limited liability was seriously contested, precisely because it would lead to abuses, to irresponsibility and a rending of the social fabric. Limited liability is not like one of the Ten Commandments, inerasably inscribed on a stone tablet. It can be attacked, modified, or abrogated without doing violence to any of our fundamental values. To the contrary: direct attacks on the concept of limited liability are likely to advance the quest for a decent society. But they might make the corporate vehicle less attractive.

How bad could that be?

Social Welfare

THERE IS, TODAY, WIDESPREAD DISCONTENT WITH THE MORE OBVIOUS abuses of corporate capitalism. Nonetheless, its proponents argue, the corporation is a vehicle not only for the enrichment of the corporate class, but also for the public good. Let us examine how that claim plays out.

THE GROWTH METRIC

Capitalism's hymn book asks us to sing along with its message that more is better than less. And more is measured by the money that is generated by economic activity. This is reflected in the way we calculate the gross domestic product (GDP), a tool commonly used to measure the overall welfare of an economy. Investopedia defines the GDP as "the monetary value of all the finished goods and services produced within a country's borders in a specific time period.... [It] includes all of private and public consumption, government outlays, investments and exports less imports." This monetary measure of wealth is a crude one: if productive activity does not generate money, it is to be ignored.

But as famed Indian scholar and ecofeminist Vandana Shiva puts it in "Two Myths That Keep the World Poor":

> [One] myth is an assumption that if you consume what you produce,
> you do not really produce, at least not economically speaking. If I grow

my own food, and do not sell it, then it doesn't contribute to GDP, and therefore does not contribute towards "growth.".... Yet sustenance living, which the wealthy West perceives as poverty, does not necessarily mean a low quality of life. On the contrary, by their very nature economies based on sustenance ensure a high quality of life measured in terms of access to good food and water, opportunities for sustainable livelihoods, robust social and cultural identity, and a sense of meaning in people's lives.[1]

Similarly, investment guru Warren Buffett has said:

If I wanted to, I could hire 10,000 people to do nothing but paint my picture every day for the rest of my life. And the [GDP] would go up. But the utility of the product would be zilch and I would be keeping those 10,000 people from doing AIDS research or teaching, or nursing...[2]

And political theorist and environmental scholar Robyn Eckersley argues that growth in the domestic product of a nation cannot adequately measure well-being, as long as it ignores the impacts on the environment, unpaid household work, care for the sick, and acts of love.[3]

Crude though the GDP metric is, it does reflect the capitalist ethos. If the GDP grows, it means that monetary wealth has grown—and growth is good. It does not matter how that growth comes about. We have seen plenty of examples of the indifference this approach breeds. The search for growth in the pile of money to be privately accumulated is to be advanced by forcing all of us to compete in free markets, using our talents and resources as we try to meet our needs and desires.

Corporations, made up by pooled capital and personnel, supported by risk-shifting corporate law, are well designed to serve this capitalist agenda. They produce goods and services and they lend and borrow money; they form a substratum for speculation, giving rise to more accumulations of money. In all of these ways, they contribute to monetary growth. Vast amounts of monetary wealth are held in, are generated by, and swirl around corporations. Their defenders emphasize these outcomes. Corporations are not just benefactors to their shareholders and personnel but, because they contribute to GDP, they are cast as positive contributors to society's overall welfare. Corporations are not just good for themselves, they are good for all of us.

If it could be maintained, this line of reasoning would blunt the impact of many of the arguments made in this work, which has questioned the legitimacy of corporate personhood for the blob and of legal immunity and limited liability for its shareholders. If corporations, in the end, are positive wealth-generating instruments, then, whatever failings are due to their special privileges, they serve a most important function and we might not be able to afford to lose them. Any limitations imposed on the separate personhood of the corporation or on the privilege of legal immunity and limited liability that threatened personal wealth would remove major incentives to invest in corporations. The supposedly daring investors would be put off by having to bear some of the costs the corporations absorb or impose on others.

This last argument, highlighting as it does the risk-averse nature of flesh-and-blood capitalists, is not one the defenders of the blob-o-sphere want to make explicitly. This is why, when pushed, they advance the utilitarian claim that corporations are an ideal tool for a well-oiled capitalist economy and a well-off society. This argument depends on two claims:

- a quantitative claim: corporations contribute positively to overall wealth in monetary terms
- a qualitative claim: corporations contribute positively to society's overall welfare in terms of quality of life

The first claim has some, albeit highly contestable, plausibility; the second, none at all. Let us turn to these two related claims.

THE TRUE COSTS OF GROWTH

In terms of numbers, though not of significance, the overwhelming majority of firms registered as corporations are very small firms. They do not serve as effective tools for growth in monetary terms, as they do not pool together lots of discrete capital that can then be more efficiently deployed than they would be individually; they do not gather together sufficient resources, experts, and people to make a real dent in transaction costs. From these perspectives, when it comes to making a contribution to the generation of monetary wealth, they are not much more effective than the individuals who run these businesses would be if they conducted them as unincorporated firms. We know, then, what these small corporations do not do. We also know what they do do, and it is not pretty.

Incorporation allows the small-firm operators to make it difficult for regulators to implement their standards as society expects them to be applied. It allows the owners, their families, and their friends to divvy up the corporation's yields so as to minimize the impost of taxes. And perhaps most importantly, incorporation gives them the oft-used opportunity to let honest creditors and workers hold the bag they have emptied out, forcing legislators to furnish band-aid remedies and victims to take expensive legal actions or rely on welfare programs to relieve their plight. These kinds of corporations undermine trust in society. Creditors and employees learn that they cannot rely on contracts, let alone on promises. The interposition of a corporate vehicle between a small-business owner and the world makes for roguish behaviour which the law, regulators, and governments—with their professed love of small business and their formalistic view of corporate law—appear unable to prevent or remedy. Incorporated small firms do not by the mere fact of their incorporation add to monetary growth, but they do undermine many aspects of our shared values and norms. By corporate capitalism's own metric, they are a bust. Why would we miss them?

In medium-sized and large corporations, there is an economic advantage to bringing parcels of capital and numbers of people together to be deployed by expert, co-ordinating managers. There could be savings on transaction costs, as the size and scope of some of these corporations should make them less dependent on outsiders. There will be more goods and services produced than otherwise would have been. There will be more diverse and innovative investment, as wealth owners spread their capital around. There will be more importing and exporting, more lending and borrowing, more speculators betting on the enterprises' success or failure, and more brokers, commission agents, professional service providers, more insurers… In short, there will be many more money-generating activities, all adding to wealth as measured by money.

But in and of itself, this does not make the case that corporations add either to overall monetary growth or to quality of life. Indeed, it is counter-intuitive to think that the corporate contributions to social welfare will be positive. As John Maynard Keynes is reputed to have said, "Capitalism is the astounding belief that the most wicked of men will do the most wickedest of things for the greatest good of all." Capitalism is anarchic: all corporations act in their own interests. It is the sum of all the blobs' selfish activities that is measured when GDP is calculated and presented as evidence that corporations contribute positively to overall social welfare. But this does not mean that the pursuit of profits by any one corporation adds to that welfare. Entrepreneurs who wrap themselves in corporate garb do it because the corporate form blesses them with certain legal privileges.

American scholar Kent Greenfield calls these privileges subsidies.[4] They are gifts from society, he argues, because the recipient corporation is expected to deliver a benefit to that same society. This means that any one corporation must demonstrate that the net result of its activities is positive for society. It is not persuasive to hold that, because corporations may add to overall monetary growth, a particular corporation has earned the right to be subsidized. Each corporation should earn its own stripes. It is not sufficient for a corporation to book a profit; it cannot be allowed to say that it has contributed merely by pointing to a healthy bank balance or the value of its dividends and shares or the wages it pays. It must subtract the costs that are imposed on others and on their physical and cultural environments. Only if the costs inflicted on the monetary and social welfare of others are smaller than the benefits that can be directly attributed to it does a corporation have a positive impact on society.

By way of example, a car manufacturer produces a number of cars and creates a number of jobs. The economic benefits this brings should be offset by the costs of its operations. There are costs to the environment, and harms done by the way resources were obtained to build the cars and then by the way those cars are used. There is an impact on congestion and on the availability of other forms of transport, a burden of health costs that includes costs to the health system and losses resulting from the inability of the injured and dead to contribute to social welfare, the costs of litigation and insurance arising from the nature and outcomes of the manufacturing, and so on.

If the corporate form is meant to serve the public, not just its promoters and investors, it can, then, be appropriate to foster it by means of subsidies. Greenfield's argument demands that we acknowledge that corporations have an enforceable social responsibility. This kind of calculus might find a lot of corporations wanting.

Take General Motors, for example. It was in the news recently because it was found that it knew for more than a decade that some of its small cars had faulty ignition switches. It did not tell anyone. The ignition switches would slip out of the "on" position, causing the cars to stall, knocking out the power steering and turning off the airbags. Accidents followed. A large number, it turns out. The admitted toll at the time of writing is 124 deaths and many more injured persons.[5] Despite the horrendous toll, GM was allowed to do a deal: it is to pay close to one billion dollars by way of a penalty in return for prosecutors deferring prosecutions for at least three years (read: likely forever) and with no indictments to be sworn against any GM employees.

Similarly, Hyundai has been prosecuted by the U.S. National Highway Transportation Administration board and paid a fine for failing to report a defect affecting its braking systems, a defect about which it knew and which led to accidents.[6] Honda had not reported (as it was required to do) that, during a ten-year period, it had received 1,729 claims in respect of injuries or deaths alleged to be due to defective Honda vehicles; again, a fine settled the issue.[7] Toyota had faulty gas pedals that would make its cars accelerate suddenly. For a while, it pretended that the cause could be blamed on floor mats but, after twelve deaths, it admitted it had concealed a known defect. Toyota paid a hefty fine.[8] Fiat Chrysler was also fined for not reporting death and injury claims it had received, based on alleged defects in its cars. It paid a fine. Even more recently, the scandal at Volkswagen around installing a so-called defeat device that reduced emissions when the cars were being tested, and allowed them to pollute when in normal use, has caused a furor. It is estimated by *Bloomberg* that the cars on the road in the United States are polluting as much as forty times the legal limit.[9]

In these cases, some specific costs imposed as a result of profit-chasing by corporations became visible. In large part, this is because they involved violations of an existing set of rules. Monetary growth was increased because cars were produced and sold, even as existing standards were violated. But imagine if all the externalized costs of these apparently routine wrongdoings were weighed against the corporate profit statements. They would sharply reduce the contribution to social benefit such a cost-displacing corporation should be entitled to claim.

So, too, with McDonald's and Walmart. These outfits, legally, pay their employees such poor wages that they know that many of them will have to rely on government aid to make ends meet. McDonald's in the United States has set up a McResources Line, a help line to teach its needy employees how to apply for food stamps and get on Medicaid, a government-funded health plan. The contribution of McDonald's to social welfare might reasonably be discounted by this transfer of costs to the public. In 2004, Walmart's pay scales were so low that the federal U.S. taxpayer had to subsidize Walmart to the tune of two thousand dollars per annum for every one of its employees, as so many of them would have to call on the welfare systems.[10] More subsidies, as if the legal one which Greenfield wants to have justified is not enough of a boon to the corporate sectors!

In a 2011 report, the Canadian Public Health Association found that alcohol is the second leading contributor to death, disease, and disability. In 2002, the costs of alcohol consumption in Canada led to an estimated $17 billion in lost productivity, an increase in $3.3 billion in health care expenses, and another $3.1 billion in law enforcement costs. Another report, done for the Centre for Addictions Research in British Columbia, found that a 10 per cent increase in liquor stores during 2002 to 2009 was associated with a 2 per cent rise in alcohol-related deaths.[11] Any claim that the incorporated breweries, wine merchants, and other alcohol-related businesses (and the revenue-reaping government) benefit society merely by their legal-ized producing and selling would have less resonance if these horrendous monetary and social outcomes were taken into account.

Similarly, we have noted how incorporated retailers benefit from shifting costs onto vulnerable workers in poverty-stricken countries. For example, in 2013 one action group, the International Labor Rights Forum, called on people to boycott the major clothing chain H&M to force it to put safeguards into place to ensure that it would not sell clothing that was made from cot-ton sourced from fields on which some two million enslaved children work in Uzbekistan. The Pulitzer Center reported that the Democratic Republic of Congo uses its powers to force children to dig for columbite and tantalum, materials needed to produce coltan, an essential component of laptops and smart phones. In 2014, Carl Gibson, summarizing the Pulitzer Center report, noted that children as young as thirteen, earning less than two dollars a day, worked without rudimentary safety protections and that some died from sheer exhaustion because the conditions of work are brutal. He goes on: "Multinational corporations like Apple, Samsung, Dell, and HP all depend on the Congolese mining ... as 80 percent of the world's coltan supply comes from the region. The children have no other option ... because school is beyond the financial means of ordinary Congolese families."[12] Again, the huge amounts of money generated for corporations by these large, intercon-nected transactions would be less of a contribution to overall welfare if the monetary and social losses incurred by others were deducted.

This is why conventional corporate defenders reject this kind of met-ric when evaluating the utility of corporations. They prefer to stick with the argument that everything is to be measured by the aggregated corpor-ate contribution to growth as measured by money. When it comes to social benefit, these people argue, overall monetary growth benefits everyone. Not necessarily to the same extent, but everyone all the same. From this start-ing point, the externalized costs paraded above do not provide them with much of a problem. The imposition of costs on others and the environment by risk-shifting blobs forces others to take actions that generate volumes of money that, in turn, add to the GDP. The increased spending on health, insurance, and litigation that is necessitated, for which there now is a voluntary demand, does wonders for growth as measured by the metric of the GDP. Thus, rather than subtract these undesired consequences, many of them should be added to the good any one corporation does.

Hey, presto, the unwanted outcomes of corporate profit-chasing do not, in and of themselves, prove that corporations do not contribute positively to overall welfare—provided it is measured by money. It is in this kind of framework, and only in this kind of framework, that a case may be made that corporations, singly and in the aggregate, contribute to overall welfare. But this is a framework devoid of sensibility to widely held human values. Acerbically, noted Canadian political philosopher John McMurtry wrote that "no more malignant mutation of value and meaning has ever occurred."[13]

WEALTH AND "ILLTH"

In all of the illustrations used—and in countless others that might have been used—there were outcomes we do not want to experience. They do not go away just because the intellectual gatekeepers for the blob-o-sphere do not attach any monetary value to them. Deaths and physical injuries affect the victims' well-being and that of their relations in monetary terms and, to this extent, they are given a value. But they also affect people in hard-to-monetize terms. Harms done to respect for laws, to the dignity of exploited people and to their cultures, to their traditional ways of life, and to the quality of their physical environments adversely affect overall social and economic welfare. The fact that by using the corporate metric these costs—these psychic, human, social, legal, cultural, environmental costs—are not counted does not make them less real. If a further example is needed to make this obvious point, let us return to a story already partly told.

In 2004, a young woman crashed her car into a tree. Her boyfriend was killed. In 2007 she pleaded guilty to criminally negligent homicide. She was spared jail time but had suffered serious depression. It turns out that the crash was due to the failure of one of those now notoriously defective ignition switches in a GM car. General Motors had not let anyone know about this problem, although its own analysis of the crash had led it to believe that there had been a mechanical malfunction. In 2014, the young woman was given a pardon. She may or may not get compensation, and it should be easier for her to get a job now that she no longer has a homicide conviction on her CV. All this makes her happier. But as she told the *New York Times*, the best part is that a great cloud has been lifted, as she no longer feels guilty about having killed her boyfriend. And she said that someday she would tell the story of her exoneration to her children: "My heart is going to be a lot lighter to be able to tell them, 'This is what happened, this horrible thing. And it wasn't Mommy's fault.'"[14]

There are many such collateral impacts, collateral in the sense that they are of no importance to the way in which corporate capitalism wants to be evaluated. They are, however, vitally important to the way in which we, non-capitalists, live our lives. They should, therefore, play a pivotal role in evaluating the status of our overall social welfare. They may well, both in quantitative and qualitative terms, rival or outstrip the supposedly positive monetary contributions made by corporations.

English art critic and social commentator John Ruskin pointed to the need to recognize that social and economic activities yield both good and bad outcomes. Ruskin observed that, as "ill" is the opposite of "well," the cleverly coined word *illth* should be juxtaposed with *wealth* to capture the two-sided impact of economic activities.[15] University of Maryland professor Herman Daly provides a catalogue of some of the ills—or "bads," as he calls them—that should be taken into account as we try to get a handle on how well we are doing under corporate capitalism:

> Climate change from excess carbon in the atmosphere; radioactive wastes and risks of nuclear power plants; biodiversity loss; depleted mines; deforestation; eroded topsoil; dry wells, rivers, and aquifers; the dead zone in the Gulf of Mexico; gyres of plastic trash in the oceans; the ozone hole; exhausting and dangerous labor; and the un-repayable debt from trying to push growth in the symbolic financial sector beyond what is possible in the real sector (not to mention military expenditures to maintain access to global resources).[16]

It is quite a list but, nonetheless, a very incomplete catalogue of the bads that accompany our chosen means of generating wealth. These long-lasting disasters or disasters-in-waiting detract from society's overall welfare, but in corporate capitalism's cost-benefit scales, they do not count. These bads are considered valueless unless their removal or repair involves the production of goods and services, government expenditures, or the like. They are ignored when corporate cheerleaders assess the blobs' contribution to welfare. The physical and environmental impacts, their visual ugliness, obviously affect the quality of our lives. More, their debilitating effect on life itself is staggering. All this is ignored. For example, in 2007, WHO (Global Atmospheric Pollution Forum) estimated that, annually, around 800,000 people died prematurely because of pollutants in the ambient air.

The American scholar Lisa Heinzerling captures the profound moral emptiness of the corporate capitalist approach.[17] Her work emphasizes what she calls the "mismatch between ethical values and economic evaluation," one that leads to distorted thinking and, therefore, inefficiencies in our efforts to lead better lives.[18] Heinzerling's argument is that knowingly killing human beings is undoubtedly seen as a moral wrong, one frequently punished by law. She contends that environmental policy-making should take this into account. The knowing creation of risks that may bring about deaths should be part of the calculus of business planners and regulators when balancing anticipated benefits against unhidden and hidden costs. Normally this is not done, even though, as she documents,

> [there] are clearly established links between many common environmental contaminants and human mortality. Fine particulates in the ambient air kill tens of thousands of people every year in the United States alone. Widely used chemicals such as vinyl chloride pose risks of lethal cancer and other diseases. Greenhouse gases contributing to climate change will cause increased incidence of human disease, in addition to having many other health-related effects ... pollution kills people and makes them sick, and in many cases we can expect death as a consequence of pollution.

Such an approach seriously undermines the claim that, on balance, the corporations' helter-skelter pursuit of growth as measured by money makes them indispensable to our overall social welfare. A more ethical starting point demands that we take life and the quality of life seriously when evaluating the contribution of activities motivated by corporate monetary growth. This is a demand for brute sanity, a commodity eschewed by the corporate world's cheerleaders. John McMurtry passionately argues that, if we allow ourselves to be caught within the framework of what he calls the pseudo-science of the dominant corporate capitalist model, there is no way to show that its premises are wrong, even as the world collapses around us.

From a life-affirming perspective, the claim that we must not inhibit the flourishing of corporations by attacking the special privileges of legal personhood, legal immunity, and limited liability loses much of its credibility. Yet the stubborn claim that corporations make a positive contribution to social welfare persists. It dominates our discourses and policy-making. This has some further grave consequences.

There is a correlation between accepting corporate capitalism's favoured evaluation technique—using an increase in money growth as the arbiter of the contribution to overall welfare—and the law's and policy-makers' failure to force corporations to take adequate precautions. Governments stand by and welcome growth activities. They have internalized the neo-liberal scholarly arguments and the corresponding messaging in popular media; they are serenaded and bribed and threatened by the blobs' emissaries and functionaries and are convinced by the self-serving claims made for profit-chasing blobs. They assume that the end result, the generation of more money wealth, justifies the assumption that corporations are engaged in virtuous activities. The processes, technologies, materials, and substances the corporations use to make money are presumed to be innocent until proved guilty beyond reasonable doubt.

This has given profit-maximizing blobs a green light. They intensify labour by introducing new technologies and more mechanization. They use more and more untested substances in workplaces, introducing harmful chemicals into the air and water all around us and into the bodies of the workers directly exposed to them. In a Mt. Sinai School of Medicine study for the Center of Disease Control in 2003,[19] one worker had ninety-five toxic elements in her body, fifty-nine of which were known carcinogens. She bristled that she had never given consent to this kind of invasion of her body. More generally, as Heinzerling documents, the ambient air and water and soil are poisoned and become inherently dangerous, rather than nurturing.

This is no accident. Corporations decide how much to invest, for what reason, and for how long. They decide where to invest, and what kinds of processes, technologies, substances, and levels of skills are required. This is called business planning. It is considered a good thing to do, because it should lead to success. But it also establishes the level of risks the corporate undertaking creates for its workers, the community, consumers, and the environment. These risks are pictured as the collateral, unintended effects of innocent and rational business planning.

This means that the initial reaction to any harms that are inflicted when the risks materialize is that they are accidents; they are regrettable, but blameless, outcomes. Regulators may bring in new rules that will require future undertakings to take some of the now-known risks into account. The framework in which this takes place—stemming from the proposition that growth is good and those who pursue it virtuous—means that even well-intentioned regulators are at a structural disadvantage. Growth, as measured by money, is the holy grail, and those who search for it are do-gooders. The means used are presumed noble. Moreover, the impact of any restraints regulators impose will be blunted by the fact that the intended beneficiaries of corporate profit-maximization are legally irresponsible and fiscally protected, inveigling them to have their corporations push back on the regulations.

The regulatory framework is, characteristically, reactive rather than proactive. And when regulators determine that they must act, they are met with a chorus of plaintive cries that they are liable to kill the goose that lays the golden eggs. That is, they are met with the argument that corporations will contribute positively to overall welfare, provided that they are left to do their own planning so that they can make money. They do not intend to do any harm; accidents will happen, but so be it. This sets a stage tilted in favour of wealth owners at the expense of everyone and everything else. Corporate capitalism's preferred metric makes corporations dangerous.

Of course, if violations of existing regulatory standards are adjudged to be due to obvious negligence, recklessness, or malevolence, they will be punished. That kind of behaviour is positively deviant. And as we have seen throughout this work, there is plenty of that; indeed, there is so much of it that it should not be seen as aberrational. The wrongdoing never seems to abate. As this is being written, a few clippings on my desk should suffice to make that point.

Bribery charges are being brought against SNC-Lavalin, one of Canada's blue-ribbon corporations, which earned such a reputation for getting its contracts by bribery that it had to agree not to bid on World Bank contracts for ten years. GlaxoSmithKline is fined for maintaining a "massive bribery network," and JPMorgan is alleged to have paid eighty thousand dollars a month to the Chinese premier's daughter. Hershey is fined for conspiracy to fix chocolate prices, an Ontario firm for fixing gas prices, and Scotiabank is named in a silver price-fixing suit. Lying remains in fashion in corporate circles, as firms are taken to task for destroying evidence or running Ponzi schemes. And the golden oldies of money laundering and dubious tax avoidance feature in the news on a regular basis.[20]

This rather random sampling should be enough: actual violations of regulatory rules and the absence of ethical consciousness are common, and they cause a great deal of harm to immediate victims, to the legitimacy of the system, and to respect for law. There is much obvious illth, but these disagreeable practices all add to wealth as measured by the favoured yardstick. Huge amounts of money are generated by these malpractices, adding to the GDP. Bad behaviour does not, in itself, mean that the blobs are making no positive contribution to overall welfare measured in this way. The money metric, the growth metric, leads to distortions which become blatantly obvious when the harms done by corporate actors are the outcome of illegal conduct.

But focusing attention on clearly deviant behaviour leads to an even more egregious misdirection. It reinforces a tendency to think that all other corporate conduct—conduct that does not actually violate an enforceable standard—is virtuous and contributes positively to our overall welfare. The ills in the long and depressing lists of such non-law-violating profit-chasing often inflict harms silently, over long periods of time. They rarely even make it to the scales that should be used to weigh the utility of the blobs. Our law- and opinion-makers look for positive bad actions when they want to assess the need to regulate or to inhibit corporate actions.

But all too often, it is the omission of taking the risks to others into account that has such detrimental effects on society. Liverpool professor David Whyte, addressing the slaughter in the U.K. workplace, argues that the evidence is in:

> We can say with little doubt that the minority of deaths caused by working can be regarded purely as "misfortunes" or "accidents" which were not avoidable. In other words, the majority of deaths at work do not result from "out of control" or haphazard circumstances, but are the result of decisions or non-decisions that could—if they were investi- gated—be traced to the authors of those decisions.[21]

The omission to take precautions becomes a routine and sensible cor- porate practice if we accept the starting point that corporations, if left alone, will make a positive contribution to overall welfare. But this is an unproven assertion, not a given truth. This is why this book has emphasized that it is the failure by those who could take action, namely, controlling shareholders, that should be held to be the active ingredient in the large numbers of wrongs done and harms inflicted. Civil or criminal actions against these controllers for their failure to diminish the risks of their profit-chasing activities have the potential to reveal the genesis of much of the illth inflicted on society. They could clarify how much harm could be avoided by refusing to accept the starting positions proffered by the blob-o-sphere's defenders.

THE ROLE OF FINANCIAL CAPITAL

The importance of financial capital as a feature of contemporary capital- ism is not to be doubted, although the implications of its significance are a matter of great controversy. This discussion of the topic merely raises some of the aspects that relate to the issue of concern here, namely, whether the corporation may have a claim to utility after all.

It is plain that a lot of money-yielding activity swirls around the blob-o-sphere. Given the preferred growth metric, there is a danger that the financial capital floating in and around corporations may be taken as part of the contributions corporations make to our overall welfare. Obviously, there is a connection between corporations and the ever-increasing financialization of capital. The fact that corporations are a component of the financial fabric from which money is spun as if it is going out of style, however, does not go to the raison d'être for corporations: they are to engage in trade and the production of goods and services. It is because they are supposed to be the best vehicle to fulfill those kinds of wealth-creating functions that they are constituted by law as they are. This is the reason that justifies the entitlements that corporate functionaries and shareholders enjoy. But corporations' core role as efficient productive engines is not advanced much by the huge pools of money that flow around them.

Corporations that want to raise money from the general public are listed on stock markets. Via stock market exchanges, investors contribute capital to corporations searching for profits by trading and by producing goods and services. A very large amount of money goes through these exchanges. Should all this money be credited to listed corporations as part of the contribution they make to monetary growth? Not all. We have already seen that not much—in fact, truly trivial amounts—of shareholders' money goes to capitalize corporations. While such investments are significant when a start-up firm is launched or when it is hard for an enterprise to raise money from lenders, they do not do anything much to advance the trading or production of goods and services by the established corporations which issue these securities. For the most part, share trading's direct contribution to growth generated by corporations' core functions is minor. The breathless moment-by-moment reports on the gyrations in the number of shares sold and bought, their overall trajectory in value, and the rise and fall in price of particular stocks are mostly about secondary trading. In other words, about shareholders selling and buying from each other, not about investors putting money directly into productive corporations.

There is a great deal of writing about the nature of share trading, about its ability to reflect the state and prospects of a particular corporate entity, or whether it is a surrogate for the state of the economy as a whole; there are a variety of theories about how investors should choose where and when to put their money. None of this need detain us here. The ins and outs of secondary share trading do not address our main concern. While vast sums change hands every day, by itself this does not signal positive contributions to overall welfare, either by the traders or by the corporations that spawn the securities that they trade.

If shareholders hang onto their shares in a corporation for the long term, they may be rewarded if it proves a good investment over time. Conversely, if the corporation does not fare well, they may suffer a loss. Trading in shares— as opposed to holding onto them—leads, in the aggregate, to quite a different outcome. It is widely accepted by the pundits that share trading is a zero-sum game. Each time people sell shares because they believe the price they can get for them is as good as they are likely to obtain, the purchasers are willing to pay that price because they believe that the value of the shares will increase. If the price does decrease, the loss by the buyers will equal the amount the sellers gain. There will have been a transfer of wealth, not a net gain. There will have been, for the purposes of the growth metric, no added wealth.

Political scientist Elmer Altvater has shown that the frenzied increase in stock market activities in the United States after the Clinton administration's deregulation had little to do with economic developments, although the money that flowed was recorded as part of the GDP's growth.[22] This does not imply that there are no individual winners and losers. Some traders might be luckier, cleverer or, although it is a no-no, have useful information that others do not have, putting them on the winning side more often than less lucky, less clever, and less informed ones. But overall, it is still a zero-sum game.

All this remains true even if the securities being traded are fancy instruments based on the normal shares issued by corporations when raising capital. Appropriately, such instruments are described as derivatives. The instruments are bewildering in their complexity and are daily being elaborated into ever more complex ones, but the central notion is not so difficult to grasp.

Let us go back to a time when, to bet at the horse races, the bet had to be placed with a bookmaker. The bookmaker would offer odds on the horses in a race, based on the bookmaker's insight into the ability of the horses, trainers, jockeys, past performances, recent track trials, and so on. Bettors would choose their horses. Behind the bookmaker stood a colleague watching the odds competing bookmakers were offering on the same field of horses. If this monitor observed changes in odds offered by other bookmakers, indicating a new plunge on a particular horse, he would assume that the competing bookmakers had shortened the odds on that horse to limit their potential losses should the horse prove victorious. Our bookmaker, advised of this "market" trend, would change his odds or place bets on that newly favoured horse. If it won, it would not cost him as much as his previously longer odds on that horse would have dictated. He would have hedged his bets. He would have reallocated the risks he had taken in the market as new price information had come to hand.

That is the role of derivatives. A variety of derivatives are used by risk-allocators. There are futures contracts. These are bets made by people on the price of the commodities in respect of which securities have been issued. Bets are taken by the parties entering into a contract with each other whereby one agrees to provide, the other to accept, delivery of the commodity at a set price by a specific date. This allows each of them to take a guess (based on research, hunch, or otherwise unavailable information) as to where the commodity price will be on a particular day. The wagerers are able to shift some of the risks they face should the price of the commodity in which they have invested unexpectedly fluctuate. These contracts may be sold on to others willing to speculate on the price of the commodity. In turn, such speculation may affect the price of the commodity, as it gives signals to the commodities markets.

The other major kinds of derivatives are called options; some are known as "puts," some as "calls." Options permit someone to buy a security at a particular price by a given date, or a seller may be forced to sell. Options can be based on the equities issued by one corporation or on the securities issued by a group of corporations in related spheres of enterprise. These calculations are not done by a human being thinking quickly on the spot at a racetrack, but by computers programmed to operate sophisticated formulas calculating chances as they process new data about market prices. This happens at lightning speed, giving it an air of scientific decision-making. But basically, it is still a bookmaking exercise. Options allow holders of interests to lay off some of the risks they have assumed in acquiring those interests.

Ultimately, while there will be some who win more consistently than others, in the aggregate this trading of instruments remains a zero-sum game. More importantly in this context, it is not so much the corporation as an engine of production that is key to this generation of monetary flows. Rather, the corporation provides a platform for these exciting chance-taking pursuits. The pursuits do not go to the core functions of vehicles perceived as efficient instruments designed to generate wealth by their enhanced productive capacities.

Colloquially, all this trading and betting is differentiated from what is termed "the real economy," where goods and services are produced and sold. This is significant. After all, special privileges showered on corporations because their legal architecture supposedly enables them to contribute more to our overall well-being, enhancing their capacity to engage in trade and to produce goods and services. It is not acceptable to change that claim to hold that the corporations' real value is tangential to that traditional form of wealth creation, that its utility to our welfare is not so much as a producer of goods and services but rather as a platform for speculation. If this is to be the justification for the corporation's existence, there is no reason why it should have legal personhood or its shareholders have legal immunity and limited fiscal responsibility. The huge flows of money that cascade around these financial markets should not be seen as an indication that the corporate form is a positive contributor to overall wealth.

Many people do profit from the churning of corporate securities: the brokers and commission agents, their paid advisers and phalanxes of analysts and technical professionals, the underwriters of those who create security devices or who incur debts to engage in the gambling game. Given that the overall result of the actual trading is merely a transfer of wealth between sellers and buyers, the commissions paid to the facilitators mean that trading results in an overall loss. The traders' exchanges offset each other, leading to no new wealth creation, but the commissions need to be subtracted. And the sums are not insubstantial. The more trading the commission agents and their technical and funding associates and professionals can encourage, the more money they are likely to earn. As was noted in chapter 6, this gives them reasons to talk up markets and prospects, to form alliances with well-placed people inside corporations, to invent new products (a term used without any sense of irony) on which to bet. There is potential for the corrosion of trust and confidence in the markets as the facilitating intermediaries compete fiercely with each other to get traders' business. This produces another ill that is hard to measure in monetary terms, but an ill nonetheless.

All this trading does have a purpose. It allows people, including corporations, to hedge some of the risks of their investments. As well, the continuous evaluation of what securities are worth, as assessed by sellers and buyers, acts as a useful price mechanism. And we noted in chapter 11 that the large amounts of money that are generated create liquidity that helps borrowing, that makes it easier to rationalize the deployment of industrial capital by facilitating mergers and takeovers. This may lead to greater efficiencies.

But in the end, what is occurring is that contemporary capitalists make more money by engaging in transactions than they do by producing goods and services to be traded in markets. The share of profits made by what is often called FIRE—the sectors comprised by finance, insurance, and real estate—has grown much faster than that of sectors of industry that lead to trade and the production of goods and services. This creates rivers of money that are looking for investment opportunities. Large investment funds have taken up some of the roles that used to be the domain of traditional banks. Private equity funds, which are non-publicly-traded enterprises, buy assets rather than engage in trade or the production of goods and services. And hedge funds—large pools of capital gathered by fund managers who accept contributions only from very wealthy people and extremely high income earners—specialize in risk allocation, rather than productive entrepreneurism. Such funds are fast replacing more traditional banks as financial intermediaries. This is forcing traditional banks to change their business model, as they become more commercial in orientation.

All of this financial activity has had immense political economic impacts. The owners and controllers of these huge amounts of money look for returns. They are willing to bet on derivative instruments that stray further and further from the assets and operations on which they were based. Thus, looking for more investment opportunities, mortgage funders (banks and other fund managers) paid commission agents to sell mortgages at any cost, even to those manifestly incapable of repaying the debts incurred. The mortgages were bundled, sold off to a special entity with a good reputation, leaving the original, rather uncaring, lending institution in the black. The holder of all these mortgages had bundles of them "appraised" as potentially safe and remunerative investment opportunities and sold them, and then, they were sold off again and again. Eventually, as the initial borrowers failed and the housing market bubble these newly enabled purchasers had help create burst, many people were left holding worthless securities. The former U.S. secretary of labor, Robert Reich, in a January 2015 blog,[23] said that the financial crisis connected to the sub-prime collapse was linked to 23 million people in the United States losing their jobs, another 9.3 million losing their health insurance, and one million their homes. Illth aplenty. Leaving aside the deceptive practices, the story is indicative of financial capitalists' ravenous hunger for ever more investment opportunities.

This frenzied drive to pursue wealth, not by producing goods and services but by financial selling and buying of instruments, has added greatly to the pressures put on governments to privatize the public services they have rendered in the past, giving the financiers more opportunities to make money. Michael Hudson, a professor of economics at the University of Missouri, writes:

Financial elites are demanding privatization sell-offs from debt-strapped governments. Pressure is brought bear on Detroit to sell off its most valuable paintings and statues from its art museums. The idea is to sell their art works for tycoons to buy as trophies, with the money being used to pay bondholders.... [A] new neo-feudal rentier class [is] eager to buy roads to turn into toll roads, to buy parking meters (as in Chicago's notorious deal), to buy prisons, schools and other basic infrastructures. The aim is to build financial charges and tollbooth rents into the prices charged for access to these essential, hitherto public services.[24]

As the new intermediaries, the makers and shakers of mammoth financial funds lend money to governments and, to ensure repayment, require governments to save money by cutting services, dismissing workforces, dampening incomes, and so forth. They have played, and continue to play, a major part in the politics of austerity.

The combination of neo-liberal ideology and the increasing financialization of capital adversely impacts workers, environmental protection, public health, safety and quality of products... A lot of illth. As well, this drive downwards and the deregulation that accompanies it also assist non-financial corporations in their pursuit for more. They are pressured to push down on wages and employment and on the precautions against risks to others by the new financial titans who are betting on a rise in value of their shares and derivatives. This brings us closer to our concern, namely, how the behaviour of financial capitalists affects the capacity of non-financial corporations to contribute to overall welfare.

Law professors Iman Anabtawi and Lynn Stout give a good account of some of the parlour tricks used by hedge funds.[25] They set out to show that these funds take shareholding or creditor positions in non-financial corporations and use their influence to force corporate managers to extract profits for them, regardless of what harm this might do to the corporation in which they hold shares. One case they discuss is that of a number of hedge funds that held shares in an incorporated insurance firm called MONY. The same hedge funds had lent money to a conglomerate, AXA. The debt instruments issued by AXA would increase in value if AXA succeeded in purchasing MONY, a much-resisted deal then under discussion. The opponents of the deal included many of MONY's management team and some shareholders. But in the end, the deal went through with the help of the hedge funds, and the hedge funds' overall position was improved as the increased value of their AXA investment outweighed the negative impact on their MONY shares. Whether this was good for either AXA or MONY was never their concern. They were making money by way of an elaborate bit of dealing, not by improving trade or increasing either corporation's production of services.

Similar games include those of hedge funds making an investment in one corporation, then getting rid of the economic risk associated with that investment by, say, shorting its stock. This means that the hedge fund borrows stock issued by that corporation from another investor in the same corporation, promising to return the stock at a later date. The hedge fund then sells the borrowed stock. If the stock's price has gone down by the time it needs to be returned, the borrowing hedge fund will make an easy profit. To ensure that this will happen, it may use its voting power in the corporation, which it still has by virtue of its initial investment, to cause the board and its executives to take actions which will drive the price down. This cunning practice, and variants of it, is so oft-used that it has led to scholarly examinations and discussions of what is called empty voting. Empty because, while the hedge fund retained its voting shares, it had actually dealt away the economic risks associated with those voting shares. Manifestly, a shareholder persuading a corporation's managers to take actions that are widely seen as deleterious to it does little for the corporation's contribution to welfare.

In sum: the power of these investment funds is such that they can, by taking large (though not majority) shareholding positions, hold boards to ransom. They can bargain with them to cut costs, to pay dividends out of earnings that the managers might want to retain to deploy later or differently, to buy back shares (which will leave remaining shareholders better off), to get rid of one division or another. They can use their voting power in one corporation to push it to bid for shares in another, knowing that the acquiring corporation's shares will go down but the target corporation's shares will go up, when their calculation is that this will leave them in a positive position. In short, the hedge funds can and do behave as self-interested bullies. As we have come to know, these shows of strength and cunning invoke testosterone-imbued attitudes. This is reflected in the names some give themselves. Anabtawi and Stout provide a short list: "Pirate Capital, Bulldog Investors, Steel Partners, Cerberus Capital." Enough said.

This thumbnail sketch of some of the machinations of the new giants of financial capital, scanty though it is, is highly relevant. It demonstrates that it is not hard to find shareholders who exercise real control over corporate affairs, even in the United States, which prides itself on the prevalence of diffuse shareholding. It is hard to classify these hedge funds as passive capitalists whose only redress, should they be unhappy with a corporation's management, is to take a walk down Wall Street or Bay Street and put their money elsewhere. Of equal significance, the games played by the new financial captains, often referred to by the popular media as the new rulers of the universe, are not, in any way, intended to use their money to advance the purposes for which any firm was incorporated. They are not at all interested in using their invested capital to help a corporation trade or produce goods and services. They are interested in making money any old how. If a corporation provides a platform, it will be used for that purpose, regardless of that corporation's needs.

This is not meant to say that financialization is of little importance. Its hugely increased prominence may well be a manifestation of a shift in the very nature of capitalism. But it does not tell us much about the utility of the corporate form as such. True, the corporation provides a base and is implicated in what goes on, but it was not designed by law to serve the purposes of financial capital. If we take those who hold on to the myth that, without the corporation, we would be worse off, their argument is not made any stronger by the dominance of the FIRE sectors of our economy. If anything, their dominance underscores the poverty of those claims.

AN ETHICAL METRIC

To return to our main argument, a last feature of legal incorporation needs to be revisited. It is the political impact of corporations on our social relations.

The corporation, as structured by law, is virulently anti-democratic. Those with the most votes, that is, those with the most skin in the game as measured by money, get to decide who shall have authority over others and how they can exercise that authority. The for-profit corporation is a top-down organization, run on a one-dollar, one-vote basis. If the corporation were a marginal actor in our political economy, this arrangement might be insignificant. But the corporation is central to our social relations, and its anti-democratic structures are like a cancer in the body politic.

Those who help in the formation of corporations, those who run them, advise them, and depend on them for their commissions, those who deal with them, and all of those who are employed by them get daily lessons in how decisions should be made and by whom. They are taught that authoritarian, undemocratic decision-making is not only efficient, but also the norm. As a result, many of us live our working lives in circumstances that directly contradict the principles that society proclaims. This is corrosive of political life. It is yet another non-monetized ill.

Even more directly, so is the enormous influence corporations wield inside contemporary governments. The threat of a capital strike, the interchanges between government and business lobbies and personnel, the funding of political parties, candidates, and causes, complemented by a large array of think tanks and university-inspired research and messaging have made governments less sensitive to majority demands. The truly wealthy benefit. This, too, is a cost imposed by means of corporations, a cost that ought to be taken into account in any evaluation of the corporate sectors' contribution to overall welfare.

Many people are conscious of the disproportionate influence wielded by corporate money, as demonstrated at rallies around the world. A sign at an Occupy Wall Street rally declaimed: "I can't afford my own politician so I made this sign." One at an Indignados rally in Barcelona pleaded: "2000 Euro for an honest politician."

Those, then, who plead for hanging on to the corporation as constituted by law are forced to make some dubious arguments. In order to ask a liberal polity and a market economy to accept the corporation as a legitimate player, they have to ask everyone to suspend disbelief. The pro-corporate crowd asks us to ignore the facts on the ground when there is a challenge to the legitimacy to the corporation. When cornered, its fallback position is that, despite all the troublesome illogicalities and false empirical claims, the corporation delivers the goods: it provides us with the welfare we crave. But this claim, too, turns out to be overblown. It only has merit if the framework within which it is made is not questioned. If social welfare is measured by growth, by the monetary value of all goods and services produced—all transactions, exports minus imports, and all governmental service and production activities—large corporate businesses do make a contribution. But this claim rests on a view of society that is of a very special kind. It assumes that we are a market society.

The eminent political economist Karl Polanyi insightfully warned that, should the economy become a market economy, then social relations would become those of a market society.[26] He saw this as a backward step. In a well-worn phrase, a market society is one that knows the price of everything and the value of nothing. Only in that kind of society could for-profit corporations claim to make a positive contribution to overall social welfare.

But as a host of thinkers and philosophers will tell us, this kind of world is not a good one. As Adam Smith wrote, "He certainly is not a good citizen who does not wish to promote by every means in his power, the welfare of the whole society of his fellow-citizens."[27] Albert Einstein reflected, "From the standpoint of daily life ... there is one thing we do know: that man is here for the sake of other men."[28] And ethicist Peter Singer paints this picture of the life well lived:

> To live ethically is to think about things beyond one's own interest. When I think ethically I become just one being, with needs and desires of my own, certainly, but living among others who also have needs and desires. When we are acting ethically, we should be able to justify what we are doing, and this justification must be of a kind that could in principle, convince any reasonable being.[29]

The kind of welfare that may be attributed to profit-maximizing corporations is contrary these hopes and aspirations. It values only growth, assigns meaning only to money. That kind of utility—and let us remember that, even by this miserable yardstick, blobs do not all that well—erodes and corrodes more humane aspirations. This is not fanciful.

In recent times, a clamour has arisen for a new metric. Organizations and scholars have taken on board the need to make happiness the criterion by which economic activity ought to be measured. The idea of giving the pursuit of happiness standing as a public policy got a kick-start in the small Himalayan kingdom of Bhutan in the early 1970s. As many people sense ever more clearly that both their material and non-material well-being have deteriorated, the idea has had an enormous rise in popularity.

During the onset of the global financial crisis, circa 2008, the unfairnesses and injustices associated with growth at any cost became obvious. The overseers of a system that seemed to be failing came under pressure. They have been looking for valves to open to relieve that pressure. Thus, in 2008, President Sarkozy of France set up a blue-ribbon commission led by leading economists Joseph Stiglitz, Amartya Sen, and Jean-Paul Fitoussi.[30] Among its many recommendations was one that urged governments to "shift emphasis from measuring economic production to measuring people wellbeing," arguing that "well-being is multidimensional." Many people and groups are attempting to find ways of doing this. Among them, a group at the University of Waterloo compiles a Canadian Index of Wellbeing.

Obviously, there are many difficulties with measuring happiness or wellbeing. It involves finding a formula that gives appropriate weight to material needs and to those that reflect subjective, spiritual, and cultural human wants and desires. How this should be done is fraught and beyond my field of knowledge. My point is not so much the merit of current attempts, but that these efforts reflect the ever-increasing sense that the growth metric does not yield satisfactory results.

Movements like Occupy Wall Street, Idle No More, the Quebec student movement, the Indignados, and the like, are evidence of discontent. When their activists are accused of having no agenda for an alternative, what is meant is that they have no agenda for an alternative way to continue to provide the kind of welfare we currently think should be our holy grail. They have no agenda to produce more and more things that can be priced in money. To the contrary, their agenda is the opposite. If the protest movements are seen as an intuitive reaction to a lack of well-being, a lack of happiness, a search for something different than growth for its own sake, those movements are more pointed than they are often said to be. Certainly, one of the more prolific writers on the need to develop a well-being metric on which to base our economic activities, Coral Graham, sees it this way. In a 2011 *Toronto Star* interview, she told Olivia Ward that "we are in a state where discontent is coming to the fore. It's not an organizational movement yet, and it's hard to tell whether it will spread or fizzle out like others.... The old economic model has failed."[31]

Another indication of how widespread the perception is that the growth model no longer satisfies the people, and by inference, that corporations that single-mindedly pursue that agenda can no longer can count on the public's support, is the anxiety among some of the current system's beneficiaries. Nick Hanauer, a founder of Amazon who says he is wealthy beyond belief, acknowledges that he is one of the ".01%ers, a proud and unapologetic capitalist."[32] Yet he warns that the huge amount of wealth in a few hands (like his) is largely unearned, and that those left behind will, as they always have, finally and probably suddenly, bring out the pitchforks to force a radical change. His is a modest plea, based on genuine fear, for a better sharing of the enormous pile of money spawned by corporate capitalism. While Hanauer is perhaps the most colourful of the dominant class articulating this view, many members of the class of the few are aware of the deep unhappiness in the population and the anger that seethes not too far below the surface. The *Guardian* recently reported, for example:

> At a packed session in Davos, former hedge fund director, Robert Johnson revealed that worried hedge fund managers were already planning their escapes: "I know hedge fund managers all over the world who are buying airstrips and farms in places like New Zealand because they think they need a getaway."[33]

Corporate cheerleaders have a tough time defending their claim that the legally created blobs serve overall welfare; many of them know that that claim is increasingly threadbare. They would prefer to avoid the last line of defence they could turn to. It is that the terrible outcomes of corporate profit-maximization are not the natural results of the way in which the corporation is constituted and acts, but that they arise from the logic of capitalism. This defensive posture holds that corporations are just vehicles designed to be efficient wealth maximizers within any given set of rules. Law-makers have the responsibility to tighten those parameters, thereby fettering capitalists and capitalism. If this is done, corporations will once again act to everyone's benefit; once again we will be able to trust them to make positive contributions to overall social welfare. This line of defence prompts two responses.

First, as always, we are asked to suspend disbelief. The hypocrisy of the argument is manifest. If anything is plain it is that the corporate sector and its defenders are adamantly opposed to having capitalists or their corporations fettered. Indeed, their economic theory and philosophy is that the market is by far the most efficient wealth-creating mechanism we have and that corporations, as vehicles for individual capitalists, are marvellously designed for efficient market participation by capitalists. Those individual capitalists should be left as free as possible. Inevitably, the argument that fetters should be imposed, even if it is made by forward-thinking capitalists trying to save the system from itself, will be met with enormous resistance from those very capitalists whose adherence to capitalism leaves their corporations no option but to inflict all that ugly illth.

Second, it is an acknowledgement that the corporation is not a self-standing institution that "cannot help itself." It is a frank admission that a corporation is an instrument: in the first place for capitalism, a system so pervasive that it is not distinct from the ambient air, and in the second place, for the human beings who gain from this system, capitalists. There are human beings who can make corporations do their bidding. This is ammunition for those persuaded by the arguments in this book to identify human targets in their struggles against corporate capitalism.

Walter Clement, a Canadian leader on corporate ownership and control, puts it like this:

> Corporations are simply structures organized for particular purposes, their prime objective being the appropriation of surplus for the private intentions of the people who control them. The apparent autonomy of corporations that led some to mistakenly attribute to them a quality they do not have; [Eric] Hobsbawm, for example, says that "Increasingly the real members of the ruling class today are not so much real persons as organizations" (1971:19), and [Paul] Baran and [Paul] Sweezy say that "The real capitalist today is not the individual businessman but the corporation" (1966:43). In reacting to the change from entrepreneurial capitalism dominated by captains of industry, to corporate capitalism, where control is collegial, these authors have over-reacted and reified corporations by abstracting them from their class base and from the people who are still very much in command of them. Organization in general, and corporations in particular, do not have objectives other than those instilled in them by people. They are legal devices created to accomplish certain ends.[34]

In sum, the case that the for-profit corporation brings overall benefits to society is a weak one. It is only defensible by using arguments which put the system the corporation serves, capitalism, and the people who motivate it to act as it does, capitalists, on the legal and political firing lines.

Let us fire at them.

13

A Step off the
Road to Serfdom

WE DON'T HAVE TO LOOK VERY FAR FOR EVIDENCE OF THE RAVAGES
of capitalism. The *Toronto Star*, for example, recently reported: "1.2 million
Canadian children go to school hungry ... [food] banks distribute 200 million pounds of canned and packaged food a year to 1.7 million people, which
works out to 8.8 pounds of food per month per person."[1] Jean Ziegler of
the UN Human Rights Council's Advisory Committee offers these sobering
stats: "Every five seconds, a child under 10 dies of hunger. Thirty-five million people die each year from hunger or its immediate aftermath. One
billion people are permanently and severely malnourished and the situation
is becoming increasingly catastrophic."[2] And Warren Buffett recently told
CNN: "There's been class warfare going on for the last twenty years, and my
class has won."[3]

This work has posited that we leave major economic decisions to a few
private profiteers hiding behind humanly devised artifices which, then, are
reified as machines with a single, unquestionable mission. As a result, we—
the many, the majority of human beings—have lost control over our des-
tinies. We are incapable of attaining our potential as autonomous sentient
beings. Material inequalities, serious deprivations for many, ecological devastation, and unhappiness are our lot.

IS THERE NO ALTERNATIVE?

When, in 1944, economist Friedrich Hayek wrote *The Road to Serfdom*, his concern was that if we left economic decisions to be made by government as a central planner, the inevitable results would be a tyrannical government and an unfree society. This convinced trailblazers like Margaret Thatcher and Ronald Reagan and their modern followers who argued that "there is no alternative" (TINA) to the reliance on private wealth creation. There is, they say, no option but to stick with corporate capitalism, if we are to thrive as a free and rich polity. This is horribly wrong. Today, our tyrants are not so much the governments Hayek feared, but human capitalists who control wealth and its uses by means of corporations. A recent *Toronto Star* headline put it well: "Super-Rich Now the World's Dictators."[4]

TINA is an idea that blunts the fight against capitalism, a fight that must be fought and won. I do not pretend to know what a new regime ought to look like, or to tell people how best to fight. Many struggles and organizations are already dedicated to finding ways to combat and reject corporate capitalism. The work is intended to put these people in a better position to defeat what is. My argument, in the end, is based on a belief: that human beings are capable of constructing a life of altruism, compassion, and caring for others and their environments and that they instinctively seek to live such a life. What they need is to see these inclinations in themselves and to understand how they are being held back from realizing their potential. As William Tabb wrote, discussing the World Trade Organization's incursions: "Change does not come about from the mere fact of oppression, but from a belief that a better alternative is not only desirable but possible, not necessarily tomorrow, but when the momentum can be turned around."[5]

The TINA mantra holds that the fundamentals of the prevailing regime cannot be bettered. This is bold, indeed, arrogant. We are asked to believe that we cannot do better than a system that ensures that some people, capitalists, get most of the spoils, that they are entitled to limit the shares of others and to command them in their daily lives. That this view has any purchase at all is to be deeply lamented. Could there really be no practical alternative to an authoritarian, anti-democratic, anti-egalitarian regime? But nonetheless, even as many are disadvantaged and chafe under the system, it is hard to mount opposition, to see how we can go beyond the boundaries and metes within which we live.

The legal argument crafted in this book is offered to assist those who want to defend us against corporate capitalism's immediate impacts and those who want to change it forever. It seeks to alter the ideological context of anti-capitalists' resistance, whatever goals they have set and whatever tactics and strategies they choose.

SEEING THE HIDDEN SHAREHOLDER

Law is intent on the retention and reproduction of the status quo. It plays a crucial role in establishing and maintaining the ideas and practices that dominate our social relations. Central to the arguments I have presented is the specific role corporate law plays in erecting a wall between capitalism and its victims. Social historian Doug Hay and lawyer Christopher Stanley identify law's invention, the corporate vehicle, as a major instrument used by law to discharge its tasks, namely, making the dominant system seem unassailable and work as if it makes perfectly good sense.[6]

This book first focused on the legal attributes of the corporation to show how the concepts and applications of corporate law further the goal of the private accumulation of socially produced wealth. The analysis, supported by data, led me to conclude that, to do this effectively, law has no choice but to undermine some of the legitimacy it has gained as a reflection and enforcer of our social consensus. A vast array of solemn legal principles are betrayed by law's need to make the blob-o-sphere work for the capitalists, who use it to accumulate and accumulate some more.

This betrayal gives anti-capitalist activists an opening, an opportunity to attack the energy-sapping strength of TINA. If the corporate form is seen as a legally created cloak hiding the truth that not the corporation but the people who are cloaked by it are the evil-doers, one of the bulwarks of the TINA fortress is severely weakened. To exploit this weakness, I have provided evidence that the primary instigators and beneficiaries of the predations

carried out by means of corporations can be identified and, by the application of normal legal rubrics, should be driven out of their legal hiding places.

Conventional capitalist wisdom needs this evidence to be ignored, especially that bit about real, live predators sitting in their safe and splendid
counting houses, counting all that money. An opposing message is sent out.
The corporation's history no longer works to discredit it. The sinister role
played by the corporation as a vital cog in the colonial and imperial periods'
pillaging has been lost in the mists of time. Corporate cheerleaders are able
to praise the blob's current benign character and to proclaim that the modern corporation is ideally designed to efficiently deliver general welfare.

That claim, it has been shown, should not be accorded any respect. The
evidence shows that it is risible. The corporation is a legally created predator. It should be damnified. Its privileged standing is based on contortions
of law and a jettisoning of available empirical data. As well, to burnish its
image, it relies on unconscious irony and a falsehood.

The irony is that the intellectual gatekeepers who normally abjure collectivized action, because it smacks of socialism, contend that it is precisely
because profit-chasing productive activity by a blob is socially organized that
it is efficient. It is the co-ordination of many inorganic and human resources inside one envelope that makes it more efficient than a real, live human
being, than a true individual. Its collectivized features, however, are intended
to benefit the few, not all the producers. The corporation is a living contradiction: a collectivized endeavour to serve the few, rather than all. This should
give corporate cheerleaders pause about their grand claims that the corporate
form dovetails with pristine market economic and liberal political principles.

The falsehood is that the corporation is a self-standing, self-driven
engine of efficiency. The unfounded conclusion is that the corporation, the
blob, the ectoplasmic legal device, is the active capitalist, not those who
motivate it and benefit from the activities it facilitates. The blobs' controlling
shareholders are to be treated as passive, helpless, irresponsible bystanders. Capitalist acts undertaken by blobs are to be perceived as being more
like natural phenomena than deliberate conduct engineered by thoughtful
human beings pursuing their interests. One aim of this work has been to

blast this mystifying and empirically false idea out of people's minds. It will only be when the true predators are identified and made responsible for the role played by the blob-o-sphere which allows them to extract and retain socially produced wealth that some of the ideological fetters that restrain anti-capitalist activists will be loosened.

In conversation with Peter Fitting, a friend and a scholar and student of cinema, science fiction, and utopia literatures, he observed that my project reminded him of a John Carpenter film, *They Live*. The story centres on a drifter who discovers some special sunglasses in a bin. When he puts them on, his world changes. He can now see a continuous series of totalitarian-advancing messages beamed subliminally at him and all the other people without sunglasses. And he can see that many respected and influential members in the non-sunglassed world are frightening humanoid aliens. In the story the film tells, earth is the third planet these outsiders have invaded. They want its resources to enjoy; they are content to deplete them and then move on, leaving the drifter's planet with climate change, food shortages, and the like. Spectacular fights add to the film's entertainment value, but the lesson to be drawn for us is plain enough. The aliens' targeted planet and its people were helpless without the sunglasses. They did not see by whom and how they were victimized.

Philosopher Slavoj Žižek, in a documentary entitled *The Pervert's Guide to Ideology*, commented:

> *They Live* is definitely one of the forgotten masterpieces of the Holly-wood Left.... The sunglasses function like a critique of ideology. They allow you to see the real message beneath all the propaganda, glitz, posters, and so on.... When you put the sunglasses on you see the dictatorship in democracy, the invisible order which sustains your apparent freedom.[7]

THE "THINKING CAPITALIST" RESPONSE

Evidence has been provided that in all small corporations and in many large private and publicly traded corporations, it is possible to name controlling shareholders who, when it comes to accepting responsibility, prefer to remain hidden. If anti-capitalists use this evidence, they will be equipped with sunglasses. If they then rely on the capitalists' claim that they believe in the rule of law and the liberal legal system, and launch legal actions to hold the now exposed aliens, the controlling shareholders, responsible for conduct by blobs that have behaved badly, they may not bring capitalism to its knees. They will, however, change the terrain on which the battles to do so are fought.

Thinking capitalists in the advanced capitalist political economies understand this danger. They have become aware of a growing anger against the dominant regime. These prescient pro-capitalists, therefore, want to relieve the pressure. They seek to establish a frame from within capitalism in which capitalists can operate without creating too much dissonance. Their concerns, as we have seen, were colourfully expressed by that self-proclaimed member of the 0.01 per cent club, Nick Hanauer. He suggested a show of benevolence lest the oppressed pick up their pitchforks. Elite guardians of capitalism echo this message in more sober terms. Thinking capitalists see every reason to regroup:

- increasingly turbulent demonstrations against capitalist organizations like the Organisation for Economic Co-operation and Development, the World Trade Organization, the World Bank, the International Monetary Fund, the G8, the G20, the EU Troika, and so on
- the vigour and resonance of the Occupy Wall Street movement, and vociferous dissatisfaction with the growth in inequality
- the anti-growth agitations undergirding the environmental movements
- the spreading student uprisings centred on the cost and nature of education
- public denunciations of market principles by the Vatican and some South American governments
- greater awareness of capitalism's displacement of Indigenous people and exploitation of their rights all over the globe

The anger over inequality in wealth, income, and political power, is becoming dangerous. Mark Carney, the prestigious governor of the Bank of England, speaking in 2014 at a tellingly named Conference on Inclusive Capitalism,[8] made a passionate plea for capitalists to reconsider the oft-expressed opposition to the return of some countervailing powers for consumers, trade unions, and the wealthless. There should be, he believes, something like a renewed acceptance of the post–Second World War social contract, which focused on attaining greater equality of opportunity and more generous outcomes for non-wealth owners and made for a more inclusive, stable capitalist society. A new social contract might include some legitimacy for trade unionism, more social welfare spending by governments, more progressive taxation systems, and a willingness to improve fairness across generations. Christine Lagarde of the International Monetary Fund made a similar plea, suggesting that, should governments not bring capitalists back to their senses, Karl Marx's prediction that capitalism would create its own gravediggers might come true.[9] Lawrence Summers and Ed Balls, as well as progressive leading economists and social scientists such as Joseph E. Stiglitz, Amartya Sen, and Jean-Paul Fitoussi, have written reports along the same lines.[10]

To sweeten the potentially bitter pill they proffer, thinking capitalists tell the plain greedy ones—and the foot-dragging governments they influence—that self-discipline by the mighty and avaricious, together with a show of tolerance for allowing the non-wealth classes to protect themselves, will ultimately benefit capitalists and the governments that support them. These reforms, after all, do not include capitalism-threatening measures, such as increased public ownership of financial institutions, self-management by workers, the promotion of non-commercial communication systems, or any such outlandish policies. Reforms of social policy are being urged that, odious as they might be to individual capitalists, will blunt the anger aimed at the regime of capitalist production.

But this subtle argument may not convince too many people who have benefited from the roll-back of the postwar social contract. While the reformers are trying to save capitalism from its practitioners, those practitioners—who are, by definition, anarchic self-seeking actors—are not all that interested in making sacrifices on behalf of a system, of an "ism." Michael Parenti once quipped that, since time began, the ruling classes have only ever wanted one thing—everything. Still, in the event that a number of these changes are implemented, some concrete limits on some of the excesses of capitalism will take hold. But this will not be enough: as long as the fundaments of the ruling system remain unchallenged, any victories will be momentary. The preservation of this potential to roll back non-capitalists' rights and entitlements lies at the heart of those thinking capitalists' project.

Nafeez Ahmed, in the *Guardian*, records that the Henry Jackson Institute, the organization behind the Inclusive Capitalism Initiative, explained its raison d'être as follows: "We felt that such was the public disgust with the system, there was a very real danger that politicians could seek to remedy the situation by legislating capitalism out of existence." The primary concern of these reforms, in other words, is to maintain the system. TINA is not to be doubted; we are still to be ruled by the same abstract naked emperor. But the emperor's clothes have to be adjusted because some of the more outrageous capitalists, imprudently, have made it too clear that corporate capitalism's promises and dominant prophets are false.

The need to see capitalism for what it is and to assault its logic remains pressing. Fortunately, an increasing number of people see this. Pope Francis, for one, has been outspoken: "How can it be that it is not a news item when an elderly homeless person dies of exposure, but it is news when the stock market loses two points?" he has asked. And further, "Unfettered capitalism is a 'new tyranny.' Just as the commandment 'Thou shalt not kill' sets a clear limit to safeguard the value of human life, today we also have to say 'thou shalt not' to an economy of exclusion and inequality. Such an economy kills."[11]

As the rich get richer and richer and more people everywhere are impoverished, the wealthy parade their wealth and arrogance. They flaunt their highly publicized ostentatious living styles. They blatantly lord it at anti-democratic gatherings. They summon the governments of the world to prestigious meetings, such as Davos and Bilderberg, to give them their marching orders. There also are a host of meetings held for their benefit—less prestigious because they have to invite functioning bureaucrats to run the meetings and draft the resolutions—such as the G8, G20, and World Bank. These are in-your-face displays of unashamed power. The conferences put fences around their lavish premises and use local police and armies to keep away those who do not want their lives and the life of the planet decided by undemocratic resolutions passed at a closed conference. Those protestors, carrying puerile signs like "What we need is an end to greedlock," are castigated as hopeless romantics or troublemakers. They are repressed and punished. After all, they are showing a willingness to reject the reign of TINA.

Despite the repressions—or maybe, because of them—the anger of those who already reject corporate capitalism is deepening, and the circles in which these sentiments are shared are widening. So-called austerity measures imposed around the globe have caused misery but also spawned resistance movements and politics, from the Battle of Seattle to Occupy Wall Street to Idle No More, to many political upheavals in Europe. This has real demonstration effects to the afflicted. It is incumbent on those of us who do not like capitalism to find ways to help maintain the rage.

This book aims to help make this growing awareness more effective and more dangerous to the rich and powerful nestled inside corporations. As the vulnerable and repressed classes begin to comprehend that behind those anonymous blobs there are real human beings, eager to profit at the expense of everyone else—that is, when they see the faces of those who are truly responsible for their plight—their devotion to TINA will likely become ever more tenuous. They will see that the mantra suits a few identifiable, rather disagreeable and unproductive human beings. They will have tangible enemies to aim at, flesh-and-blood human beings who, if knocked off their TINA-constructed pedestal, will feel pain. If such pain is seen to be imminent, capitalists might be more willing to take steps to avert it. Immediate reforms might be easier to obtain. Each reform, though, should be treated as a step in the right direction but not the end point of agitation.

SEPARATING THE SHAREHOLDER FROM THE BLOB

More standing and leverage for unions, a more progressive income tax, the encouragement of employee ownership. Raising of the minimum wage, better protections against dismissal, and granting women greater parity. Spending more on job-creating projects, such as bridges, roads, ports, and schools. These are all reforms floated by some of these thinking capitalists, and they are to be welcomed. But remember why they are on offer. They have been put on the table by TINA preservers in order to save capitalism and capitalists.

Many of the recommendations made by the thinking capitalists replicate demands already made by those lobbying on behalf of the non-wealthy. Those at the bottom of the pile have had little success with these demands. There has been recent regress rather than progress. Demands made by the vulnerable have been rejected by governments keen to further the capitalist agenda, as demanded by the anarchic, unthinking wealthy. In this context, fighting for reforms is seen as valiant when unions, NGOs, and other activists are the demanders. This perception is bolstered by the vigour with which they have been repulsed by governments and the corporate sectors. But at best, these are campaigns to go back to the conditions that existed not so long ago, at a time when capitalists had to make some concessions in order to have a stable economy and polity in which to chase profits. Michael Lebowitz notes that these kinds of struggles are akin to what Marx termed the fighting of a guerilla war against the impacts of an existing system, as opposed to a war against the system:

> The great failing is that we have lost sight of an alternative. And, because we have no grand conception of an alternative (indeed, we are told we should have no grand conceptions) then the response to the neo-liberal mantra of TINA ... has been: let's preserve health care, let's not attack education, and let's try for a little more equality and a little more preservation of the environment. Because of our failure to envision an alternative as a whole, we have many small pieces, many small NGOs; indeed, the only feasible alternative to barbarism proposed has been barbarism with a human face.[12]

Reforms that would confront the fundamental features of corporate capitalism are not put on the table by the thinking capitalists. There is no suggestion militating for economic democracy. Nothing in the reforms speaks about workers having a say not only in how to do things but also over what things should be done. There is no suggestion that—as the most immediately affected by new technologies, processes, and materials used in production—workers should have the final say on what is to be used, when, and to what extent. There is no recommendation that banks be nationalized to centralize the provision of credit. This is strange, because the thinking capitalists were pivotal members of the elites that, in the aftermath of Lehman Brothers and the subsequent failures, bailed out banks, in effect took them over for a while, allowing them to get back to financial health and then—perversely from a non-capitalist point of view—setting them free to make private profits by issuing credit once again.

There is not a whisper about putting important sectors of industry under state control, or about slowing down the fervent privatization of services run by governments. There is no coherent set of reforms on these thinking capitalists' agenda to deal with environmental practices that, in pursuit of growth, threaten life on the planet. These are just a few of the kinds of demands that anti-capitalist activists have to make the centre of their politics. Many activists understand this, but find it difficult to do so from the framework within which they must fight.

Let us use the reforms on offer as a platform for radical change, not as ends in themselves. Let the platform be a staging point for translating capitalist-compatible reforms into demands that reject capitalism's crass logic. The changes to be put on the agenda should envision a system of social relations which does not proclaim greed and monetary growth to be the pinnacle of human achievement. Anti-capitalist activists might be better positioned to do this if they asked everyone to put on the sunglasses the thinking capitalists have kept hidden in their bin.

If the arguments in this book are persuasive to them, activists should add to their arsenal the bringing of civil, regulatory, or criminal actions against those controlling shareholders who are inflicting the pains they are seeking to alleviate. These irresponsible capitalists are to be seen as responsible for the many ugly outcomes of corporate capitalism, to be characterized as belonging to a class of unproductive gamblers and exploiters. They are to be brought out as toxins in our body politic.

Dan Plesch and Stephanie Blankenburg, of the School of Oriental and African Studies in London, argue:

> While the mantra of "no rights without responsibilities" is used to regulate the behaviour of poor people who benefit from social security payments—from single mothers to the unemployed, from the homeless to the "self-inflicted" sick—, "The Unaccountable Few" enjoy feudal privileges. It is, by no means, an exaggeration to note that owner-shareholders (and by extension manager-directors) are beyond the law to an extent not enjoyed by the Central Committees of Communist Parties, similar to the despotic monarchies, dictators and tribal leaders over which liberal Western societies claim moral supremacy and akin to the aristocracy in the Ancien Regimes of pre-enlightenment Europe.[13]

THERE IS A NEW ALTERNATIVE

With activists advancing these arguments, TINA will come under increasing scrutiny and with that, the potential to develop and pursue alternative visions of society may be greatly improved. This may sound a little fanciful, but consider what impacts a systemic, sustained campaign of this sort, accompanying demands for concrete changes, might have. The unveiled visages and flesh-and-blood bodies of those instigating the machine-like, hard-to-get-personally-angry-with blobs will come into view. They, not some intangible blob or "ism," will be seen as the persons profiting directly and grossly from all the illth that is visited on the many and their fragile environments. Once it is seen that this is what TINA—as implemented by means of the corporation—inevitably produces, the notion that something radically more humane ought to be devised may gain more adherents and political salience. The alien nature of capitalism will be much harder to defend.

Used to eons of privilege, the controllers of blobs can be expected to fight back fiercely. They will claim that the majesty of established law does not allow for such attacks on the vehicle that gives them so much comfort. This book has shown that, while it may be costly, good technicians on the other side should be able to deal with these roadblocks. More significantly, if the ruling class has to defend the blob-o-sphere, the burden of political and ideological proof will shift to them. Their vehicles, subsidies, and claims of utility to overall welfare, and crucially, of their legally defended immunities, will be the subject of debate. No longer will the controllers of blobs be able to assume their privileges and advantages are beyond challenge. No longer will they enjoy the luxury of not having to prove anything.

This work is dedicated to giving anti-capitalists weaponry for just such debates. Let corporate cheerleaders try to defend the existence of one-person and other small incorporated firms: the evidence is in. These firms are incorporated not to be true participants in the market but to shift risks onto others. They add nothing to our welfare. If this fact becomes public knowledge, a dent is likely to be made in the assertions that, on balance, corporations are fine tools by which to create wealth from which everyone benefits.

Similarly, if the blobs' defenders are forced to argue—as opposed to having it assumed—that limited liability is necessary to garner capital for welfare-creating corporate endeavours, the evidence is there to show that this is pure malarkey. The privilege is then more likely to be seen as a gift to people who want to profit without doing anything and without taking responsibility for any costs incurred by others.

Moreover, inasmuch as limited liability is made the fulcrum of debate, it will become more visible that it is the players of the stock market and the rather useless people who circle like vultures around it who profit from this legally created gambling sphere. The frenzied pursuit of share and derivative trading will no longer be seen as a mysterious world in which incomprehensible but useful things are done. And if controlling capitalists, in apprehension of being made responsible for a corporation's infliction of harm, are forced to bring out the nonsense argument that the blob's conduct had nothing to do with them, they can be countered with a good deal of evidence and persuasive legal arguments.

In such a context, how easy will it be for the corporate masters to maintain that they do it all for us, that they are wealth creators rather than wealth destroyers? How difficult might it become for them to argue that the pernicious influences exercised by the corporations they own and control over our legislators, regulators, educational institutions, and media have nothing to do with them, that they do not make the one-person, one-vote system a sad mockery? How much more awkward might it be for them to claim that they, being the few, are endangered by a political system that allows the masses to exercise too much power over them? How difficult might it become to pretend that they are not more like feudal lords and aristocrats than citizens in a liberal polity? How easy will it be to assert, as controlling shareholders do now, that they as individuals should have the right to decide who should benefit from essential services, and that therefore, elected government should privatize these tasks to allow them be done by their profit-driven blobs?

Imperilling the legal safety of the corporations' controllers forces a resistance by them that, in turn, allows activists to change the ideological and political setting for struggle. Capitalists will no longer be able to say that it could be no other way. They will be asked to prove it. Anti-capitalists may begin to proclaim that TINA should really stand for "there is a new alternative." By itself, outing controlling shareholders and menacing them with legal actions and sanctions will not bring down capitalism. It may, however, demonstrate the threadbare nature of the claim that there is no alternative but to accept an anti-democratic, authoritarian, non-inclusive regime. A regime bent on measuring welfare and merit by money, that creates and supplies wants and ignores needs, that thrives on inequality. More people may be persuaded that capitalism's TINA is based on such a weak justification that we should be open to other ways of doing things. The many efforts already in existence to do other to become other (to borrow a phrase from Leo Panitch and Sam Gindin) could get much more traction.

If the analysis and data furnished in this book encourage activists to step through the revealed holes in the corporate fences that currently keep them penned in and marching along capitalism's road to serfdom, I will be content. I am optimistic about people's potential to flourish once they free themselves from these artificially created corporate shackles on their imaginations.

Acknowledgements

RELYING ON MY TRAINING AS A LAWYER, THIS BOOK IS MY MODEST effort to help people prevent the ongoing, continuous infliction of egregious harms by corporations and those who control and benefit from their actions. I was spurred by the distress I felt because so many people think these outcomes have to be borne with resignation, as if they were merely collateral damage of what is, on the whole, a superior system of welfare creation. Despite the accounts of the many wrongs and disasters it offers, the book is not written in despair. I believe real change is possible. I believe this because I am an optimist: I have faith in the capacity of people to be decent. I owe this faith to two sets of people, my parents and *la famille* Souquet.

My parents were of the European generation that became teenagers during the First World War. They married and began family life as the Great Depression took hold. They suffered privations and stress. Even as there seemed to be a flickering light on the far side of the tunnel, they had to flee their home as the Nazis and their fanatical anti-Semitism rolled into Belgium. They became refugees in France and, while their experiences were tough, they survived. Shortly after the war, they decided that Europe would never be safe for them and migrated. They came to a land where their occupational qualifications were of no use and the language, customs, and culture were alien. They remained poor for the rest of their lives. We did not have a house, a car, or anything else that was considered an ordinary necessity of life at that time. But my parents were never bitter. There was joie de vivre in our house. We enjoyed each other. Not having the means to buy tickets to costly entertainment events, we sang and listened to music and read plays together. My parents were the embodiment of the idea that one does not have to be wealthy to enjoy non-material beauty and pleasures. There was nothing to spare, but whatever there was was cheerfully shared with any who came to the house or had greater need. Hospitality and generosity were the greatest virtues. They had been taught this by their experiences. They respected others, in large part because others had respected them.

After they had fled to France, they were hidden by *la famille* Souquet, who owned a subsistence farm in the Lot & Garonne region. The Souquets hid seven to thirteen Jewish refugees in a stable behind their house for four and a half years. They took enormous risks as both Vichy and German troops combed the area in search of Resistance fighters and undocumented foreigners. They suffered hardship. Their farm barely provided for their own needs, yet they shared what they had with those penniless, non-contributing refugees. And it turned out that hundreds of people were saved in much the same way by other farmers in that region. No one was betrayed. When, as an adult, I asked *la famille Souquet* why they had done what they did, they looked bemused. *"Si le besoin s'en fait sentir, on doit faire quelque chose"* (If there is a need, something needs to be done), they told me.

This is why I am an optimist. My family and *la famille* Souquet provide compelling evidence that human beings are capable of decency, altruism, compassion, and respect for each other. Conscious of the limitations my professional expertise imposes on me, this work is not intended as a full-blown program on how to overthrow the existing scheme of social relations. I have written this book to provide a set of legal tools to aid people to resist the current coercive and co-opting regime that pushes them to give in to greed, cupidity, and venality. Human beings are capable of being so much better. As the Souquets said: *"On doit faire quelque chose."*

Finally, inasmuch as this work has any felicity, it is largely attributable to the care lavished on the manuscript by the editor, Tilman Lewis, and the staff at Between the Lines. Thank you.

Notes

Following the numbered endnotes for each chapter are elaborations of the issues and arguments, for readers interested in further pursuing them.

INTRODUCTION

1   R.H. Tawney, *The Acquisitive Society* (London/Glasgow: Fontana Library, 1961, first pub. 1921), 30–31.

2   Stéphane Hessel and Edgar Morin, *The Path to Hope*, trans. Antony Shugaar (New York: Other Press, 2011), 2.

3   Throughout this work, Canadian, New Zealand, Australian, U.S., and English illustrations and commentaries are used to support the arguments advanced. This book does not attempt to say anything about legal systems with vastly different histories and cultures.

4   Doug Hay, "Time, Inequality, and Law's Violence" in Austin Sarat, ed., *Law's Violence* (Ann Arbor: University of Michigan Press, 1992).

In this chapter, I assert that anti-capitalist activists should see controlling shareholders, human beings, rather than their principal tool, corporations, as their target. They should recognize that the ills they want to redress are attributable to the greed of flesh-and-blood human beings, promoted and laundered by means of corporations. Some elaboration of the way greed has developed as an acceptable trait follow, and some data are provided to show that it is a tiny number of individuals who profit from the pursuit of greed.

Defenders of capitalism are unabashed in their celebration of greed. In other settings, greed is viewed, as it always was, unfavourably. Before capitalism became as dominant as it is today, many scholars, religious leaders, and students of philosophy and ethics argued that other human characteristics and tendencies had a better claim to be prized and fostered than did naked self-regard. The older wisdom acknowledged that impulses such as greed, avarice, and selfishness always threatened to surface, but, as they were ugly aspects of human nature, their push should be resisted and jettisoned. As late as the seventeenth century, the drive to acquire things and to serve oneself was regarded as the most terrible of all "passions," one of the deadliest of all sins threatening a decent society. Influenced by these teachers and philosophers who set the standards of morality during an age of humanism and reason, Adam Smith, the intellectual and philosophical father of contemporary market capitalism protagonists, decried the vulgarity and inutility of selfish conduct: "To what purpose is all the toil and bustle of this world? What is the end of avarice and ambition, of the pursuit of power, and preeminence?" Manifestly, a change in ethical thinking had to accompany the advent of market capitalism to make self-serving behaviour and the satisfaction of greedy impulses appear so natural that it makes sense to enjoy them and see them as virtues, not as toxic brews.

. As market capitalism took hold, selfishness and greed were stamped as virtues because they came to be associated with efficiency. They emerged as the essential building blocks for a well-functioning market economy. The market economy posits that, if each of us uses our resources and talents to meet spontaneous demands, and if we do this in a setting in which none of us can dictate the price of our goods or services because we have to compete with profit-driven actors who are using their resources and talents to the same ends, the goods and services provided will meet the demand for them at the best price possible. Further, because no one tells anyone that they must demand a particular good or service, our discrete competitive efforts to meet these spontaneous demands will produce just the right amount of goods and services for the cheapest price. As Adam Smith famously put it in *The Wealth of Nations*: "It is not from the benevolence of the butcher, the brewer, or the baker that we expect our dinner, but from their regard to their own interest."

Motivated by unbridled, undirected greed, we will ensure the most efficient use of our aggregate resources and talents. This insight is what made Adam Smith dilute his earlier harsh judgment of greed as a moral quicksand. *Le douce commerce*, he now argued, diminished the ugliness of greed's vulgarity and nastiness. When aimed in the right direction, self-serving greed would do more good than harm. It would bring more material abundance for all. To this day, this understanding is perceived to trump any reservations we might have about the detrimental impact the promotion of greed might have on our social cohesion and values. Barbara McDougall, as Canadian minister for finance, for example, said: "There is one underlying motive in business shared by all—it is greed. We support it wherever it happens" (D. Olive, *Just Rewards: The Case for Ethical Reform in Business* [Markham, ON.: Penguin Books, 1987], 23).

While in our non-commercial lives, in our relationships with friends and relatives, most of us still consider greed and selfishness to be character flaws, we accept and tolerate these same flaws as necessary attributes when competing for our material spoils. We are schooled, by our experiences and by our teachings, to think of this as unremarkable, as normal. Market capitalism has gained a patina of moral acceptability, even as, in our more personal relationships, we continue to think of its fundamental building block, *greed*, as a grave character flaw. There ought to be, indeed there is, something of a disconnect. This is why capitalism's legitimacy is reinforced in other ways.

The system does generate a great deal of wealth, some of which goes towards the welfare of all citizens. It claims to do this efficiently because the contemporary mode of operation of capitalism is reliant on the operations of competitive markets, an instrument that is adamantly proclaimed as the embodiment of economic efficiency. This is why capitalism presents itself as *market* capitalism. The market mechanism, like liberal law, relies on and celebrates the creed of the individual as a sovereign, autonomous actor. The pivotal idea is that all individuals make their own economic choices and decisions. And, as more and more of the decisions affecting lives are made by individuals acting as market participants, the less need there is for anyone to plan how our national assets (once referred to tellingly as the *common* wealth) ought to be used, and the less need there is for political decision-making by elected governments. Milton Friedman, in his book *Capitalism and Freedom* (Chicago: University of Chicago Press, 1962), boasted that the free market mechanism lessened the danger to the rights of individuals presented by the heavy hand of majoritarian governments. In this way, economic market capitalism is cleverly twinned with individual civil and political freedom. This constitutes a platform on which wealth owners stand as they oppose government regulatory activities that do not directly benefit them. The problems to which this gives rise are taken up in this book.

The point made in this chapter is that the greed game we are asked to play begins on a very uneven terrain. This should be beyond debate. Yet those who defend the system pretend that, most of the time, the highly visible inequality ought not to disturb us. Somehow or other it will all work out and we will live happily ever after. But recently, it has become apparent that it is not going all that smoothly; the Occupy Wall Street movement gains its impetus from the massive inequalities that mar the capitalist landscape.

The less wealthy and the wealthless constitute a whopping majority of the people in any one nation state. Ajay Kapur, Niall Macleod, and Narrenda Singh, in *Equity Strategy—Plutonomy: Buying Luxury, Explaining Global Imbalances* (2009), report on a memorandum written by Citigroup to its clients, congratulating them on belonging to the superclass and suggesting that Citigroup would be happy to advise them as to how to invest their money. The memorandum, rather boastfully, set out how, at that time, wealth was divided in the United States: 1 per cent of U.S. households, i.e., about one million households, had a share of overall income that was only slightly less than the aggregate of 60 per cent of households, i.e., 60 million households. The same top 1 per cent (the clients) accounted for 33 per cent of net worth, a greater share than the bottom 90 per cent of households put together enjoyed; and that same top 1 per cent of households accounted for 40 per cent of the financial net worth of the nation, greater than the combined total of the bottom 95 per cent of households. These numbers go a long way towards explaining the welcome extended to Thomas Piketty's *Capital in the Twenty-First Century*, tr. Arthur Goldhammer (Cambridge/London: Bellknap Press of Harvard University, 2014), with its rich documentation of inequality and its argument that this inequality was built into the workings of capitalism. The evidence detailing the disproportionate flow of benefits spawned by corporate capitalism is overwhelming; see David Rothkopf, *Superclass: The Global Power Elite and the World They Are Making* (Farrar, Strauss & Giroux, 2009); Cynthia Freedland, *Plutocrats: The Rise of the New Global Super-Rich and the Fall of Everyone Else* (New York: Penguin, 2012). Statistics Canada's National Household Survey, 2013, revealed the growing gap between rich and poor in Canada. One example, among many proffered, showed that the top 1 per cent of Canadians received an average income of \$381,300 per year, while the bottom 90 per cent earned an average of \$28,000.

The number of people that constitutes the superior class is truly puny, matched only by its members' obscene wealth. A recent report out of the United Kingdom (James Henry et al., Tax Justice Network, *The Price of Offshore Revisited*, 2012), documented the number of wealthy folks who park their money outside the countries in which they live and are expected to pay taxes. The finding was that somewhere between 21 trillion and 32 trillion dollars resided happily in offshore tax havens, contributing little or nothing to governments' revenues. Whenever this kind of "cleverness" is exposed, as it was by the Tax Justice Network, the unfairness of it all, the extra burden imposed on those who obediently do pay their democratically imposed taxes, shocks the collective conscience. Even more so because, amazingly, \$9.3 trillion of this enormous amount of untaxed wealth is owned by 92,000 individuals. While 92,000 is quite a large number when it describes the attendance at a football game, it represents 0.001 per cent (one thousandth of 1 per cent) of the world's population. This tiny group of flesh-and-blood capitalists has managed to squirrel away incomprehensible amounts of money. In 2014, Oxfam produced even more startling data. Its report claimed that a mere 85 individuals had as much wealth as the bottom 50 per cent of the world's population. It might be said that these kinds of numbers prove that capitalism has generated a great deal wealth in the world. Yes, it does show that, but here, where we are concerned with the distribution of that wealth and its impacts, the significance of this evidence is that only a handful of single-minded, self-seeking people own most of the wealth and they have used their wealth-based power to keep it for themselves. The following is attributed to a successful nineteenth-century American business person, Frederick Townsend Martin: "We are the rich. We own America, we got it, God knows how, but we intend to keep it."

To drive the point home, note that a 2006 United Nations report showed that the richest 10 per cent of individuals own 85 per cent of all of the planet's assets; at the other end of the scale, three billion people share 1 per cent of the globe's assets. The rich are not a majority. They are the most and best protected minority we have.

1. A CORPORATION IS BORN

1   I discussed the numbered companies 630903 Ontario Inc. (Bilt-Rite) and 550551 Ontario Limited (Westray) extensively in chapters 4 and 5 of *Wealth by Stealth: Corporate Crime, Corporate Law, and the Perversion of Democracy* (Toronto: Between the Lines, 2002).

In this chapter, the nuts and bolts of the legal creation of a corporation are set out. This note emphasizes the peculiarity of the process.

Much of the pretending that needs to be done when creating a person by legal pronouncement is there for all to see. For instance, as the corporation must have a slew of people who will think and act for it for a registrar to declare it to be a person with the capacities of a human being, a slate of initial directors must be named in the application so that the registrar may pretend that a real person with the ability to cogitate and do things is to be given a licence. The artificiality of it all comes into view: How can a corporation choose its directors before it has begun life? As is the case with much of what goes on in this sphere of legal hocus pocus, a trick is played. The named directors are appointed only until they can be approved by a meeting of the corporation that they are to call as soon as the entity is registered.

2. COOKING THE BOOKS

1   Michael Winship, "Jack Lew's Footprints in Cayman Sand," *Consortium News*, March 10, 2013.

2   Aaron Sankin, "Jonathan Frieman, California Political Activist Asks, 'If Corporations Are People, Can They Ride in the Carpool Lane?,'" *Huffington Post*, Jan. 7, 2013; Brett Wilkins, "Judge Rejects Jonathan's Frieman's Corporate Personhood Carpool Lane Argument: Appeal Vowed," *Moral Low Ground*, Jan. 7, 2013.

The Frieman story was obviously an effort to bring attention to the absurdity of thinking of corporations as if they are human beings. For a similar imaginative effort to raise awareness, see "Seattle Woman Marries Corporation in Intimate Downtown Ceremony," posted by Cienna Madrid on *Slog*, July 17, 2012. It tells the story of Angela Vogel, who was issued a marriage certificate to wed someone called Corporate Person. She expressed her excitement although she feared the marriage would be set aside as Corporate Person was not an adult, being only 1.5 months old. In the event, the local administrators, giving no reasons, issued a statement that the marriage certificate had been issued in error and refunded the $64 application fee.

3   *Business Day*, April 22, 2013, 26.

4   Carl Gibson, "Tax Shelter from the Cuts on Tax," *Reader Supported News*, March 11, 2013.

5   Robert Scheer, "If Corporations Don't Pay Taxes, Why Should You?," *Truthdig*, March 12, 2013.

6   David Sirota, "Microsoft Admits Keeping $92 Billion Offshore to Avoid Paying $29 Billion in US Taxes," *International Business Times*, Aug. 22, 2014.

7   Jana Kasperkevic, "Forget Panama: It's Easier to Hide Your Money in the US Than Almost Anywhere," *Guardian*, April 6, 2016.

8   Gabriel Zucman, *The Hidden Wealth of Nations: The Scourge of Tax Havens* (Chicago: University of Chicago Press, 2015).

9   Laureen Snider, "The Sociology of Corporate Crime: An Obituary," *Theoretical Criminology* 4,2 (2000), 169; Laureen Snider, "Relocating Law: Making Corporate Crime Disappear" in E. Comack, ed., *Locating Law: Race/Class/Gender Connections* (Halifax: Fernwood Press, 2007).

10   *New York Times*, April 16, 2014.

11   However, as I demonstrated in *Wealth by Stealth*, they often violate laws that they see as a drag on profit-making.

In this chapter, the abuses made possible by the grant of separate legal personhood to each and every corporation is discussed. One manifestation is the use of revenue and democracy–sapping tax havens. This raises the question of the undue influence wielded by corporate actors. The following notes are concerned with U.S. attempts to curtail some of that political power and the apparent inability of governments everywhere to blunt corporate tax avoidance schemes and scams.

The kind of anti-corporate personhood activism evidenced by the car-pooling and pretend wedding stunts noted in this chapter arise out of the anxiety created throughout the United States by the Supreme Court's holding in *Citizens United* v. *FEC*, 2010, in which it was decided that a corporation, as a person, could contribute directly to a politician's campaign. The perceived skewing of the political process that followed this decision has given a spur to a movement that has always had traction in the United States. This is to argue for the revocation of corporate licences when corporations misbehave. The theoretical work of David Korten (*When Corporations Rule the World*, 3rd ed., Barret-Koehler, 2015), has been influential in this thrust, and the political efforts of the Program on Corporations Law and Democracy (see my *Wealth by Stealth* [Toronto: Between the Lines, 2002]) are well known. More recently, because of *Citizens United*, the movement has been demanding that corporations no longer be granted personhood in the first place. Move to Amend is a coalition of activists that promotes the passing of resolutions by communities and municipalities for their state legislatures to consider. The notion is to have the state governments go forward to demand a constitutional amendment. Typically the resolutions say: "Corporations and unions are legal entities that arguably help the economy, but that does not mean they are, in fact, people deserving of Constitutional personhood rights. We the People, actual human beings, will benefit when we clearly establish through a Constitutional Amendment that legal entities such as corporations, unions and, for that matter, the government, are meant to serve us, not the other way around" (http://movetoamend.org). Carl Gibson, in "Campaign for Finance Reform—That'll Shut 'Em Up" (*Reader Supported News*, July 11, 2014), reports that by July 2014, 487 local, county, and state entities had passed resolutions calling for a constitutional amendment that would end corporate personhood and the status of the use of money as an exercise in free speech.

On the tax issues raised in the chapter: headlines even before the Panama Papers scandal heightened the temperature captured the anxiety that pushes the G20 to deal with tax avoidance: "G20 Summit: States Chase Tax Evaders with Plan to Swap Data Globally," Simon Bowers, *Guardian*, Sept. 4, 2013; "G20: How Global Tax Reform Could Transform Africa's Fortunes," Kofi Annan, *Guardian*, Sept. 5, 2013. In the United Kingdom, domestic action was being urged to deal with the outflow of money after scandalizing newspaper reports such as "Wealth Doesn't Trickle Down—It Just Floods Offshore, Research Reveals," Heather Stewart, *Observer*, July 21, 2012; "HMRC Criticised as Just One of Top 30 Tax Fugitives Caught," theguardian.com, Aug. 9, 2013. The then legislative riposte was the *UK Corporate and Individual Tax and Transparency Bill 2013–14*, introduced on July 23, 2013.

The unpromising prospects for the mooted reforms are captured by a report of the International Consortium of Investigative Journalists that noted that 340 corporate entities (including Canada's Public Sector Pension Board) had signed tax deals with Luxembourg, a state known as a notorious tax haven. SBS, on November 6, 2014, reported that 1,600 companies listed their address as 5 rue Guillaume Kroll, Luxembourg. This was part of the information released on November 4, 2014, that became known as the Lux Leaks. Twenty-eight thousand documents on so-called tax rulings (advice given to accountants and lawyers as to how their corporate clients' income earned in Luxembourg would be treated) were published; see Wayne, Leslie, Carr, and Kelly, "Lux Leaks Revelations Bring Swift Response around the World," *International Consortium of Investigative Journalists*, Nov. 6, 2014; Boland Rudder and Schillis Gallego, "Luxembourg Leaks Stories around the World," *International Consortium of Investigative Journalists*, Nov. 6, 2014. Carol Goar (*Toronto Star*, Sept. 24, 2014), reported that in Canada, the Professional Institute of the Public Service of Canada was complaining as fifty members of the newly established international anti-tax avoidance department were to lose their jobs as the Harper government was defunding the exercise. This kind of disjuncture between the promise of a tougher stance and an actual downgrading of monitoring and enforcement is far from unusual. For instance, Robert H. Tillman and Henry N. Pontell, in "Corporate Fraud Demands Criminal Time" (*New York Times*, Opinion pages, June 29, 2016), noted that corporate securities fraud in the United States costs approximately $380 billion and that, despite the huge scandals that emerged out of the 2007–08 financial meltdowns, the number of FBI officers available to investigate white-collar crime dropped by 36 per cent so that by 2015, the number of prosecutions had sunk to their lowest ebb for twenty years.

So it is no surprise that, when the Lux Leaks revelations pushed the European Union to take steps to attack the tax haven problem, it was noted that the prospects were not rosy. For one thing, the European Commission's president is Jean-Claude Juncker, who had been the leader of the Luxembourg government for eighteen years (*Toronto Star*, Nov. 22, 2014, A31), that is, a government heavy of the very nation that had attracted the opprobrium of the International Consortium of Investigative Journalists' report. This kind of symbiosis between the blob-o-sphere and the political elites bubbles underneath the arguments made in this book; it facilitates wealth owners' ability to use the malleability of the blob to advantage themselves as governments legalize the manipulations.

Despite all the proclaimed outrage by the political classes, there appears to be a never-ending flow of reports on schemes and scams. There are reports that Walgreens, under immense public pressure, has abandoned its intention to use a technique known as "inversion" (giving all assets to a subsidiary in a low-tax locale, while not changing anything else about its operations), but, despite this apparent setback, the technique remains favoured by a lot of corporations. An embittered and saddened President Obama weighed in, calling these corporations who, after all, are using the magic of corporate law as they are legally entitled to do "deserters" (*Toronto Star*, Aug. 9, 2014). Recently, Margrethe Vestager, the European Union's competition commissioner, issued a demand that the Irish government recover $14.5 billion from Apple, the amount that Apple got from that government's favourable tax rulings in 1991 and 2007. She claims that the government had given preferential treatment to Apple in contravention of EU laws. She noted that Apple's effective European tax rate had been well below 1 per cent; see Armine Yalnizyan, "Will Apple Make or Break Europe" (*Toronto Star*, Sept. 2, 2016).

The difficulties of developing unified preventative action are on stark display. The Irish government obviously feels that it is to Ireland's advantage to do what it did; the U.S. government feels aggrieved by the ruling as it feels that, if anyone should be allowed to get at Apple, it should be the United States and they are afraid that the European Union would be the sole beneficiary of this ruling against the U.S. multinational Apple. But the U.S. government, like all others, has no effective means to garner some of the money it feels it ought to have had. One of the tools in the rather empty kit is to give tax haven users amnesty, but this does not work out so well. Robert Reich, in "Standing Up to Apple" (on his website, robertreich.org, Sept. 2, 2016), notes that during the last such tax amnesty, corporations were allowed to repatriate all their money with the assurance that it would be taxed at 5.25 per cent, rather than the normal 35 per cent which the tax haven seekers had been so keen to avoid. The hope was that some of this largesse for legal tax-avoiding outfits would persuade them to invest some of the repatriated money in the United States. But Reich records that 92 per cent of that money was not reinvested; rather, it was paid out in dividends to shareholders, share buy-backs, and bonuses. As the editors of the *Toronto Star* (Sept. 2, 2016), echoing Barack Obama, lamented, "Legal or not, Apple's arrangement is a scandal.... Canadians and corporations have stashed some $200 billion in offshore tax havens, resulting in a loss of tax revenue of about $8 billion a year.... Closing tax loopholes and ending sweetheart deals [is]... not tax gouging, just basic justice."

Meanwhile, in Canada, an exposé produced by the CBC and the *Toronto Star* has revealed that, when Canada Revenue Agency sat down with the to-be-taxed corporations (here we have the symbiosis again), it was decided to accept the corporate sectors' argument that, if they could not move their assets to tax havens, they would be at a competitive disadvantage. Hence, while proclaiming that it was trying to close existing loopholes, the government, ever so quietly, entered into Tax Information Exchange Agreements with a number of tax havens. This enabled the targets of the closing-of-the-loophole exercise to get legitimacy for moving their assets around more easily. The exposé claims that, since 2010, some $55 billion worth of tax money was lost by Canada (*Toronto Star*, June 17, June 20, 2016).

The Panama Papers, as the text notes, created a new furor around the tax avoidance issue. In part, this may have been due to the political points that could be scored when the first release of the papers occurred. It was noted that favourite Western media punching bags, such as Russia's president Putin, the family of the president of China, and some well-known drug lords in Mexico, had made use of Mossack Fonseca's services. Indeed, some conspiracy theorists observed that this might well have been an objective of those who funded the investigative journalists and helped them with access to the leaked data. For instance, Pepe Escobar, in "The Real Target of the Panama Papers" (teleSUR, May 11, 2016), pointed to the fact that the International Consortium of Investigative Journalists is funded by the Soros Foundation, which, he suggests, may have an interest in deflecting attention from the more important tax havens (Hong Kong, Switzerland, United States, and another nine nations that rank ahead of Panama) that the wealthy and their corporations prefer to use. Certainly, the initial media focus was on political "enemies" and reputed criminals, rather than systemic tax avoidance by "respectable" blobs and their owners.

Finally, note that the use of the corporate form to avoid the incidence of taxation is not restricted to the much-discussed tax havens' schemes. Michael Wolfson, Mike Veall, and Neil Brooks, in "Piercing the Veil: Private Corporations and the Income of the Affluent" (available from Mike Wolfson, mwolfson@uottawa.ca), have shown how putting money in Canadian-controlled private corporations (referred to as CCPCs), and paying themselves or their families incomes and/or dividends or postponing the payment of any income from these corporations, enable wealth owners to hide a great deal of money from the Canada Revenue Agency, aggravating the already yawning gap in income equality in the country. Note also that this set of manoeuvres supports the argument made in the book that 10 per cent ownership of shares gives substantial control over corporations, control here exercised to direct cash flows to minimize taxes, endorsing another point made in the book, namely that small corporations often are used for anti-social, uneconomic purposes.

3. GAMING THE SYSTEM

1   *Refac Industrial Contractors Inc.*, [1990] O.E.S.A.D., No. 83, decision of Robert Brown.

2   *Re Avant Lithographies,* [1991] CarswellOnt 1092, E.S.C. 2868.

3   *Lee v. Lee's Air Farming Ltd.,* [1961] A.C. 12 (Privy Council).

4   Harry Glasbeek, "The Legal Pulverization of Social Issues: *Andar Transport Pty. Ltd.* v. *Brambles Ltd,*" (2005), 13 *Torts Law Journal,* 217.

5   *Lian v. J. Crew Group Inc.* (2001), 54 OR (3d) 239 (Ont. S. Ct.).

6   Harry Glasbeek, "Contortions of Corporate Law: James Hardie Reveals Cracks in Liberal Law's Armour," (2012), 27 *Australian Journal of Corporate Law,* 132.

7   Mark J. Roe, "Corporate Strategic Reaction to Mass Tort," (1986), 72 *Virginia Law Revue,* 1; A. Ringleb and S. Wiggins, "Liability and Large Scale, Long-term Hazards," *Journal of Political Economy* 98 (1990), 574.

8   The Supreme Court of Canada pronouncements on piercing the veil are taken from *Kosmopoulos v. Constitution Insurance Co. of Canada,* [1987] 1 S.C.R. 2, specifically the judgment of Wilson, J.

The topic of when courts do, should, or could pierce the corporate veil takes up undue time in law schools and space in academic journals and books. I am guilty of participating in this rather sterile debate, sterile because actual piercing hardly ever happens. For my legal elaborations and discussions of the literature, see *Wealth by Stealth*, particularly chapters 4 and 5, where many other examples of astute uses of the blob to avoid legal imposts are furnished.

9   Harry Glasbeek, "Preliminary Observations on Strains of, and Strains in, Corporate Law Scholarship," in Frank Pearce and Laureen Snider, eds., *Corporate Crime: Contemporary Debates* (Toronto: University of Toronto Press, 1995).

Throughout this book a good deal of emphasis is put on the on-the-ground vulnerability of the wealthless and on law's role in sustaining the pretense that these imbalances are adequately offset by our laws and policies. Law allows the use of blobs to help wealth owners to extract more with little risk; it purports to hold that contracts contain the terms and conditions that the vulnerable voluntarily accept, giving it justification for the enforcement of harsh terms and conditions; it holds that the owners of wealth who manipulate the blob and the law in order to avoid such restrictions on their contractually based powers as do exist are not guilty of any sinful plots. The notes to this chapter provide illustrations of many other instances and circumstances in which controllers of corporations deploy the legal vehicle to exploit non-wealth owners while staying within the letter of the law. The emphasis is how workers' lives are rendered precarious by the "clever" use of law.

In this chapter, the Brambles case is used as an illustration of the conscious use of corporate letter-of-the-law doctrine to destroy the spirit of the law. Brambles, by its machinations, was trying to overcome the few victories workers had won after a century or more of struggles and hardships. In early capitalism—well into the late nineteenth century—employers were allowed to say that any injuries suffered by their employees were not compensable because the relationship was one of pure contract, and therefore, the employee must be taken to have agreed to any risks that the workplace threw up. Similarly, at that time, even if the employee could show that the employer had contributed to the injury by their negligence, the employee was still out of luck if the employee's own conduct had been careless in any degree. Contributory negligence in those unfettered laissez-faire days was a complete defence. Moreover, if an injury could be attributed to the careless conduct of a fellow employee, the employer was let off the hook by courts that accepted the argument that any employee voluntarily assumed the risk of having to deal with careless and incompetent fellow workers. In this legal setting, workers were defenceless, and the carnage and economic hardships forced them into political battles.

Eventually, these battles led to the legislative abolition of the contributory negligence rules and the common employment rules; more importantly, it led to the development of a workers' compensation system in which employees need only show that they had been engaged at work when hurt in order to recover something for their injuries. The courts, acknowledging that their adherence to pure contract doctrines had become an anachronism, gradually agreed to impose duties on employers to provide a safe work system, lest they be held liable by courts for the injuries inflicted on workers. Employers would now be liable to them by having a different head of law, tort law rather than contract law, apply in these circumstances. In addition, employers became vicariously responsible for the negligence of their workers should they harm third parties when carrying out their duties for their employers. All in all, judicial law had come to the position that since an employer could control the risks of the enterprise better than its employees, it should assume some of the responsibilities when those risks materialized. This is an important development to the thrust of this book's central argument, which is that controlling beneficiaries should be saddled with legal responsibilities.

Thus, whereas once an employer could rely totally on the judicial pretense that an employment contract was one between equals who assumed risks voluntarily, this assumption of true voluntarism, while left in place conceptually, is modified when applied in various circumstances. This irritates employers. Brambles used the separate corporate personality doctrine to pretend that it had nothing to do with the risk-bearing assumptions of another person who, once upon a time, it would have wanted to be legally treated as an obedient, risk-assuming employee. This, then, is an example of how the corporate form and corporate law are twisted—legally—to avert obligations imposed by other rules of that self-same legal system. There is much cunning and little shame. The levels of low cunning know no limits.

Sara Mojtehedzadeh, in "Just Energy Focus of Class Action" (*Toronto Star*, Aug. 8, 2016, GT1), provides an example of a variant on the Brambles scheme. Seven thousand people whose task it was to go door-to-door to sell gas and electricity contracts on behalf of a corporation called Just Energy have brought a class action to have themselves declared employees and, therefore, entitled to minimum legislated terms and conditions mandated for employees' benefit. These complainants earned much less than the minimum but had signed a contract with Just Energy that described them as independent contractors. They are claiming that this characterization is negated by their actual terms and conditions. Just Energy has responded by arguing that the demands it made for training, the wearing of certain Just Energy identifying clothing items, and the provision of suggested sales techniques were simply aids and recommendations and did not indicate that Just Energy controlled these contractors as it would if they had been real employees. The jurisprudence suggests that the outcome of this legal dispute is far from certain. There is a relatively low rate of success for complainants in these kind of cases, a signal reason why this cost-avoiding strategy continues to thrive.

In the text it is suggested that the cogs in the Eliz Wong retailers' chain of production stretching down to an impecunious small operator, Rebecca Wong and her Eliz World, might be classed as agents of the retailers. This should not be a startling proposition. The corporations at the top end often will describe their links in the chain in that way. The *Toronto Star* reporter Rick Westland (Oct. 13, 2013), tells about a manufacturer in Bangladesh who had allegedly sacked workers trying to unionize. Westland interviewed executives of a Canadian retailer, Reitmans, that sold garments made by the anti-union Bangladeshi employer. He quotes a Reitmans executive as saying that Reitmans knew nothing about the alleged sackings as they do not "contract directly to them but sometimes ... use agents for this work and [they] may have in this case." The corporate separation allows principals to hide behind a veil of pretended ignorance. It is corporate law thinking that resists taking into account the actual functioning of corporate businesses as deliberately devised by them; it is law's rigid formalism about corporate separate personhood that is manipulated by clever lawyers and accountants.

By comparison, respect is paid to the functional nature of relationships elsewhere in law. When an enterprise is sought to be made vicariously responsible for the damage done to a third party by a person who appeared to be acting on behalf of the enterprise, or when a claim for payments to be made towards a social welfare fund for employees is at issue, or when an injured person seeks workers' compensation, or when a union seeks recognition as a bargaining agent and the employer claims that the persons wanting to bargain are independent contractors rather than employees, and so on, the fundamental issue for the courts and legislation has been whether the enterprise can be said to be in functional control. Jurisprudence and legislation have developed to see whether people are functionally part and parcel of the enterprise or are dependent, rather than independent, contractors. Once they are classified as being under control or as being part and parcel of the enterprise, the enterprise will be on the hook.

The core of the argument to be made later in the text is that actors with control over others from whose conduct they seek to benefit (like the retailers discussed in this chapter) should be liable for that conduct. Here it suffices to say that the element of control matters morally, socially, and economically and, therefore, should matter legally. Thus, in the same *Toronto Star* article cited above, Westland noted that the Bangladeshi manufacturer had been forced to reinstate the unionizing workers. The manufacturer bitterly said that this was a signal to foreign retail chains that, from now on, his products would be more expensive and that they would punish him, thereby hurting the very workers about whom everyone seemed so concerned. To support his claim, he told the *Star* reporter that a Canadian retailer, Fame Jeans, had cancelled a contract worth $150,000 as a result of the episode. Fame Jeans denied any knowledge of the sackings and riposted that it always reserved the right to cancel orders for poor performance or untimeliness. Whatever the truth of the matter, it is clear that all participants understand where the control and power in these kinds of relationships reside.

The vast jurisprudence and literature on the many means to deal with the ability of large capitalists to organize themselves so as to rupture their direct legal relationships with those who are a vital part of their profit-making activities is a clear acknowledgement of the facts that the corporate form facilitates this risk-shifting and that capitalists take advantage of it in many ingenious ways. One of the most common is the use of labour hire agencies. Employers contract with a labour hire corporation that collects a pool of workers. The labour hire firm, for a fee, dispatches workers as required by a business. There are endless questions about which of the enterprises is responsible for, and to, the hired workers. Different answers are provided in different jurisdictions; different answers are provided in any one jurisdiction depending on why the question arises. The details are not pertinent here, but four points emerge: first, the question is not whether the worker is an employee, but who the employer is, a refocusing of the problem, one that disadvantages the employees; second, the labour hire firm places workers as demanded, i.e., as if they were so much equipment; third, the labour hire firms and the enterprises with which they contract are overwhelmingly corporations and therefore unlikely to be considered integrated departments of the corporation to which they supply labour, or to be thought of as the producing site's agent or employee; fourth, this rupturing of direct personal relationships to avoid the obligations of law that are incidental to direct personal contracts is much in vogue. For instance, one such large labour hire firm, Adecco Worldwide, is a Fortune 500 company with annual revenues of 16.3 billion Euros and 28,000 employees. The Economic Development Committee of the State of Victoria in Australia records that Adecco claims to place 312 workers every minute.

4. THE SHAREHOLDER AS GAMBLER

1   Milton Friedman, *Capitalism and Freedom* (Chicago: University of Chicago Press, 1962).

2   *Automatic Self-Cleansing Filter Co. v. Cunninghame*, [1906] 2 Ch. 34 (Court of Appeal).

3   Gerda Reith, ed., *Gambling: Who Wins? Who Loses?* (Amherst, NY: Prometheus Press, 2003); Gerda Reith, *The Age of Chance: Gambling in Western Culture* (London: Routledge, 1999); I. Nelson Rose, "Compulsive Gambling and the Law: From Sin to Vice to Disease," *Journal of Gambling Behavior* 4,4 (1988), 240; Roger Munting, *An Economic and Social History of Gambling in Britain and the U.S.A.* (Manchester: Manchester

University Press, 1996); David Dixon, *From Prohibition to Regulation: Bookmaking, Anti-Gambling and the Law* (Oxford: Clarendon Press, 1991).

4 Darrell W. Bolen and William H. Boyd, "Gambling and the Gambler: A Review and Preliminary Findings," *Archives of General Psychiatry* 18,5 (1968), 615; Jerome H. Skolnick, *House of Cards: Legalization and Control of Casinos Gambling* (Boston: Little, Brown, 1978); Reith, *Gambling*, ch. 19; Francis Allen, *Borderland of Criminal Justice: Essays in Law and Criminology* (Chicago: University of Chicago Press, 1964).

5 *Securities and Exchange Commission* v. *W.J. Howey Company and Howey-In-The-Hills Service Inc.*, 328 U.S.203; *Hawaii (State) by Its Commissioner of Securities* v. *Hawaii Market Center, Inc,* 485 P.2d 105 (Sup. Ct. Hawaii); *Pacific Coast Coin Exchange of Canada* v. *Ontario (Securities Commission)*, [1978] 2 S.C.R 112 (S.C.C.).

6 Adam Smith, *An Inquiry into the Nature and Causes of the Wealth of Nations*, ed. Edwin Cannan (New York: Modern Library, 1994), bk. III, ch. 1.

7 Adolph A. Berle and Gardiner C. Means, *The Modern Corporation and Private Property* (New York: Commerce Clearing House, 1932).

8 Diana Gordon, *The Return of the Dangerous Classes: Drug Prohibition and the Policy Politics* (New York: W.W. Norton, 1994).

9 Charles Loring Brace, *The Dangerous Classes of New York* (Echo Library, 2010, first pub. 1872).

The notes to this chapter contain a short account of way in which the law and economics school sees the nature of the corporation and some criticism of this perspective. There is also an acknowledgement of an alternative view of the corporation by scholars who see the corporate form as a potential tool for progressive action. There is an account of the legal limits on shareholders' right to be hands-on. The coincidence between gambling and investing in corporate shares is explored further, as is some of the anti-corporate sentiment in the early days of corporate law.

The law and economics school is guided by a belief that the corporate form is just a convenience. It is merely a shorthand way of describing a nexus of contracts between autonomous individuals, shareholders, lenders, and employees, who all are acting as market actors should. Milton Friedman argued that the use of a corporation when chasing profits was completely consonant with the idealized market model that envisaged individuals acting on their own accounts, provided that "enterprises are private so that the ultimate contracting parties are individuals." How clever: neither liberal nor market principles are a problem if a corporation is just a nexus of contracts. The utility of this claim to corporate cheerleaders is manifest. Thus, statutory benefits and rules, such as limited liability and directors' duties to the corporation, are to be seen as terms of contracts that would have been expressly negotiated if the principals were left to their own devices. The legal interventions that write in these conditions are, like the company form, merely cost-saving conveniences. For a review of the vast literature on, and critique of, these ideas, see my *Wealth by Stealth* and "More Direct Duties for Directors: Much Ado About … What?," (1995), 25 *Canadian Business Law Journal*, 416. While the law and economics adherents do see shareholders as principals (a position that leads them to justify the entrenched idea that the interests of the corporation and that of the shareholders are congruent), they do not want them to be held responsible as principals when the corporation commits wrongs or leaves debts to be paid. This peculiar tension-filled stance is defended on claimed empirical grounds, grounds that are challenged later in the body of the text.

There are other theories of the corporation that posit that shareholders are not its principals and should not be held to account for its behaviour. The argument is that the corporation is a living thing, in its own right. The point of shareholders' capital becoming the corporation's property so as to enable it to dispense it as it wills is to create a stable fund, one that does not in any way depend on the whims of shareholders; see M. Blair and L. Stout, "Team Production Theory of Corporate Law," (1999), 85 *Virginia Law Revue*, 247. This argument sees the corporation as an ideal vehicle for long-term planning and, thereby, increased welfare for all, and as being perfectly suited to look after the interests of stakeholders other than shareholders. But this attractive line of reasoning is countered by facts on the ground that speak to the schizophrenia of corporate law. Should a corporation's life be terminated, if it has met all its outstanding obligations, shareholders are entitled to a proportion (matching their proportion of investment) of the residual property of the now defunct corporation. That is, after saying categorically that the shareholders have no rights over the property of the corporation, in the end, they are said to have some right to it. Moreover, the same facts on the ground show that the directors and executives of corporations, apparently unaware of the theory, do believe that their primary obligation is to their shareholders.

The legal approach that denies shareholders the right to participate in operational decision-making, even very important decision-making, might be thought of as leaving the power *to* do things to the corporation's functionaries, while the power *over* the corporation might still be vested elsewhere. Indeed, at the centre of this book is the argument that ultimate control over the fate of a corporation rests with some shareholders, even though they never seem to be engaged in operational matters. For a strong, early judicial acknowledgement that, despite the strong statements that shareholders have no role to play, directors and managers have not usurped all powers over the corporations, see the judgment of Greer, L.J., in *John Shaw & Sons (Salford) Ltd. v. Shaw*, [1935] 2 K.B.113: "A company is an entity distinct alike from its shareholders and its directors. Some of its powers may, according to its [constitution] be exercised by directors; certain other powers may be reserved for its shareholders in general meeting. If powers of management are vested in the directors, they and they alone can exercise these powers. The only way in which the general body of shareholders can control the exercise of the powers vested by the articles in the directors is by altering the articles, or, if opportunity arises under the articles, by refusing to re-elect the directors of whose actions they disapprove. They cannot themselves usurp the powers which by the articles are vested in the directors any more than that the directors can usurp the powers vested by the articles in the general body of the shareholders."

For the equation of shareholders with low-level gamblers, see Thomas Lee Hazen, "Rational Investments, Speculation, or Gambling?: Derivative Securities and Financial Futures and Their Effect on the Underlying Capital Markets," (1992), 86 *Northwestern University Law Review*, 987. It may be jarring to some, although the analogy is frequently made. Robert J. Shiller, "Financial Speculation: Economic Efficiency and Public Policy," a background paper prepared for the 20th Century Fund, Jan. 1991, quotes Theodore Roosevelt: "There is no moral difference between gambling at cards or in lotteries or on the race track and gambling in the stock market. One method is just as pernicious to the body politic as the other kind and in degree the evil worked is far greater." *Roget's II: The New Thesaurus* (Houghton Mifflin, 1980), provides the following description of a gamble: "To bet: 'We bet on the winner'; to gamble, to put, to stake, to take a flyer." For its overlap with share market players, see the thesaurus's description of speculation: "Speculator: one who speculates for quick profit; 'stock market speculators'; one who bets; equivalent for gambler."

And for an example of the way in which stock markets resemble promoters of the gambling industries, see *Business Day, The Age*, March 17, 2014, relating how markets react to published and unreliable statistics about employment: "It suits the vested interests of the financial markets and the media to ignore the Bureau of Statistics' advice and focus on the volatile seasonally adjusted estimates rather than the more reliable trend estimates." The coincidence between gambling and investing on corporate outcomes suggests, strongly, that gambling is part of the essence of capitalism as it exists, rather than as it portrays itself. Thus, Vicki Abt et al. in *The Business of Risk: Commercial Gambling in Mainstream America* (University of Kansas Press, 1985), note that capitalism hails the virtue of equality of opportunity while concretely it manifests itself as supporting massive substantive inequality. In this setting, gambling/speculation provides "a safety valve for … unfulfilled hopes," as there always is a chance that it will work out for some of the gamblers. The relationship between gambling and productive enterprise is also real. Jerome Skolnick (who was cited in this chapter) tells the story of how mining in Nevada was a speculative entrepreneurial endeavour, but one that was tolerated because of its kinship with to-be-encouraged market activity. At the same time, recreational gambling was legislatively resisted. But when mining fell into disarray, licences for recreational gambling became a major source of government revenue, one argument justifying it that it was not all that different to betting on a bonanza in a mine enterprise.

The creation of an atmosphere of getting something by relying on the way the ball bounces, rather than by dint of effort and/or thought, is pivotal to much of what goes on in the markets for financial products. It should not escape our attention that the instruments that create these financial opportunities are referred to as products, even though, all too often, they are only remotely connected to the production of any material good or service.

Even formally, the resemblance between shareholders and socially useless gamblers is understood to be a close one. Legislative provisions have had to be enacted to ensure that securities do not fall foul of the regulatory restrictions on gambling; see Christine Hurt, "Regulating Public Morals and Private Markets: Online Securities Trading, Internet Gambling and the Speculation Paradox," (2005), 86 *Boston Law Review*, 371, who notes that buying a passive interest in a corporation is seen as legal by default but, when governments want to inhibit online gambling (because it is hard to get revenues from it), they are forced to craft exceptions for online share trading, lest it be inhibited by anti-gambling legislation. This is not the only embarrassment spawned by the promotion of share purchasing and trading.

The standard legal definition of a security reproduced in the text dovetails with the Marxist view of the essence of capitalism. Marxism posits that, at its core, capitalism is the appropriation by individuals of value produced by a collective. This is what they see as a characteristic of a class-divided political economy. The mainstream definition of a security (an investment of money to be managed by another so as to extract profit from the productive labour of others) suggests an unwitting acknowledgement that shareholders are protected to the extreme extent they are because they are members of the ruling class (although many shareholders, as will be discussed, are not shareholders who hunt for profit but are looking for security). They belong to a class of individuals whose appropriation of collectively produced wealth is to be privileged by law. This should be discomfiting to those who hold fast to the proposition that class war is a figment of out-of-step theorists and malcontents.

The *Law Times* cited in the text was only one of many progressive voices that expressed disgust at the shielding of investors by the limited liability device. On Feb. 11, 1842, *Emporium and True American*, a Democratic newspaper, expressed anxiety about the unpaid debts the privilege would leave: "Should an incorporation, simply because it is an incorporation, have the privilege to contract debts, squander their capital, and leave the community to suffer, while, individually, the persons interested are in affluence? Should they have privileges that are denied to individuals?" In Canada, reformer William Lyon Mackenzie, in the lead-up to the Upper Canada Rebellion, 1837–1838, in the Nov. 15, 1837, issue of his newspaper, *The Constitution*, presented a Draft Constitution that he hoped would become the basis for a proposed constitutional convention. One of its provisions was: "S. 56: There shall never be created within this State any incorporated trading companies or incorporated companies with banking powers. Labour is the only means of creating wealth."

One of the commentaries on the early doubts of the legitimacy of corporations was by J.W. Hurst, 1970. For more recent questioning of the potential legitimacy problems created by limited liability, see T. Ornhial, ed., *Limited Liability and the Corporation* (London: Croom Helm, 1982); J. Ziegel, "Is Incorporation (with Limited Liability) Too Easily Available?," (1991), *Les Cahiers de Droit* 31; Harry Glasbeek, *Wealth by Stealth*. Of course, there were always many (and ultimately triumphant) protagonists who were totally happy about what the *Law Times* considered an outrage. B. Cataldo, "Limited Liability with One-Man Companies and Subsidiary Companies," [1953], *Law and Contemporary Problems* 18, cited Charles W. Eliot, the then president of Harvard University as saying that "limited liability is by far the most effective legal invention ... made in the 19th century."

The worries expressed about the apparent gap between ownership and control are due, in part, to the understanding that, in a world in which greed and self-advancement are seen as natural, as to be promoted, trust and obligation come to be seen as unnecessary luxuries indulged in at one's peril. In such an imagined world, it is to be expected that opportunities to satisfy greed and self-advancement will be pursued with vigour by those in a position to do so. Shirking and looting are natural, if not to be promoted. Shirking and looting by avaricious types come at the expense of others who also would like to satisfy their greed and self-interest at the expense of everyone else. This is why it is hoped that, as between those who belong to the greedy opportunistic class, the opportunistic takings from others will be sorted out by the very mechanism that gives them their opportunities, the market and its tool, the corporation. It follows that the movements that push for directors and executives to use their discretion to use the steady fund of corporate capital for altruistic reasons, that is, in a corporate responsible way, start behind the eight ball. The intended beneficiaries, and the directors and functionaries, all favour the maximization of profits. They may differ on how to divide the spoils produced by means of the corporation; they are united on the need to produce as much as they can for them to fight over.

This has not stopped liberal reformers from arguing that the gap between ownership and management has laid the ground for managers to search to deliver a reasonable profit (an oxymoron if ever there was one!) that will keep the gambling shareholders happy, leaving the managers free to pursue the public good by utilizing corporate funds to attain desirable social goals. In the immediate aftermath of the publication of the Berle and Means study cited in the text, E.M. Dodd, "For Whom Are Corporate Managers Trustees?," (1932), 45 *Harvard Law Review*, 1145, made a famous argument to this effect. This led to a Berle response, arguing that managers owed a primary responsibility to maximize the owners' interests. Eventually, Berle was to soften that stance, and a host of 1950s and 1960s scholars—for example, E. Mason, ed., *The Corporation in Modern Society* (Atheneum, 1966)—urged a quasi-public role on corporate managers; see also C.H. Schmithoff, "Salomon in the Shadow," [1976], *Journal of Business Law* 305; E. Kamenka and A. Tay, "Social Traditions and Legal Traditions" and "'Transforming' the Law and 'Steering' Society" in Kamenka and Tay, eds., *Law and Social Control* (St. Martin's Press, 1980). Today, these ideas are reflected in the corporate social responsibility movement to be discussed later in the body of the book. It will be argued that this movement, based as it is on frail premises, will not bring the rewards its many well-meaning proponents seek. The fundamentals of corporate capitalism get in the way.

Marxism-inspired scholars regard the claim that there is a gap between management and investors as a mistaken analysis that sees individuals and groups as determining what the nature of the business is. They argue that the nature of the business system, capitalist relations of production, determines how individuals and groups must act. Marxists see them as persons joined by a common goal, namely, to expand the capital invested in the corporation. In the end, the personal motivation of the managers and investors will be subjugated to their joint goal, which is to rule the corporation in the wealth-owning class's interest; see P. Sweezy, "Galbraith's Utopia," *New York Review of Books* X,18 (1973), a response to one of the chief proponents of managerial sovereignty and the potential for good this entailed. Moreover, Marxists argue—and this is important to the conclusion reached in this book—that, despite the apparent control by corporate directors that worried Berle and Means and their followers, the investing class, actual capitalists, had not disappeared even as the corporate form seemed to give that impression. Berle and Means, by contrast, were worried that capitalism, with its notion of individual entrepreneurship, was becoming endangered. The reference to private property in the title of Berle and Means's study is illuminating—the authors were concerned that red-blooded capitalists, by becoming shareholders, were losing control over *their* private property. It may be that the fear expressed in this study got more play than it might have had if it had it been published in an era when a Depression was not looming, that is, at a time when serious questions about the utility of capitalism were being raised. The notion that there should be no gap between ownership and control is conceptually important to capitalism. After all, as noted in the text, the danger of the separation of ownership from control had been pointed out by Adam Smith. Thorsten Veblen, in *The Theory of the Business Enterprise* (New York: Scribner's, 1904), had already written about the inefficiencies that inhere in the use of corporations. It also may be speculated that the Berle and Means concerns may have stemmed, in part, from their instinctive appreciation of Marxist-informed scholarship which saw incorporation leading to the transformation of individualized private capital into socialized capital as the owner of the collective capital, the corporation, became the active capitalist. This is not an idea that would have appealed to them.

5. THE SHAREHOLDER AS TOXIN

1   Friedman, *Capitalism and Freedom*; "The Social Responsibility of Business Is to Increase Its Profits," *New York Times Magazine*, Sept. 13, 1979; Friedrich Hayek, *The Road to Serfdom* (Chicago: University of Chicago Press, 2006, first pub. 1944).

2   Lee Drutman and Charlie Cray, *The People's Business: Controlling Corporations and Restoring Democracy* (San Francisco: Berrett-Koehler, 2004).

3   Henry Blodget, "The Green Investor: Virtue Has a Price," reproduced in *Australian Financial Review*, Jan. 2008.

4   Michael J. Sandel, *What Money Can't Buy: The Moral Limits of Markets* (New York: Farrar, Strauss & Giroux, 2012).

5   Ibid., 138.

6   E.J. Mishan, "The Rise of Affluence and the Decline of Welfare," in Herman E. Daly, ed., *Valuing the Earth: Economics, Ecology and Ethics* (Herman E. Daly, 1980).

7   Matt Taibbi, *The Divide: American Injustice in the Age of the Wealth Gap* (Melbourne/London: Scribe, 2014).

8   Ana Marie Cox, "Private Prisons: The GOP's Real Shame on the Border," *Guardian, UK*, July 22, 2014.

9   In The Public Interest (ITPI), *Criminal: How Lockup Quotas and Low Taxes Guarantee Profits for Private Prison Corporations*, 2013.

10 ACLU, *Banking on Bondage: Private Prisons and Mass Incarceration*, Nov. 2, 2011.

11 Sarah Schweitzer, "A Matter of Policy: Suit Hits Wal-Mart Role as Worker Life Insurance Beneficiary," *Boston Globe*, Dec. 10, 2002; Ellen E. Schultz and Theo Francis, "Valued Employees: Worker Dies, Firm Profits—Why?," *Wall Street Journal*, April 19, 2002; "Why Secret Insurance on Employees Pays Off," *Wall Street Journal*, April 25, 2002; "Why Are Workers in the Dark?," *Wall Street Journal*, April 24, 2002; "Big Banks Pile Up 'Janitors Insurance,'" *Wall Street Journal*, May 2, 2002; "Death Benefit: How Corporations Built Finance Tool out of Life Insurance," *Wall Street Journal*, Dec. 30, 2002; Ellen E. Schultz, "Banks Use Life Insurance to Fund Bonuses," *Wall Street Journal*, May 20, 2009.

12 Sandel, *What Money Can't Buy*.

13 G. Geis, "The Heavy Electrical Equipment Anti-trust Cases of 1961," in M.B. Clinard and R. Quinney, eds., *Criminal Behaviour Systems* (New York: Holt, Rinehart & Winston, 1967).

14   G. Geis and R.F. Meyer, eds., *White-Collar Crime* (New York: Free Press, 1977).

15   Steve Tombs and David Whyte, *Safety Crimes,* ed. H.Croall (Cullompton: Willan, 2007).

16   Marshall B. Clinard and Peter C. Yeager, *Corporate Crime* (New York: Free Press, 1980).

17   F. Pearce, *Crimes of the Powerful: Marxism, Crime and Deviance* (London: Pluto Press, 1976); F. Pearce and M. Woodiwiss, eds., *Global Crime Connections: Dynamics and Control* (Toronto: University of Toronto Press, 1993); J.E. Parkinson, *Corporate Power and Responsibility: Issues in the Theory of Company Law* (Oxford: Clarendon Press, 1993); Celia Wells, *Corporations and Criminal Responsibility* (Oxford: Clarendon Press, 1993); Stephen Box, *Power, Crime, and Mystification* (London/New York: Tavistock Press, 1983); D. Ellis, *The Wrong Stuff* (Toronto: Collier-McMillan, 1986); J. McMullan, *Beyond the Limits of the Law: Corporate Crime and Law and Order* (Halifax: Fernwood Press, 1992); L. Snider, *Bad Business: Corporate Crime in Canada* (Toronto: Nelson, 1993); Geis and Meier, *White-Collar Crime*; M. David Ermann and Richard J. Lundman, *Corporate and Governmental Deviance: Problems of Organizational Behaviour in Contemporary Society,* 2nd ed. (New York/Oxford: Oxford University Press, 1982); Henry N. Pontell and G. Geis, eds., *International Handbook of White-Collar and Corporate Crime* (New York: Springer, 2007); Russell Mokhiber, *Corporate Crime and Violence: Big Business Power and the Abuse of Public Trust* (New York: Random House, 1989); Gary Slapper and Steve Tombs, *Corporate Crime* (London: Longman, 1999); Steve Tombs and David Whyte, *Unmasking the Crimes of the Powerful* (New York: Peter Lang, 2003); Steve Tombs and David Whyte, *The Corporate Criminal: Why Corporations Must be Abolished* (New York: Routledge, 2015).

18   *Lewis K. Liggett v. Lee,* 288 U.S. 517, 1933.

19   Glasbeek, *Wealth by Stealth.*

20   Ian T. Shearn, "ExxonMobil's New Guinea Nightmare," *Nation,* May 1, 2014.

21   MiningWatch Canada, June 18, 2014; Canadian Centre for International Justice, June 18, 2014.

The notes to this chapter deal with aspects of corporate social responsibility, offer more data on janitors' insurance and private prisons as well as a commentary on the extent of corporate illegalities and the different treatment of regulatory and criminal law.

There is a conceptually persuasive defence for the approach that proclaims that directors and managers have a primary duty to shareholders and that neither they nor the shareholders they endeavour to benefit should be too concerned about any social or economic impacts this might have on others. In addition, there is much anecdotal evidence that this approach is internalized by corporations and the shareholding class. Friedman, in a much-quoted article whose title said it all—"The Social Responsibility of Business Is to Increase

Its Profits," *New York Times Magazine*, Sept. 19, 1979—wrote that there was no sensible way for directors and executives of a corporation to balance profits versus all sorts of other goals. Acerbically, he said that arguments for the imposition of a duty on corporations to act in a socially responsible manner (other than the maximization of profits) were "notable for their analytical looseness and lack of rigor." Hayek's argument, in *The Road to Serfdom*, first published in 1944, was more frankly political. He argued that, if unelected administrators of private corporations had to look out for what *they* might believe to be the common good, they would have no standing to make such decisions and, likely, no expertise. It would be anti-democratic and possibly inefficient to ask them to impose their views on society. It is not happenstance, of course, that these advocates for private buccaneering became the intellectual heroes of the right-wing political regimes from Margaret Thatcher onwards.

Their line of thinking gives vigour to the way in which corporations soldier on even as they offend everyone outside their sphere. None of the publicity around its shamelessly implausible claims and callous conduct appears to restrain the tobacco industry. George Monbiot, *Guardian*, Nov. 5, 2013, notes that, when Australia decided that cigarettes should be sold in plain packets marked with shocking health warnings, Philip Morris asked an international trade tribunal to award it compensation pursuant to a free trade agreement between Hong Kong and Australia. Its argument was that its intellectual property rights protected under that deal were about to be infringed. The intellectual property rights were its "right" to design its packets as it deemed fit. At this time, the outcome of this dispute is not available, but the action demonstrates that, if a plausible argument defending profit-making can be made, it will be made, no matter how anti-social, how anti-democratic it turns out to be.

There are daily examples of how corporate actors maximize their profits even as it offends the public's sense of decency. It was noted in the text that, when it comes to making money, the question for a pharmaceutical company is not whether a needed and useful drug should be manufactured but whether it is likely to yield more profit than a frivolous compound such a skin lotion. Of course, if the need for a drug is great and its availability limited, it is highly prized and priced by such a corporation. The *Toronto Star*, Sept. 23, 2015, A2, carried the following headline: "CEO to Roll Back Pills' 5,000% Price Hike." Marin Shkreli, an entrepreneur who had bought another corporation, the sole provider of Daraprim, a vital antidote to a deadly parasitic disease, toxoplasmosis, used his vendor's power to stick it to consumers who had no choice if they wanted to live. The outcry in this instance led to a promise of an unspecified reduction in price. But while one corporation, Valeant, and a brash executive were identified as scoundrels by the drama of the story, the logic of keeping needed drugs away from those who cannot pay pervades the industry.

Mylan, another pharmaceutical corporation, has sole control over a medical device known as EpiPen, which has the capability of saving the lives of people who suffer anaphylaxis attacks. The original research was initiated by the Pentagon; Mylan's only real input has been the provision of the medicine to be injected. It costs Mylan very little. Since 2012, Mylan has raised the price of EpiPens some 600 per cent, making it prohibitive for many would-be users. Public outrage has been fuelled by revelations that Mylan's CEO's wage packet has increased by 671 per cent since 2007, the year that Mylan gained monopoly control. By 2015, her salary was an eye-popping $18.9 million; see Ben Popken, "Mylan Execs Gave Themselves Raises as They Hiked EpiPen Prices," *NBC News*, Aug. 24, 2016; Jim Hightower, "How Can a CEO Feel Good about Price Gouging to Get Rich?," *AlterNet*, Aug. 31, 2016. In the same vein, Deena Beasley, *Reuters*, Jan. 10, 2016, wrote a story head-lined "Pfizer Hikes US Prices for Over 100 Drugs on Jan. 1," and Charles Davis penned "Children Are Dying from Pneumonia, but Greed Is the Real Killer," teleSUR, March 6, 2016; Lee Fang, "Pharmaceutical Company Funding Anti-Pot Fight Worried about Los-ing Business, Filings Show," *Intercept*, Sept. 12, 2016, details how drug manufacturers of fentanyl (whose abuse is said to be responsible for many deaths) are opposing marijuana legalization because its similar anti-pain properties may diminish the market for fentanyl; for a more comprehensive account, see Fran Quigley, "Corporations Killed Medicine: Here's How to Take It Back," *Foreign Policy in Focus*, Feb. 5, 2016.

Or take the way corporations try to please their shareholders, as told by the headline above a Thad Moore story in the *Washington Post*, July 25, 2015: "US to Investigate Airlines for Using Amtrak Crash to Increase Rates." Devastation for some may provide wonderful profit opportunities for others; shareholders are never reluctant to take advantage of the misery of others. Indeed, they often express their anger when this is not done: "Wal-Mart Stock Drops 3% after Wage Hike," *Toronto Star*, Aug. 19, 2015, S8.

This context makes it clear that the use of janitors' insurance is not just a bizarre manifestation of greed by a few anti-social corporate actors. Rather, it is an illustration of a norm which entails a repulsive venality produced by careful business planning, a point to which I shall return later in the body of the book. Thus, in the janitors' insurance case, once a new means to exploit workers had been invented, it was pursued earnestly, even though it was likely to fill anyone who learned about it with indignation. Michael Sandel, whose work is relied on in this chapter, summarizes the findings of the exposes he cites: by the early 2000s, Corporate-Owned Life Insurance (COLI) constituted 25 to 30 per cent of all life insurance sales. By 2008, U.S. banks held $122 billion of life insurance on their employees, even though there once had been a requirement that such COLIs could only be bought in respect to the employees with the highest one-third of pay in any one firm. Some states still require lower-ranked employees' consent. What Walmart did in response was to offer free insurance policies for benefits up to $5,000 while getting their consent to take out policies on employees that would pay out several hundred thousand dollars to

Walmart when they died. It is important to note that, in Canada, the purchase of life insurance policies by third parties is permitted only in Quebec, Nova Scotia, New Brunswick, and Saskatchewan.

Overall, then, there is little embarrassment if profits are made. Lee Fang, "Gun Industry Executives Say Mass Shootings Are Good for Business," *The Intercept*, Dec. 3, 2015, tells the story that market analysts, who need information to advise potential investors, hassle gun manufacturers after a mass shooting. They know that there will be a lot of fuss about reform of gun laws, but they also know that, after such tragedies, there will be an invigorated demand for guns. Experience has taught them this. After the first trading day following the homophobic slaughter in Orlando in 2016, Smith & Wesson shares went up $1.50; see Jennifer Wells, "Another Rise in Firearm-Maker Shares after Tragedy Hits," *Toronto Star*, June 15, 2106; she also noted that, after the horrible shootings in Paris and San Bernardino in 2015, Remington reported a sharp increase in profits. Thus it is that the analysts want to know whether they can safely tell their clients that the gun manufacturers are ready to take advantage of the intensified demand after a shocking life-taking event. They know that their clients, these would-be shareholders, will be more than happy to make money out of death, even as their actions increase the likelihood of more deaths.

Equally cynical was the statement of CBS's CEO, Leslie Mooves, who, at an investors' conference, chortled about the Trump campaign: "It may not be good for America, but it's damn good for CBS.... The money's rolling in ... this is going to be very good for us ... a terrible thing to say. But, bring it on Donald. Keep going" (as told by Lindsay Ellefson, ITE *Media*, Feb. 29, 2016). While political analysts and peace activists express anxiety about the renewed raising of tensions between Russia and the United States and its NATO allies, arms sellers see profits looming. The end of the Cold War, a retired general and now vice-president of a defence contractor noted, had meant that peace had broken out all over and that defence budgets had shrunk. The current tensions between the United States and Russia and the United States and China are furnishing an opportunity to convince governments to reverse that trend; see Lee Fang, "US Defense Contractors Tell Investors Russian Threat Is Great for Business," *Intercept*, Aug. 21, 2016. Arms manufacturers have sent their lobby groups into action to persuade legislators to spend more by pointing to the Russian danger. They know that their shareholders do not care how money is made! The examples tumble out of the media.

The *Economist*, March 12, 2016, reports that U.S. and U.K. corporations are lending money at 16 to 18 per cent interest to divorcing litigants who are fighting over assets. The only danger is amicable settlement, and the lending corporations are seeking guarantees from the involved lawyers. Their concern is that the parties will conclude a money-losing (for them) deal. This should be seen as an anti-social ploy, but that does not worry the profit-seekers too much. This is standard. Writing about the private incarceration system, Ana Marie Cox, "Private Prisons: The GOP's Real Shame on the Border," *Guardian, UK*, July 22, 2014, reports that more than half of the detained immigrants were housed in private prisons, generating circa $250,000 a day for the private prison complex. Matt Taibbi, in *The Divide: American Injustice in the Age of the Wealth Gap* (Melbourne/London: Scribe, 2014), comments on the fact that not only does the persecution and detention of so-called illegal immigrants fill the coffers of private prison operators, but it also allows local government and private service providers to charge desperate people exorbitant prices for goods and services: "Ironically, the very brokest people in America, Hispanic immigrants, are one of America's last great cash crops" (217). Betsy Woodruff, "Prison Gets Rich Locking Up Preschoolers," *Daily Beast*, Sept. 8, 2015, writes that "the latest quarterly finance report from Corrections Corporation of America, a for-profit prison company, indicates that its contract with Immigration and Customs Enforcement to manage a detention center packed with immigrant mothers and children is very helpful to its bottom line." Chico Harlan, "US Skipped Standard Bid Procedure in $1 Billion Deal with Prison Company," *Washington Post*, Aug. 15, 2016, reports that Corrections Corporation of America was on the brink of bankruptcy when the boon of immigration detention followed the 9/11 attacks. He also notes that the same corporation has engineered a new contract where it will get paid a set sum whether or not its cells and beds are put to use.

When it comes to judicial corruption spawned by the privatization of prisons, the ACLU report *Banking on Bondage*, tells us that the judge discussed in the body of the text was convicted in February 2011. In February 2009, CBS reported that two judges had pleaded guilty to charges that they had received one million dollars in kickbacks from private entrepreneurs to send youthful offenders to private detention centres; one judge sent 1 in 4 of convicted youths to detention centres while the state-wide average was 1 in 10; see Wilkes-Barre, "2 Pa. Judges Admit Jailing Kids for Cash," www.cbsnews.com, Feb. 12, 2009.

The "respectability" of making money from the misery of those who fall afoul of the law is underscored by the fact that blue-ribbon businesses (a self-proclaimed status), such as the investment firm Smith Barney, which is a part-owner of a prison in Florida, or American Express and General Electric, which also are invested in private prisons, are happy to make money by becoming shareholders in private prison firms; see Eve Goldberg and Linda Evans, "The Prison Industrial Complex and the Global Economy" (Prison Activist Resource Center, 2004). The same article describes how private firms are more than eager to have prisoners do work otherwise done by more expensive "free" labour. Prisoners are safe, are not permitted to strike, and their outside employers do not have to pay into a workers' compensation plan. Alice Speri, "Prisoners in Multiple States Call for Strikes to Protest Forced Labor," *Intercept*, April 5, 2016, reports that half of the U.S. prison population is made to work in government or privately run prisons, that is, 870,000 people, many making as little as seventeen cents per hour, generating wealth even though they are not counted in the national employment statistics.

Goldberg and Evans illustrate the cynicism of profit-seekers who use the Oregon prison system to deliver for their shareholders: "The Oregon Prison Industries produces a line of 'Prison Blues' blue jeans. An ad in their catalogue shows a handsome prison inmate saying, 'I say we should make bell-bottoms. They say I've been here too long.'" The excuse for this shameless exploitation is that prisoners are being rehabilitated. As might be expected, prisoners resent their treatment and Alice Speri recounts the spread of strikes as complaints about not being credited with time against work done and/or about having to make co-payments of about a hundred dollars should they require medical attention are providing tipping points. And in September 2016, Ben Rosen, "Inmates on Strike: Will It Shift the Conversation about US Prisoners' Rights?" (www.csmonitor.com), reported that a national prisoners' strike had just been initiated.

On the pervasiveness of illegal behaviours: as noted in this chapter, the heavy electrical equipment conspiracy was seen as a blot on capitalism. Yet, even then, the justice system found it hard to get tough with the miscreants. Having expressed outrage, the presiding judge imposed what he thought to be stiff sentences. The largest conspirator, General Electric, was fined $437,500 dollars for having participated in a scheme that cost consumers close to $1 billion in 1960 dollars. It was the equivalent of a $3 fine for a man making $175,000 per annum. Four executives got jail time, ranging from three to four months; see Gilbert Geis, cited in endnotes.

Many of the illegalities recorded by the studies on corporate crime and deviance referred to in this book are violations of regulatory laws, a description to characterize some offence-creating laws as different, as not being criminal law proper. There is a vast literature on the nature of regulatory law. My own views have been elaborated in *Wealth by Stealth*, ch. 8, and in "The James Hardie Directors: A Case of Missing Directors and Misdirections by Law," (2013), 28 *Australian Journal of Corporate Law*, 107; "Missing the Targets—Bill C-45: Reforming the Status Quo to Maintain the Status Quo," *Policy and Practice in Health and Safety*, 11,2 (2013). The starting point is that what are being regulated are activities that give rise to disputes within a sphere of shared interests. This is reflected in the way we create a regulatory scheme. The starting premise for regulators and the judiciary is that for-profit pursuits are worthwhile, that the actors are virtuous; see F. Haines and A. Sutton, "The Engineer's Dilemma: A Sociological Perspective on Juridification and Regulation," (2003), 39 *Crime, Law and Social Change*, 1. Transgressions—and there always will be some—are treated as aberrations. Rarely will they be perceived as meriting denunciation or stigmatization. Offenders may have to be penalized, but they are unlikely to be seen or portrayed as "real" criminals. To maintain faith in what is essentially a non-punitive approach, carefully refined methods of enforcement have had to be advocated and crafted. Persuasion, via warnings, mediations, conciliations, and the like are to bring wrongdoing profiteers to understand their obligations. The prosecution for regulatory violations by private entrepreneurs is to be the remedy of last resort; see I. Ayres and J. Braithwaite, *Responsive Regulation: Transcending the Deregulation Debate* (Oxford: Oxford University Press, 1992); B. Fisse and J. Braithwaite, *Corporations, Crime and Accountability* (Cambridge: Cambridge University Press, 1993); J. Braithwaite and T. Makkai, "Trust and Compliance," *Policing and Society*, 1994, 1; C. Delitt and B. Fisse, "Civil and Criminal Liability under Australian Securities Regulation: The Possibility of Strategic Enforcement" in C. Delitt & B. Fisse, eds., *Securities Regulation in Australia and New Zealand* (Oxford: Oxford University Press, 1994). Generally, this approach is known as the pyramid approach to regulatory enforcement. In Canada, it is a commonplace in the area of occupational health and safety to speak of internal and external enforcement, with a strong preference for schemes fostering an internal (largely private) responsibility system and marginalizing the public external enforcement system.

While, in form, regulatory laws resemble criminal ones, they are treated quite differently because they are truly different. They are concerned with the promotion of what is prima facie desirable conduct, rather than the inhibition of what is viscerally sensed to be bad conduct. The standards are not enacted to protect our most important shared values and social mores.

The standards imposed by regulation, therefore, do not, despite their criminal format, demand enforcement whenever violated. The regulators and courts have a delicate political role to play, one without precise guidelines. Their unstated but understood role is to ensure that the inevitable crises of capitalism do not become crises for capitalism, as neatly stated, albeit in a different context, by S. Resnick and R. Wolff, "The Economic Crisis: A Marxian Approach," *Rethinking Marxism: A Journal of Economics, Culture and Society* 22 (2010), 170.

This self-imposed tolerance toward wrongdoing in the blob-o-sphere is what is reflected in the cited passage from the Brandeis judgment found in the text of this chapter. For more populist statements to the same effect, see John K. Galbraith's citation in *The Great Crash of 1929* (Mariner Books, reprint ed., 2009), of Nelson D. Rockefeller's bons mots: "The American Beauty Rose can be produced in the splendor and fragrance which bring cheer to its beholder only by sacrificing the early buds which grow up around it.... This is not an evil tendency in business. It is merely the working-out of a law of Nature and a law of God." In a more academic manner, Richard Posner, *The Economics of Justice* (Cambridge: Harvard University Press, 1983), 83–4, wrote that "only the fanatic refuses to trade off lives for property, although the difficulty of valuing lives is a legitimate reason for weighing them heavily in the balance when only property values are in the other pan."

6. THE SHAREHOLDER AS VICTIM

1   Glasbeek, "Contortions of Corporate Law"; Harry Glasbeek, "The James Hardie Directors: A Case of Missing Directors and Misdirections by Law," (2013), 28 *Australian Journal of Corporate Law*, 107.

2   Colin Mayer, *Firm Commitment: Why The Corporation Is Failing Us and How to Restore Trust in It* (Oxford: Oxford University Press, 2013), 27.

3   Nancy B. Kurland, "The Ethical Implications of the Straight-Commission Compensation System: An Agency Perspective," *Journal of Business Ethics* 10 (1991).

4   Harry Glasbeek, "Enron and Its Aftermath : Can Reforms Restore Confidence?" in Anita I. Anand, Justin A. Connidis, and William F. Flanagan, eds., *Crime in the Corporation* (Kingston, ON: Queen's Annual Business Symposium, 2004); Donald C. Langevoort, "Information Technology and the Structure of Securities Regulation," (1985), 98 *Harvard Law Review*, 747; Thomas Lee Hazen, "Rational Investments, Speculation, or Gambling?: Derivative Securities and Financial Futures and Their Effect on the Underlying Capital Markets," (1992), 86 *Northwestern University Law Revue*, 987.

5   Bethany McLean and Peter Elkind, *The Smartest Guys in the Room: The Amazing Rise and Scandalous Fall of Enron* (New York: Portfolio, 2013).

6   T. Hadden, *Company Law and Capitalism* (London: Weidenfeld & Nicholson, 1972), 14.

7   Taibbi, *The Divide*, 194.

8   Jenny Anderson, "In Britain Libor-Rigging Conspiracy Case Is Also a Test for Regulators," *New York Times*, May 24, 2015.

9   T. Hadden, "Fraud in the City: The Role of the Criminal Law," [1983] *Criminal Law Review*, 500.

10   W. Adams and J.W. Brock, *Dangerous Pursuits: Mergers and Acquisitions in the Age of Wall Street* (New York: Pantheon, 1989).

11   Charles H. Ferguson, *Predator Nation: Corporate Criminals, Political Corruption and the Hijacking of America* (New York: Crown, 2012).

12   Taibbi, *The Divide*, 174.

13   John Kenneth Galbraith, *The Great Crash of 1929* (Mariner Books, republished ed., 2009).

14   www.bata.com.au

15   Eduardo Porter, "The Spreading Scourge of Corporate Corruption," *New York Times*, July 10, 2012.

16   E.F. Schumacher, *Small Is Beautiful* (New York: Harper & Row, 1989), 24.

17   Harry Glasbeek, "More Direct Directors' Responsibility: Much Ado About … What?," (1995), 25 *Canadian Journal of Business Law*, 416.

18   Snider, "Relocating Law."

19   Daniel Vogel, *The Market for Virtue: The Potential and Limits of Corporate Social Responsibility* (Washington, DC: Brookings Institution, 2006).

20   Judy Molland, "Care2Success! New York Establishes Benefit Corporations," www.care2.com, Dec. 18, 2011.

These notes give some more details on the James Hardie affair to underscore the indifference of shareholders to bad behaviour. There is a comment on corporate managers as employees and the social and legal difficulties this potential characterization lays bare; in particular, the vexed question of executive compensation is given a new twist. Some more details of the LIBOR and other financial scandals are furnished.

More on James Hardie: The gap between the way in which outsiders and insiders of a corporation are treated is starkly illustrated by the aftermath of the James Hardie affair. The compromise reached after the commission of inquiry had delivered its harsh verdict was that James Hardie was to make sure that 35 per cent of its annual cash flow be made available to an entity set up by the corporation and the government of New South Wales to administer and distribute the funds. Later, the New South Wales and federal governments set up a plan to make up any shortfalls in any one year, should James Hardie's contributions be inadequate. In 2014, it was reported that James Hardie had called on this back-up money, as it could not meet its obligations under the agreement made with the New South Wales government. Despite the corporation's shortness of funds for its victims, it had found a way to pay its shareholders dividends of circa $600 million over the past two years. The shamelessness of the gamblers/shareholders and the way in which they push corporations into shady behaviour is hard to miss. Shareholders were obviously happy to remain, or to become, invested in a corporation that had committed horrendous wrongs and had been caught trying to scam and scheme its way out of its obligation; shareholders were happy to take money that they knew could have been paid to deserving folk; see Timothy Binstead and Simon Evans, "Why Taxpayers Underwrite the James Hardie Asbestos Compo Fund," *Sydney Morning Herald*, Sept. 14, 2014.

The chapter makes the point that the duties imposed by corporate law on directors and senior managers to be loyal, to act in good faith in the interests of the corporation (read: shareholders) and not to serve themselves at the expense of the corporation are similar to the duties imposed by employment law on run-of-the-mill employees. This does not lead to the conclusion that directors and senior managers are just employees. When looting and shirking is suspected, there is a tendency among the victims to want to reduce directors and senior managers to the status of "mere" employees. But it is conceptually controversial. In labour relations law, it is understood that the employment relationship entails a superior-inferior nexus. This is why the analogy with employees troubles people who are uncomfortable with attributing the status of an inferior to any functionary, such as a director or executive who is given so much discretion and power in an incorporated firm. They are not under anyone's direct command when it comes to the doing of their operational tasks. Still, they do have to share some of the responsibilities with shareholders, and this suggests that their superiority is far from absolute, not truly like that of an unincorporated owner of a firm. It is all a bit murky. Law tends to characterize directors and senior decision-makers as occupying a hybrid status, something in between employer and employee, as an agent, as a trustee, or as an office holder, or even as occupying a special, otherwise unknown place in law. Law being what it is, the choice made when characterizing a person in one or another category will lead to different duties and obligations being imposed on that person. Once again, we are into an area of uncertainty, beloved by litigating lawyers and academics and vexing to all others. Some scholars believe that all these attempts to classify directors and executives as neither employers nor employees are unconvincing; see Robert Flannigan, "The Employee Status of Directors," (2014), 25 *King's Law Journal*, 370.

On the LIBOR affair, for a very good description of the machinery and the built-in features that make it a target for those who would like to game it, see the prescient piece by Donald MacKenzie, "What's in a Number," *London Review of Books*, Sept. 25, 2008. If that piece had been heeded by regulators, some serious harms might have been avoided. On the scope and scale of those harms, see John Lanchester, "Are We Having Fun Yet?," *London Review of Books*, June 4, 2013. He tallies the sums major banks have already had to pay out, with many more claims and settlements to come. Barclays' settlements with various British and U.S. agencies amounted, in mid-2013, to 290 million English pounds; UBS had forked out 970 million English pounds; RBS a total of 390 million English pounds. Other major banks, like Deutsche Bank, Citigroup, Credit Suisse, and JPMorgan Chase were still negotiating. The sums were expected to be gargantuan. Lanchester notes that, in one case brought by Baltimore municipalities, $10 billion was the claimed loss as a result of the manipulation of interest rates. A large number of similar claimants have yet to come forward. It is hard not to notice that many of these manipulating banks were among the same ones that had to be bailed out by governments during the preceding financial crisis of 2008. They seem to be slow learners and/or incorrigible.

Lanchester tells the story of another rip-off by the same English banks. It is about the payment protection insurance scam, PPI. Banks sold insurance to people who feared that they might not be able to repay their mortgage or credit card debt due to a loss of job, illness, or the like. In some cases, the banks sold these policies without telling their clients they were buying them; but mostly the wrongs done consisted in selling PPI to people who, to the banks' knowledge, could never collect any benefits under the policies. There were hard-to-detect and undisclosed exclusions for the self-employed and for people with pre-existing diseases. The banks are now making provisions to repay their deceived clients, adding interest foregone and opportunity lost. Again the amounts are mindboggling: the money owed, according to Lanchester, is circa 16 billion English pounds or, as he puts it colourfully, about twice the much-criticized cost of the London Olympics.

But it is not just the amounts that arrest attention. It is the nature of the behaviour: straightforward deception/fraud is part of the modus operandi of the financial titans of the world; see Steve Tombs, "Corporate Theft and Fraud: Business as Usual," (2013), 94(1) *Criminal Justice Matters*, 14/15. In the United States, an eerily similar scandal broke when it was revealed that Wells Fargo, a bailed-out bank, had pressured its lowly (and low-paid) employees to open unauthorized accounts for vulnerable customers, yielding millions in illegal fees for the bank. The bank dismissed 5,300 of its hapless employees and, finally, the CEO was forced to resign but, thus far, with much of the bonus payments he had "earned" still in his keep; see Stacy Cowley, "Voices from Wells Fargo: 'I Thought I Was Having a Heart Attack,'" *New York Times*, Oct. 20, 2016.

Of course, whenever these kinds of outrages are publicized, a new round of reforms is put on the table, usually with a great deal of fanfare. But as these regulatory reforms rarely go to the core of the problem, they are quickly seen to be ineffective. In a survey of 1,223 senior, middle, and junior financial service workers, the researchers found that little had changed when it came to ethical attitudes after the scandals and reforms of the new century's first decade. Ann Tenbrunsel and Jordan Thomas, *The Street, the Bull and the Crisis: A Survey of the US and UK Financial Services Industry* (University of Notre Dame and Labaton Sucharow LLP, May 2015), found that, if anything, ethical attitudes had become even more degraded. For example, their findings showed that 47 per cent of respondents believed that that their competitors had engaged in illegal or unethical conduct; 51 per cent of respondents earning more than $500,000 believed this to be true; even more startlingly, 23 per cent of respondents believed that their fellow employees had engaged in illegal or unethical conduct. In any other sphere of society, this kind of amorality and immorality would engender a panic about the viability of society. But not when that sphere is that in which corporate capitalism reigns. A low level of ethics is expected. Peter J. Henning, "When Lies Are Allowed in Business Deals," *New York Times*, April 18, 2016, reports that in three recent Court of Appeal decisions, it was held that lying will not be treated as fraud unless it goes to a material issue (another of these slippery legal terms). One of the courts wrote that "it is not unusual for parties to conceal from others their true goals and values, priorities, or reserve prices in a proposed transaction ... to state the obvious, they will often try to mislead the other party about the prices and terms they are willing to accept. Such deceptions are not criminal." The corrosion of our shared values and norms spoken about in the chapter is taken to be normal and acceptable.

The chapter suggests that the executives of major corporations have very cozy relationships with some people that may be detrimental to the corporation and its shareholders. Sometimes these conflict-rich ties are exposed for all to see. One grubby example is provided by United Airlines' replacement of its CEO and other senior executives. It is investigating whether the CEO's friendship with the chairman of the Port Authority of New York and New Jersey, with which it had commercial relationships, may have had any influence on United Airlines offering a special flight route to an airfield where the chairman of the Port Authority has a summer home; see Kate Zernike and Jack Mouawad, "United C.E.O. Is Out Amid Inquiry at Port Authority," *New York Times*, Sept. 8, 2015 (also noting that the chairman of the Port Authority had allegedly been of assistance when Governor Christie allegedly blocked a freeway to embarrass a mayor who had refused him political support, a little nugget of information hinting at the close relationship between the political and the economic).

One of the things that sticks in the ordinary person's throat is the crudeness, the knowing smart-aleck attitude of many of these captains of finance as they manipulate the blob-o-sphere. The *Associated Press*, June 26, 2013, released the contents of telephone calls made by the senior executives of the Anglo Irish Bank as it asked for a bail-out. In order to inveigle the government to help it get German loans, the amount needed was greatly understated. The bank officials assured the government only 7 billion euros would be needed, a far cry from the actual 30 billion euros eventually required. On the tapes, the then-head of capital markets at the bank is asked how he came by the figure of 7 billion euros. His response: "I picked it out of my arse." In the story, the *Independent* newspaper is cited as telling the story that the same man sang the German national anthem and chortled as he discussed the prospect of German money flowing in after the Irish government had guaranteed the bank's deposits which it believed "only" needed a top-up of 7 billion euros.

The appalling incidents of financial delinquency and scamming are not aberrant. They are integral to the legal architecture of the Anglo-American corporation. They recur in history. The episodes are well-documented; e.g., see M. Blair, ed., *The Deal Decade: What Takeovers and Leveraged Buyouts Mean for Corporate America* (Washington: Brookings Institute, 1993); R. Sobel, *Panic on Wall Street: A History of America's Financial Disasters* (New York: MacMillan, 1968); C. Kindleberger, *Manias, Panics and Crashes: A History of Financial Crises*, 4th ed. (New York: Wiley, 2000); R. Brenner, *The Boom and the Bubble: The US in the World Economy* (London: Verso, 2002). The titillating aspects of the corporate shenanigans during the late twentieth century in the United States spawned a series of films, like *Wall Street* and *Other People's Money*, television series, like *Traders*, and many muckraking books. The situation is much the same in all parts of the Anglo-American corporate law system. In Australia, this century has witnessed the HIH and One-Tel affairs, the Centro matter and James Hardie and AWB scandals, among others. Indeed, the first decade of the twenty-first century has been spectacularly deviant-prone in Australia; see Adam Schwab, *Pigs at the Trough: Lessons from Australia's Decade of Corporate Greed* (John Wiley & Sons, 2010). Some of the many like crises and failures in England and Canada were detailed in the body of the book.

7. THE IDEAL OF INDIVIDUAL RESPONSIBILITY

1   Joachim Dietrich, "The Liability of Accessories under Statute, in Equity, and in Criminal Law: Some Common Problems and (Perhaps) Some Common Solutions," (2011), 34 *Melbourne University Law Review*, 106.

2   *Toronto Star*, July 12, 2014, A16.

3   *Dorset Yacht* v. *Home Office*, [1970] A.C. 1004 (House of Lords).

4   *Racz* v. *Home Office*, [1994] 2 A.C. 45 (House of Lords).

5   Charles Woolfson and Aruna Juska, "Neoliberal Austerity and Corporate Crime: The Collapse of the MAXIMA Supermarket in Riga, Latvia," *New Solutions* 24,2 (2014), 129–52; "Postscript: A Very Baltic Tragedy: The Collapse of the MAXIMA Supermarket in Riga, Latvia," in Jeffrey Somers and Charles Woolfson, eds., *The Contradictions of Austerity: The Social Costs of the Neo-Liberal Baltic Model* (Abingdon/New York: Routledge, 2014).

6   *Bazley* v. *Curry*, [1999] 2 S.C.R. 534 (Sup. Ct. Canada); *London Drugs Ltd.* v. *Kuehne & Nagel International Ltd.*, [1992] 2 S.C.R. 299 (Sup. Ct. Canada).

7   *Lloyd* v. *Grace Smith & Co.*, [1912] A.C. 716 (House of Lords).

8   A much more wide-sweeping class of managers in the corporation than are considered the guiding minds and wills of a corporation for the purposes of the identification doctrine.

9   Wendy Gillis, "Victim Wins Right to Sue T.O. Police," *Toronto Star*, July 22, 2016, GT1.

10   *Stewart* v. *Pettie*, [1995] 1 S.C.R. 131 (Sup. Ct. Canada).

11   *Dryden (Litigation Guardian of)* v. *Campbell Estates*, [2001] OJ No. 289.

12   42 U.S.C. #9601–75 (1994 & Supp. V 1999) (CERCLA).

13   *U.S.* v. *Fleet Factors* (1990) F.2d 1550, 11th Circuit Court of Appeals.

14   28 U.S.C. 1350 (2007).

15   *Doe I* v. *Unocal Corp.*, 395 F. 3rd 932 (9th Cir. 2002).

16   *Sosa* v. *Alvarez-Machain* (2004), 542 U.S. 692 (Sup. Ct. U.S.).

17   Doug Cassel, "Corporate Aiding and Abetting of Human Rights Violations: Confusion in the Courts," *Northwestern Journal of International Human Rights* 5 (2008), 304.

18   There are too many cases involved in the Chiquita litigation to list, but a useful overview is provided by David Voreacos, "Chiquita Executives Must Face Claims over Colombia Torturers," *Bloomberg*, June 2, 2016; EarthRights International (USA), "Victims of Colombian Death Squads Can Move Forward with Case against Former Chiquita Executives," June 2, 2016; teleSUR, "Colombian Paramilitary Victims Fight Banana Giant in US Court," June 15, 2016.

19   *Kiobel* v. *Royal Dutch Petroleum Co.* 132 S. Ct. 1732 (Sup. Ct. U.S.) (2014).

20   Anthony J. Colangelo, "The Alien Tort Statute and the Law of Nations in Kiobel and Beyond," (2013), 44 *Georgetown Law Journal*, 1329.

21   There are too many reported cases to list here; useful summaries include Joyce Nelson, "Ecuador vs Chevron, by Way of Canada," *Counterpunch*, Sept. 16, 2015; Sean Fine, "Ecuadoreans Can Sue Chevron in Canada, Supreme Court Rules," *Globe and Mail*, Sept. 4, 2015; Nicole Hong and Kim Macrael, "Canada's Top Court Rules in Favor of Ecuador Villagers in Chevron Case," *Wall Street Journal*, Sept. 4, 2015.

22   Shawn McCarthy, "CBA Drops Plans to Intervene for Chevron at Supreme Court," *Globe and Mail*, Oct. 16, 2014.

23   *Trial of Bruno Tesch*, the Zyklon B case, 1 Law Reports of Trials of War Criminals, 93 (Brit. Military Court, 1946).

24   *Trial of Otto Ohlendorf and ors. (Einsatzgruppen case)*, 4 Trials of War Criminals before the Nuremberg Military Tribunals under Control Council Law No. 10, 572.

25   Christopher Reynolds, "Judge Blames Broken System in Acquitting Inmate of Assault," *Toronto Star*, July 22, 2016, A9.

26   *Choc* v. *Hudbay Minerals Inc.*, 2013, ONSC 1414 (Supreme Ct of Justice, ON).

These notes expand on the seduction of using controlled, but legally separable, producers in impoverished countries. They also give many illustrations of the way in which law, in widely disparate sets of circumstances, is willing to hold controlling beneficiaries of other people's conduct responsible for that conduct. The nature of the connection required by law to impose such responsibility is elaborated.

In historical terms, requirements such as a legislated floor for wages, the facilitation of unionization, and relatively well-enforced occupational health and safety and environmental protections are not very old. Unsurprisingly, aided by technologies and free trade agreements, mobile for-profit corporations are eager to return to the good old days. They search out nation states where, hungry for investment, governments do not impose such costly requirements. If they succeed, they then resist any efforts at losing their newly gained advantage by having parent corporations made responsible for the outcomes in cheap and dirty locales. Lauren Carasik, "The Uphill Battle to Hold US Corporations Accountable for Abuses Abroad," america.aljazeera.com, Aug. 8, 2014, details how efforts by various nations at the United Nations to hold multinational corporations responsible for conditions at their outsourced sites of production have been defeated again and again. Similarly, the *Toronto Star*, July 24, 2015, A4, reported that the UN's human rights committee had noted that Canada should set up an independent body to deal with human rights abuses committed by, or on behalf of, its companies abroad. To no avail, as was noted by the contesting parties in the Hudbay case discussed in the text of this chapter. To get any action at all, corporations have to be shamed into it. Highly publicized tragedies are necessary. In this sad sense, the Rana Plaza collapse was useful.

The Bangladesh Worker Safety Initiative of the Alliance for Bangladesh Worker Safety was entered into by 180 U.S. apparel companies and 12 unions. It has led to the hiring of 110 engineers who are to conduct inspections. The *Toronto Star* story quoted in the text is about the consequences of some of those inspections. Pressure also has been generated to promote the formation of unions in Bangladesh. These pressures have been reinforced by the U.S. government removing Bangladesh as a beneficiary of trade benefits under the *Generalized System of Preferences*. At the time of writing, this ban is still in force. It is too early to say that the conditions of workers have improved and/or that buildings are much safer, although there are some reports of success on this front. It is impossible to know the extent to which external vigilance and enforcement will stay in place. For a pessimistic view, see Beryl ter Haar and Maarten Keune, "One Step Forward or More Window-Dressing?: A Legal Analysis of Recent CSR Initiatives in the Garment Industry in Bangladesh," [2014] *International Journal of Comparative Labour Law and Industrial Relations*, 5. Reports such as the one from Associated Press, found in thestar.com, Sept. 10, 2016, about an explosion at Tampaco Foils Inc. just near Dhaka that killed twenty-three people give little reason for comfort. The police instantly blamed poor safety conditions at the factory. Tampaco Foils makes snack-food packs for the likes of Nestlé and cigarette packs for British American Tobacco. Similarly, while the large clothing retailer H&M claimed that it was doing its best to monitor its suppliers' compliance with the practices its signing off on the new protocols required, there are reports from the Asia Floor Wage Alliance that in 11 out of 12 such suppliers to H&M surveyed, women were terminated because they were pregnant and in 9 out of 12 supplying enterprises, sexual harassment was rampant; see Sirin Kale, "The Women Who Make H&M's Clothes Are Fired for Getting Pregnant," *Broadly*, Sept. 30, 2016.

The United States made its own arrangements after European multinationals had entered into a similar, seemingly more enforceable, set of protocols; see *Accord on Fire and Building Safety in Bangladesh*. Largely these kinds of reforms have been welcomed as acknowledgements that large corporations at the top of supply chains can be pushed towards better behaviour. It is worth noting that it remains true that those at the coal face, those who are being pushed and shoved by the large corporations at the top to squeeze their employees, are treated much more harshly when harm due to exploitation becomes visible. The Associated Press in Dhaka reported that the Rana Plaza building owners and owners of factories using that building have been charged with culpable homicide, as well having to face charges for the violation of regulatory rules governing safety at work (*Guardian*, June 1, 2016). Both the criminal charges and safety regulation ones are levelled against controlling human beings, a far cry from the sanctions found in the protocols designed by controlling corporations in faraway jurisdictions. This draws attention to the central argument of the book to the effect that we know that sentient human beings have to be identified and pursued if we want to educate profit-seekers into accepting our values and norms.

For my elaborations on the identification doctrine and the *Criminal Code* amendments, see *Wealth by Stealth* and my "Missing the Targets—Bill C-45: Reforming the Status Quo to Maintain the Status Quo."

For superior court decisions that echoed the tangible connection test discussed in the text, see *Lister* v. *Hesley Hall Ltd.*, [2001] UKHL 22 (House of Lords); *Jacobi* v. *Griffiths*, [1999] 2 S.C.R. 534 (Supreme Ct Canada); for a textbook analysis to the same effect, see J. Fleming, *The Law of Torts*, 9th ed. (Thomson Professional, 1998). There always is anxiety about the vagueness of the connection test; intricate legal arguments have been developed as to whether there needs to be a finding of incidental risk, of introduced risk, of enhanced risk, etc.; for examples of the slightly different wordings used (that allow lawyers to develop nuanced refinements about the nature of the connection needed), see *Dubai Aluminium Co. Ltd.* v. *Salaam*, [2002] UKHL 48 (House of Lords) and *Maga* v. *Archbishop of Birmingham*, [2010] 1 W.L.R. 1441; J. Steele, *Tort Law, Text, Cases and Materials*, 2nd ed. (Oxford: Oxford University Press, 2010); P. Morgan, "Distorting Vicarious Liability," (2011), 74 *Modern Law Review*, 932. But these legal tussles merely contest the scope of the accepted principle that a creator/controller of an organization should be held accountable for the conduct of sovereign others, even prohibited conduct. The issue is not whether it is legally appropriate but rather, whether, in some as yet unspecified circumstances, it might be appropriate to curtail the application of this general principle.

This holds true in cases dealing with the liability of liquor licensees for the conduct of their patrons. The rule of thumb is that, even if the licensees did not exercise reasonable care when selling alcohol to inebriated customers, they will be excused if the intoxicated customer drove home safely before setting out again and doing harm to another. But this will not always work. In one case, the drunken patron drove himself and his friend safely to his friend's home. But they then set off to another place to drink and, subsequently, when driving away from the second alcohol-providing site, had an accident. Both drinking establishments were held legally liable for the ensuing damages; see *Holton v. MacKinnon*, [2005] B.C.S.C. 41 (BC Sup. Ct.). Note that the sovereignty of the patron, that is, the complete separateness of the immediate wrongdoer, is recognized in these cases: the licensees are usually held only contributorily negligent for the damages awarded, the largest part of the blame being accorded to the drinking driver (or the overly aggressive drunk who assaults some other patron on the licensee's premises, see *Mellanby v. Chapple*, [1995] O.J. No. 1229). In employer vicarious liability cases it is legally possible, although practically useless, for an employer to bring an action against the employee who actually inflicted the injury that leads to litigation. The employer's insurer, who has to pay on behalf of the employer, is entitled to claim any payments so made from the employee who acted wrongfully; see *Lister v. Romford Ice and Cold Storage Co. Ltd.*, [1956] A.C. 555 (House of Lords); *Douglas v. Kinger* (2008), 92 O.R. (3d) 721 (Ont.Ct.Appeal).

All this demonstrates that, if law is to help maintain the legitimacy of the private pursuit of profits, it must show itself willing to pursue those who make bad things happen, as well as those people who act as their instruments. This pressure is felt in many spheres and jurisdictions. On March 10, 2016, *Electronic Intifada* published a story by Charlotte Silver that related how Palestinians and Palestinian-Americans had lodged lawsuits against a bunch of charities and their sponsors, including well-known Israel supporters such as Sheldon Adelson and Haim Saban. The allegations are that contributions are made to the tax-exempt charities and that it is known by the charities that they will be used to pursue criminal activities, such as funding the theft and destruction of private property, enabling the commission of discriminatory practices, such as the creation of Jewish-only towns and highways, to facilitate the use of force against Palestinians, thus aiding and abetting genocide, torture, etc. Where this will go is not yet determined but, again, the notion that controllers could and should be held responsible is thought of as an eminently justifiable basis on which to found legal responsibility.

In addition to CERCLA (which was accompanied by the establishment of a superfund to finance environmental clean-up at waste sites; see the *Superfund Amendments and Reauthorization Act* [SARA] 1986), there are other U.S. state and federal statutes with similar provisions; see Karl Hofstetter, "The Ecological Liability of Groups: Comparing US and European Trends," in G. Teubner, L. Farmer, and D. Murphy, *Environmental Law and Ecological Responsibility: The Concept and Practice of Ecological Self-Organization* (Chichester: Wiley, 1994). Hofstetter also reports that, in Germany, a parent company has been held to have the onus of proving that it was not heedless of what went on in its subsidiaries' practices if it wishes to avoid the imposition of liability for one of its subsidiaries' harm-causing conduct. The French and Swiss will, in certain circumstances, treat a parent corporation as if it were a director of one of its subsidiaries and, therefore, liable for making good the damage inflicted by that subsidiary because it failed in its directors' and/or fiduciary duties to it. The underlying principle seems nearly universal. Its actual application, however, requires a balancing of profit-seekers' freedom and the need to appear evenhanded.

In other examples: U.S. gun manufacturers whose product was used by criminals have been held responsible because their modus operandi allowed for the sale of guns in states with little monitoring of purchasers, enabling potential wrongdoers to get easy access to these weapons; sometimes this kind of action succeeds, sometimes it doesn't (see my *Wealth by Stealth*, 160). It depends on the predilection of the judge, but the deep-seated legal principle that responsibility might attach is not in issue. Similarly, a drive-by shooting in Toronto led to a family launching an action against Toronto public housing authorities because, it was alleged, the authorities' reduction of security personnel had contributed to the tragedy (*Globe and Mail*, Dec. 6, 2011). While at the time of writing, there has been no public resolution of this initiative, the widely held belief that legal responsibility might attach in these kind of circumstances, as it did in the Borstal Boys case, is plain. The *Toronto Star*, Aug. 14, 2015, A1, reports that a class action by victims of abuse at a residential school run under government auspices (much like the Borstal Boys institution), known as the Huron Regional Centre, had been settled. The same day, the *Star* reported that a provincial government had been held responsible to a former inmate of a prison who had been assaulted by another prisoner.

Legal responsibility for the wilful acts of others notionally under the control of an overseeing authority is obviously deemed appropriate in many different kinds of situations. In Japan, a bereaved family has brought an action against the Tokyo Electric Power Co. for its role in the nuclear meltdown and subsequent tsunami. The wife and mother of the family had become distressed by the loss of everything and had committed suicide. A court found that there *might* be a case to answer (*Toronto Star*, Aug. 22, 2014, A9). Similarly, a human rights tribunal refused to dismiss a case brought against McDonald's as the franchisor of legally independent franchisees who had allegedly discriminated against the complainants (Lancaster House, July 29, 2014, eAlert 373). This refusal to rule out franchisors at a preliminary stage of proceedings is common (*Philip* v. *Giant Tiger Stores*, 2009 HRTO 1227; *Wozenilek* v. *McDonald's Restaurants of Canada*, 2010 HRTO 1120); for similar strategies of avoidance by major corporations that might attract similar responses, see "Walmart & Contractor Settle $21 million Wage Theft Suit, Days after Obama Praises Penny-Pinching Retailer," *Democracy Now*, May 15, 2014.

Sara Mojtehedzadeh, "Cleaners Caught in Contract World," *Toronto Star*, Dec. 1, 2015, GT1, provides another example of a frequent use of the cost-cutting method used in the Eliz World example in the text. Dream Office REIT, a corporation with assets worth $15 billion, had contracted out its cleaning services to an outfit that, in turn, contracted out its obligations that finally were to be met by a one-person company. Workers were left holding the bag, having been paid less than the legislative minimum. Dream Office REIT's spokesperson said that the wage dispute had nothing to do with it: "We have no involvement in this matter." This, of course, is an argument made based on the formality of law, not on the actual facts on the ground. This leads to angry demands for changes to the law. The factual issue in these cases, then, is whether the formal separation between controller and victim is convincing; in line with this chapter's argument, the principle that the principal might be legally responsible is seen by many as desirable and by an increasing number of tribunals and courts as acceptable. Only the tribunal's or court's view of the facts is in issue, not the principle.

There are actions and decisions in relation to a bunch of circumstances where plaintiffs claim a different kind of wage theft by franchisees of outfits like fast food ones, such as Burger King and Jimmy John—the allegations are that, in order to please the franchisor whose rules they think drive them to do so, they finagle their computer systems to reduce the number of hours for which they should pay their employees. For instance, Burger King's franchise agreement contains the following clause: "You must construct, operate your Restaurants in accordance with BKC's standards and specifications. You must use fixtures, signage, improvements, décor, supplies, other products and equipment, including computer and point of sale hardware and software that meets BKC's specifications." Unsurprisingly, the franchisee perceives the franchisor as being in command. It is not hard to see why some courts and tribunals also might see that the control lies with the franchisor (or a housing authority or a utility corporation or the retailer at the top of a long manufacturer chain) and that the default liberal principle to the effect that those who exercise or could exercise control over activities that will benefit them could/should be held responsible for the materialization of risks created should kick in. This explains why, after the Rana Plaza disaster, retailers felt they had to do something lest the law-makers did something that the public and legal principles demanded be done. In all these cases, the argument is that the formally legally unconnected owner of the enterprise may owe a duty in its own right and be held responsible for the acts of others because it is in a position, and has a duty, to control the behaviour of the direct inflictor of harm. It is in this general sense that the claim of the chapter that vicarious responsibility is not as exceptional as it is often said to be, that it, in fact, reflects a general principle.

The process as to whether functional controllers will be held to account, then, does not require new legal thinking. Understanding this, large corporations fight back. It is a political process and, therefore, grubby political biases, rather than rationality, sway the outcomes. On Sept. 22, 2014, Stephanie Clifford, writing in the *New York Times*, reported that, after ten years of litigation, the Arab Bank had been held responsible by a jury under the *Anti-Terrorism Act*. The allegation had been that the bank had supported Hamas in some way and that Hamas had been responsible for acts of terrorism by other individuals against the plaintiffs in and around Israel. In a parallel, in late September 2016, the U.S. Senate passed the *Justice Against Sponsors of Terrorism Act* that may allow lawsuits to be brought in the United States against Saudi Arabia for its connection to the 9/11 attacks; see Azeezah Kanji, "White House Fears Justice for the 'War on Terror,'" *Toronto Star*, Oct. 6, 2016. These instance of the willingness to hold controlling persons responsible on the basis of some rather hard-to-pinpoint connection to the wrongdoing contrast sharply with the eagerness displayed by the U.S. Supreme Court when it curtailed the reach of the *Alien Tort Claims Act* in its *Kiobel* decision. The large corporations had campaigned vigorously for this kind of judicial restraint. This is the kind of evidence that led some commentators to think that the reach of the *Alien Tort Claims Act* might be restored when the circumstances are right; see Anthony J. Colangelo, "The Alien Tort Statute and the Law of Nations in *Kiobel* and Beyond," (2013), 44 *Georgetown Law Journal*, 1329; the ongoing litigation in the Chiquita case cited in the text supports this reasoning.

The success large corporations enjoyed in the *Kiobel* case should not have surprised anyone. The corporate sectors in the United States have fought successfully to stack the august court with people it can trust, much as their predecessors accused Franklin Delano Roosevelt of stacking the same court with judges who favoured his New Deal legislation. The Corporate Accountability Coalition, an advocacy alliance promoting political and economic transparency reported that, in 2013, the U.S. Chamber of Commerce spent $75 million on lobbying; the top ten corporations raised $157 million to this end. The resulting pro–large corporate atmosphere must have enveloped the judges. During the 2102–13 term, the Supreme Court of the United States sided with the Chamber of Commerce 82 per cent of the time. *Citizens United* and *Kiobel* are jewels in this rich crown of corporate successes. This kind of partiality—tough on the Arab Bank, much easier on U.S. corporations maximizing profits by exploiting foreigners—does not negate the basic principle. It illustrates the malleability of law in the hands of clever lawyers; see Carasik, "The Uphill Battle."

The discussion on the *Hudbay* case noted that the defendant argued that the action brought by the plaintiffs was a novel one and that, to establish the existence of a duty of care in novel situations, the plaintiff not only has to establish that the injuries were foreseeable and proximate (both terms having the usual annoying qualities of elasticity, giving judges a great deal of discretion), but also that there was no public policy that would make the imposition of a new duty unacceptable (another opportunity for much manipulation by lawyers and judges). This was a correct statement of the law; *Anns* v. *Merton London Borough Council*, [1978] A.C.728 (House of Lords) and *Kamloops (City of)* v. *Nielson*, [1984] 2 S.C.R. 2 (Sup. Ct. Canada). The Hudbay Minerals plaintiffs' success at this early stage, then, will not translate automatically into success when the foreseeability, proximity, and policy issues are considered at any ensuing trial. The point made in the *Hudbay* case by the defendants to the effect that there have been proposals for the imposition of a duty on Canadian corporations engaged in business elsewhere has new salience. The argument will get new attention as human rights activists in Honduras have pleaded with Prime Minister Trudeau to act to ensure that its corporations do not cause Canada to be in breach of international environmental and human rights standards and not be part to the displacement of local communities without prior consultation; Marina Jimenez, "Honduras' 'No. 1 Enemy' in Limbo", *Toronto Star*, Aug. 17, 2016, A4; see also The Justice and Corporate Accountability Project, "The 'Canada Brand': Violence and Canadian Mining Companies in Latin America" (Osgoode Hall Law School, York University, Oct. 24, 2016).

The *Hudbay* litigation is an outcome of yet another of the legion of cases in which large corporations from wealthy nation states exploit resources and labour where conditions for profits are much better, in part, because workers and human environments are much less protected, where their welfare is sold off so cheaply. Often these exploits and exploitations are accompanied by corruption and violence. The allegations of rape and killings in the *Hudbay* case are, regrettably, not untypical; see *Garcia* v. *Tahoe Resources Inc.*, filed in British Columbia on June, 18, 2014, and discussed in chapter 5, and *Araya* v. *Nevsun Resources Ltd.*, filed in British Columbia, Nov. 20, 2014, alleging the use of forced labour, torture, and slavery at a mine in Eritrea. In chapter 5, reference was made to Barrick's adventurism in Peru and of Exxon's in Papua New Guinea. Because of their sheer numbers, Canadian resource firms are very likely to be involved in these kinds of cases. The law firm McCarthy Tétrault, reporting on mining and the courts, records that more than three-quarters of the world's mining and exploration companies are based in Canada. More than 50 per cent of world's publicly listed exploration and mining corporations have Canadian headquarters; there are some 1,500 of them with interests in 8,000 properties in 100 countries. In this context, it is interesting that Hudbay Minerals' legal defence depended on the argument that the Canadian government had failed to pass legislation to stop such abuses. In essence the argument was that our wealthy government was willing to be complicit in violations of international norms and human rights in order to allow corporations to do what they do best: deliver for their shareholders. Corporate capitalism is forced into some strange arguments to maintain and perpetuate itself.

8. THE IDEAL ABANDONED

1   Arturo Bris, "Do Insider Trading Laws Work?," *European Management* 11 (2005).

2   Jeff Gray, "After 17 Years, the Bre-X Case Finally Closes," *Globe and Mail*, April 23, 2014.

3   "Too Big to Indict," *New York Times*, Dec. 11, 2012; Glenn Greenwald, "The Untouch-
      ables: How Obama's Administration Shielded Wall Street from Prosecutions," *Guardian,*
      UK, Jan. 23, 2013; Bill Black, "Pervasive Fraud by Our 'Most Reputable Banks,'" *Reader*
      Supported News, Feb. 28, 2013; John Cassidy, "The Justice Department's 'War' on Wall
      Street: Still No Criminal Charges," *New Yorker*, Aug. 8, 2013; David Olive, "JP Morgan
      CEO Jamie Dimon Is a Clear and Present Danger to the World Banking Systems," *Toronto*
      Star, thestar.com, May 11, 2012; "JP Morgan Doubles CEO Jamie Dimon's Salary Despite
      Billions in Fines," Associated Press, Jan. 25, 2014; and by way of contrast: "Executives at
      Collapsed Iceland Bank Jailed for Fraud," Thomson Reuters, Dec. 28, 2012.

4   Taku Dzimwasha, "20 Global Banks Have Paid $235 Billion in Fines since the 2008
      Financial Crisis," *International Business Times*, May 24, 2015.

5   Ravender Sembhy, "Banks Hit with Record $5.7B Fines for Rigging Forex Markets,"
      International Business Times, May 20, 2015.

6   Matt Taibbi, "Eric Holder, Wall Street Double Agent, Comes in From the Cold," *Rolling*
      Stone, July 10, 2015.

7   Edward Wyatt, "Promises Made, and Remade by Firms in S.E.C. Fraud Cases," *New*
      York Times, Nov. 7, 2011.

8   Kara M. Stein, "Dissenting Statement Regarding Certain Waivers Granted by the Com-
      mission for Certain Entities Pleading Guilty to Criminal Charges Involving Manipula-
      tion of Foreign Exchange Rates," May 2, 2015.

9   Ezra Wasserman Mitchell, "Deferred Corporate Prosecution as Corrupt Regime: The
      Case for Prison," Feb. 1, 2015, Case Legal Studies Research Paper No. 2015-06, avail-
      able at SSRN: http://ssrn.com/abstract=2558748.

10   Charles H. Ferguson, *Predator Nation: Corporate Criminals, Political Corruption,*
      and the Hijacking of America (New York: Crown Business, 2012), 1.

11   CBC News Toronto, June 26, 2015.

12   Norm Keith, "After 10 Years, Bill C-45 Yields Few Prosecutions," *Canadian Occupation-*
      al Safety, www.cos-mag.com, April 23, 2014; S. Bittle, "Beyond Corporate Fundamen-
      talism: A Marxian Class Analysis of Corporate Crime Law Reform," *Critical Sociology*
      41,1 (2013).

13   "Asleep at the Switch," editorial on the Transportation Safety Board of Canada, *Toronto*
      Star, Aug. 20, 2014, A12.

14   David Sharp, "U.S. Bankruptcy Judge Approves $446 Million Settlement for Victims of
      Fiery Derailment in Lac-Megantic," *National Post*, Oct. 9, 2015.

15   CBC News, "Lac-Megantic Families Welcome Charges against MM&A Railway Work-
      ers," May 13, 2014; Canadian Press, "Accused in Lac-Megantic Disaster Won't Face
      More Charges," *Toronto Star*, Sept. 11, 2014.

16 Eric Atkins and Verity Stevenson, "Six Former Employees Charged in Lac-Megantic Disaster," *Globe and Mail*, June 22, 2015.

These notes offer a brief discussion of how adult corporations are treated as if they were juvenile delinquents who need to be re-educated. An account of how the corporate world saw Westray's C.H. Frame after the tragic events and a recounting of a historical parallel make the point that the pursuit of wealth is admired as a goal howsoever and by whom-soever it is pursued. There is a contextualization of the Lac-Mégantic happening and its aftermath. Some of the literature on the regulation of safety enforcement is referenced, and the way in which regulators who tend to be soft on corporate actors and their major decision-makers try to assure the public that they are doing something to safeguard it is discussed.

The readiness of regulators to do deals, known as deferred prosecutions agreements in the United States, with those corporations considered too big to fail is not only at odds with the norms of criminal law, but it also has a strange history. The idea springs from the authorities' desire to rehabilitate young offenders and delinquents. Rather than treat immature kids as hardened criminals, there is a trend to want see them as having drifted from the straight and narrow path and that they could be, with firm guidance, brought back to righteousness. Prophylactic, rather than punitive, remedies were developed to these ends. That a scheme designed for juvenile delinquents is applied to corporate persons (fully mature and mostly giant in size and that supposedly base all their actions on rational thinking by someone qualified to do so) tells us a lot about the skewed thinking imposed on us by corporate law and corporate power; see Jed Rakoff, "Justice Deferred Is Justice Denied," *New York Review of Books*, Feb. 19, 2015; Brandon L. Garrett, *Too Big to Jail: How Prosecutors Compromise with Corporations* (Bellknap Press/Harvard University Press, 2014). As if to reinforce this tenderness towards corporate wrongdoing, note that settlements often are made in secret. The *Toronto Star* editorialized rather angrily that Canada Revenue Agency's failure to release the names of taxpayers with whom they had made a deal was out of line with the principles of criminal justice, which assume that the public has a genuine interest in knowing who perpetrators of wrongs were and how they were dealt with by our institutions. Canada Revenue Agency responded by saying that it was forbidden to release details not in the public domain, and as the deals were made behind closed doors, they were to be kept secret; "Expose Tax Cheats," *Toronto Star*, June 28, 2016, A10.

The apparent legal invisibility of C.H. Frame to the legal authorities was not due to his disappearance from the corporate world. Even after Westray, he kept on making corporate waves. Fresh from his adventures in Nova Scotia, he was established as the chairman of Mining Resources Corporation. It was the owner and operator of the Cassiar chrysotile mine. Mining Resources engineered a takeover bid of a junior Australian mining company. Frame's reputation had gone before him, and it was said to be part of the reasons why the target's shareholders rejected the bid. This did not seem to harm Frame's corporate career as, in addition to remaining chairman of the board of Mining Resources, he was also appointed as CEO of the corporation whose name had now been changed to Cassiar Mines & Metals Inc., a corporation associated with another risky operation for workers and the environment, namely asbestos. Eventually, this firm was taken over by another and C.H. Frame's tenure as chairman and CEO was terminated as the new controllers wanted their own nominees in charge of their investment, a point to be remembered when reading the next chapter: there are some people who can have their way with the corporation. The story has been told to show that, in the corporate world, C.H. Frame was not shunned by investors/shareholders because of his misadventures at Westray. To them the most important question is whether this kind of person can bring them profits; if they believe he might give them what they seek, his checkered history about how he goes about maximizing profits, his character, will rarely worry them.

Another example is the treatment of two mining promoters in the early 1960s. The story of the MacMillans bears a strong resemblance to that of Walsh and Felderhof in the Bre-X affair. The MacMillans managed to convey the impression that their drilling was yielding spectacular results. They did not actually say that but slyly led the public to believe it. A wave of speculation followed that allowed them and their corporation to cash in handsomely. As well, a royal commission that was struck to inquire as to how this kind of manipulation had been allowed to take place found that stockbrokers had treated the Toronto Stock Exchange as a private gaming club. They had pursued trades for clients as well as on their own behalf, taking advantage of outsiders' ignorance. The MacMillans were convicted of unrelated financial misbehaviours but, because they had not explicitly told the investing public any lies, they were never convicted of any wrongdoing in respect of their virtually salted gold mine. Mrs. MacMillan, the acknowledged ringleader, lived until she was ninety and received the Order of Canada; see Christopher Armstrong, *Moose Pastures and Mergers: 1940–1980* (Toronto: University of Toronto Press, 2001).

There is a voluminous literature on the Westray affair, ranging from descriptions of the tragedy, the legal processes, and the ensuing amendments of criminal law that were spawned by it; see S. Bittle, *Still Dying for a Living: Corporate Criminal Liability after the Westray Mine Disaster* (UBC Press, 2012); S. Comish, *The Westray Tragedy* (Halifax: Fernwood, 1993); D. Jobb, *Calculated Risk* (Halifax: Nimbus, 1994); H. Glasbeek and E. Tucker, "Death by Consensus: The Westray Story," (1993), 3 *New Solutions*, 14; H. Glasbeek, "Missing the Targets—Bill C-45: Reforming the Status Quo to Maintain the Status Quo," *Policy and Practice in Health and Safety* 11,2 (2013), a special issue to mark the twentieth anniversary of the Westray Mine explosion. There also is much writing on the Bre-X saga: Diane Francis, *Bre-X: The Inside Story* (Key Porter, 1997); Douglas Goold and Andrew Willis, *The Bre-X Fraud* (McClelland & Stewart, 1997); Jennifer Wells, *Fever: The Dark Mystery of the Bre-X Gold Rush* (Penguin, 1998); Brian Hutchinson, *Fool's Gold: The Making of a Global Fraud* (Alfred Knopf, 1997).

In addition much work has been done inquiring into why it has been so difficult to hold corporations criminally responsible, how technical difficulties might be overcome, how various jurisdictions have sought to overcome the technical hurdles, the extent to which corporate behaviour should be left to the regulatory sphere rather than to the criminal one, the need to impose more direct responsibility on senior officers within corporations, and how the Anglo-American approach compares to that taken in European jurisdictions. Even an abbreviated list is a long one; see Karen Wheelwright, "Goodbye Directing Mind and Will, Hello Management Failure: A Brief Critique of Some New Models of Corporate Criminality," (2006), 19 *Australian Journal of Corporate Law*, 287; Rick Sarre and Jenny Richards, "Responding to Culpable Corporate Behaviour: Current Developments in the Industrial Manslaughter Field," (2005), 8 *Flinders Journal of Law Reform*, 93; T. Woolf, "The Criminal Code Act 1995: Towards a Realist Vision of Corporate Criminality,"(1997), 21 *Criminal Law Journal*, 257; Darcy L. McPherson, "Extending Corporate Criminal Liability?: Some Thoughts on Bill C-45," (2004), 30 *Manitoba Law Journal*, 253; T. Archibald, K. Jull, and K. Roach, "The Changed Face of Corporate Criminal Liability," (2004), 48 *Criminal Law Quarterly*, 367; H. Glasbeek, "Crime, Health and Safety and Corporations: Meanings of Victoria's Failed Crimes (Workplace Deaths and Serious Injuries) Bill and Its Equivalents Elsewhere," Working Paper No. 29, CELRL (University of Melbourne, 2003). For the Dutch position, see S. Field and N. Jorg, "Corporate Liability and Manslaughter: Should We Be Going Dutch?," [1991] *Criminal Law Review*, 156; for a short account of the German and French positions, see Guy Stessens, "Corporate Criminal Liability: A Comparative Perspective," (1994), 43 *International and Comparative Law Quarterly*, 493; see also Celia Wells, *Corporations and Criminal Responsibility* (Oxford: Clarendon Press, 1993); V.S. Khanna, "Corporate Criminal Liability: What Purpose Does It Serve?," (1996), 109 *Harvard Law Review*, 1477; John C. Coffee Jr., "Emerging Issues in Corporate Criminal Policy," foreword to Richard Gruner, *Corporate Crime and Sentencing* (Michie, 1994); for the European recommendations on how to deal with corporate criminality, see Council of Europe, Recommendation No. R (88) 18, 1988. J. Gobert and M. Punch, *Rethinking Corporate Crimes* (London: Butterworths, 2003) report that Italy, aiming primarily at financial crimes, has enacted legislation that punishes structural negligence, that is, conduct that constitutes organizational fault. In Japan, too, there are similar developments; see Tomomi Kawasaki, "White-Collar Crime and Reaction of the Criminal Justice System in the United States and

Japan" in H. Pontell and G. Geis, eds., *International Handbook of White-Collar and Corporate Crime* (New York: Springer, 2007), 552.

On the ongoing compensation struggles in respect of Lac-Mégantic, Canadian Press, April 11, 2016, reported that four thousand people have been offered settlements out of funds contributed to by twenty-five companies (this group did not include Canadian Pacific) and that, thus far, $50 million has been paid out in respect of moral claims and $113 million for material losses suffered; more payments are to follow but four hundred people have lodged complaints about the amounts allocated to them.

The political and legal aftermath of Lac-Mégantic is following a well-established pattern. Just as in the Westray disaster, the politicians, prosecutors, and media concentrated on the immediate causes and outcomes. This leads to the elimination of the questioning about the nature of corporate capitalist system these horrible outcomes might otherwise spawn. It is what the Norwegian scholar Thomas Mathieson has called a process of pulverization. It fragments and decontextualizes the events from larger social relations. Yet what should be significant is the context in which private actors and governments alike work as wealth is sought to be generated by the individual pursuit of profits. When it came to rail transport, Canada's federal government undertook to deregulate the sector in 1985. The government trusted the market to punish those who did not meet customer-satisfying services. But this faith in the market's capacity always is misplaced and it was very much so in this sector. Greg Cormick (*Toronto Star*, Aug. 22, 2014, A13), a transportation writer and policy adviser, noted that the weaker competitors, in their zeal to satisfy stockholders, did all they could to keep their heads above water. Here this meant cutting expenses on safety. All this came to a head as existing pipelines have no more capacity and the building of new ones is extremely controversial. As shippers turned to rail they made do, as much as possible, with existing tracks and trains. The business decisions made can only be understood from the perspective of actors who were looking for cheap ways to transport fuels. The routes chosen were circuitous. The fuels that exploded in Lac-Mégantic had come from the Bakken oil fields in North Dakota and were on their way to Saint John, New Brunswick, travelling across the breadth of the continent through many dense population centres. This is manifestly dangerous and the shippers did not provide population centres with information about the cargo they had shipped. They liked their already built circuitous routes. Notably here, the shippers were content to use the nearly 100-year-old Montreal and Maritime Atlantic railway line as part of their delivery system. Its state of repair and level of maintenance had been in question for some time. They operated the trains with as few employees as the deregulated industry allowed. They did not see fit to replace the single-hulled cars with what they knew would be the safer double-hulled ones. The context made sure a disaster would occur. The only mystery was when and where it would occur. It was no accident. The circumstances of the Westrays, the Lac-Mégantics, are consciously created. This point is of considerable importance to the central argument of this book: we must find a way to make profit-chasers understand that they will no longer be allowed to pretend that they could not possibly have done anything, that collateral damage is inevitable, that it should not attract blame.

The tendency to the pulverization of complex events helps us to understand why regulators and prosecutors are able to concentrate on workers as major culprits rather than on the investors who influence managers to force workers to implement profit-seeking activities in circumstances in which obvious risks have not been eliminated. This is what happened in the Metron Construction, Westray, and Lac-Mégantic cases. The politicians and authorities believe that, by showing how tough they are on workers at the coal face, they are assuring the public that they play no favourites, that they apply criminal law to everyone, even people within corporations. Thus, when the decision was made to charge the engineer in the Lac-Mégantic disaster, the police descended on his house, with sirens screaming and automatic weapons drawn. He was led away in handcuffs. The engineer's lawyer had undertaken that, should charges be laid, his client would surrender himself voluntarily to the court. Of course, you can only fool all of the people some of the time. At the laying of the charges, the accused were, as reported by Roger Annis, "Oil-by-Rail on Trial in Lac-Megantic, Quebec and in Maine," *Truthout*, June 3, 2014, treated with respect and even some sympathy by the attending public: "'They're not the ones who should be there' ... 'I believe there should be charges, but for the right people,'" said [a woman who] lost her daughter in the explosion. 'The big boss—he should be the first.'" The "show" aspect of charging workers is all the more remarkable as the amendments to the *Criminal Code* that followed the Westray legal fiasco were aimed at making it easier to convict organizations; there was never any technical problem with charging individuals as such.

9. TOO HARD TO FIND? THE ANECDOTAL RIPOSTE

1   Canadian Press, "Paul Desmarais's Funeral Draws A-List of Politics Past and Present," *Globe and Mail*, Dec. 3, 2013.

2   James Hedley, ed., *Canada and Her Commerce: A Souvenir of the Dominion Commercial Travellers' Association* (Montreal: Sabiston, 1894); Gustavus Myers, intro by Stanley Ryerson, *A History of Canadian Wealth* (Toronto: James Lorimer & Co., 1972, first ed. 1914); Libby and Frank Park, *Anatomy of Big Business* (Toronto: James Lewis & Samuel, 1973); Thomas A. Naylor, *History of Canadian Business, 1867–1914* (Toronto: James Lorimer & Co., 1975); Walter Clement, *The Canadian Corporate Elite: An Analysis of Economic Power* (Toronto: McClelland & Stewart, 1975); Michael Bliss, *Northern Enterprise: Five Centuries of Canadian Business* (Toronto: McClelland &

Stewart, 1986); Diane Francis, *Controlling Interests: Who Owns Canada?* (Toronto: Macmillan, 1986), *Who Owns Canada Now?: Old Money, New Money, and the Future of Canadian Business* (Toronto: HarperCollins, 2008); Graham Taylor and Peter Baskerville, *A Concise History of Business in Canada* (Toronto: Oxford University Press, 1994); Peter C. Newman, *The Canadian Establishment* (Toronto: McClelland & Stewart, 1975), *The Canadian Establishment, vol. II* (Toronto: McClelland & Stewart, 1981), *Merchant Princes* (Toronto: Penguin, 1991), *Titans: How the New Canadian Establishment Seized Power* (Toronto: Penguin, 1998).

3   Dana Flavelle, "Shareholder Group Slams Tim Hortons Merger," *Toronto Star*, Nov. 13, 2014; Anthony Davis, "Art of the Deal: Behind the Scenes of the Burger King Purchase of Tim Hortons," *Lexpert Magazine*, Sept. 2015; Marlene Leung, "A Closer Look at 3G Capital, the Firm behind the Tim Hortons Deal," CTV News, Aug. 27, 2014.

4   Per Brown, J., *Hale v. Henkle*, 201 U.S. 43 (1906).

5   Moyers and Company, "Too Big to Jail?," billmoyers.com.episode/too-big-to-jail, Oct. 3, 2014.

These notes begin with remarks on how the desire by controlling investors to limit their liability has always been central to corporate law developments. Controllers of wealth have always sought not to be held responsible for the uses they make of their wealth. The desire of so-called entrepreneurs to eliminate risks is patent. In this context, a recent grant of relief to accountants and lawyers by means of the revival of an old idea, a limited liability partnership, is noted. As well, there is an elaboration on how the nature of law and economics school thinking negates the potential of initiatives to promote corporate social responsibility. A couple of examples of the shared understanding—despite legal theorization—that it matters who the controlling shareholders are offered.

The predecessors of the modern corporation were unincorporated joint stock companies. They were, in effect, large partnerships. They were used to attract large numbers of investors to fund explorations (like the East India Company) and large infrastructure endeavours. As legal instruments, they presented several related technical problems. Because they were partnerships, contractors and others who wanted to hold the company (a non-person at law) accountable had to find a way to sue the individual members of the company (a word that, as it does today in some circumstances, suggested a social, not legal, association). A major difficulty existed for those investors who wanted to pull their capital out of the company and/or alienate their interest in the company to other investors, both natural impulses in a thriving capitalist system. The development of the modern corporation with its ability to overcome these problems was slow and, meanwhile, many investors sought refuge by relying on limited partnerships where they could take a profit-seeking position, but one that did not make them liable for the partnership's obligations unless they had exercised some kind of managerial control or influence over the partnership's operations. This kind of partnership persists to this day and, it will be noted, the rule that, should a limited partner take control over the firm, that partner will be responsible for the outcomes, dovetails with the argument made in chapter 7; see also Robert Flannigan, "The Political Path to Limited Liability in Business Trusts," (2006), 31 *Advocates Quarterly*, 257.

The recent turn to limited liability partnerships by professional firms arises from similar impulses. It is somewhat paradoxical. Law and accountancy, as professions, have been allowed to regulate themselves. The logic is that they are professions that accept that their primary duty is to serve the public interest, rather than their own. They are to develop and enforce rules of probity and set appropriate standards of skill. Their own interests, unlike those in business more generally, are to be subjugated to their public duties. In that context, members of a firm stand behind all acts done by the other members in the name of the firm. The development of limited liability partnerships appears to run counter to this logic. It was put on the agenda after the notorious savings and loans scandals in the 1980s in the United States where highly prestigious accountancy firms were to be saddled because of the complicity by their branch managers and partners with the imprudent lending and speculating by savings and loans banks in disparate regions of the country. The main offices of these accountancy firms claimed that this was unfair and they needed protection. They got it as new limited liability partnership arrangements were made statutorily available to them. Law firms soon were allowed to follow suit. It is worth noting that these firms never reject their share of the profits made by members of their firms elsewhere. But that is a cheap shot. What is important is that this is another example of how the shedding of responsibility for acts done under one's potential control requires exceptional treatment by the law.

The chapter's evaluation of the way in which the corporate cheerleaders, here identified as law and economics scholars, justify the current legal position that defends the idea that individual contractors have created a nexus of links through which they can pursue their self-interest more efficiently is, admittedly, somewhat rudimentary. For my earlier, hopefully more thorough, efforts see *Wealth by Stealth* and "More Direct Directors' Duties." It is notable that the argument that the corporation is really a convenient way for a lot of individuals to enter into contracts with one another suits the opponents of the imposition of anything akin to social responsibility on corporations. The question of what purposes the corporation ought to serve becomes irrelevant to those who think that self-standing individuals do not have any responsibility to do good or, indeed, any particular thing. When leading exponents of the law and economics school's dogma, F. Easterbrook and D. Fischel, *The Economic Structure of Corporate Law* (Harvard University Press, 1990), were confronted by "interesting" questions such as "What is the goal of the corporation? Is it profit and for whom? Social welfare more broadly defined? Should corporations try to maximize profits over the long term or the short term?" they responded with a cavalier "Who cares?"

The chapter notes how seriously investors take the character of the to-be-controlling human shareholders when they make judgments about a corporation. The hard-nosed approach by the same folks who run 3G Capital and who purchased Tim Hortons is at issue in a contretemps in Australia. There a corporation called AB InBev, dominated by 3G Capital, is about to merge with a major Australian brewery. The local union is up in arms because it believes that the cost-cutting 3G Capital modus operandi will cost them their jobs. In an analogous way, Jennifer Wells, "Will the Hershey Legacy of Philanthropy Endure?," *Toronto Star*, July 6, 2016, B1, asks whether a projected takeover will spell the end for what (she clearly admires) was the support of the original owner of Hershey Chocolate for local schools and anti-poverty programs. Everyone knows that it matters who the human beings behind corporations are, even as law asks us to ignore this verity.

10. TOO HARD TO FIND? THE EMPIRICAL RIPOSTE

1   R. Flannigan, "Corporations Controlled by Shareholders: Principals, Agents or Servants?," (1986–7), 51 *Saskatchewan Law Revue*, 23.

2   *Hindu*, May 10, 2014; *Wall Street Journal*, Oct. 15, 2014.

3   Jordan Brennan, "A Shrinking Universe: How Concentrated Corporate Power Is Shaping Income Inequality in Canada" (Ottawa: Canadian Centre for Policy Alternatives, 2012).

4   Robert Paul Wolff, "The Future of Socialism," *Seattle University Law Review* (2012), 1403, 1424.

5   For the studies relied on in this chapter to discuss the level of the concentration of corporate ownership, see: John Porter, *The Vertical Mosaic* (Toronto: University of Toronto Press, 1956); Tom Hadden, Robert E. Forbes, and Ralph L. Simmonds, *Canadian Business Organizations Law* (Toronto: Butterworths, 1984); P.S. Rao and Lee Sing, "Governance Structure, Corporate Decision-Making and Firm Performance in North America" in R.J. Daniels and R. Morck, eds., *Corporate Decision-Making in Canada* (Calgary: Calgary University Press, 1996); Aviv Pichhadze, "Mergers, Acquisitions, and Controlling Shareholders: Canada and Germany Compared," *Banking and Finance Law Review* 18 (2005); Rafael La Porta, Florencio Lopez-de-Silanes, and Andrei Shleifer, "Corporate Ownership around the World," *Journal of Finance*, LIV,2 (1999), 471; Randall Morck, Michael Percy, Gloria Tian, and Bernard Yeung, "The Rise and Fall of the Widely Held Firm: A History of Corporate Ownership in Canada" in Randall Morck,

A History of Corporate Governance around the World: Family Groups to Professional Managers (Chicago: University of Chicago Press, 2005); Randall K. Morck, David A. Strangeland, and Bernard Yeung, "Inherited Wealth, Corporate Control and Economic Growth: The Canadian Disease?" in R. Morck, ed., *Concentrated Corporate Ownership* (National Bureau of Economic Research, 2000); Randall Morck, "Shareholder Democracy in Canada," NBER Working Paper no. 16558.

6   "Sears Sells Most of Limping Canadian Stake to Raise $380 M," *Toronto Star,* Oct. 2, 2014.

7   "More Problems for Eddie Lampert's Empire: Sears Canada CEO Quits," *Fortune*, Sept. 25, 2013.

8   See Clifford G. Holderness and Dennis P. Sheehan, "The Myth of Diffuse Ownership in the United States," *Review of Financial Studies* (2009), 1377 (identifying 650 publicly traded corporations with majority shareholders); Nina A. Mendelson, "A Controlled Approach to Shareholder Liability for Corporate Torts," (2002), 102 *Columbia Law Review*, 1203 (noting that 79 per cent of close corporations had one shareholder with more than 51 per cent of the corporation's equity); Harold Demetz, "The Structure of Ownership of the Firm," (1983), 26 *Journal of Law and Economics*, 138 (reporting that close to 50 per cent of large U.S. corporations fall into the owner-controlled category); Harold Demetz and Belen Villalonga, "Ownership Structure and Corporate Performance" (2001, on file with *Columbia Law Review*) (finding that the five largest shareholders in 60 per cent of 223 large U.S. firms held more than 20 per cent of the voting rights).

9   B.E. Eckbo, "Mergers and the Market for Corporate Control: The Canadian Evidence," *Canadian Journal of Economics* 19 (1986), "The Market for Corporate Control: Policy Issues and Capital Market Evidence" in R.S. Khemani, D. Shapiro, and W.T. Stanbury, eds., *Mergers, Corporate Concentration and Corporate Power in Canada* (Montreal: Canadian Institute for Research on Public Policy, 1987).

10   Judy Rebick, *Toronto Star,* Oct. 8, 2014.

11   April 4, 2014.

12   Adam Harmes, *Unseen Power: How Mutual Funds Threaten the Political and Economic Wealth of Nations* (Toronto: Stoddard, 2001).

13   Jennifer Taub, "Able but Not Willing: The Failure of Mutual Fund Advisors to Advocate for Shareholder Rights," (2009), 34(3), *Journal of Corporation Law.*

14   David Olive, "Why Shareholders Need to Stand Up and Vote," *Toronto Star*, Business, Aug. 5, 2013.

15   Jennifer Hill, "Visions and Revisions of the Shareholder," (2008), 48(1) *American Journal of Comparative Law*, 39.

16   Marvin Lipton, Theodore Mirvis, and Jay Lorsch, "The Proposed 'Shareholder Bill of Rights of 2009,'" May 12, 2009, https://corpgov.law.harvard.edu.

17   *Toronto Star*, Nov. 13, 2014, 8.

These notes address the issue of whether the conventional wisdom that (a) there is a gap between ownership and control and (b) this creates difficulties for the corporation's efficiency and governance raises any serious questions. There is a clarifying note on the significance of distinguishing between small and large corporations, followed by evidence of the economic importance of mega-corporations and their controlling shareholders. Some surprising data about the United States are included. Some examples of the uses made of legal personhood by large controlling corporations and their controllers are proffered, leading to the observation that the oppression remedy is supposed to offset (in part) the dangers this controlling shareholders' power entails for other shareholders and just others. The oppression remedy's nature and reach is contextualized. An illustration of the impact of pyramids, by using the example of two Canadian families, is provided. Finally a note on what is called passive shareholding is offered.

Much of this chapter sets out to engage with the conventional wisdomeers' best justificatory argument, in particular, the claim that corporations are characterized by widely dispersed shareholding that has robbed owners of their birthright, namely the capitalists' sacrosanct right to control their property. This 1932 finding by Berle and Means still has corporate lawmakers, scholars, and activists in its spell. On one side, there is a fear that corporations might become inefficient and that the controllers without property, the directors and executives, might serve themselves all too well. On the other side of the fence, the glass is seen as half full. It is hoped that independent directors and executives might use their discretion to act for the public good. Both sides take off from the premise that there is a gap between the interests of red-blooded capitalists who gave away their property, and directors and managers of corporations, and that the former cannot be held responsible as if they were real capitalists in charge of their own affairs. Because these are conventionally accepted arguments, this chapter takes aim at them as if they make eminent sense. But in fact, as was observed in the notes to chapter 4, Marxist scholars have persuasively argued that the conventional claims are highly disputable, which explains why the justifications on which they rely prove to be threadbare.

Some might cavil at the claim in this chapter that corporate law does not differentiate appropriately between, say, one-person corporations and multinational corporations. After all, it is legally accepted that some allowances for size and nature must be made in respect of legal accounting treatment and reporting requirements and for some technical adjustments in respect of quorums and meetings. But these adaptations arise from practical needs; they do not challenge the fundamentals of the legal nature of registered corporations. Regardless of the size or nature of a corporation, there is to be no deviation from the legal privileges that make corporations a special kind of business organization.

In Canada, it is clear that the sixty mega-corporations that dominate the publicly traded blob-o-sphere also produce the most highly paid executives and the wealthiest people as shareholders. Much of the vaunted Canadian 0.1 per cent come from this enclave; *Toronto Star*, Nov. 22, 2013, reported that, through their family-controlled corporations, the Thomson wealth was measured at $26.1 billion, that of the Westons at $10.4 billion, of the Irvings at $7.85 billion, and of the Rogerses at $7.6 billion; see Jordan Brennan, "A Shrinking Universe" (Canadian Centre for Policy Alternatives, 2012). The thousands of small investors are really small by comparison in all jurisdictions; see Ruy Texera, "The Myth of the Investor Class: And Why Small Investors Still Rely on Government," *American Prospect*, Summer 2003, A11; Edward N. Wolff, *Recent Trends in Household Wealth in the United States; Rising Debt and the Middle-Class Squeeze—an Update to 2007*, Levy Economics Institute of Bard College, March 2010; Rob Larson, "Hitting the Class Ceiling," *Z Magazine*, July/Aug. 2010 (the lower 80 per cent of Americans owned 8 per cent of the values of stocks held, the richest 10 per cent owning 81 per cent of all stocks by value, making the holdings of most investors truly tiny). Even in the United States, then, where the claim of dispersed ownership is most justified, the numerous small investors have very little sway inside the corporations in which they invest. William W. Bratton and Michael L. Wachter, "Shareholders and Social Welfare," (2013), 36 *Seattle University Law Review*, 489, using these data, have come to the view that, despite the large number of people who now hold shares directly and indirectly, "the shareholders' overall socioeconomic status has remained largely unchanged. The model shareholder in the data is rich, old, and white." They conclude that one of the justifications for shareholder primacy, namely that, because shareholding is such a widespread phenomenon, advancing shareholders' interests is a means to advance overall welfare, making profit maximization a central part of democratic practices, is unfounded. It turns out that, except for a relatively few large publicly traded corporations, most U.S. corporations have a small number of substantial shareholders; see Clifford G. Holderness and Dennis P. Sheehan, "The Myth of Diffuse Ownership in the United States," (2009), *Review of Financial Studies*, 1377 (identifying 650 publicly traded corporations with majority shareholders); Nina A. Mendelson, "A Controlled Approach to Shareholder Liability for Corporate Torts," (2002), 102 *Columbia Law Review*, 1203 (noting that 79 per cent of close corporations had one shareholder with more than 51 per cent of the corporation's equity); Harold Demetz, "The Structure of Ownership of the Firm," (1983), 26 *Journal of Law and Economics*, 138 (reporting that close to 50 per cent of large U.S. corporations fall into the owner-controlled category); Harold Demetz and

Belen Villalonga, "Ownership Structure and Corporate Performance"(2001, on file with *Columbia Law Review*, found that the five largest shareholders in 60 per cent of 223 large U.S. firms held more than 20 per cent of the voting rights). Of course, these shareholders might themselves be corporations.

In this chapter, the argument is that all too often, there are shareholders who are in control of business firms, incorporated or not. When it was argued earlier that liberal law requires that those with control over undertakings and who intend to benefit from those undertakings be held legally responsible, a number of instances were proffered to demonstrate how control could be or was exercised. Indeed, corporate cheerleaders who resist the notion that controlling shareholders (if findable) should be held responsible for corporate wrongdoing cheerfully celebrate such controlling shareholders when they use their clout to steer the corporation in the right direction by cutting costs and rewarding shareholders; *Bloomberg's* Scott Deveau, "Largest CP Rail Shareholder Sells Stake," *Toronto Star*, Aug. 5, 2016, GT8, tells the story of how Bill Ackman, the controlling shareholder of an investment firm, bought 6.7 per cent of CP Rail's shares and then used his voting power to install a better CEO and turn a corporation around. To underscore an argument raised in the book, note how a relatively small number of shares in a relatively widely held corporation may bestow a critical amount of decision-making power—for good and evil doings. Legal control, as defined in the book, is not crucial. Control by easily identified individuals can be obtained in many ways.

To emphasize the point, note how parent corporations consciously use subsidiaries to attain their profit-maximization ends, i.e., how they not only have control but also exercise it over legally sovereign entities. Michael West, "Clive Palmer's Antics Are the Very Same Ones Multinationals Use," WAtoday.com, April, 15, 2016, tells how Chevron in the United States borrowed money in the United States and then lent it at nine times the rate at which it had borrowed to its Australian subsidiary, lowering that Australian subsidiary's tax bill dramatically, so dramatically that the local revenue authorities forced it to pay $73 million in additional taxes; this is being appealed (of course!) but, however it comes out, the story shows that there are persons in command in these kinds of corporate families. Indeed, Shell acknowledges its treatment of its Australian subsidiaries as dependent by renaming them Shell in Australia, while Google's supposedly independent Australian corporate outlet has only one Australian resident on its board of directors, the other two members residing in the United States.

The oppression remedy has now been mentioned twice. The remedy stems from law dealing with disputes between partners. In those very personality-rich firms, remedies were needed when a partner abused their power to oust a notional equal from entitlements. The corporate firm, legally distancing the investors from the corporation and its directors and operators, but often replicating the functional relationships of a partnership, needed similar remedial tools. Gradually, this tool, the oppression remedy, came to be applied to the large, and functionally totally different, corporate firm; moreover, it has been expanded to allow stakeholders other than shareholders to use it. Naturally, this has been seen as a major exercise in social engineering and has attracted an enormous amount of practitioners' and academics' interest. The promise of the remedy seems immense. It is, however, not unlike a similar innovation, the unconscionability doctrine in contract law (that came about for analogous reasons, namely to help the apparently hapless). It, too, attracted way more attention than its concrete results warranted. Arthur Leff, "Unconscionability and the Code: The Emperor's New Clause" (1967) noted that he had counted over 100 articles on the imaginative aspects and promise of the new unconscionability doctrine but only three successful uses of it. The oppression remedy is widely used, mostly by minority shareholders in small corporations (that is, by persons resembling the disaffected partners of yore). It has delivered less than those who hoped, and continue to hope, for a more effective means to make corporations accountable to the outside world. Indeed, when the Supreme Court of Canada was confronted by the extent to which the controllers of a corporation could be held to account by shareholders and other stakeholders, it was extremely cautious. In *People's Department Stores Inc. (Trustees of)* v. *Wise*, [2004] 3 S.C.R. 461, it stated that a board of directors was entitled, but was not obliged, to take legitimate interests into account (of investors, workers, creditors, the corporation itself) even if this meant disadvantaging other legitimately interested persons (shareholders, other stakeholders), giving them a sound defence against claims of prejudicial dealings.

The potential danger of rule by the few that inheres in the use of pyramids underpinned the anxiety felt by policy-makers when it seemed as if the Argus Corporation and the Power Corporation might be melded into one gigantic firm. Both these corporations were pyramids whose tentacles spread through the Canadian economy. Argus was under the sway of two individuals, McDougall and Davis (Conrad Black was later to take over this mini-empire) and Power was (and still is) controlled by the Desmarais family. The panic led to the setting up of a major inquiry into the extent and nature of corporate concentration in Canada, the Bryce Report, 1978. Here it is sufficient to note that it was understood that a few individuals or families could command our economy by means of corporate pyramids. And while it is outside the purview of this work, it should be noted that interlocking ownerships allow a relatively few major corporations (and behind them, a few very wealthy individuals) to control a huge proportion of global wealth. A. Coghlan and D. MacKenzie, "Revealed—the Capitalist Network That Runs the World," *New Scientist* 2835 (2011), report that (out of a universe of 37 million companies) 43,000 multinational corporations linked by a network of share ownerships controlled by (a now trivial number) 1,318 interlocked companies controlled 20 per cent of the world's assets. And, within the 1,318 mega-controllers, a min-iscule 147 companies held 40 per cent of that one-fifth of the world's wealth.

Many equity purchasers do not want to play a role in corporate decision-making. This does not mean that a block of such shareholders has no impact. Robert Flannigan, "The Political Imposture of Passive Capital," (2009), 9 *Journal of Corporate Law Studies*, 139, argues that, should there be some shareholders who want to be active in the affairs of the cor-poration, the existence of a large block of passive capital aids them in their quest to control the de jure decision-makers in respect of the assets of corporation as it allows them to take risks with some backing behind them. Passive shareholders are willing to be so used because it relieves them of the obligation to monitor managers. That is, their complicity strengthens active capital. On another front, when some directors/managers are under pressure from active shareholders, they may use passive shareholders to form a counterweight. In short, passive capital, even when it is not doing anything to imperil its limited responsibility pos-ition, may be more influential than it appears to be on the surface. By contrast, when small shareholders want to exercise their voice to have the corporations consider the interests of stakeholders other than shareholders, they are seen as obstructive nay-sayers. John Engler, president of the very influential think tank and lobbying group Business Roundtable, wrote in "How Gadfly Shareholders Keep CEO's Distracted," *Toronto Star*, May 31, 2016, A13, that "small-stake investors take advantage to flood companies with frivolous ballot measures … the overwhelming majority of shareholders don't abuse the proposal system. Investors who have a real skin in the game don't want to undermine a company's operations."

11. THE ROLE OF LIMITED LIABILITY

1   *Economist*, Dec. 18, 1926, 118.

2   T. Gabaldon, "The Lemonade Stand: Feminist and Other Reflections on the Limited Liability of Corporate Shareholders," (1992), 45 *Vanderbilt Law Revue*, 1387.

3   Mark J. Roe, "Corporate Strategic Reaction to Mass Tort," (1986), 72 *Virginia Law Revue*, 1; Dan Plesch and Stephanie Blankenburg, "Corporate Rights and Responsibil-ities: Restoring Legal Accountability," Royal Society for the Encouragement of Arts, Manufactures and Commerce, May 13, 2007.

4   A. Ringleb and S. Wiggins, "Liability and Large Scale, Long-term Hazards," *Journal of Political Economy* 98 (1990), 574.

5   H. Hansmann and R. Kraakman, "Toward Unlimited Shareholder Liability for Cor-porate Torts," (1991), 100 *Yale Law Journal*, 1879; P. Halpern, M. Trebilcock, and S. Turnbull, "An Economic Analysis of Limited Liability in Corporation Law," (1980), 30 *University of Toronto Law Journal*, 117; C. Witting, "Liability for Corporate Wrongs,"

[2009] *University of Queensland Law Journal* 28; N. Mendelson, "A Controlled Approach to Shareholder Liability for Corporate Torts," (2002), 102 *Columbia Law Journal*, 1203.

6   A. Rogers, "Reforming the Law Related to Limited Liability," (1993) 3(1) *Australian Journal of Corporate Law*, 137, 140.

7   Justin Fox and Jay W. Lorsch, "What Good Are Shareholders?," *Harvard Business Review* (July–August 2012), 48.

8   Adolf A. Berle, *The American Economic Republic* (New York: Harcourt Brace World, 1963).

9   Doug Henwood, *Wall Street* (London: Verso, 1997).

10   Marjorie Kelly, *The Divine Right of Capital: Dethroning the Corporate Aristocracy*, foreword by William Greider (San Francisco: Berrett-Koehler, 2003).

11   Leo Panitch and Sam Gindin, *The Making of Global Capitalism: The Political Economy of American Empire* (London: Verso, 2012).

These notes briefly discuss the initial repugnance of the notion that shareholders should be granted limited liability. The major concern was what now seems a quaint concern for the plight of workers exploited by investors hiding behind a blob.

The transition from seeing limited liability as a special privilege that entailed great dangers to an entitlement that is not to be challenged is well captured in the history of protection for unpaid wages owed by corporations. Eric Tucker, "Shareholders and Director Liability for Unpaid Workers' Wages in Canada: From Condition of Granting Limited Liability to Exceptional Remedy," (2008), 26 *Law and History Review*, 57, brings out the radical change that capitalists have managed to engineer. As the struggle to be allowed to incorporate as a matter of right unfolded, the claim that those who invested capital should have their liability for corporate debt limited to the extent of their investment was a stumbling block. Opponents relied heavily on the hardship this might inflict on vulnerable employees who, despite being considered sovereign contracting parties, could not protect themselves adequately. Tucker reports how, early in the piece, limited liability was granted in a limited fashion: shareholders and directors would be responsible for unpaid wages, although their other fiscal responsibilities might be limited. But over time, the judiciary, wedded to the purity of contract law doctrines, whittled down this worker protection by what the reader now ought to recognize as typical judicial finessing. They read the definitions of employees and wages in the various corporate law statutes more and more narrowly. In the end, hardly any of the protections first crafted had any real life left. In due course, this forced legislatures to enact new safeguards to allow unpaid employees to recover what was owed, but for the most part, this is done without confronting the sacrosanct nature of limited liability for shareholders.

Of particular interest is some of the thinking that infected those who doubted that the limited liability corporation could be of much value to society. One example should suffice. Tucker, talking about the battle for incorporation of limited liability firms in the mid-nineteenth century in New York, cites a couple of passages from a Senate Committee on Manufactures, chaired by Thomas Barlow. They indicated the doubts felt about exonerating capitalists from having to pay debts incurred by their enterprises: "What class shall thus be favoured, in whole or in part?... Shall it be the farmer, the merchant, the blacksmith, the day laborer, the lawyer, the doctor, the carpenter, the mechanic of any kind? No, not any one man, nor men in common, but the capitalists, and those of all others best able to pay their debts." This perspective was informed by the disrespect felt for an argument that pretended that investing capitalists were not in control of the corporations in which they had sunk their money, that they were not the real contractors who had employed the workers: "If they do not do it in person, they do by officers or agents of their own choosing, for whose acts they are justly responsible.... Large tears may be dropt in their advocacy, but they roll from the eyes of hungry crocodile. In short, corporate rights are hostile to the very spirit of our institutions, unjust and oppressive to the rights of individuals"; see Tucker, 2008, citing from New York State Senate, Report 143, Nov. 22, 1847. It is this kind of thinking that needs to be brought back. This is a major theme of this book.

12. SOCIAL WELFARE

1   *Ode* 28 (2005).

2   Janet C. Lowe, *Warren Buffett Speaks: Wit and Wisdom from the World's Greatest Investor* (New York/Toronto: Wiley, 1997), 165. Buffett used GNP, gross national product, rather than GDP, but the terms are more or less interchangeable for these purposes.

3   Robyn Eckersley, *The Green State: Rethinking Democracy and Sovereignty* (Cambridge, MA: MIT Press, 2004); "The Age," *Business Day*, Feb. 22, 2012.

4   Kent Greenfield, "New Principles for Corporate Law," [2005] *Hastings Business Law Journal* 87.

5   David Shepardson, "GM Compensation Fund Completes Review with 124 Deaths," *Detroit News*, Aug. 24, 2015.

6   US National Highway Transportation, "Hyundai Fined $17.35 Million by US for Delayed Reporting of Brake Defect," Staff Wire report, Aug. 7, 2014.

7   Katie Lobosco and Chris Isidore, "Honda Underreported 1,729 Deaths and Injuries," CNN, Nov. 25, 2014; "Honda Fined Record $70 M US for Failing to Report 1700 Death and Injury Claims," CBC News, Jan. 8, 2015.

8   Danielle Douglas and Michael A. Fletcher, "Toyota Reaches $1.2 Billion Settlement to End Probe of Accelerator Problems," *Washington Post*, March 19, 2014.

9   Jeff Plungis, "Volkswagen Admits to Cheating on US Emissions Test," *Bloomberg*, Sept. 18, 2015, "Carmaker Cheating on Emissions Almost as Old as Pollution Tests," *Bloomberg*, Sept. 23, 2015.

10   Democratic Staff of the House of Representatives Committee on Education & Workforce, "Everyday Low Wages: The Hidden Price We Pay for Walmart," Feb. 16, 2004.

11   Dr. Edward Xie, "Steep Societal Cost of Alcohol," *Toronto Star*, July 11, 2013.

12   Carl Gibson, "How the iPhone Helps Perpetuate Modern-Day Slavery," *Reader Supported News*, Sept. 10, 2014.

13   John McMurtry, "Breaking Out of the Invisible Prison: The Ten-Point Global Paradigm Revolution," *The Bullet*, Feb. 25, 2015.

14   Rebecca R. Ruiz, "Woman Cleared in Death Ties to G.M.'s Faulty Ignition Switches," *New York Times*, Nov. 24, 2014.

15   John Ruskin, *Unto This Last* (Library of Congress, 1860); George Bernard Shaw, *The Basis of Socialism*, 1889.

16   Herman Daly, "Dear Paul Krugman: Is GDP Growth Making Us Richer or Poorer?," *Daly News*, May 10, 2014.

17   Lisa Heinzerling, "Knowing Killing and Environmental Law," (2006), 14 *NYU Environmental Law Journal*, 521.

18   Frank Ackerman and Lisa Heinzerling, *Priceless: On Knowing the Price of Everything and the Value of Nothing* (New York: New Press, 2004).

19   Robert Chernomas and Ian Hudson, "Labour in the Time of Cholera and Cancer," *The Bullet*, July 1, 2013.

20   "Former SNC-Lavalin VP Charged with Bribery," *Toronto Star*, Sept. 25, 2014; "SNC-Lavalin Unit Wins Contract Despite Ban," *Toronto Star*, Aug. 1, 2013. These articles tell the story of charges against, and settlements by, one of Canada's blue-ribbon corporations that earned such a reputation for getting its contracts by bribery that it had to agree not to bid on World Bank contracts for ten years. An ABC News headline, Sept. 25, 2014, read: "GlaxoSmithKline Fined $488M for 'Massive Bribery Network'"; the headline in the *Sydney Morning Herald,* Nov. 15, 2014, was "JPMorgan Allegedly Paid $80,000 a Month to Wen Jiabao's Daughter." Price fixing, like bribery, is still in vogue: "Hershey Fined $4 M for Conspiracy to Fix Chocolate Prices—Cadbury Got Immunity from Prosecution," *Toronto Star*, June 22, 2013; "Ontario Firm [les Petroles Global Inc] Guilty for Role in Price-Fixing Gas 'Cartel,'" *Toronto Star*, Aug. 10, 2013; "Scotiabank Named in Silver Price-Fixing Suit," *Toronto Star*, July 29, 2014; "Japanese Partsmaker Fined $2.45M in Bid-Rigging (in Ontario)," *Toronto Star*, Aug. 21, 2014; "Apple

Conspired to Fix Ebook Prices, US Judge Rules," *Toronto Star*, July 11, 2013; Jonathan Stempel, "Goldman, BASF, HSBC Accused of Metals Price-Fixing in U.S. Lawsuit," Reuters, Nov. 26, 2014; Jenny Anderson, "4 Banks, Including JP Morgan, Fined in Europe Over 'Cartel' Behavior," *New York Times*, Oct. 21, 2014. Lying never goes out of fashion and is holding its own in corporate circles: Kevin McCoy and Rick Jervis, "Halliburton to Pay $1.1B for Destroying Deepwater Horizon Evidence," *USA Today*, Sept. 2, 2013. And the age-old Ponzi schemes that require a lot of lying never seem to go away: "Sino-Forest Reaches 'Fair' Court Settlement," *Toronto Star*, July 22, 2014, details the fact that a corporation had misled investors by claiming it had large stands of forest where there were precious few trees. And, talking about golden oldies among wrongdoings, new allegations and findings of money laundering and dubious tax avoidance schemes are in the news on a regular basis, as in Jill Treanor's story in the *Guardian*, Feb. 15, 2015: "Swiss Bank Searched as Officials Launch Money-Laundering Inquiry." This article told of HSBC's willingness to clean up "dirty" money that rich people did not want the revenue departments to see. While the affair is still unfolding, HSBC has issued an apology in full-page advertisements, proclaiming that it is now on the straight and narrow while acknowledging that, in the past, the current, much better, standards had not been in place.

21   David Whyte, "Naked Labour: Putting Agamben to Work," (2009), 31 *Flinders Feminist Law Journal*, 57.

22   Elmer Altvater, "The Growth Obsession" in Leo Panitch and Colin Leys, eds., *Socialist Register* (London: Merlin, 2002).

23   Jan. 27, 2015.

24   Michael Hudson, "From the Bubble Economy to Debt, Deflation and Privatization," *Counterpunch*, July 5–7, 2013.

25   Iman Anabtwai and Lynn Stout, "Fiduciary Duties for Activist Shareholders," (2008), 60 *Stanford Law Review*, 1255. On the use of the empty voting techniques, see Henry T.C. Hu and Bernard Black, "Empty Voting and Hidden (Morphable) Ownership: Taxonomy, Implication, and Reforms," (2006), 61 *Business Law*, 1011; Shaun Marin and Frank Partnoy, "Encumbered Shares," [2005] *University of Illinois Law Review*, 775. For more general discussions of the hedge funds' operations, see Mara Der Hovanesian, "Attack of the Hungry Hedge Funds," *Business Week*, Feb. 20, 2006; William W. Bratton, "Hedge Funds and Governance Targets," (2007), 95 *Georgetown Law Journal*, 1375.

26   Karl Polanyi, *The Great Transformation* (Boston: Beacon, 1957).

27   Adam Smith, *Theory of Moral Sentiments*, part VI.

28   Albert Einstein, *Living Philosophies* (New York: Simon & Shuster, 1931).

29   Peter Singer, *How Are We To Live?* (Melbourne: Text, 1993).

30 Joseph E. Stiglitz, Amartya Sen, and Jean Paul Fitoussi, *Report by the Commission on the Measurement of Economic Performance and Social Progress*, Government of France, 2008.

31 Nov. 5, 2011.

32 Nick Hanauer, "The Pitchforks Are Coming . . . for Us Plutocrats: Memo from Nick Hanauer to My Fellow Zillionaires," *Politico*, Jan. 27, 2015.

33 Alec Hogg, "As Inequality Soars, the Nervous Super Rich Are Already Planning Their Escapes," *Guardian*, Jan. 26, 2015.

34 Clement, *The Canadian Corporate Elite*, 23.

These notes illustrate some ways in which the ceaseless, anarchic drive for more leads to collateral damage that detracts greatly from the argument that the corporation is needed to create overall welfare. Some of this collateral damage inflicts personal tragedies and environmental catastrophes, as noted. Our collective marginalization of these easily observable outcomes is documented. The sin of omission is posited as equal to the sin of commission. As the chapter deals with financialization, the nature and utility to social welfare of trading in shares and derivatives is addressed. Theories about the way those investments are undertaken are summarized, as is the recent frenzy generated by High Frequency Trading. The centrality or not of the financialization of capital is addressed, and the perverse uses made of pension plan investments is sketched out.

The assertion in this book that the fundamental logic of capitalism is a ceaseless push for private accumulation based on a relentless drive for economic growth is accepted by conservative political economists. The dynamic nature of capitalism, Joseph Schumpeter wrote, was the defining character of capitalism: "Stationary capitalism would be a *contradiction in adjecto*," a contradiction in terms, oxymoronic; see his *Essays* (Cambridge: Addison-Wesley, 1951). This single-mindedness concerns progressive people who do not like the outcomes and leads some to beg for a relaxation of the goal, to ask for more corporate social responsibility. Kent Greenfield's 2005 argument, relied on in this chapter, goes beyond not only that made by the social responsibility movement, but also beyond the U.S. trend to push for defined benefit corporations (discussed earlier). Like the social responsibility movement, the defined benefit corporation movement appeals to the goodwill of the corporate sectors. It makes no demands of them. And when no enforceable demands are made of vehicles legally designed to satisfy the greed of legally irresponsible actors, it is inevitable that a high risk of injuries and harms will accompany the drive for profits by the greedy and unfettered.

A story in the *New York Times*, Jan. 26, 2014, by Michael Corkery and Jessica Silver-Greenberg, reports that large lending institutions associated with automobile dealers are making money available to dealers to inveigle even those with truly low incomes to buy cars. The loans are then packaged into bundles by the lending institution and, having been given a high credit rating by analysts, sold to investors who have money to burn now that the housing subprime market has gone the way of the dodo. Serious concerns are being raised whether a similar series of defaults will occur as did in the housing market. The sums involved are large, such securitized loans (secured by the original contract made by the vehicle purchasers) said to be worth $20.2 billion in 2010. It is all legal, of course (subject to a finding that lenders knew that the borrowers lied about their ability to pay back the original loan), and may work out well, although the subprime mortgage history suggests otherwise. The point is that the scandals and failures of similar schemes in the immediate past do not prevent profit-seekers from trying the same thing again. The Volkswagen story mentioned in this chapter furnishes more evidence. The still unfolding saga illustrates some of the main arguments made in this book.

First, it is clear that the inexorable drive to maximize profits will often lead to the skirting of regulations. Volkswagen's defeat device was not the first of its kind. In 1972, Ford had been fined $7 million for the use of a similar device to fudge the pollution readings; Volkswagen itself was fined $120,000 a year later and, in 1974, Chrysler had been forced to recall 800,000 cars because such devices were hidden in their radiators (*New York Times*, Sept. 23, 2015). In May 2016, the president of Mitsubishi Motors stepped down after the corporation admitted to having exaggerated fuel consumption performance by 15 per cent and the chairman of Suzuki left his post when that corporation acknowledged that its mileage performance testing had differed sharply from the government-required methods. Lying and cutting corners is far from unusual. In the Volkswagen case, the deception appears larger and more blatant, but it is hardly aberrational. Moreover, when looking for someone to blame, the CEO, as the hands-on operator, was pinpointed. But it did not take long to note that, even though Volkswagen is one of the giants among publicly traded corporations, it is controlled by a few easily identified flesh-and-blood persons. The descendants of Ferdinand Porsche own a bloc of controlling shares and they have an agreement to vote them as a bloc. They direct all policies and, when they want to, all operational decisions. To illustrate this point and reinforce another, the German business papers were scathing when the chairman of the supervisory board, a grandson of Ferdinand Porsche, appointed his fourth wife, a former kindergarten teacher who once had been his governess, to the company's supervisory board. This appointment led to complaints by other shareholders, but to no avail (*New York Times*, Sept. 24, 2015).

The harm done by Volkswagen's use of the defeat device goes well beyond deception leading to reduced value of the cars it sold. It added copious amounts of harmful pollutants to the ambient air, likely contributing materially to illnesses and, perhaps, premature deaths. As seen in this chapter, Heinzerling observes that to engage in conduct that is certain to inflict serious harm or death is ethically unacceptable and should be considered a crime, as should the many other polluting activities engaged in by profit-seekers who do not have to prove their productive methods safe ere they embark on them.

For a dramatic and thoroughly documented study of how exposure by particular workers to untested, and deemed to be innocent, chemicals led to horrendous outcomes, see Jim Brophy et al., "New Occupational Breast Cancer Study Challenges the Cancer Establishment," *The Bullet*, April 3, 2013; M. Firth, J. Brophy, and M. Keith, *Workplace Roulette: Gambling with Cancer* (Toronto: Between the Lines, 1997); J. Brophy and M. Keith, "Breast Cancer Risk in Relation to Occupation with Exposure to Carcinogens and Endocrine Disruptors: A Canadian Case Study," *Environmental Health*, 2012. The impact of the huge number of chemicals and substances discharged into our workplace and living environments has been termed "the largest uncontrolled experiment in history" by David Rosner and Gerald Markowitz, "How You Became a Guinea Pig for the Chemical Corporations," TomDispatch.com, April 29, 2013. In our parts of the world, the slavish devotion to think of the chase for more as inherently virtuous and with the attendant useful mantra that processes, technologies, equipment, materials, and substances used in the pursuit of more are to be deemed innocent until proved guilty, there is very little check on the potential noxious effects of chemicals in use and to be put in use. Robert Chernomas and Ian Hudson, "Labour in the Time of Cholera and Cancer," *The Bullet*, July 1, 2013, report that the United States Environmental Protection Agency, a far better funded and more active outfit than its Canadian counterpart, has required testing of a mere 1 per cent of commercially available commercial chemicals, regulating five of them, and has not banned the use of any since 1991. This compares unfavourably with corporate capitalist nations in Europe that have had to deal with a longer history of social democracy. These writers note that the European Union has a Registration, Evaluation and Authorization of Chemicals authority that employs a precautionary principle. It demands that would-be users of chemicals prove to the authority that they are safe. The starting point is that the substances are guilty unless proved innocent. As well, the authority is implementing a plan to take 1,400 known-to-be-dangerous chemicals off the market over the next ten years. All these more stringent precautions point to the fact that we, in the Anglo-American corporate sphere, practise the most primitive form of capitalism. It underscores how our law has enabled the polity to give our blobs more reach to do harms than they would be given if they set up in other kinds of blob-o-spheres.

The argument in this chapter that it is really an omission to take precautionary steps that lead to the harms to society links to the discussion in chapter 7, where it was argued that law abides by an overarching principle that those who have control over the conduct of an undertaking should be held responsible for the fallout. One of the conceits of law is that positive acts are required to attribute responsibility and that this does not include *omissions.* But that is mere sophistry. An omission to put in precautions in an organizational setting is, in actual fact, a *positive* act. For these reasons, critical observers who worry about the extent of illth inflicted by corporations have crafted definitions of corporate crime that takes this reality into account. F. Pearce and S. Tombs, *Toxic Capitalism: Corporate Crime and the Chemical Industry* (Toronto: Canadian Scholars Press, 1998) defined corporate crime as "illegal acts or omissions punishable by the state under administrative, civil or criminal law which are the result of deliberate decision making or culpable negligence within a legitimate formal organization. These acts or omissions are based in legitimate, formal, business organizations, made in accordance with normative goals, standard operating procedures, and/or cultural norms of the organization, and are intended to benefit the organization itself"; see also Steven Box, *Power, Crime, and Mystification* (London/New York: Tavistock, 1983); Steven Bittle, *Still Dying for a Living: Corporate Criminal Liability after the Westray Mine Disaster* (UBC Press, 2012).

On the financialization of capital front: rarely is there as much agreement about anything as there is about the fact that the selling and buying of shares lead to a transfer in wealth, rather than to the creation of new wealth. As early as 1880, Friedrich Engels argued that as the bourgeoisie had been displaced by joint stock companies as industrial capitalists, "the capitalist has no further social function than that of pocketing dividends, tearing off coupons, and gambling on the Stock Exchange, where the different capitalists despoil one another of their capital." Modern scholars support this early Marxist hypothesis on the basis of their empirical observations; see Lawrence H. Summers and Victoria P. Summers, "When Financial Markets Work Too Well: A Cautious Case for a Securities Transaction Tax," (1989), 3 *Journal of Financial Services Research*, 261; Jack L. Treynor, "Types and Motivations of Market Participants" in Katrina F. Sherrerd, ed., *Execution Techniques, True Trading Costs, and the Microstructure of Markets* (Association for Investment Management and Research, 1993); John C. Coffee Jr., "Market Failure and the Case for a Mandatory Disclosure System," (1984), 70 *Virginia Law Revue*, 717; William J. Baumol, "Speculation, Profitability, and Stability," (1957), 39 *Review of Economics and Statistics*, 263; Lynn A. Stout, "Are Stock Markets Really Costly Casinos?: Disagreement, Market Failure, and Securities Regulation," (1995), 81 *Virginia Law Revue*, 611. Stout has observed that the misplaced optimism of those who sell and buy shares and derivatives speaks volumes about the irrationality of traders as a class. It seems that each one believes that they will be a winner and the inevitable offsetting losses will be suffered by others.

For an easily accessible piece on the strategies advocated by experts who claim to be able to guide those who want to trade in securities, see John Cassidy, "Smart Money," *New Yorker*, Oct. 6, 2003. He reviews some of the major literature: Benjamin Graham, *The Intelligent Investor* (HarperBusiness, 2003; on value investing, a method dear to Warren

Buffet's heart and wallet); Burton G. Malkiel, *A Random Walk Down Wall Street: The Time-Tested Strategy for Investing*, 11th ed. (W.W. Norton & Co., 2015; on how individual stocks fluctuate randomly, even if the overall market for shares reflects all the economic data available at any one time, the so-called Efficient Market Hypothesis); those who believe in behavioural science to inspire them to bet contra the irrational herds (a favourite ploy of George Soros); and those who believe that buying cheap stocks and hanging onto them is the best way to go. In the end, guessing is in, gambling is in; see chapter 4.

The exponential increase in the kinds of financial instruments, derivatives and derivatives based on derivatives, seemed to take off in the late 1980s and early 1990s, as the provision of goods and services was running out of steam, leading to the tech bubble; see Doug Henwood, *Wall Street* (London: Verso, 1997); E. Helleiner, *States and the Emergence of Global Finance: From Bretton-Woods to the 1990s* (Ithaca: Cornell University Press, 1994).

The incredible amounts of money that can be made by facilitating trading in shares and securities has been highlighted in recent times by the sheer inventiveness of the many commission agents chasing lucrative deals. It has led to something called High Frequency Trading (HFT), in essence, new technology applied to trading. It acts as a replacement for the slow trading on the floors of the stock exchanges conducted by brokers who were real human beings who executed sell and buy orders. Being human, they could only get access to a limited amount of information as they were confronted by the need to make instant decisions. They had to decide to buy and sell by calculating the pros and cons, that is, the risks, in their heads, based on experience and primitive chance calculation methods. Today, electronic platforms carry the information about orders and whizz-bang computer systems can see and analyze the orders in nanoseconds (billionths of a second). If a broker with a faster computer/analyzing system can see an order before anyone else can, that broker can take advantage of that knowledge to buy and sell before anyone else can or to make a purchase for itself, knowing that there may be buyers out there. The analysis depends on the complicated application of algorithms that have a very large number of scenarios built into them and will activate sell or buy orders by themselves. The speed of any one broker's machinery depends on how close it is to an electronic platform, how long a distance an order has to travel before a broker's watching equipment gets to see it (the physical proximity may be shortened or lengthened by how the wiring is done), leading to jostling for ideal physical locations.

Michael Lewis, *Flash Boys: A Wall Street Revolt* (W.W. Norton & Co., 2014) has written a bestseller describing the development of HFT mechanisms. It is a riveting story of ingenuity, knowledge of qant theories, computer programming, and physics. It is a tale of money making by "making" and "taking" deals (the maker of a deal gets more of a fee than the taker and this leads to jockeying by brokers to formulate the deal to get the benefit of being a maker rather than a taker). See Scott Patterson, *Dark Pools: The Rise of A.I. Trading Machines and the Looming Threat to Wall Street* (Crown Business, reprint 2013); Michael Edesess, "Who Benefits from High Speed Trading?," *Advisor Perspectives Inc.*, Aug. 28, 2012. It has created a large sphere of lightning and voluminous trading that, on the positive side, provides market actors with easy access to money (liquidity) and, on the negative side, makes it very hard for regulators to monitor the mindboggling number of the trades, many of them across platforms not seen by the whole of the market. It all has a rather tenuous relationship with the argument that the *corporate form* is essential to growth, to overall welfare; see L. Snider, "Interrogating the Algorithm: Debt, Derivatives and the Social Reconstruction of Stock Market Training," (2014), 40(5) *Critical Sociology*, 747.

The literature on the so-called financialization of capital is truly voluminous, speaking to the sense that something significant is happening to capitalist relations of production. Greta R. Krippner, "The Financialization of the American Economy," (2005), 3 *Socio-Economic Review* provides a helpful list of the many different meanings scholars attach to the phenomenon of financialization. I have taken her starting point as mine for the purposes of the discussion in this chapter: "I define financialization as a pattern of accumulation in which profits accrue primarily through financial channels rather than through trade and commodity production ... 'financial' ... refers to ... the provision (or transfer) of liquid capital in expectation of future interest, dividends, or capital gains" (174–5). Krippner also notes that the current spurt in financialization has had precursors. This time things may be different to these earlier periods of financialization because of different political circumstances (for instance, the extent of globalization, the state of nation states), the new production and financial technologies (new instruments, algorithms, etc.), and the sheer size of the phenomenon; time will tell. It certainly has led a large number of socialist writers to see this emphasis on financial capital and its often heavy-handed role in political affairs of nation states, together with the large "too big to fail" institutions' large failures (requiring mass state rescue interventions), as an indication that capitalism is nearing its end; see David McNally, *Global Slump: The Economics and Politics of Crisis and Resistance* (Oakland, CA: PM Press, 2011); David Harvey, *A Brief History of Neo-liberalism* (Oxford University Press, 2007); *The Enigma of Capital*, 2nd ed. (Oxford University Press, 2014); *Seventeen Contradictions and the End of Capitalism* (Profile Books, 2014).

For a different view that sees financialization as a natural support system for capitalism (and on which some of the tentative points in this chapter on the interrelationship between financial capitalists and non-financial corporations are based), see Leo Panitch and Sam Gindin, *The Making of Global Capitalism: The Political Economy of American Empire* (London: Verso, 2012). One of the intriguing issues for political activists is that pension funds, that is, funds constituted by contributions out of workers' foregone wages to provide for their non-working lives, are increasingly invested in newly privatized services. This is perverse; see Kevin Skerrett, "Can We Defend Our Pension *without* Challenging Financialized Capitalism?," *The Bullet*, Oct. 29, 2014. As well, many of the pension plans invest workers' funds in the private markets, giving workers a reason to support activities that harm them. Perverse, indeed. The Canada Pension Plan Investment Board, which controls $153 billion of workers' money, has invested in the Royal Bank of Canada, Apple Inc., Barrick Gold, Monsanto, Asahi Breweries, Galaxy Entertainment (a Macau casino outfit), and other enemies of the people. Michael Rozworski, "How Not to Fund Infrastructure," *The Bullet*, Aug. 25, 2016, E-bulletin 1296, reports that the investment manager for a large union pension plan, the Ontario Teachers' Pension Plan, while acknowledging that it was unfair for governments to allow private profiteers to exact tolls from road users who had paid for the road in the first place, shrugged his shoulders as he defended investing workers' money into toll roads; see also Kevin Skerret, "Pension Funds Investing in Privatization of Infrastructure," *Counterpoint*, June 26, 2016.

There is a growing literature on redefining what a society aimed at a different kind of well-being (happiness indices) would look like and on what kinds of policies will be needed to attain the aims of such an economy; see Ed Diener and Robert-Biswas Diener, *Happiness: Unlocking the Mysteries of Psychological Wealth* (Oxford: Blackwell, 2008); R. Kamman, "The Analysis and Measurement of Happiness as a Sense of Well-Being," (1984), 15 *Social Indicators Research*, 91; Richard Layard, *Happiness: Lessons from a New Science* (Penguin, 2005); and of course, the surveys prepared for the Bhutan initiative and the French Commission referred to in the text; see also Coral Graham, *Happiness around the World: The Paradox of Happy Peasants and Miserable Millionaires* (Oxford University Press, 2010); *The Pursuit of Happiness: An Economy of Wellbeing* (Washington: Brookings Institute, 2011).

13. A STEP OFF THE ROAD TO SERFDOM

1   *Toronto Star*, Nov. 19, 2014.

2   Jean Ziegler, *Destruction massive: Géopolitique de la faim*, trans. Siv O'Neill (Paris: Seuil, 2011), 19.

3   CNN, Sept. 30, 2011.

4   *Toronto Star*, Jan. 4, 2014.

5   William Tabb, "The World Trade Organization? Stop World Takeovers," *Monthly Revue* 51 (2000), 8.

6   Doug Hay, *Albion's Fatal Tree: Crime and Society in Eighteenth-Century England* (London: Verso, 2011); Christopher Stanley, "Corporate Personality and Capitalist

Relations: A Critical Analysis of the Artifice of Company Law," (1988–89), 97 *Cambrian Law Journal,* 19–20.

7   Slavoj Žižek in *The Pervert's Guide to Ideology*, video, dir. Sophie Fiennes, 2013.

8   Mark Carney, "Inclusive Capitalism: Creating a Sense of the Systemic," Conference on Inclusive Capitalism, London, May 27, 2014.

9   Christine Lagarde, "Economic Inclusion and Financial Integrity," ibid.

10   Lawrence Summers and Ed Balls, *Report of the Commission on Inclusive Prosperity,* Center for American Progress 52,1 (March 2015); Stiglitz, Sen, and Fitoussi, *Report by the Commission on the Measurement of Economic Performance and Social Progress.*

11   Heather Saul, "'A New Tyranny': Pope Francis Attacks Unfettered Capitalism and Says Rich Should Share Wealth," *Independent*, Nov. 26, 2013, citing passages from an apostolic exhortation by the Pope entitled *Evangelii Gaudium.*

12   Michael Lebowitz, *Build It Now: Socialism for the Twenty-First Century* (New York: Monthly Review, 2006), 43.

13   Plesch and Blankenburg, "Corporate Rights and Responsibilities."

In these notes, I set out the political theories that influenced me to write the book in the way I did. I state my hoped-for outcomes as plainly as I can. I note some of the many writings that led me to where I find myself politically. I am conscious that my chosen path to bring about change may lead to reforms of the existing system, rather than to a rejection of its workings and ideas. I take strength from much evidence, manifested in the recent uprisings and protest movements noted below, that suggest that my hopes are not romantic. I note how relatively easy it has been for capitalism to repress many of these uprisings and to marginalize many of these protests. But this does not signify that, if better armed, movements for radical change will never meet with success.

I am painfully aware that not to prescribe what kind of alternative world anti-capitalists must aim to develop may be taken as a weakness. But I am equally aware of my shortcomings: I have narrow training and limited experiences. I find comfort in the fact that such prescriptions, even when proffered by better and better-placed people, might be fraught. David Graeber, *Fragments of an Anarchist Anthropology* (Prickly Paradigm Press, 2004), makes the point as I would like to have: "Normally, when you challenge the conventional wisdom— that the current economic and political system is the only possible one—the first reaction you are likely to get is a demand for a detailed architectural blueprint of how an alternative system would work, down to the nature of financial instruments, energy supplies, and policies of sewer maintenance. Next, you are likely to be asked for a detailed program of how the system will be brought into existence. Historically, this is ridiculous. When has social change ever happened according to someone's blueprint? It's not as if a small circle of visionaries in Renaissance Florence conceived of something they called 'capitalism,' figured out the details of how the stock exchange and factories would someday work, and then put into place a program to bring their visions into reality. In fact, the idea is so absurd we might well ask ourselves how it ever occurred us to imagine this is how change happens to begin."

My view that another world is to be fought for is based on the belief that human beings are desirous of another kind of society, one in which compassion, care, and altruism ground our actions. To the status quo defenders who contend that anti-capitalists must have a detailed positive blueprint to be credible, this notion is fanciful. Yet moral, ethical, and religious teaching, preaching, and the inculcation of altruistic and mutual support vales have informed cultures across a wide swathe of the globe for centuries. Graeber has argued that, if we treated each other—friends, families, lovers, neighbours, even strangers—only on the basis of seeking competitive advantage, there would not be sufficient cohesion to keep a society together. The Nobel Prize winner Elinor Ostrom (and her increasing number of followers)—*Governing the Commons* (Cambridge University Press, 1991); Elinor Ostrom et al., eds., *The Drama of the Commons* (Washington, DC: National Academy Press, 2002)—documents that human beings live in a web of social relations infused with norms and values and that these are posited on the basis that we are intrinsically co-operative as opposed to innately self-obsessed. This, she and her many adherents argue, makes collective action possible, which may militate towards sustainable and equitable governance practices. More, her evidence shows that these kinds of societal relations are likely to be more efficient, in terms of generating material welfare, than the ones currently in favour. Community regulation of the commons is the most promising way to ensure preservation of our resources, environments, and communities. Socialists, of course, share this view of the potential of human beings to forge a society in which they are more likely to develop as better and more fulfilled persons; see, e.g., Michael Lebowitz, *The Socialist Alternative: Real Human Development* (Monthly Review Press, 2010). It is these very real impulses and aspirations that motivate so many disparate groups to engage in political agitation for a different world, as has been documented by Richard Swift, *SOS: Alternatives to Capitalism* (Toronto: Between the Lines, 2014), and as reflected in the many contemporary efforts to compile happiness indices that refuse to measure happiness and contentment by the money metric dear to capitalism. As Coral Graham points out in this chapter, anti-capitalists' ideas are as well-anchored in human nature, if not better, than the depressing view that, innately, we are self-oriented. It is that idea, that greed is our primordial driver, that led Margaret Thatcher to proclaim that there is no such thing as society and it is that idea that all of us who like living in a collaborative society firmly believe to be untrue.

The work is infused by some of the political ideas suggested by Erik Olin Wright, *Class, Crisis, and the State* (New Left Books, 1978). He argues that, within any one system, there is no resonance for demands for change that have no anchor in the existing regime of social relations. Within feudalism, it would make no sense for those without land to push for redistribution by seeking legislative reforms. Feudal power was not institutionally subject to the legislature. In any event, the legislature, such as it was, was constituted by the landowners. What would make sense, however, was to occupy lands and lay claim to them by dint of physical possession. This was the way in which the landlords got it in the first place. Violent repression might have to be faced but the physical movement would have legitimacy, and therefore political standing, within the scheme of existing arrangements. Wright argues that activists for change should make demands that are functionally compatible with the dominant system's bases, but the least compatible with them at that time as possible. Each time concessions are won, the mark for what is least functionally compatible will change. In Wright's latest work, "How to Be an Anticapitalist Today," *Jacobin*, 2015, he argues that, as people are born into existing circumstances that constrain their actions, they should aim at regulating those who wield power, and this can be done in advanced democracies by social democratic struggles. He calls this taming capitalism because it does not overthrow the system, merely makes it more bearable. He then suggests a series of strategies that will erode the existing schemes of domination and exploitation and, thereby, move the goal posts. The aim of this work is to make it easier for that erosion to take place by pointing to the non-neutral technologies used to exploit and dominate, by documenting how the harms done greatly outweigh the supposed benefits of the extant regime and how, ideologically, the justifications for capitalist relations of production offend the very social, cultural, and legal principles by which corporate capitalism seeks to legitimate itself.

This approach underlies the arguments being made in this last chapter. There is a manifest danger that this approach might lead to reforms and not radical change. It will be crucial for activists to keep their end goal, their desire for radical change, firmly in mind as they engage in battles for the least functionally compatible changes.

The protest movements referred to in the text were generated by widely shared discontent with current outcomes of corporate capitalism's practices. They have been dismissed by corporate capitalism's gatekeepers. Central to their marginalizing arguments is their claim— as Graeber, above, predicted—that the movements only express discontent and do not provide feasible, practical alternatives. Jeff Madrick's foreword to Stephane Hessel and Edgar Morin, *The Path to Hope*, tr. Anthony Shuugar (New York: Other Press, 2011) observed that this riposte missed an essential aspect of Occupy Wall Street and other movements, such as the Arab Spring, the Indignados of Spain, the occupiers of St. Paul's in London, the economically hammered and angry Israelis in the streets, and, he might have added, maddened Greeks and the Idle No More movement. He argued that, in brutal dictatorships, as those railed against during the Arab Spring, the dissentients wanted democratic institutions; in so-called democracies, they were averring, as Occupy and Idle No More clearly did, that there was no point in having a voice if there were no listeners. There are "no sounds in the forest when the tree falls and no one is there" (xv). They felt the legislators were not there and the media appear to be intent on clapping their large hands over everyone's ears. They had and have no choice but to bypass the existing institutions. This critique of the conventional response makes eminent sense, but does not seem to have had much bite.

The protest movements were effectively portrayed as too diverse, as unfocused, as impractical, as unacceptably contemptuous of the privileges of the people they claimed to represent. It was an article of faith among government spokespersons, opinion leaders, and the media that it was natural that leaderless collectives, with their inefficient and romantic attempts at free and open discussions, using apparatuses like the symbolic open mic, could not and did not expound a coherent set of demands, let alone a viable alternative to the regime they blamed for their unhappiness.

There is a sense in which this line of argument by status quo advocates is persuasive: Occupy and most of these movements were extremely diverse and open-ended. But this does not mean that the dissidents and protestors did not have identifiable goals and aims. In line with their anarchist sensibilities, Barbara Epstein in her "Anarchism and the Anti-Globalization Movement," *Monthly Review* 53,4 (2001), 54, noted that the folks in the streets do not want new political *leaders* taking them to a promised land. The Chilean student movement adapted the old slogan "The People United Shall Never Be Defeated" to read "The People United Move Forward without Political Parties." This attitude is also evident in the Nuit Debout movement that is gripping France as these lines are being written.

The many varieties of contemporary protest movements are rebelling against authoritarianism and are instinctively instilling their political actions with processes and practices that negate the creation of leaderships. They want more participation, more on-the-ground democracy, leading them to adopt slow, time-consuming consensus decision-making practices, possibly blunting their political effectiveness. And while they have no specific political program, their marches, actions, and organizations are not without aims. They coalesce around values such as altruism, economic and political egalitarianism, concern for the vulnerable, respect for different lifestyles, and notably, the decommodification of the environment. While they may not yet know how to reach their goals, it is simply wrong to think that they have no values that inspire their actions. More importantly, if their values could be given life they would clash sharply with the values and culture of a market capitalist regime, indeed, would be totally incompatible with them. As Madrick notes, they do not just want an end to poverty or economic inequality, but an end to injustice. This does present a challenge to the dominant class, one whose ruling logic has no concept of justice other than formal justice.

I write in 2016 and, thus far, capitalists and their allies have found it relatively easy to marginalize the current expressions of dissatisfaction. They acknowledge that it may well be that the dominating regime, that is, the current way of producing general welfare, inflicts some collateral damage, but, they argue, it continues to generate more overall wealth than any other political economic system ever has. As Andre Tosel, "Prefazione to Costanzo Preve" (Naples: la Citta del Sole, 2007), put it: "A for now victorious neo-capitalism has proved capable of developing the productive forces at a prodigious rate, despite the enormous damage it has inflicted on humanity and nature. It has been able to legitimate itself as the only possible order by reference to the virtues of the market, representative democracy, the religion of human rights and the seductions of a generalized consumerism." In short, precisely because capitalism is a holistic system, one that pervades and shapes all political, economic, social, and cultural aspects of people's lives, it is hard to confront it effectively.

As non-capitalists struggle against economic and political oppression, they find themselves using the economic and political machinery designed to maintain and perpetuate capitalism as a system. This makes for uneven, unfocused politics of opposition, not necessarily for anti-capitalist struggles. Too often, anti-capitalist activists find themselves resembling flies unwittingly taking the side of the spiders in whose webs they are caught. This may be why many contemporary anti-capitalist theorists, such as Callinicos, *An Anti-Capitalist Manifesto* (Cambridge: Polity Press, 2010); Graeber, cited above; and Elliott, *Ends in Sight: Marx/Fukuyama/Hobsbawm/Anderson* (London/Ann Arbor: Pluto Press/Between the Lines, 2008) suggest that the contradictions of the dominant scheme's workings will not automatically make for its demise. Conditions must be created to make this a more realistic prospect. In this work, a helping hand is offered.

On the point that capitalists claim that there is nothing paradoxical about promoting the corporate form as an efficient one because it produces wealth by a socialized mode of production, they are forced to argue that the essential goal is *private* accumulation of the yielded surplus, not the sharing of wealth or directing the management of resources for a made-up public good. But a gnawing problem remains: why should non-producers get anything? The gap between the claim that the private appropriation of the wealth produced socially is defensible because, somehow, putting capital to "work" is the direct equivalent of producing wealth by personal effort is, to say the least, controversial. Here it suffices to note that TINA has such a hold that this controversy, well known to theorists, is not raised in public discourse. Occasionally it threatens to come out because facts on the ground make it clear that some people benefit from not working. The recent austerity measures imposed on working classes to permit financiers to recover lost money and to make new money point strongly to the fact that they will be making money by denying others the opportunities to enjoy wealth they have already earned and denying them the opportunity to create some more. Bini Adamczak, "The End of the End of History, and Why the Era of Revolutions Is upon Us," www.nationofchange.org, pithily summarizes how capitalism's austerity remedies leads to such contradictions: "In the U.S. and Spain, people are forced to live in tents—because too many houses were built. In Italy, the high youth unemployment is lamented—and the retirement age is raised. In Germany, labor productivity increases and overtime increases, too. In Greece, to prevent a national bankruptcy that would cause social impoverishment, social impoverishment is increased (which might result in national bankruptcy)."

They Live was based on a story, "Eight o'Clock in the Morning," written by Ray Nelson. Nelson later collaborated with Bill Wray to turn it into a comic book anthology named *Nada*. Many similar films have been made, including fairly recent ones like *Terminator* and *RoboCop*. Commercially they are sold as action/fantasy genre films, rather than meaningful ones about the nature of our political economy. But because of that underlying motif, films such as *They Live* do attract the attention of serious cultural studies critics.

On the fears that the rich have, see Alice Cooper, "Arming Goldman Sachs with Pistols," *Bloomberg*, Dec. 3, 2009, who reported that "senior Goldman people have loaded up on firearms and are now equipped to defend themselves if there is a populist uprising against the bank"; see also Robert Frank, "Why the Rich Fear Violence in the Streets," *Wealth Report*, July 6, 2011.

Index